SURVIVING SLAVERY
IN THE BRITISH CARIBBEAN

EARLY AMERICAN STUDIES
Series editors:
Daniel K. Richter, Kathleen M. Brown,
Max Cavitch, and David Waldstreicher

Exploring neglected aspects of our colonial,
revolutionary, and early national history and culture,
Early American Studies reinterprets familiar themes
and events in fresh ways. Interdisciplinary in character,
and with a special emphasis on the period from about
1600 to 1850, the series is published in partnership with the
McNeil Center for Early American Studies.

A complete list of books in the series
is available from the publisher.

SURVIVING SLAVERY
IN THE
BRITISH CARIBBEAN

RANDY M. BROWNE

PENN

UNIVERSITY OF PENNSYLVANIA PRESS

PHILADELPHIA

Published by
University of Pennsylvania Press
Philadelphia, Pennsylvania 19104-4112
www.upenn.edu/pennpress

Printed in the United States of America on acid-free paper
1 3 5 7 9 10 8 6 4 2

Library of Congress Cataloging-in-Publication Data
Names: Browne, Randy M., author.
Title: Surviving slavery in the British Caribbean / Randy M. Browne.
Other titles: Early American studies.
Description: 1st edition. | Philadelphia : University of Pennsylvania
    Press, [2017] | Series: Early American studies | Includes
    bibliographical references and index.
Identifiers: LCCN 2016056687 | ISBN 978-0-8122-4940-8
    (hardcover : alk. paper)
Subjects: LCSH: Slaves—Guyana—Berbice—Social conditions—
    19th century. | Slaves—Guyana—Berbice—Social life and
    customs—19th century. | Slaves—Legal status, laws, etc.—
    Guyana—Berbice—History—19th century. | Slavery—Social
    aspects—Guyana—Berbice—History—19th century. | Slavery—
    Social aspects—Caribbean, English-speaking—History—19th
    century. | Slavery—Law and legislation—Guyana—Berbice—
    History—19th century. | Survival—Guyana—Berbice—History—
    19th century. | Violence—Guyana—Berbice—History—19th
    century.
Classification: LCC HT1140.B4 .B76 2017 | DDC
    306.3/62098815—dc23
LC record available at https://lccn.loc.gov/2016056687

CONTENTS

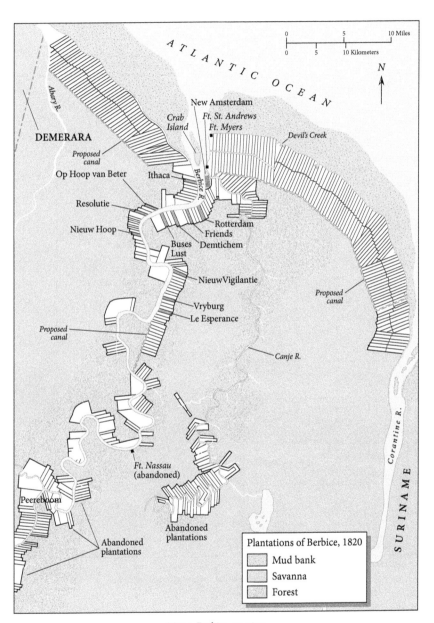

Map 1. Berbice, ca. 1820

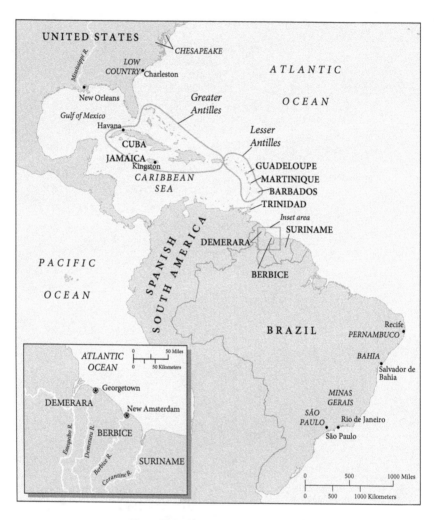

Map 2. Major Plantation Societies, ca. 1820

Introduction

Everyone dies, but few people face the horror of being sealed in a coffin while still alive. One man who did was Harry, an enslaved African laborer on a coffee plantation along the Berbice River (in present-day Guyana). Along with thousands of other African captives, Harry had been taken to Berbice, a British colony on the Caribbean coast of South America, toward the end of the eighteenth century. By 1825, when Harry was in his mid-thirties, he had endured decades of brutal work in one of the deadliest slave societies in the Americas. When Harry got sick, it would have come as no surprise, but by June, Harry was so ill that "he swelled all over [and] he was able to do nothing," according to his friend Billy, another enslaved African. Several months of medical attention did nothing to improve Harry's condition, and his owner, Richard Bell, grew impatient. He tried flogging Harry to force him back to the field, but that did not work. Harry was barely breathing by the time Bell sent him to the plantation's "sick house." Expecting Harry to die soon, Bell ordered an enslaved carpenter, Demerara, to make a coffin. Billy described the gruesome scene that unfolded when Demerara went to where Harry was lying. Harry opened his eyes and saw Demerara holding a measuring stick over him. He knew what was happening. He struggled briefly to sit up, then gave up and "hung down his head." Horrified, Billy protested to his owner's wife that it was "not good nor right fashion" to make a coffin for a living man. His owner responded by ordering Billy and two other men to dig a grave. A few hours later, Harry, still "frothing at the mouth," was "put in the coffin & was nailed up."[1]

What is remarkable about this case is not so much its horror—this was a society full of atrocities—but that we know it at all. We know about the final hours of Harry's life because Billy was angry enough to complain to a militia officer, who, complying with his official responsibility, forwarded the case to Berbice's fiscal, the legal authority in charge of investigating enslaved people's complaints. The fiscal summoned Billy, his owner, and other witnesses to Berbice's capital, New Amsterdam, to testify. When questioned by the fiscal and other members of the Court of Criminal Justice, Billy emphasized the utter lack of compassion Bell showed Harry even in death. Indeed, Bell was apparently angry with Harry for dying on him. Harry was a "bad negro," Bell told the men who buried Harry, and said "lazy had killed him." "Finding I could get no redress," Billy told the court, "I came here to complain." For his part, Bell denied most of Billy's accusations, including the charge that he ordered a coffin made before Harry's death, and dismissed Billy, too, as "a very lazy idle negro."[2]

Ultimately, the court believed Billy's account but did not find Bell's actions criminal. The court was "sorry to observe that Bell has shown a want of proper feeling in causing a Coffin to be made for a negro previous to his death (although his fate appeared to have been inevitable)," which was "not in itself a Criminal act [but] might yet operate prejudicially on the minds of his negroes by creating discontent." The court "admonished" Bell before handing Billy over to him to be punished at his discretion for having complained without a legal case. Billy, who had experienced floggings so severe that he vomited blood and fainted and seen Bell force a man to drink cow urine, must have known all too well what kind of sadistic tortures he would soon endure for having made a formal complaint against his owner.[3]

Billy's story was one of several hundred preserved in the remarkable and little-used archive that distinguishes early nineteenth-century Berbice from other American slave societies. These records of enslaved people's complaints offer striking first-person testimony of the tremendous physical and emotional suffering they endured and an imperfect record of their responses. Like Harry, the overwhelming majority of enslaved Africans and their descendants suffered greatly and died all too soon, worked to death by greedy and callous enslavers. In addition to the litany of horrors one would expect to find, these records also reveal a less familiar story about enslaved people's efforts to navigate the brutal worlds they inhabited and, in particular, their engagement with the colonial legal system to claim rights and protection. In Berbice, thousands of enslaved people turned to the fiscal and other officials, using the law to protest abuses, negotiate complex relationships, and struggle to survive under desperate conditions. Listening closely to their voices challenges us to rethink our assumptions about the power relationships of Atlantic slavery. In particular, viewing slavery through the eyes of enslaved people themselves, or at least over their shoulders, prompts us to reconsider enslaved people's well-known struggle against slavery as first and foremost a fight for sheer survival.[4] *Surviving Slavery in the British Caribbean* therefore takes the problem of survival as its starting point for a reconsideration of slavery and power.

Historians have long known that Caribbean slave societies were death traps. African captives who did not die during the forced migration from the African interior to the coast, which consumed between 5 and 40 percent of all captives, or during the notorious Atlantic crossing, which claimed at least 10 percent more, usually succumbed within a few years of arrival in the West Indies, victims of a lethal combination of unrelenting work, a hostile disease environment, inadequate nutrition, and physical violence.[5] Children born under slavery fared little better, with most infants dying well before their first birthdays.[6] The rare men and women who lived into their forties or fifties, old age by the standards of plantation slavery, had watched hundreds if not thousands of shipmates, friends, and kin perish.[7] In the century and a half before the abolition of the British transatlantic slave trade in 1808, some 2.7 million captive Africans were brought to the British West Indies. Yet by 1808, the total British Caribbean slave population was barely a third that number—about 775,000. After the arrival of new African captives to Britain's Caribbean colonies ended, the population plummeted as slaves died faster than they could reproduce; by 1834, only about 665,000 slaves were still alive. Enslaved people were therefore painfully aware of what historians have generally recognized only as a demographic fact: that the basic problem of Atlantic slavery was one of survival.

This human catastrophe is familiar, but only recently have historians begun to explore its social and cultural ramifications. Recent scholarship has helped us understand how the specter of death and terror shaped the experiences and mentalities of enslaved Africans from the Atlantic crossing to New World plantations.[8] *Surviving Slavery in the British Caribbean* joins this conversation, asking how the daunting challenge of staying alive shaped a wide range of social relationships, cultural practices, and political strategies in a notoriously brutal society.

The basic premise of this book is that the struggle to survive was at the center of enslaved people's experience. When they negotiated with plantation managers or drivers for reduced workloads or more food, protested domestic violence or the legitimacy of the floggings they endured, or used the illicit Afro-Caribbean healing complex known as obeah to treat disease, their most urgent goal was to stay alive. While historians have long been preoccupied by enslaved people's fight for "freedom," this Western abstraction had little ideological resonance for Africans and even less practical relevance for people trying to cope with the daily realities of enslavement.[9] First and foremost, enslaved people in Berbice and similar societies fought for survival. This shift in perspective challenges some of the unspoken assumptions that continue to shape the study of slavery, including the notion that enslaved people's primary goal was freedom and that their lives can best be understood by focusing on the hot and cold wars they waged against their enslavers.

For several decades, much scholarship on Atlantic slavery has emphasized enslaved people's efforts to rebel, resist, and wrest some measure of autonomy from their enslavers. Such work remains an important corrective to earlier arguments that enslaved people passively accepted domination or were too traumatized to resist. Yet, as critics have argued, focusing too narrowly on enslaved people's struggles with their enslavers runs the risk of exaggerating their agency and, more important, reducing complex lives to a single-minded fight for freedom. As the eminent anthropologist Sidney Mintz wrote two decades ago, "only a tiny fraction of daily life [on Caribbean plantations] consisted of open resistance. Instead, most of life then, like most of life now, was spent living."[10] An exclusive emphasis on domination and resistance obscures the many other important relationships—and conflicts—that shaped enslaved people's lives.[11]

In *Surviving Slavery in the British Caribbean*, I show how enslaved people and their enslavers not only struggled with each other but also navigated complex relationships with peers and third parties. Competition for authority, power, and material resources created both predictable antagonisms and unexpected alliances between drivers and field laborers, husbands and wives, obeah practitioners and clients, and plantation managers and legal officials. Moreover, all of these relationships, at least in Berbice, were negotiated in the midst of unprecedented imperial intervention, as metropolitan politicians, absentee planters, reformers, colonial authorities, and abolitionists grappled with the place of slavery in a changing empire.

Mapping these relationships is key to understanding how enslaved people navigated the concrete obstacles enslavement posed, including poverty, disease, and violence. As they interacted with one another, with their enslavers, and with legal officials such as the fiscal, enslaved people in Berbice developed and refined what historian Vincent Brown has described as a "politics of survival."[12] Although some of their survival strategies tested the limits of the slave system, many others, such as becoming a driver to secure badly needed material resources, reinforced the hierarchies that made slavery possible. Other actions, like stealing food from other slaves or using obeah to detect a suspected poisoner, pitted enslaved people against one another, fostering divisions that made collective resistance more difficult. Focusing on survival thus not only reminds us how difficult life was in Atlantic slave societies, but also enhances our understanding of the complex social worlds in which enslaved people and their enslavers confronted each other.

Early nineteenth-century Berbice is perhaps the most well-documented slave society in the Americas due to its unique historical development. Established by Dutch colonists in the seventeenth century and developing slowly until the late eighteenth century, when the British conquered it, Berbice harbors the rich and unique records of the fiscals and other crown officials known as protectors of slaves.[13] These documents are the product of two developments that converged in Berbice in the early nineteenth century. First was a Dutch legal system—continued under British rule—in which enslaved people possessed limited legal rights and could air their grievances before the fiscal, who could prosecute slaveowners and other free colonists in court or rule summarily on cases brought before him. Second was the British government's experiment in "amelioration," in which it sought to gradually reform slavery through new laws meant to grant slaves legal rights, improve their treatment, and prepare them for emancipation. The responsibility for enforcing the new regulations fell to a newly created office: the protector of slaves. The records of the fiscals and protectors, with cases that range from a few sentences to dozens of pages, span from 1819 to 1834 and feature near-verbatim testimony from thousands of individual slaves, free people of color, and European colonists. They include detailed accounts of the fiscals' and protectors' investigations, prosecutions, and punishments of enslaved people for a range of actions, from theft and neglecting work to running away and insolence. They also feature an especially valuable body of evidence: thousands of complaints from enslaved people themselves against plantation overseers and managers, slaveowners, merchants, and, less commonly, other slaves. Due to the peculiarities of British imperial history, there are no comparable sources for better known West Indian colonies, such as Jamaica or Barbados, where the traces of the voices of enslaved people are much harder to find and where enslaved people's legal rights were more limited and more difficult to enforce.[14]

Taken together, these records are the single largest archive of first-person testimony from and about enslaved people in the Americas. They offer powerful insights into the perspectives of hundreds of individual people who struggled to build lives on the shifting and perilous terrain of Atlantic slavery some two centuries ago. They reveal, in astonishing and often painful detail, the world that enslaved Africans and their descendants confronted, their hopes and fears, and their efforts to survive horrific conditions. The stories that emerge from Berbice undoubtedly had their parallels in other Atlantic slave societies, where slaves faced similar challenges, but nowhere were the ordeals of ordinary enslaved people documented as regularly or as thoroughly as they were in Berbice. The evidence from Berbice thus allows for an unusually intimate study of enslaved people's daily lives, as seen largely through their eyes and told in their voices.

As rich as the archive that distinguishes Berbice is, it is also problematic and requires careful handling. Only some enslaved people took the considerable risk of making a formal complaint, and those who did may not be representative of the colony's slave population. Moreover, complainants generally went to officials not simply when they felt aggrieved but rather when they thought they had a decent chance of having their complaint upheld, and so Berbice's legal culture filtered the types of grievances that were recorded. For those who did testify, the judicial process itself shaped the ways that events and actions were described, with complainants, witnesses, and defendants— enslaved and free—telling outright lies or at the very least trying to craft persuasive narratives that would lead to a favorable outcome.[15] In short, Berbice's legal grievance apparatus did not simply shine a spotlight on the lives of the colony's slaves and enslavers; it also shaped those lives, in ways that are difficult to assess. How were enslaved people's aspirations and strategies affected by the existence of colonial officials with the authority to intervene in the most intimate aspects of their relationships with their enslavers and one another? What difference did it make that enslaved people in Berbice had certain legal rights and formal mechanisms for asserting them? And what did it mean to be a "master" in a society where slavery and plantation management were subject to imperial surveillance and legal regulation? Even as such questions resist precise answers, they remain central to this book.

Also important to remember is that the recorded testimony at the core of this study is not a literal transcription of spoken speech but rather the product of several translations. Clerks transformed enslaved people's creole into standard English, paraphrasing and summarizing what they heard, adding and removing narrative details. Nevertheless, there are many indications that they attempted to record testimony as precisely as possible and interfered only minimally.[16] The presence of many African-derived and creole words, the frequent use of the first person, and the nonstandard punctuation and grammar found in many records all suggest that this archive is the closest we are likely to come to the actual voices of enslaved people in the Atlantic world. When triangulated with the other kinds of evidence from nineteenth-century Berbice, including punishment record books that detail the "offences" enslaved people committed and slave registration returns that identify individual slaves by name, birthplace, age, occupation, and other biographical details, the fiscals' and protectors' records offer an unparalleled glimpse into the world of the enslaved.

I read these records with different questions than the fiscals and protectors who created them. They usually were only interested in finding out enough about a particular event to determine whether the law had been violated and what verdict to reach—what anthropologist James Scott would call the "public transcript." Although I necessarily begin with such "public transcripts," the record of the alleged customary or legal right that had been violated and the redress sought, I am more interested in uncovering "hidden transcripts," that is, in what complaints tell us about how enslaved people viewed their world, understood their relationships, and sought some semblance of justice.[17]

At the same time, it is important to read these records "with the grain," foregrounding the legal and cultural context in which they were produced and the ways that the competing motivations of different participants shaped what they did—and did not—reveal.[18] Rather than smoothing over the conflicting claims of different witnesses and pretending that it is always possible to determine what really happened, my inclination is to present competing claims transparently and, wherever possible, to allow historical subjects who are too often rendered silent to speak for themselves.

Finally, to help contextualize and interpret the information that can be gleaned from the records that document slavery in Berbice, throughout this book I make occasional use of evidence from other Caribbean slave societies, especially Jamaica. Such comparisons both highlight the features of Berbician slave society that were particular and reveal the many ways that enslaved people's struggle to survive was universal.

The upheavals of the early nineteenth century transformed the plantation complex throughout the Atlantic world, including Berbice. At the end of the eighteenth century, when the Dutch lost Berbice to the British, the colony was rapidly expanding, with dozens of new plantations soon making it a leading producer of coffee and cotton and an important site of sugar production. Yet at the same time planters were flooding Berbice and other new southern Caribbean colonies like Trinidad, Demerara, and Grenada—collectively, Britain's last frontier of slavery—with tens of thousands of captive Africans, antislavery activists were gaining momentum in their fight to close the transatlantic slave trade.[19] Their success left slaveowners entirely dependent on the unlikely possibility of a slave population that could reproduce itself. Abolitionists hoped this economic incentive would improve conditions for enslaved people, as planters realized that the survival of colonial slavery was predicated on the survival of their enslaved laborers. But instead, overextended planters faced additional economic challenges and tried to extract more work from a declining population, and slaves continued to suffer and die. By the 1820s, Berbice had become a central site in the metropolitan government's amelioration program, with new legislation and new mechanisms of surveillance designed to regulate the treatment of enslaved people and their relationships with their enslavers. These experiments ultimately failed, however, and Britain abolished slavery in 1834.

Enslaved people in Berbice thus experienced a slave system that first expanded dramatically and then began to fall apart. The first chapter of *Surviving Slavery in the British Caribbean* introduces Berbice and locates its spectacular rise and fall in the larger world of Atlantic slavery. It focuses on the conditions slaves encountered during the rapid development of Berbice after its incorporation into the British Empire, which transformed a marginal Dutch backwater into one of the most dynamic and important slave societies in the early nineteenth century. Chapter 1 also compares Berbice to other Atlantic slave societies, emphasizing its unique geography and especially its legal culture. The omnipresence of water and the need to protect low-lying land from flooding created special challenges for plantation development in Berbice while also contributing to a particularly adverse disease environment. Berbice's legal system, shaped by its Dutch heritage and by new reforms enacted during amelioration, was even more important than its physical environment in structuring social relationships. Unlike slaves in British North America and most other West Indian colonies, enslaved people in Berbice had legal rights, however limited, and official mechanisms for enforcing them.

The following chapters show how enslaved people's struggle to stay alive intersected with their many other concerns. Each chapter focuses on a distinct set of characters and thus emphasizes the wide range of overlapping relationships enslaved people had to negotiate. Taking survival as the starting point throughout provides an opportunity to reconsider some of the key

themes and issues in the history of Atlantic slavery, from violence and punishment to labor, cultural and spiritual practices, family life, and the slaves'
economy.

Chapter 2 is about the impact of enslaved people's legal recourse upon
their relationships with their enslavers (including overseers, managers, and
owners). In particular, it asks how limits placed on the violence that enslavers
could inflict affected the ways that both groups negotiated power. Physical
violence was a major threat to slaves' survival, a central target of abolitionists'
and reformers' criticism, and a major point of conflict between masters and
slaves. This was especially true during the era of amelioration, when a new
disciplinary regime circumscribed enslavers' autonomy with new laws on the
treatment of slaves. Enslaved people regularly turned to the law to protect
themselves from violence or seek redress after the fact, challenging one of the
key "rights" masters had long claimed. This chapter also charts the process of
going to the fiscal or protector in order to explore enslaved people's strategies
for navigating the legal system and the possible outcomes.

Chapter 3 turns to the inner workings of Berbician plantations, exploring
the role of drivers as crucial go-betweens for enslaved laborers and plantation
management. Most drivers lived longer, less materially difficult lives than
other slaves, such as field laborers. Yet as the men—and they were almost always men—tasked with carrying out their enslavers' orders, keeping other
slaves at work, and inflicting punishments, drivers struggled to maintain authority among their subordinates. While drivers used a variety of tactics to
stifle dissent and earn other slaves' cooperation, their most effective strategy
was cultivating the support of overseers, managers, and planters, who shared
their interest in keeping plantations running and reinforcing the official hierarchy. Becoming a driver thus helped certain enslaved men survive while at
the same time perpetuating the slave system.

The fourth chapter examines marriage as a complex and dangerous site of
power negotiation among enslaved men, enslaved women, and the colonial
government. Enslaved people in Berbice sometimes turned to plantation officials and legal authorities for help regulating the behavior of their spouses,
often after their own efforts failed. Focusing on a range of domestic conflicts
that preoccupied enslaved people and reformers to varying degrees—
including adultery, separation, and physical violence—this chapter shows
how enslaved people tried to construct marital relationships that suited them.
Given the patriarchal assumptions of colonial legal officials and plantation
authorities, enslaved men in Berbice were much more successful than

enslaved women in getting what they wanted. If family life could be a source of resilience and insulation from the violence and trauma of slavery, it could also be a source of threats to the survival of women.

Chapter 5 explores the practice and politics of obeah, a catchall term for a wide range of spiritual healing rituals that were prohibited—by penalty of death—under colonial law. This chapter focuses on the events that led to the criminal prosecutions of two enslaved men who claimed the ability to manipulate spiritual powers. At different times and on different plantations, both of them were accused of having organized the "Minje Mama" (Water Mama) dance, a ritual designed to identify the root cause of otherwise inexplicable illnesses and deaths. Yet while the dance was supposed to "set the estate to rights," it turned out to be violent, dangerous, and in one case fatal. This chapter asks how obeah practitioners fashioned themselves as spiritual and political authorities that could rival official authorities like drivers and even planters, and why enslaved people turned to obeah despite its well-known risks.

The final chapter examines the most important economic claims enslaved people made—some based on generations of hard-fought negotiation and custom, others grounded in statute law—and their strategies for securing them. Enslaved people demanded the right to be provided with regular "allowances" of food and clothing in exchange for their labor, to control private property such as livestock and produce, and to participate in the colonial economy, exchanging goods and small sums of cash, bartering services, and collecting payment for work done on their own time. Taken together, these rights not only played a central role in enslaved people's struggle to deal with the concrete challenges that enslavement posed, including poverty and malnutrition, but also challenged much of what it meant, legally and customarily, to be a slave. In claiming rights normally associated with free wage-earners rather than people who were themselves legally considered property, and in using a variety of labor bargaining strategies, Berbician slaves anticipated many of the battles over labor, land, and property that would soon play out in British Guiana and other plantation societies after emancipation.

The voices at the heart of this book tell many stories. Theirs are not familiar tales—stories of rebels, Maroons, or "Atlantic Creoles," the kinds of extraordinary heroic characters who have rightly attracted much attention from historians for their efforts to escape or destroy the societies that enslaved them.[20] Instead, the stories in this book document the lives of some of the many unheralded enslaved women and men who are often the most difficult to find in historical sources. *Surviving Slavery* recounts the unromantic struggles of the all too often anonymous people who lived, worked, and died under slavery. Millions of enslaved Africans and their descendants fought to get by in slave societies throughout the Americas, but how many of them do we know by name? How well do we understand their world? Listening to the voices from nineteenth-century Berbice allows us to better consider enslaved people's ordeal and especially their struggles, successes, and failures in a world of violence, terror, and uncertainty. Their stories bear witness to remarkable courage, and human frailty. They are surprising, horrifying, and haunting. When we listen to them together, we are able to see Atlantic slavery at its core—a world where the central problem was one of survival.

CHAPTER 1

Slavery and Empire on the Wild Coast

Although the African captives crammed into the holds of the *Barbados Packet* had no way of knowing it, the ship's captain wanted them to survive the Atlantic crossing. Adam Bird was a veteran captain and one of a hundred or so Liverpool-based slave traders that sailed to Africa in 1805. He knew that every person who died during the voyage represented a financial loss. Bird and his thirty-four-man crew began trading near the mouth of the Grand Mesurado River, a sparsely populated region in what is now Liberia, in November 1805. Within a few months they had transformed their ship into a floating prison for 270 captive Africans. Bird was probably eager to set sail, given the higher than average likelihood of revolt on the Windward Coast, the hazards of sailing in a region with few natural harbors and steep beaches pounded by heavy surf, and, most important, because the longer he stayed, the more captives he would lose. As Bird knew all too well, transporting human commodities was a risky business infused with death.[1]

As the ship full of captives followed the trade winds south into the Atlantic, it was not destined, as its name suggested, for Britain's oldest West Indian colony, where the soil had been depleted after a century and a half of intensive sugar cultivation. Instead, it headed toward a former Dutch colony five hundred miles south of Barbados that had recently become the new frontier of Caribbean slavery: Berbice. By late March 1806, after some two months at sea, the *Barbados Packet* approached its destination. Navigation along the Guianas—a nine-hundred-mile stretch of muddy coastline between the Orinoco and Amazon Rivers—was dangerous and difficult. The brackish water was shallow, and a seemingly endless series of shoals, sandbars, and mudflats shifted faster than cartographers could update their maps.[2] Thousands of rivers and creeks carved through the continent, dragging silt dozens of miles into the Atlantic, but none provided a natural harbor.

Figure 1. New Amsterdam and the Berbice River. *Gezigt van de stad Nieuw-Amsterdam a Rio de Berbice,* foldout color frontispiece in Abraham Jacob van Imbijze van Batenburg, *Kort historisch verhal van den eersten analog, lotgevallen en voortgang der particuliere colonie Berbice . . .* (Amsterdam: C. Sepp Jansz, 1807). This image represents Berbice's capital and only town, New Amsterdam, near the time that Great Britain occupied the colony. The artist emphasizes the town's frontier quality, depicting it as a thin strip of muddy land sandwiched between the Berbice River, which dominates the foreground, and uncultivated land immediately beyond. There are no discernable roads or wharf, a few dozen scattered buildings, and only a handful of pedestrians. The modest fort at the far left, near the Atlantic coast, protects the entrance to the Berbice River, the colony's major artery. Courtesy of the John Carter Brown Library at Brown University.

Even the captives, who had no experience with open-ocean navigation and no idea where they were headed, could see that they were nearing land. The first clue was the change in the ocean's color, which transformed, as another British traveler observed, "from being hitherto as clear as an emerald" to "thicker and more impregnated with mud" as the ship neared the coast.[3] But even once land was in sight, it offered few landmarks to help navigators. The "very low and woody land," one captain cautioned, "appears in all parts so much alike, that the most experienced Pilots are frequently deceived."[4] A virtually endless line of mangrove forest backed by swampy savannas was only occasionally interrupted by sparse signs of human settlement: planters' whitewashed homes, slaves' thatched roof cottages, and fields of cotton and sugar that stretched to the horizon.[5] Unlike his disoriented captives, Captain Bird was familiar with this coastline, having delivered his most recent cargo of slaves to Berbice's western neighbor, Demerara, the previous April.[6]

Toward the end of March, the *Barbados Packet* reached its port of call: the mouth of the three-hundred-mile-long Berbice River, divided in two by Crab Island and guarded by the modest battery of Fort St. Andrews on the east bank. A couple miles upriver, sandwiched between the Berbice and its tributary, the Canje River, was New Amsterdam, the colony's ramshackle capital. It was an unimpressive sight—scattered wooden houses and offices, a couple of brick buildings in disrepair, and unpaved streets bordered by canals.[7] The few thousand residents of the town, most of whom were enslaved, probably smelled the *Barbados Packet* before they saw it, so bad was the stench of slave ships after months at sea. The blood, urine, vomit, and feces produced by hundreds of captives made a noxious mixture. Of the human cargo, 247 Africans had survived the Atlantic crossing, while 23 died somewhere en route, their bodies thrown to the sharks. Yet as Bird and his crew began preparing the survivors for presentation to potential buyers, he may have congratulated himself on a successful voyage.[8] There had been no major outbreak of smallpox, yaws, or dysentery; no insurrection; and the 9 percent mortality rate was predictable "wastage," a normal part of doing business in human flesh.

For Berbice's European colonists, the arrival of the *Barbados Packet* was an exciting spectacle. They turned out in droves to buy new laborers or simply gawk at the newly arrived saltwater slaves. Few transatlantic ships and even fewer slavers landed directly at Berbice. The river's channel was too narrow and shallow for large vessels. Moreover, just seventy miles to the west, captains found a better harbor, easier coastal access, and a larger market for slaves at the mouth of the Demerara River.[9] Whenever a slave ship did arrive

Group of Negros, as imported to be sold for Slaves.

Figure 2. Recently arrived African captives. *Group of Negros, as imported to be sold for Slaves*,
engraving by William Blake after John Gabriel Stedman, *Narrative of a Five Years' Expedition
Against the Revolted Negroes of Surinam*, 2 vols. (London: J. Johnson and J. Edwards, 1796), vol. 1,
plate 22, following p. 200. This highly romanticized image of a group of smiling, semi-naked
African captives represented a planter's fantasy of the transatlantic slave trade. Ironically,
Stedman's text—where the engraving was published—acknowledged the physical suffering and
emotional trauma that characterized the arrival of African captives in the Americas, even as
Stedman defended slavery and the slave trade. To Stedman, the captives seen here, being driven
by a sailor with a bamboo stick after arriving in Paramaribo, Suriname, were a "sad assemblage" of
"walking Skeletons." Nevertheless, he claimed that instead of the "horrid and dejected
countenances" found in antislavery propaganda, he "perceived not one single downcast look"
among them. Courtesy of the John Carter Brown Library at Brown University.

in Berbice, crowds gathered at the open space behind Government House, near the riverside "stelling" (wharf), treating it like a "holyday, or a kind of public fair," according to one witness. Planters came from all over the colony, some with their families, "all arrayed in their gayest apparel." As the naked Africans were forced to mount a chair, buyers scrutinized their bodies—were they strong or weak? sick or healthy?—"with as little concern as if they [were] examining cattle in Smithfield market."[10]

The physical condition of the captives after months at sea was shocking even to those familiar with the brutality of Atlantic slavery. Although they had been washed, oiled, and shaved in a vain attempt to hide evidence of the violence that had brought them to Berbice and make them attractive to buyers, "the odour proceeding from their bodies was most unpleasant," as a soldier observed after witnessing the sale of a slave ship cargo in 1806—the same year the *Barbados Packet* arrived.[11] Slaveowners clamored to purchase slaves, in part because they knew the transatlantic slave trade to British ports would soon end, but if they expected healthy people who could be put to work right away, they were sorely disappointed. The captives before them "were such a set of scarcely animated automata, such a resurrection of skin and bone . . . they all looked so like corpses just arisen from the grave."[12]

Less immediately visible than their physical suffering, but no less important, was the intense emotional trauma the captives faced during this new phase of their harrowing forced migration. The day they were sold may have been one "of feasting and hilarity" for colonials, as one British traveler observed, but "to the poor Africans it was a period of heavy grief and affliction." They had been separated from friends and family by death and sale at every stage of their journey—from capture and enslavement in the Windward Coast interior to the march to the coast and ultimately the Middle Passage across the Atlantic. Strangers who had become shipmates would now "be sold as beasts of burden—torn from each other—and widely dispersed about the colony, to wear out their days in the hopeless toils of slavery."[13]

What did the captives from the *Barbados Packet* make of their arrival in Berbice? The sights and sounds must have been overwhelming as they made their way from ship to shore, surrounded by merchants and hucksters, stevedores and planters, slaves and soldiers. What was it like to be "examin[ed] . . . limb after limb, . . . just as the dealers do with horses in our fairs in England?"[14] As buyers and sellers haggled, captives would have heard a jumble of languages—Dutch and English, the local creole known as Berbice Dutch, and, from other newcomers, a variety of Central and West African languages, including Kikongo, Twi, and Igbo.[15] As they followed their new owners to the plantations, houses, and workshops where they would soon be put to unfamiliar tasks—picking coffee, ginning cotton, grinding sugarcane, and preparing European foods—they may have searched the faces and bodies of other enslaved people for signs of home. The "country marks" some Africans bore may have helped them identify people from their homeland or neighboring West African societies—people who might answer their questions, or offer advice and solace.[16] Captives from the Windward Coast were relatively rare, though, in Berbice, and the *Barbados Packet* captives would have seen many more strangers from Central Africa, the Bights of Benin and Biafra, and the Gold Coast than people who spoke their language and shared their culture. Other sights—slaves working in chains, white men cracking whips and barking orders—would have confirmed that the horrors they had become familiar with at sea would follow them on land. Many captives would soon die, unable to endure the "seasoning" or adjustment period to the West Indian environment, but those who survived would never forget the shipmates who endured the journey with them.[17]

As the *Barbados Packet* captives struggled to adapt and learn how to survive the plantation world, the future of West Indian slavery itself was increasingly uncertain. To be sure, planters were eager to build on the dramatic recent growth of slavery in Berbice and its neighbors, but they faced a number of obstacles. Berbice had been established in the seventeenth century by the Dutch, but was captured by the British in 1796, along with neighboring Demerara and Essequibo. For a short time, Britain's new Guiana colonies were at the center of an expanding British slave system in the southern Caribbean after the Haitian Revolution (1791–1804).[18] Between British occupation and the close of the transatlantic slave trade to the British colonies in 1808, a major blow to planters, some 270 voyages delivered at least 70,000 captives to British Guiana.[19] Thousands more arrived from older West Indian colonies over the next four years, not counting those smuggled in.[20] These enslaved laborers, combined with massive investment of British capital and the region's famously fertile soil, were making Britain's Guiana colonies the most productive and important slave societies in the West Indies. At the height of expansion, however, they were beset by a series of economic crises and imperial experiments in "amelioration" that threatened to bankrupt planters and destroy colonial slavery.[21] Nineteenth-century Berbice was thus the site of two intersecting battles, as planters, lawmakers, and reformers fought to determine the fate of slavery and the plantation system. Meanwhile, enslaved

Africans and their descendants struggled to make viable lives under desperate conditions. Ultimately, and ironically, the survival of the slave system was dependent on the survival of the very people it destroyed.

A Wet Country Between the Tropics

The world that confronted African captives taken to nineteenth-century Berbice had been created by more than two centuries of imperial rivalry and by efforts to develop plantation agriculture in an especially challenging physical environment. The Caribbean coast of South America was unknown to Europeans until the end of the fifteenth century and not colonized for another hundred years. Christopher Columbus's fleet got its first glimpse of the continent (near modern-day Venezuela) in 1498, on his third voyage, but made no effort to settle there. Europeans were soon calling the area between the Orinoco River in the west and the Amazon delta in the east "Guiana," from an indigenous word meaning "land of many waters." It was a fitting name for a region dissected by thousands of rivers and pounded by torrential rains that flooded the land most of the year.

After Columbus, European explorers mostly ignored the Guianas in favor of more lucrative prospects for the next century and a half. Those who did come were looking for quick riches, not places to plant colonies. Englishman Walter Ralegh, the most famous early modern explorer of the Guianas, went looking in the 1590s for the fabled golden city of "Manoa," said to be located on a lake far up a tributary of the Orinoco and ruled by a king who covered himself in gold, "El Dorado." Ralegh's wildly exaggerated account of his 1594–95 voyage, *The Discoverie of the Large, Rich, and Bewtiful Empyre of Guiana* (1596), became an instant publishing success, fed the El Dorado legend, and inspired others to seek their fortunes in the Guianas.[22] Over the next several decades the English, French, and Dutch jockeyed for access to the region, but most failed spectacularly or decided not to pursue settlement.

The Dutch were the first colonists to get a firm foothold in the central Guiana coast, beginning with a series of trading posts in the 1590s. They called it the *Wilde Kust* (Wild Coast) since it was controlled not by Europeans but by *wilden*, native groups that included Arawaks (Lokono), Caribs (Kali'na), Warraus (Waraos), and Akawaios.[23] The colonization of Berbice as a slave society began in 1627, when Abraham van Peere obtained from the recently formed Dutch West India Company a *patroonship* (land grant) ninety miles up the Berbice River, where he built a house on a tall bluff that he called *Peereboom* (Pear Tree). Van Peere and his descendants traded with Berbice's native groups, exchanging manufactured goods like knives and fish-hooks for food, wood, and slaves; cleared the tropical forest to cultivate tobacco and later sugar; and anchored the fledgling colony for the next century. They sold the colony in 1714 to a group of Amsterdam investors who founded the Company of Berbice in 1720 and slowly developed the colony over the eighteenth century. By the 1760s, there were eleven large, Company-owned sugar plantations and perhaps 120 smaller, privately owned estates that produced coffee, cacao, and cotton along the Berbice and Canje Rivers. Though the plantations were located far enough inland to be relatively safe from maritime attack, occasional raids from French privateers and others kept the 350-odd colonists on their guard. The fifty or so soldiers stationed at two small forts near the coast and another, Fort Nassau, some fifty-five miles up the Berbice River, were poorly equipped to defend the colony. Plantation labor came from 4,000 to 5,000 enslaved Africans—many from the Gold Coast—and creoles, as well as 300 native slaves. Beyond the plantations and forts was an impenetrable tangle of "bush," sprawling savannas and jungles that terrified Dutch colonists, inhabited by natives, some of whom had signed treaties with the Dutch pledging to assist them in the event of an invasion or insurrection.[24]

Dutch slaveowners' nightmares became reality in February 1763, when a massive slave rebellion erupted.[25] It turned into a nearly two-year-long civil war that pitted rebels not only against the Dutch and their Native allies but also against one another, ultimately reducing the already small population to just 3,370 slaves and 116 whites.[26] The rebellion—the largest and longest lasting in the Caribbean before the Haitian Revolution—was only barely crushed with the help of indigenous allies, including Caribs recruited from Essequibo, and left dozens of destroyed plantations in its wake. Afterward the Company found it nearly impossible to attract new settlers to a colony associated with a bloody revolt, and many planters sold their estates at a loss and left.[27] A decade later the Dutch government would draft a new slave code, designed to prevent future rebellions, which would have a major impact on slavery in the colony for more than a century.[28]

Even before the brutally repressed 1763–64 rebellion, Berbice and the other "lesser Guiana" colonies, Demerara and Essequibo, lagged far behind the development of other Caribbean plantation societies, all of which (in contrast to North American slave societies) were dependent on the transatlantic slave trade. In Berbice, as in all Caribbean plantation societies, slaves died faster

Figure 3. Dutch Berbice, ca. 1700. *Naauekeurige Plattegrond van den Staat en den Loop van Rio de Berbice*, engraving by Jan Daniël Knapp (Amsterdam: Directeuren van de Kolonie Berbice, ca. 1700). This map, with the Atlantic Ocean on the far right, shows the concentration of plantations along the Berbice and Canje Rivers around 1700, when plantations were clustered dozens of miles inland to deter seaborne attacks against the fledgling colony. It highlights the lack of colonial settlement beyond the thin plantation belt, where savannas (lighter shading) and dense forests or "bush" (darker shading) dominated the landscape. It also reveals the general shape of Berbician plantations, which had narrow frontages along the river but extended deep inland. Later in the eighteenth century and especially after Britain occupied the colony, the gravity of plantation development would move downriver and onto the Atlantic coast, near the new capital of New Amsterdam, leaving many of the plantations seen here abandoned. NG-477, Rijksmuseum, Amsterdam, Netherlands.

than they could reproduce. But planters had trouble getting the number of captives they wanted. Dutch slave traders and merchants preferred to do business with Suriname, a major slave society that bordered Berbice to the east, across the Corantine River, and the island of Curaçao.[29] As early as 1712—less than half a century after the Dutch permanently took Suriname from the English—the colony had 200 plantations and 12,000 slaves.[30] And Berbician slaveowners did not have access to British slave ships, which dominated the slave trade in the eighteenth century.[31] Only about 7,000 African captives, according to surviving records, arrived in Berbice between 1627 and 1760.[32] By one estimate, more than 160,000 slaves disembarked in Suriname during the eighteenth century, whereas only about 34,000 arrived in Berbice.[33] By 1770, Suriname's slave population had grown to 50,000, which was ten times the number of slaves in Berbice on the eve of the 1763 rebellion (4,500–5,000).[34] Compared with colonies such as Saint Domingue, where some 300,000 captives landed between 1700 and 1760, or Jamaica, which imported more than half a million captives in the same period, Berbice was a minor player in the eighteenth-century slave trade.[35]

In the middle of the eighteenth century, however, a de facto British takeover began that would transform Berbice, Demerara, and Essequibo from sparsely populated backwaters into the most profitable plantation societies in the southern Caribbean.[36] Colonial Dutch officials, frustrated by meager military support and investment from their mother country, began in the 1740s to attract foreign—especially British—settlers along with their capital and slaves to Demerara. They enticed potential migrants with generous land grants, tax exemptions, and promises of virgin soil.[37] British planters, "sparing effort nor zeal nor investment," according to the governor of Essequibo, were soon abandoning the "utterly depleted" fields of established colonies like Barbados and Antigua for the Guianas in numbers large enough to concern men like Barbados governor Thomas Robertson, who complained to the British Board of Trade about the exodus.[38]

British planters, however, like their Dutch predecessors, had to contend with an especially challenging physical environment. The Guiana coast was—and is—a land ruled by water. Heavy rains fell much of the year, swelling the colony's rivers, creeks, and canals as they carried sediment and sewage to the sea with the outgoing tides. Incoming tides fought back, dragging the waters of the Atlantic several miles inland. Almost all of the land that was inhabited—and where crops were grown—was below sea level and thus susceptible to flooding at high tide.

Water was both a blessing and a curse. Waterways were the only practical means of carrying people and goods from one place to another. Enslaved people used small dugout canoes known as *corials* to visit spouses and friends on other plantations and run errands for their enslavers. On sugar plantations, flat-bottomed punts were used to transport freshly cut canes from field to mill, replacing the mule carts used in West Indian islands. Colonials traveled to and from town on "tent boats" rowed by teams of slaves. "Colony schooners" connected Berbice to Demerara. Even in New Amsterdam, the Berbice River was virtually, as Pinckard noted, "the only private path, and the only public road."[39] Water also irrigated fields, but too much—or too little—could be disastrous; floods and droughts were constant worries. To control the flow of water, planters developed an elaborate maze of dams, trenches, and sluices that made their estates veritable islands. For enslaved people, the waterways that surrounded them were often deadly.

As colonial maps illustrate, Berbice's population was concentrated in narrow belts along the seacoast and riverbanks well into the nineteenth century.[40] The colony's total land area was large when compared with most West Indian colonies, stretching some sixty miles east to west, from the Corantine River to the Abary Creek, and extending several hundred miles to the south, but the labor and expense of protecting land from flooding discouraged inland settlement beyond the riverbanks. Past the plantations and woodcutting establishments was a seemingly endless hinterland of savanna and bush.

In the wet season, water's power was especially obvious, particularly to newcomers.[41] Pinckard complained that he was "compelled daily to walk mid-leg deep in moist clay, or to drag [his] limbs through a path still deeper in mud."[42] Thomas St. Clair, who praised the quality of Berbice's roads during the dry season—"smooth and level as a bowling-green, without a stone or hill"—found that "in the rainy season, owing to the quantity of clay, they frequently become impassable." On one excursion St. Clair struggled with "horses sinking up to their knees at every step," and on another he complained of being "wet to the skin, which is a common occurrence with travelers in the rainy season." "Here it never rains but it pours," St. Clair explained to his readers, unfamiliar with the tropical climate, "and I will defy greatcoats to resist it."[43] If St. Clair wondered what it might have been like to pick coffee or plant sugarcane under such conditions, he did not write about it.

The stagnant waters of the ubiquitous swamps, puddles, and canals meant that no one could escape "the sharp bitings of myriads of musquitoes."[44] Pinckard recalled a two-mile walk in Demerara that put him and his companions "in danger of being devoured by those annoying insects the mosquitoes."[45] His first night in the colony was a memorably restless one, thanks to the "quadrillions of hungry mosquitoes" who "thrust their lancets into" his flesh.[46] Missionary John Smith similarly began complaining of "moschettos" as soon as he arrived in Demerara: their bites swelled his feet so badly that his shoes no longer fit, and the constant swatting of his bare-legged enslaved congregants distracted him while preaching.[47]

The soggy Guiana environment was uncomfortable for men like Smith, but for the tens of thousands of enslaved people who worked barefoot and were barely clothed—exposed to rain, mud, and waterborne pathogens for hours at a time—it could be fatal. Modern scholarship has confirmed what many colonists and travelers claimed: Berbice's disease environment was "singularly unhealthy."[48] British officials reported in 1816 that the climate "in general [was] proverbially bad, even in comparison with the most sickly of the British West India Islands." The major problem was "the extensive marshes and swamps to which the plantations are for the most part adjacent, and the intersection of all the fields by ditches full of stagnant water." This environment, which led to "much sickness and mortality among the Europeans," was "also extremely unfriendly to the negroes." "Fevers, fluxes, and other diseases of debility" abounded in this "wet country between the tropics."[49] Enslaved people regularly drank from contaminated water sources, which helped make diarrhea the single largest cause of death, killing one in ten.[50] Water was also the perfect breeding ground for mosquitos that transmitted a particularly virulent strain of malaria endemic to the Guianas.[51] Thanks in large part to geography—combined with brutal plantation labor—Berbician slaves had the highest morbidity rate in the nineteenth-century West Indies.[52]

Berbice's environment not only threatened slaves' survival but also presented special challenges for plantation agriculture, which is part of the reason it had not been developed more during the eighteenth century.[53] Controlling water for irrigation and drainage was especially problematic in the nineteenth century since much of the land used for cultivation in that period was manmade, or *empoldered*—reclaimed from the sea and protected by large embankments. Plantations thus needed an elaborate system of dams, seawalls, canals, and sluices to direct the flow of water and protect crops from flooding. Dams or seawalls at the front of plantations prevented saltwater from encroaching and also served as wharves. Large sluices, known as *kokers,* opened at low tide to drain excess fresh water carried by hundreds of miles of trenches and canals that zigzagged the fields, connecting the "front dam" to the "back dam." Plantations were long, narrow rectangles, usually at least 500 or 1,000 acres in size, with frontages of 100 roods (120 feet) and depths of 750 roods, minimizing the expense of constructing and maintaining the front dam or seawall.[54] Every estate, Bolingbroke observed, was "an island within itself," separated from its neighbors by waterways and connected by small foot-bridges.[55] Maintaining these canals and trenches required constant labor, and enslaved workers moved millions of tons of wet clay each year. "Trenching" was a brutal task that enslaved workers hated and one of many ways that the swampy environment shaped—and shortened—their lives.[56] Despite such challenges, the Guianas had geographic advantages—chief among them large tracts of fertile, well-irrigated land—that would help make them the center of a rapid expansion of plantation slavery during the Age of Revolution.

British Capital, Industry, and Perseverance

In the late eighteenth century, the Dutch lost Berbice and its western neigh-bors to the British—first temporarily and then permanently. The global im-perial conflicts that began with the Seven Years' War and ended with the French Revolutionary and Napoleonic Wars led to a series of naval block-ades, occupations, and military skirmishes throughout the Caribbean, in-cluding the Guianas. Between 1780 and 1803, Berbice, Demerara, and Essequibo changed hands some half dozen times, but by 1803 the British were permanently in control of the colonies.[57]

Despite the dizzying changes in imperial control during the Age of Revo-lution, development in Berbice and its neighbors accelerated rapidly, espe-cially after British occupation. The late eighteenth and early nineteenth centuries were a period of remarkable prosperity for planters and investors in newly conquered and largely undeveloped colonies like Berbice, which bene-fited from integration into the British Empire at the same time the plantation economy in Saint Domingue was disintegrating and before Cuba would be-come a major competitor.[58] British capital and colonists flooded into the Gui-anas, lured by vast tracts of fertile land, easy credit, a climate suitable for year-round sugar cultivation, and a southerly location that provided protec-tion from the hurricanes that routinely devastated West Indian islands.[59] En-glishman Henry Bolingbroke, who lived in Demerara during the transition from Dutch to British rule, guessed "the planters of Barbadoes [had] as much capital employed in the [Guiana] colonies on the continent, as they [had] actually in Barbadoes."[60] British slave ships, meanwhile, were free for the first time to call on Guiana ports, where captives fetched higher prices than in the older colonies that had reached their limit of expansion. Slave traders probably delivered as many Africans to British Guiana between 1796 and 1807 as the Dutch had during the entire previous century.[61] Despite horrifyingly high death rates and low birth rates, Berbice's slave population nearly doubled in just three years, from only 8,232 slaves in 1796 to almost 15,000 in 1799. By 1802, the slave population had grown to nearly 18,000, and by 1807 it had exploded to more than 28,000.[62] For abolitionists, this was a nightmare: a new, rapidly expanding, and immensely profitable slave society that was entirely dependent on the transatlantic slave trade for its growth.[63]

Bolingbroke and others, however, celebrated the economic opportunity Britain's new colonies offered, especially in the hands of his countrymen, who were supposedly more entrepreneurial than Dutch planters.[64] "Guyana present[ed]," Bolingbroke wrote, "such a boundless track of country to cultivate."[65] "British capital, industry, and perseverance," Bolingbroke claimed, "had accomplished in eight years, what would not have been done by any other means in half a century." What had until recently been "a low marshy sea coast, covered with overgrown timber and underwood, inundated by every rising tide, [had] now grown into a colony, bestowing riches on its founders and support to several thousand individuals."[66] Bolingbroke was right: Britain's Guiana colonies were, as historian Seymour Drescher has shown, "the very epitome of British expansionism between 1797 and 1807."[67]

British investment—most of it in the form of laboring bodies—transformed Berbice and its western neighbors into important producers of sugar and the leading producers of coffee and cotton in the British Empire.[68] Planters made legendary profits as they increased production of plantation staples that sold at high prices. Between 1789 and 1802, sugar exports rose 433 percent, coffee exports rose 233 percent, and cotton exports rose a staggering 862 percent.[69] It was rumored that in the Guiana colonies "a slave would pay his purchase in twelve months."[70] Though Berbice, Demerara, and Essequibo (along with Trinidad, which Britain conquered from Spain in 1797) had much smaller populations than older West Indian colonies like Jamaica, they were far more productive in the early nineteenth century. Together, Berbice, Demerara-Essequibo (the colonies were united in 1814), and Trinidad produced an average of nearly 20 percent of the total British Caribbean sugar output between 1814 and 1823. Between 1823 and 1834 they produced one-third of the total sugar output, which was as much as Jamaica and all other colonies combined. British Guiana alone produced one-fourth of all British Caribbean sugar between 1823 and 1834.[71]

In Berbice, which was never a sugar monoculture, other crops were also profitable in the years after British occupation. Cotton production surged to meet the demand of British textile mills.[72] A cotton planter in 1799 could supposedly make a profit of £6,000 on a crop of 60,000 pounds.[73] Cotton and coffee cultivation expanded until about 1810, when their prices on the British market peaked, and only then did Berbician planters begin devoting serious attention to sugar.[74] Even two decades later, when the number of sugar estates had grown significantly, less than half of all slaves lived on sugar plantations.[75]

Unfortunately for planters and even more so for their slaves, Berbice's extraordinary economic boom was short-lived. The "golden age" that began in the 1790s ended two decades later with a series of economic crises that jeopardized slaveowners' profits and led to harsher conditions for enslaved workers.[76] The first major blow came in 1806, when the ban on the transatlantic slave trade to newly acquired colonies like Berbice cut off the supply of laborers at the height of demand. Slaveowners, who had invested heavily to expand production during the boom years, thus faced the challenge of creating a self-sustaining labor force in one of the most unhealthy disease environments in the West Indies.[77] The Guianas were extraordinarily profitable, but they were also death traps. Their populations had grown through immigration, not reproduction, like all Atlantic slave societies other than North America.[78] As observers like Bolingbroke recognized, the immediate end of the transatlantic slave trade "would be almost utter destruction" to the Guianas' plantation economy.[79] Although planters could legally purchase some slaves from other British colonies until 1828, restrictions on the intercolonial slave trade combined with the declining slave populations of other West Indian colonies meant that the number of slaves available would never be enough to satisfy demand.[80]

Planters in both Berbice and Demerara struggled after losing access to the transatlantic slave trade, but conditions were especially bad in Berbice. Demerara planters were better able to import slaves from other colonies—including Berbice—because the extraordinary productivity of the more numerous sugar plantations there allowed them to pay the highest prices for slaves in the nineteenth-century British Caribbean. Demerara was one of only three net importers of slaves after 1807.[81]

On the heels of losing access to the transatlantic slave trade, planters faced other crises: the collapse of the cotton and coffee industries around 1810, followed by the decline of the sugar industry that was supposed to be the colony's savior. Competition from the rapidly expanding cotton kingdom of the southern United States, which produced more cotton than the West Indies and at cheaper prices and which became Great Britain's largest supplier of cotton by 1800, devastated Berbice's cotton planters.[82] Producers of coffee suffered too, with falling prices on the British market made worse by the metropolitan government's refusal to allow exports to the United States.[83] Unable to profit from their principal crops as they once had, planters with sufficient capital turned to sugar, while many others lost their properties and their slaves to overseas creditors. Between 1809 and 1824, 111 cotton plantations and 21 coffee estates were abandoned; 19 were converted to sugar, but the majority simply sat idle and were reclaimed by the bush.[84] Sugar cultivation, moreover, was no panacea: the price of sugar on the international market declined after 1816, when sugar from Brazil, the East Indies, and Cuba began flooding the market, pushing prices to their lowest point in 1822–23— years of crisis in more ways than one for Berbician planters.[85]

As the cotton and coffee economies collapsed in Berbice, large numbers of Berbician slaves were torn from their homes, friends, and kin to work on Demerara sugar estates.[86] Berbice's slave population declined by nearly one-third between 1807 and 1834 (compared with 14 percent for the British Caribbean as a whole)—the result of high death rates, low birth rates, and the transfer of thousands of slaves to Demerara.[87] What investors and planters experienced as economic crisis was, for the enslaved, a human catastrophe.

Living and Dying on Slavery's Frontier

Nineteenth-century Berbice remained a frontier colony that never rivaled the large slave societies of the eighteenth-century Caribbean, such as Jamaica or Saint Domingue, and much less nineteenth-century Cuba, Brazil, or the United States. Enslaved people continued to die, and planters could no longer replace them. As a late-developing or "third-phase" West Indian colony, Berbice was structured—and hampered—by its short-lived and intense participation in the transatlantic slave trade under British rule.[88] Its slave population never came close to that of other early nineteenth-century British colonies like Jamaica (348,825 slaves), Barbados (75,000 slaves), or Demerara-Essequibo (80,915 slaves).[89] From a peak of just 28,480 in 1807, the slave population declined to only 19,360 by emancipation in 1834.[90]

Like other third-phase colonies, the majority of Berbice's population was

African-born. At the end of the transatlantic slave trade, some three-fourths of Berbician slaves were recent arrivals from Africa, such as those who arrived on the *Barbados Packet*, and as late as 1819, nearly 54 percent of all slaves were African.[91] Berbice's African majority distinguished it from most West Indian colonies, which had stopped expanding by the mid- or late eighteenth century and subsequently only imported captives to replace those who died, and from the southern colonies of North America, where the slave population began to reproduce itself as early as the mid-eighteenth century. In Britain's oldest Caribbean colonies, unlike Berbice, most slaves were creoles. Among British colonies, only the other third-phase colonies of Demerara-Essequibo (54.7 percent) and Trinidad (54.4 percent) had marginally higher proportions of Africans in their slave populations.[92] Berbice was thus one of the most demographically—and culturally—African places in the British Caribbean.

The enslaved Africans taken to Berbice had diverse origins. Slave registration returns from 1819 suggest that more Africans came from Central Africa (22.5 percent) and the Bight of Benin (22.2 percent) than other areas. Significant numbers also came from the Bight of Biafra (16.5 percent), the largest supplier of captives to the British Caribbean as a whole in the late eighteenth century, and the Gold Coast (14.8 percent). Captives from other regions were less prominent, with 10.1 percent from Senegambia, 8.2 percent from Sierra Leone, and only 5.7 percent from the Windward Coast—the origin of the *Barbados Packet* captives.[93] Adding to this geographic diversity was the fact that every slave-exporting region contained multiple ethnicities, speech communities, and polities. Ports of embarkation collected people from several societies that often stretched a hundred or more miles inland.[94] The largest ethnolinguistic groups in Berbice, according to the registration returns, were, in descending order: Kongo (from Central Africa), Coramantee (from the Gold Coast), Popo (from the Bight of Benin), Igbo (from the Bight of Biafra), and Malinke (from Senegambia).[95] Africans enslaved in Berbice thus carried with them diverse memories of home and a multitude of cultural practices and ideas about the ways societies ought to function.

The transatlantic slave trade also created uneven sex ratios in Berbice and other third-phase colonies. Slave ship cargoes contained many more men than women—a consequence of African preferences for retaining women as well as American buyers' willingness to pay higher prices for men. As a result, Berbice had one of the highest male-to-female sex ratios—128.4 males per 100 females in 1817—of all British West Indian colonies in the nineteenth century.[96] This preponderance of men would have important consequences for enslaved people's family lives and make it that much more difficult for the slave population to reproduce itself.

If Berbice's frontier status was not immediately obvious to African captives who were landed at New Amsterdam, the colony's capital and only town, it was to European visitors.[97] When George Pinckard arrived as part of the British occupation in 1796, it was "yet an embryo." "The whole scenery at New Amsterdam," Pinckard wrote, "betrays the infant state of the colony. The dreariness of the land, just robbed of its thick woods—the nakedness that prevails around the Government house—the want of roads and paths—the wild savanna—the heavy forests; in short all that meets the eye conveys the idea of a country just emerging from its original wildness, into cultivation."[98] Dwellings were made of timber at a time when other West Indian port cities were more likely to use brick or stone.[99] Beyond the town and the fort a couple miles downriver Pinckard saw only a "deep and wild savanna" full of "enormous snakes, alligators, loud-roaring frogs, and other reptiles." This "naked waste," as it appeared to Pinckard, "extend[ed] to a great distance, and [was] bordered by dark forests" where "Indians range[d] wild and free" among the "tigers" (jaguars), monkeys, and parrots.[100]

Henry Bolingbroke was more generous than Pinckard, but he also recognized the town's shortcomings. He praised the Dutch for having "paid every attention to health and convenience" in planning the town, making each quarter-acre lot "an island within itself," separated from its neighbors by canals that filled at high tide and "empt[ied] themselves every [low] tide, by which means all the filth and dirt is carried off before it has time to stagnate." The "very long and narrow" houses faced the water and had "galleries on either side for the purpose of walking and smoaking in the shade." The Government House and attached buildings were "laid out in a splendid manner" and made of brick, but "even these [were] not perfect." As Bolingbroke saw it, "the eye and the taste [were] both insulted on looking at this fine pile of buildings from the river," because only twenty yards away was a boatbuilder's yard full of black artisans. The governor and his family were therefore "obliged to wade through a group of negroes at work, a heap of chips, boiling pitch pots and many other delicate etcæteras to embark on board [their] yatcht." Visitors like Bolingbroke found little in the way of public entertainment, though they did have their choice of two taverns where they might play billiards, get their boots cleaned, drink their fill of sangaree and wine, and, at night's end, sling their hammocks from the rafters.[101]

New Amsterdam was home to perhaps 2,000 enslaved people—many of them *winkel* ("shop") slaves the British Crown inherited from the Dutch when it seized the colony—and a few hundred free people of color.[102] At least 90 percent of the colony's slaves lived outside of town. There were no more than 250 whites. Although the town grew under British rule, it never became a large urban center like Kingston, Jamaica (17,954 slaves in 1817); Bridgetown, Barbados (9,284 slaves in 1817); or even Georgetown, Demerara (3,589 slaves in 1813 and 6,676 by 1832).[103] As late as 1818, some thirty years after New Amsterdam was founded, people still referred to it as the "new town."[104]

Berbice's white population was remarkably small, even by the standards of the West Indies. Few Europeans were eager to live in a crude society that lacked the comforts of home and where many goods were prohibitively expensive; the region's reputation as the unhealthiest in the Caribbean must have made it an especially unattractive destination.[105] Whenever possible, planters preferred to stay in Europe, entrusting the management of their plantations to resident attorneys, managers, and overseers—middling and poor whites who often lacked other employment opportunities. In contrast to many slaveholding regions in the United States, where the majority of enslaved people lived on small landholdings with resident owners and in close contact with non-slave-owning whites, Berbice was characterized by large plantations, nearly two-thirds of which were owned by absentees who lived in Britain, the Netherlands, and Austria.[106]

The colony also had one of the most extreme black-to-white ratios in the Americas, with more than 95 percent of its population African or African-descended. Slavery in the American South, in contrast, was mainly characterized by black minorities and significant numbers of whites. Even in Lowcountry South Carolina, the only North American region with a significant black majority, blacks outnumbered whites only by about two to one "at the peak of black predominance."[107] Berbice, in contrast, was overwhelmingly black. In 1799, just before the British permanently occupied the colony, there were only 428 whites, compared with 14,792 slaves and 242 free people of color.[108] Roughly a decade later, with a much larger slave population, there were still only about 500 whites in the entire colony, and blacks outnumbered whites 46 to 1.[109] A decade and a half later, the white population had barely increased to 570.[110] And because nearly half the colony's white population lived in New Amsterdam, the black majority was even more pronounced in the plantation zone, where estates of 100 or more slaves—normal for Caribbean sugar colonies or Brazil but not at all typical of the United States—might only have one resident white.[111]

The vast majority of Berbician slaves were condemned to short, brutal lives on rural estates where they planted, harvested, and processed cotton, coffee, and sugar. By custom and eventually by law, the typical workday lasted twelve hours, six days a week (Sunday was supposed to be a day off). Slaves rose before sunrise to begin work at 6:00 a.m. and stayed in the fields until 11:00 a.m., when they were supposed to have a two-hour break during the hottest hours of the day to cook and prepare their first meal. They were to return to work by 1:00 p.m. and finish by 6:00 p.m. or sundown. Starting and stopping times were signaled by the crack of a driver's whip, bells, or gunfire. In practice, however, overseers, managers, and drivers often forced enslaved people to work longer hours. Slaves assigned to task work—which coexisted with gang labor in Berbice—often found their workload so onerous that they were obliged to skip the midday break, and during the weeks- or months-long harvest season on sugar plantations, slaves processed cane in mills and boiling houses at a breakneck pace through the night. Many slaveowners, moreover, ignored the prohibition on Sunday labor and assigned additional work as punishment. Working conditions worsened after British occupation and especially after the slave trade to Berbice ended, as overextended planters sought to extract more work from smaller gangs of slaves, curtailing many of the customary privileges or rights enslaved people had under Dutch rule, including much-needed time to cultivate the gardens and provision grounds that supplemented their scanty rations of food. The switch from cotton and coffee to sugar—the most labor-intensive crop—made matters even worse for enslaved workers on sugar estates.[112]

These deteriorating conditions may have been the spark that prompted several dozen enslaved people to plan a revolt in February 1814. That month, a plantation manager on Berbice's western Atlantic coast reported, according to the governor, "that undue Night Meetings took place upon some adjoining Estates." He knew this thanks to a "trusty Negroe" who said that he "had been invited to join [the rebellion], but had refused." The manager ordered the informant "to join the Party & acquaint him with the Progress." When the governor heard about the conspiracy, he immediately summoned the Court of Policy and then went to Fort St. Andrews "to consult with the commanding officer of the Troops . . . respecting the most effective steps to be taken to seize the ringleaders, without creating any alarm." The governor commandeered three ships to transport sixty troops across the river to thwart the revolt. They traveled by night and "arrived on the Estates on the West Coast at the moment the Negroes were turning out to their work." They arrested thirty-six slaves—and detained several dozen more—and brought them to trial.[113]

The governor concluded that the would-be rebels "intended to murder the Whites & take possession of the Estates for their own benefit," rather than destroying them by arson, as previous rebels had done. According to one of the enslaved conspirators, they had appointed "a King, several Governors, Fiscals, a Lawyer, a Captain of the Fort," and designated "the Negroes who had no appointments Soldiers." Only men participated in the plotting; they "exile[d] their wives & every woman from their Meetings."[114]

The rebellion was only narrowly thwarted because of the conspirators' delay in acquiring rum, probably for a loyalty oath ceremony. According to Thomas, one of the plotters, an enslaved man he identified as "old Banaba" was "King of the whole," and they had been waiting "only for the arrival of one more Jug of rum which was expected by the return of Captain Tobias belonging to [plantation] No. 22 to commence their march straight to town, and fight with White people." After the rebellion, Banaba planned to occupy the governor's residence. Quamina (also known as Oxford) similarly confessed that they had planned "to fight Buckras," and that Banaba and his co-leader John "were to take the Country" for themselves.[115]

The punishments inflicted on the conspirators were predictably harsh, designed to serve, the governor wrote, "as a dreadful Example to deter others from attempting the same."[116] Six men were executed. Twelve others were banished from the colony and sold abroad. The rest were sentenced to brutal floggings or to work in chains for periods of up to six months.[117] The informants, meanwhile, including a driver named Alexander, were rewarded with official recognition of their "fidelity & attachment to the Whites" with annual cash payments, commemorative silver medals and staffs, and annual bonuses of clothing.[118] After the trial, the government took steps to prevent future acts of resistance, more strictly enforcing laws on enslaved people's movements, forbidding slaves to dance until the following year, providing the militia new equipment, and resuming paramilitary drills.[119] Slaveowners and colonial officials were thus reminded in 1814 of what they had always known: that some slaves hated slavery enough to risk their lives trying to escape it, that their grip on control was fragile, and that public spectacles of violence and terror were necessary to thwart resistance. The role of the state, however, and in particular its legal authorities in regulating slavery, would become an especially contentious issue over the next several decades.

Slave Law, Imperial Intervention, and Amelioration

The legacy of Dutch colonialism left its imprint on Berbice long after the British takeover, distinguishing it from other British plantation societies in important ways. The colony's physical landscape was the most visible legacy of the Dutch, who had perfected the use of *polders* and *kokers* in the old world before using them to establish plantations in the Guianas, but there were other clues to Berbice's difference. Plantations carried names like Op Hoop van Beter, Rotterdam, and Niewen Hoop. Newspapers printed notices in Dutch and carried news of ships recently arrived from Amsterdam. Berbice Dutch could be heard on many estates. Colonists calculated costs and paid debts in guilders.[120] Perhaps a third of all plantations were still in Dutch hands.[121] But by far the most important thing the Dutch left in Berbice was a distinctive legal regime that profoundly shaped the relationships between enslaved people, their enslavers, and colonial authorities. In nineteenth-century Berbice, enslaved people took advantage of the colony's Dutch legal heritage— as well as new reforms instituted as part of the British government's experiment in "amelioration"—to claim rights and struggle for survival in ways that were much more difficult, if not impossible, in many other Atlantic slave societies.

The most important feature of the legal system in Berbice was the presence of a powerful legal official known as the fiscal. This institution was a holdover from Berbice's Dutch period, which concluded in 1803 with a treaty that surrendered the colony (along with Demerara and Essequibo) to the British and guaranteed that Dutch customs and laws, including their slave codes and judicial processes, would be maintained.[122] As a result, even several decades after the British takeover, Berbice was a British colony with a largely Dutch-based legal system that differentiated it from other West Indian colonies and the United States and where enslaved people could appeal to a powerful government official for redress.[123]

The office of the fiscal was unique in the British Caribbean to Berbice and Demerara.[124] Bolingbroke described the fiscal to British readers, who would have been unfamiliar with this official, as "chief magistrate, public accuser, and attorney general, to prosecute in all cases for the sovereign."[125] One of the fiscal's major roles was to enforce the Rule on the Treatment of Servants and Slaves, a Dutch code enacted in 1772 to make the rights and obligations of enslaved people and enslavers explicit and, Dutch officials hoped, diffuse the sort of tensions that had led to the 1763 rebellion. Enslaved people could appeal to the fiscal for redress, and slaveowners or their representatives could also make formal complaints against their slaves. The Dutch had adopted the institution from the Spanish, who had inherited it from the Romans. When the British seized the Dutch Guiana colonies, they maintained the office.[126] The fiscal continued to hear enslaved people's complaints against their enslavers (and sometimes against one another) as well as complaints from free people against slaves.[127] Berbice was thus one of the only places in the Anglo-Atlantic world where enslaved people had formal access to legal intermediaries through whom they could negotiate their relationships and make claims, distinguishing it from both the United States and other British Caribbean colonies.

The fiscal had wide-reaching authority and was well compensated. He could summon anyone to testify, and he usually handled cases summarily, levying fines against overseers, managers, and slaveowners when he found in favor of enslaved complainants, and, more commonly, sentencing enslaved people to corporal punishment or imprisonment when he determined that they complained without cause or lied. The fiscal had his own police force, known as *dienaars*, who assisted him in investigations that often took place on plantations themselves.[128] Before 1814 he received one-third of all the fines and fees he levied (on top of his £3,000 annual salary), thus giving him a financial incentive to encourage slaves' complaints and to rule in their favor.[129] After 1814 his salary was increased to between £6,000 and £8,000 a year, making him the highest paid official in Berbice.[130]

Although the fiscal had the power to punish slaveowners, managers, and overseers, he was no more impartial than the law of slavery itself, which was designed primarily to stabilize slavery, not protect slaves. Moreover, as a European, a high-ranking colonial official, and a slaveowner, the fiscal was generally sympathetic to the priorities of his peers—other white men who owned or managed slaves and who viewed enslaved people as dangerous, lazy, and prone to complaining without cause.[131] Michael Samuel Bennett, the long-serving fiscal appointed in 1809, owned several domestic slaves and was part owner of two large sugar plantations.[132] He believed slaves were "in the habit of exaggerating their complaints and, indeed . . . very often [their complaints] are unfounded; nine times in ten they proceed from the most indolent and worthless negroes."[133] Not surprisingly, enslaved complainants usually had their cases dismissed.

Nevertheless, the very fact that slaves in Berbice had an official mechanism for making their grievances known—and that slaveowners could be held accountable for certain kinds of illegal mistreatment—distinguished the colony from most other Anglo-American slave societies, where enslaved people had no regular access to the legal system and where slaveowners were generally able to ignore laws governing the treatment of slaves with impunity. Slaves in Berbice had learned under Dutch rule that they had legal rights in addition to the customary ones they had won through hard-fought negotiation. They had also learned how to appeal to a powerful official when their rights were violated, and knew that sometimes they could succeed. By the time the British occupied the colony, Berbician slaves thus had a robust tradition of legal activism. They would build on this foundation during the 1820s, when the Crown clarified and expanded the law of slavery as part of its plan to ameliorate slavery.

The 1820s were bad years for Guiana planters. News from Britain about intensifying debates over abolition—reprinted in colonial newspapers and communicated in private letters—made slaveowners nervous. Developments in 1823 were especially troubling. The prices of coffee, cotton, and sugar had reached their lowest point, exacerbating the economic crisis that began more than a decade earlier.[134] But the most ominous development was a reinvigorated antislavery movement that enjoyed broad support in Britain for abolishing or at least reforming colonial slavery.

In January 1823, veteran abolitionists reorganized themselves as the Society for the Mitigation and Gradual Abolition of Slavery Throughout the British Dominions (better known as the Anti-Slavery Society). Antislavery activists realized that closing the transatlantic slave trade to British colonies had not, contrary to their hopes, brought about the decline of slavery or improvement in the conditions slaves faced, so they refocused their energies on softening and ultimately ending slavery through appeals to the public and Parliament.[135] In May, William Wilberforce introduced a petition in the House of Commons for emancipation. Two months later he published *An Appeal . . . in Behalf of the Negro Slaves*. Thomas Clarkson's *Thoughts on the Necessity of Improving the Condition of the Slaves* appeared the same year. Abolitionists portrayed the West Indies as a backward colonial space that required direct metropolitan intervention to reduce the arbitrary power of slaveowners, Christianize and civilize slaves, and pave the way for a peaceful transition to free labor.[136] Thomas Buxton, president of the Anti-Slavery Society and Member of Parliament, petitioned Parliament to enact a comprehensive slave code that would promote gradual emancipation, expand missionary activity, and prepare enslaved people and slaveowners alike for emancipation.[137] His proposal combined elements from various reform movements and experiments that went back more than half a century, including domestic penal reform and efforts by planters themselves to make plantation slavery more "rational," drawing on Enlightenment-inspired managerial theories.[138]

Absentee planters, acutely aware of the rising tide of antislavery, responded with their own, more conservative plan for the "amelioration," or gradual improvement, of slavery, seeking a compromise that would satisfy calls for reform and soften the public image of slavery enough to preserve it.[139] Parliament adopted the proposals of the West India Committee as the blueprint for the imperial government's amelioration program.[140] And circulars the Colonial Office sent West Indian governors later that year announced the Crown's commitment to amelioration and instructed local legislatures to revise their laws as necessary. The year 1823 thus marked a major shift in imperial policy, with the Crown now committed to reforming slavery through new legislation—and new means of enforcement.[141]

Colonial opposition was predictably fierce, especially among resident planters, who claimed that they had already done much, on their own initiative, to ameliorate slavery and that mere mention of additional reforms would prompt slaves to rebel and destroy the West Indian economy.[142] Such fears were understandable: news of parliamentary legislation regarding slavery had helped ignite a rebellion in Barbados in 1816.[143] And in August 1823, as the transatlantic debate over amelioration raged on, planters' worst fears were realized when a rebellion of some 10,000 to 12,000 slaves erupted in Demerara. The Demerara rebellion, like many others, was sparked by a ubiquitous rumor that the Crown had endorsed amelioration or emancipation but local authorities were hiding "the new laws" from slaves.[144] Colonial Office dispatches had begun arriving in Demerara in early July, and slaveowners were quick to blame abolitionists and especially missionaries for the rebellion. The enslaved rebels were indeed well informed of metropolitan debates. They spoke of the new rights they were to be granted and of "the powerful men in England" thought to be on their side, such as Wilberforce.[145] Though the rebellion was quickly and brutally suppressed, it strengthened colonial opposition to amelioration, with many colonies passing measures explicitly opposing the Crown's calls for reform.[146] In the Guianas, opposition to metropolitan interference and especially missionary activity was so fierce that the London Missionary Society's John Smith, who had lived in Demerara since 1817, was convicted of instigating the rebellion and sentenced to death. During Smith's trial, his fellow missionary in Berbice, John Wray, had his chapel burned down in what was likely arson meant to intimidate him.[147]

Despite colonial backlash, the Crown pressured its colonies to enact new laws to ameliorate slavery in the mid-1820s, beginning with a March 1824 Order in Council that applied to Trinidad—the first site of the British Empire's experiment in amelioration.[148] Demerara reluctantly followed suit later that year, drafting its own code based on Trinidad's. And in Berbice, after procrastinating for two years, the council of government enacted a forty-four-clause slave code—based largely on Demerara's—to ameliorate slavery.[149]

Berbice's 1826 slave code—the first under British rule—was a wide-ranging document that codified and expanded enslaved people's rights, clarified the mutual obligations of slaves and enslavers, and enacted new enforcement mechanisms. Among other things, the law limited the extent to which slaves could be punished, permitted slaves to formally marry, allowed them to own most kinds of property, affirmed their access to Christian worship, and permitted them to purchase their freedom without an owner's consent ("compulsory manumission"). Those who violated the new law could be fined, imprisoned, or banned from supervising slaves. Together, these stipulations were meant to lessen slaves' material suffering, reduce the arbitrary power of enslavers, and prepare both parties for emancipation and the shift to wage labor.[150]

The most radical provisions of the 1826 slave code—and the ones that would have the largest impact on enslaved people's daily lives—were its enforcement mechanisms. Antislavery activists, reformers, and politicians had long argued that the unenforceability of laws regulating slavery was a major obstacle to amelioration. By the early nineteenth century, many colonies had protective clauses in their slave codes, but they were rarely enforced. The 1750 observation of Jamaican governor Edward Trelawny that "many wholesome Regulations enacted in this Island for the Government of Slaves . . . as they can be enforced only by due Course of Law, they are not and cannot be enforced at all, and every one in fact, does as he lists with his own Slaves," remained a fairly accurate description into the late eighteenth and early nineteenth centuries.[151] Colonial officials—most of whom were slaveowners— lacked the political will and the resources to supervise the treatment of slaves or prosecute crimes against enslaved people.

Early proposals to create a comprehensive slave code that could actually be enforced went nowhere. One such proposal came from Edmund Burke, who in 1780 drafted a "Sketch of a Negro Code."[152] Taking his cue from Spanish and French slave codes, Burke argued that enslaved people should not "be under the sole guardianship of their Masters, or their Attornies and Overseers." They should have the right, Burke insisted, to present their grievances before a "protector of negroes." The protector would be authorized to investigate slaves' complaints and report violations of the law. He would have help from official "Inspectors," to be "placed in convenient districts in each island." The inspectors would visit plantations and submit reports to the protector regarding "the state and condition of the negroes in their districts." The protector would have the authority to order that slaves who had been "cruelly and inhumanly treated" or who labored under an overseer with "particular malice" be sold to another, presumably better, owner—a practice known in Spanish colonies as *papel*. Floggings were to be limited to no more than thirteen "blows" or "stripes," unless a justice of the peace authorized more severe punishment.[153] The kind of changes that Burke called for were far too radical for the imperial government in the late eighteenth century, and abolitionists were far more concerned with drumming up the support needed to ban the transatlantic slave trade—their immediate goal—than they were with slavery itself, so nothing came of proposals like his.

Yet by 1823, Parliament had endorsed strikingly similar legislation, recognizing that enforcing protections for slaves required a strong government committed to surveilling colonial slavery in new ways. The amelioration laws of the 1820s, including Berbice's, forced West Indian colonies to implement an unprecedented system of supervision and record-keeping that subjected slaveowners, plantation managers, and local officials to the scrutiny of the imperial government. This expansion of Crown authority was also a limited yet important move toward incorporating enslaved people into the body politic of the British Empire, expanding their rights and giving them a legal personality. Central to these transformations were the new powers the Crown exerted through its colonial officials.

In Berbice, the responsibility for advancing amelioration fell primarily to the protector of slaves, a newly created official who took over and expanded the fiscal's role in hearing enslaved people's complaints. The office of the protector, like other aspects of amelioration, was modeled on precedents borrowed from Spanish (for example, *protector de esclavos*, *protector de índios*, and *síndico procurador*) and French (for example, *procureur général*) colonies. Like the Dutch, the Iberians had a Roman legal tradition that provided a modicum of official protection for slaves. Shortly after Britain conquered Trinidad from Spain, the Colonial Office adopted the office of protector as part of its experiment in amelioration.[154] In Berbice, before the 1826 slave code, the fiscal also served as protector. Afterward the protector became a distinct, full-time, salaried position, to be staffed by a man prohibited from owning slaves or plantations. The colony was divided into districts with their own civil magistrates, who were also designated assistant protectors of slaves. Like the fiscal, the protector could examine witnesses in his New Amsterdam office, conduct investigations on plantations, and punish owners, managers, and overseers who violated laws on the treatment of enslaved people by summarily applying fines or referring cases to the fiscal for prosecution in criminal court. He was an intermediary between slaves and masters, colony and metropole.

Secretary of state Henry Bathurst instructed Berbice's new protector of slaves, David Power, that he should not feel obliged to "wait to receive complaints from the Slaves themselves." If Power "hear[d] of any unwarrantable treatment to which any Slave, or gang of Slaves are exposed," he was to travel "to the estate, and there institute a diligent inquiry into the conduct of the persons who may be responsible upon the occasion." Bathurst cautioned, however, that Power not undermine slaveowners' authority. His responsibility was "to secure all the legal rights of the proprietor as well as of the Slave," and although he was to communicate to slaves that he was their "vigilant friend and protector," he was also to let them know that he was "entirely determined to discountenance any frivolous and unfounded complaints which may be preferred against their masters."[155]

One of the protector's major responsibilities was to collect and analyze several new kinds of documents meant to track the progress of amelioration. The most important of these were "Punishment Record Book[s]." The law required that slaveowners (with more than six slaves) or their representatives keep detailed accounts of all punishments they inflicted. The colonial government distributed standardized forms with blanks for the name and sex of the enslaved person punished, the time and location of punishment, the "offence" committed, the names of witnesses, and "the number of stripes actually inflicted on the offender" or the length of time in confinement. Anyone convicted of failing to document a punishment or falsifying records was subject to a substantial fine.[156]

Punishment records were designed to subject the behavior of enslavers and the enslaved alike to the scrutiny of colonial officials and thereby expand the reach of state power into previously private realms. A civil magistrate who explained the 1826 reforms to slaves was explicit about their dual purpose, echoing Bathurst's instructions to Power: "I made it a point to impress upon their minds that the Punishment record book was meant not only as a check on the conduct of the managers towards the slaves, but also as a record . . . to know such of the Negroes whose characters are really bad and that such as appeared often in that book would be debarred of many of the benefits afforded to the slaves of good characters by the provisions of this code."[157]

The protector of slaves collected punishment records twice a year and used them, along with other evidence he was required to solicit, when preparing his reports. These reports included "Abstract[s] of Offences committed by Male and Female Plantation Slaves," quantifying the violence inflicted on slaves and the various "offences" they had supposedly committed, as well lists of slaves who had been manumitted and formally married, the amounts that had been deposited in a new "savings bank" for slaves, and accounts of the progress that had been made in converting enslaved people to Christianity. The lieutenant governor then reviewed these reports, adding his own remarks before sending them to the Colonial Office, which combed through piles of documents generated by amelioration to gauge compliance with the new laws.

Metropolitans were deeply interested in the records coming out of Berbice and other Crown colonies in the era of amelioration and especially in slaves' complaints to the fiscals and protectors of slaves. The House of Commons' *Parliamentary Papers* and abolitionist periodicals such as the *Anti-Slavery Reporter* often published enslaved people's complaints verbatim.[158] Abolitionists argued that such records "admit[ted] [readers] into the interior, the very penetralia of the slave system, which they exhibit[ed] in all its height and length and breadth and depth of deformity."[159] The thousands of documents that crossed the Atlantic made it possible, in theory, for any literate metropolitan to know what was happening to enslaved people on the other side of the Atlantic.

The reports of the fiscals and protectors of slaves, moreover, were only part of the disciplinary paperwork generated by amelioration. The 1826 slave code also required that every plantation have a "hospital" or "sick-house," and "that a book or register be kept in every such hospital, in which the names and treatment of all such slaves be respectively entered by the medical attendant." Similar surveillance accompanied the treadmill, a new and supposedly humane punishment invented in England in 1818 and quickly exported to the West Indies.[160] The "Regulations for the Tread Mill" stipulated that a "Jail Surgeon" was to "examine all Persons before they are put to work on the Mill, and declare their fitness, and whether he considers them able to bear the full punishment that may be allotted to them or a more limited number of spells." The regulations also provided that the "under-sheriff, or his Assistant, shall attend during the whole time the Mill is working" and keep written "Mill Books," or "Monthly Return[s] of Slaves Worked on the Tread Mill."[161]

These enforcement mechanisms ultimately did less to soften slavery than to redefine and in some cases destabilize relationships between slaves and masters, colonies and metropole. Transforming colonial slavery, however haphazardly, required the Crown to begin to treat enslaved people less like the personal property of autonomous slaveowners and more like nascent British subjects with at least some legal protections and access to the legal system.[162] Reconstructing slave–master relationships by reducing the power of colonial slaveowners was, in this respect, a first step toward eroding slavery.[163] As Mary Turner has argued, "to dismantle chattel slavery meant beginning the transition to wage work, preparing slave workers and slave-owners to become servants and masters, employees and employers. This process required first and foremost that owner–slave relationships be defined by law and systematically applied to both parties by enhancing the powers of the colonial state."[164]

For enslaved people in Berbice, the laws and institutions created during amelioration expanded their possibilities for seeking redress and asserting their rights. As they had long done under Dutch colonialism, they turned to legal officials who represented an imperial government increasingly seen by slaves as a potential ally, especially in their efforts to limit the authority of overseers, managers, and slaveowners. Moreover, in taking the risk of making their grievances known, enslaved people created a rich archive that allows us to reconstruct their daily struggles and understand their politics during a transformative period in the Atlantic world.

It took a great deal of courage to turn to the colonial legal system for redress. Failure was likely and retribution almost certain. And yet, despite the risks, thousands of enslaved people in early nineteenth-century Berbice did just that. Every week, men and women, Africans and creoles, left the plantations, homes, and workshops where they were enslaved—alone and in groups, with or without permission—and traveled to government offices in New Amsterdam.[165] They turned to the fiscal and protector of slaves, as one enslaved woman put it in 1826, "to get my right."[166] Taken together, the thousands of pages produced by enslaved people's legal activism make it possible to hear their voices, however muffled or incomplete, in ways that are unimaginable for most Atlantic slave societies.[167]

When we listen to those voices, filled with fear and anger, determination and hope, we hear painful stories about trying to make tolerable lives under horrific conditions. They are stories not only about the many conflicts enslaved people had with overseers, managers, and slaveowners, but also the challenges they faced in their relationships with other slaves and colonists. Field laborers sought protection from sadistic managers who flogged them while pregnant, locked them in dark cells for "insolence," and exceeded the legal limits on corporal punishment. Others complained about drivers who forced them to stay in the fields while sick or were otherwise too strict in enforcing their enslaver's orders. Married men complained about their wives' infidelity, and women, in turn, told stories about physically and sexually abusive men. Enslaved people also told officials about practitioners of obeah who used spiritual power to heal—and to kill. They complained about slaveowners who refused to provide the food and clothing they needed, neighbors who broke into their homes and stole their property, and free people of color who refused to settle their debts. When woven together, these individual stories represent enslaved people's dogged fight to survive. And although they rarely got the redress they sought, the mere act of voicing their complaints was itself an act of survival.

CHAPTER 2

Challenging the "Right of a Master to Punish"

An enslaved man named Bob went to Berbice's deputy protector of slaves in November 1827 to complain about a brutal beating he had endured at the hands of an overseer. "A month and a half ago," Bob began, "my arm was broken. It happened one night after distilling rum that I went & laid down before the furnace, where I was making fire under the still & I fell asleep." When the overseer found Bob asleep, he took a stick used for stoking the fire and struck Bob on the arm, jolting him awake. "Massa you have broken my arm," Bob cried out. The overseer retorted that he would not have cared even if he had broken Bob's neck, and continued the beating. Bob ran out of the distillery, hoping to find the manager. But the overseer caught him and ordered him locked in the stocks within a stifling cell known as the "darkhole." Somehow, Bob managed to get the attention of the "sicknurse." She confirmed that his arm was indeed broken and then released him so that he could go to the manager. This put the manager in a difficult position: should he reinforce the authority of his overseer, or discipline him for severely injuring an enslaved laborer?[1]

When the deputy protector heard Bob's story, he faced a similar problem. He had to decide whether to dismiss Bob's complaint or investigate it. He chose the latter, soliciting testimony from several people on the sugar plantation where Bob worked. One of the men who labored with Bob in the distillery testified that the overseer had beaten Bob so badly that he almost fainted. "Me see him hit Bob on the arm," he said, "one time Bob's eyes began to turn round and he fell down. Bob cried out no hit me so on my arm, he da broke." But the overseer "kept on licking him till Bob got up and ran away." The overseer admitted to the deputy protector that he gave Bob "one or two cuffs on the head," but maintained that he "did not hear any thing of Bob's arm being broken until he got to the sickhouse." He also claimed that the manager—his employer—had sent Bob to complain in retaliation for a dispute between the two of them. If this were true, it might explain why the manager took Bob's side. He told the deputy protector that on the night in question he had seen Bob's broken arm, that the "other wrist was swelled," too, and that Bob had not been able to make the trip to town earlier because "yesterday was the first time he ha[d] been out of the sickhouse," having "been very ill since the arm was broken." He added that he was the one who sent Bob to complain. When the deputy protector completed his investigation, the evidence against the overseer was overwhelming, and so he forwarded the case to the fiscal.[2]

Bob's complaint against the overseer challenged one of the core principles of slavery—what one slaveowner called "the right of a master to punish." Bob and many other enslaved laborers in Berbice were able to challenge the legitimacy of the violence their enslavers inflicted thanks to a momentous shift in the way the British imperial government regulated colonial slavery. During the era of amelioration, enslavers' "right" to punish enslaved people as they saw fit could no longer be taken for granted. To be sure, the physical suffering of enslaved Africans on slave ships and West Indian plantations had been criticized by antislavery activists for more than a century, and calls to make slavery less violent had gained momentum during the eighteenth century, as the rise of humanitarianism and the spread of Enlightenment ideas sparked a range of initiatives to discipline working people and punish criminals on both sides of the Atlantic in supposedly more humane ways.[3] Even some planters advocated less violent methods of control as part of a broader effort to "improve" plantation slavery. Most slaveowners, however, continued to justify violence as the sole means of controlling enslaved people, and it was only in the nineteenth century that the imperial government took direct action to regulate the violence of slavery.[4] In Berbice, intervention took the form of a new, comprehensive slave code—enacted less than a year before Bob's complaint—that set new standards for punishment, instituted new mechanisms of enforcement and record-keeping, and appointed a full-time protector of slaves to hear slaves' complaints.[5]

The laws and institutions that people like Bob used to set limits on their enslavers' violence were the result of a decades-long conflict between enslavers, abolitionists, and imperial officials over how enslaved people ought to be treated and disciplined. Why, by the early nineteenth century, had the physical violence of slavery become a problem that imperial officials felt obligated to address, and to what end? Berbice's 1826 slave code allows us to see in great detail how abstract ideas about punishment and discipline were supposed to work in practice and, in particular, how officials planned to replace the most egregious forms of violence with new, supposedly better disciplinary mechanisms. What kinds of violence would be tolerated? And what enforcement mechanisms did officials use to pressure reluctant slaveowners and their employees to comply with the new disciplinary regime?

Enslaved people's many complaints to the protector of slaves and fiscal about the punishments their enslavers inflicted let us see what impact these reforms had on the ground and, in particular, how enslaved people tried to protect themselves from violence. How did enslaved people decide whether or not to complain about a particular act of violence, given the many risks involved in publicly challenging their enslavers and subjecting themselves to the colonial judicial system? As Bob's story suggests, enslaved people did not complain simply because they were mistreated or abused—that was to be expected—but instead only when the violence they endured was, by the standards of West Indian slave society, excessive, unmerited, or illegal. When they did decide to lodge a complaint, what strategies did they use to persuade officials that they were telling the truth and deserved redress? How did they deal with overseers, managers, and slaveowners who responded to their complaints by undermining their character or arguing that the violence they inflicted was merited? And what happened when enslaved complainants succeeded or, far more often, failed?

Plantation authorities resisted the new disciplinary regime and resented the intrusion of officials like the protector of slaves, but they also tried to use the government's increased interest in regulating punishment for their own purposes. Particularly striking are cases in which enslavers themselves went to the fiscal or protector of slaves and asked him to punish the enslaved people they owned or supervised. In what circumstances would enslavers choose to abrogate their presumed responsibility to discipline a slave, and what did they hope to gain by involving colonial officials?

Penal Reform and the Law of Slavery in Berbice

The rise of British humanitarianism in the late eighteenth century made the physical suffering of enslaved people increasingly controversial. The more progress European penal reformers made in replacing the "Bloody Code" of early modern justice—with public corporal punishment at its core—with a new system of purportedly more humane modes of "correction," such as incarceration, the more deviant and backwards colonial slavery looked.[6] While corporal punishment was becoming less common for most free people in the English-speaking world, slaves in British America continued to face intense violence, most of it perfectly legal.[7] Colonial authorities, slaveowners, and their employees were convinced that violence was necessary to assert their authority, and so they continued to whip, beat, and mutilate slaves long after these practices became uncommon, if not illegal, in Britain. In some cases, enslaved people executed for crimes such as rebellion or practicing obeah were decapitated or mutilated, their severed heads and dismembered body parts placed in prominent locations to terrorize other slaves.[8] And although certain punishments, such as castration and dismemberment, were less common by the late eighteenth century than they once were, that was little comfort to those who were subjected to such horrific violence.[9] Slaveholders knew that their control rested on violence and terror.[10]

The imperial government's amelioration reforms were designed to initiate a new penal regime in the West Indies. They took their inspiration not only from emerging metropolitan ideas about crime and punishment, but also from the experiments of self-styled "enlightened" planters like Joshua Steele, who in the second half of the eighteenth century began proposing new methods of managing enslaved labor forces that relied less on physical force. Steele owned several sugar plantations in Barbados and was an advocate of agricultural "improvement" in the West Indies, which included a version of amelioration that predated imperial intervention by several decades. Planters like Steele argued that more "rational" methods of cultivation—more efficient use of land, labor, and other resources—would increase productivity, create a self-reproducing slave population, and improve slaves' living conditions, all at no added cost to slaveowners.[11] Decades later, some slaveowners continued to endorse similar experiments, including absentee Demerara planter John Gladstone.[12] Central to such efforts, which encountered strong local opposition while earning praise from moderate abolitionists and supposedly progressive planters, were changes in punishment. For example, Steele banned the use of the whip on his plantations and replaced it with a system of rewards as incentives to labor.[13]

Planters like Steele were cited by defenders of West Indian slaveowners several decades later as evidence that slavery was much less violent than before and that individual slaveowners and colonial legislatures had already done much to ameliorate slavery out of both rational self-interest and humanitarianism. "The treatment of negroes," Saint Vincent planter David Collins wrote in 1803, "is much improved within the last twenty years." A generation earlier, Collins admitted, slaveowners could do whatever they wanted to their slaves, but "now the enactments of law are in favour of their protection."[14] Henry Bolingbroke, who lived in Demerara and visited Berbice during the transition from Dutch to British rule, similarly argued that the "painful punishments" under the Dutch—"the severe floggings with a cart whip," "the inflicting of tortures by the rib rack"—were less common under the British. Only one person, he noted with patriotic approval, had been sentenced to the rib rack "since the colonies became British in 1796." It would be "a source of gratification to every philanthropic heart to know," Bolingbroke assured his readers, that such violence—"the greatest evil which the negroes laboured under"—would "in a short time be completely eradicated."[15]

Nevertheless, even after some West Indian legislatures began in the 1780s enacting protections against the most egregious forms of violence, such as willful murder, and setting limits on the number of lashes slaves could be given, enslaved people in Berbice and other British colonies continued to face the threat of extreme physical violence.[16] New metropolitan attitudes toward physical suffering, combined with the wide gap between the letter of the law and its enforcement, prompted the imperial government to intervene directly in colonial slavery in the 1820s rather than trusting local governments to enact ameliorative legislation on their own.

The penal reforms in Berbice's 1826 code were both consistent with evolving attitudes toward punishment and, at the same time, a testament to the Crown's new commitment to enforcement. The new law prohibited drivers and overseers from "carry[ing] a whip, or any other instrument of punishment, into the field or elsewhere, either as a badge of authority or a stimulus to labour," thus making illegal one of the defining features of plantation life.[17] It also set the number of lashes enslaved men could be given at twenty-five and banned outright the flogging of enslaved women, despite protests from slaveowners that women were often harder to control and that the lash was necessary. The code also specified several alternative punishments, from solitary confinement in plantation cells to hand- and feet-stocks.[18] To make it possible to quantify crime and punishment, slaveholders (with more than six slaves) and managers were henceforth required to keep a detailed "Punishment Record Book," a new type of document that was to be reviewed by the protector of slaves, the colony's governor, and then the Colonial Office twice a year.[19] Colonists convicted of violating any of the new regulations could be assessed a fine or imprisoned. And anyone convicted "of inflicting upon any slave any cruel and unlawful punishment" a second time would incur a double penalty and be prohibited from owning or managing slaves.[20] Taken together, these provisions illustrate the major ways that reformers tried to regulate the physical violence of slavery: changing the style and subject of corporal punishment, transitioning from whipping to supposedly more humane punishments, and creating a surveillance apparatus that would give officials unprecedented tools to monitor plantation discipline (see Appendix).

Reformers sought to modify corporal punishment by making three types of changes to the most common form of violence enslaved people faced: whipping. First, they reduced the number of lashes plantation authorities were permitted to inflict at one time, based on the straightforward reasoning that lessening the quantity of physical damage done to the body was a worthy goal. The first effort to regulate whipping in Berbice was an 1810 law that stipulated that private persons (e.g., managers, drivers) could not administer more than thirty-nine lashes "on One Day or at One Time." The framers of that law also recommended that slaves be treated "with such humanity, that Love and not Fear may operate, as motives for their good conduct to their Masters." The law also stipulated how slaves were to be whipped: they were not to be flogged "on any other part than on the *Breech* [buttocks]," and they were to be "laid flat on the ground," with "hands and feets [*sic*] tied sufficiently to prevent [their] vital parts being injured," before the lash, usually a "bush rope" or vine called "carra-carra" but often cowhide leather, struck flesh. Violations could be punished with fines ranging from 300 to 1,000 guilders (approximately £200 to £700).[21] The maximum number of lashes was lowered to twenty-five under Berbice's 1826 slave code and fifteen under the consolidated slave code of 1831.

Reformers also hoped to standardize whipping, making it easier to control its severity by depersonalizing it.[22] Had they waited a few years they might have adopted British penal reformer Jeremy Bentham's rotary whipping machine, described in his *Rationale of Punishment* (1830) as a mechanized wheel with "rods of cane or whalebone, the number and size of which might be determined by law." If a judge stipulated the speed and force that the wheel would turn, Bentham explained, "everything which is arbitrary might be removed." The major problem with flogging, penal reformers argued, was that its intensity was difficult to regulate because it depended too much on the strength, effort, and emotions of the person wielding the whip.[23] By the early nineteenth century, even some West Indian officials and reform-minded planters had begun to frown on spontaneous violence sparked by individual "passion," consistent with metropolitan arguments that punishment should be impersonal and dispassionate. In 1812, for example, when the Barbados

Figure 4. Enslaved woman tied by wrists to a tree and flogged. *Flagellation of a Female Samboe Slave*, engraving by William Blake after John Gabriel Stedman, *Narrative of a Five Years' Expedition Against the Revolted Negroes of Surinam*, 2 vols. (London: J. Johnson and J. Edwards, 1796), vol. 1, plate 36, following p. 340. This image depicts the flogged woman's bloody, lacerated body as helpless object of sympathy and of sexual desire. The contrast between the fully clothed white overseers or managers and the nearly naked woman enhances the voyeuristic and pornographic qualities of the scene. According to Stedman, the eighteen-year-old woman, identified as a "samboe" because of her complexion, was given two hundred lashes for having refused to have sex with an overseer. The drivers, seen at the bottom right with long whips, were ordered to inflict the punishment.

Agricultural Society drafted "a plan for the regulation of plantations with a particular reference to the treatment of slaves," it urged enslavers to never strike slaves in anger. Punishment, the Society argued, should be an "act of cool deliberation" and inflicted with "formality."[24] The 1826 Berbice slave code similarly stipulated that when enslaved people were to be flogged, "such punishment must be inflicted with reason, and without cruelty or passion." Moreover, slaves were not to be punished in the field or immediately after committing an infraction, but on the following day, presumably to ensure that flaring tempers did not lead to excessive abuse.[25]

The final major challenge to whipping during amelioration was the effort to place enslaved women beyond the reach of the lash. Abolitionists had long criticized the flogging of enslaved women, and the lacerated, semi-naked enslaved woman's body became one of the enduring images of antislavery propaganda, dramatizing slaves' supposed helplessness and vulnerability. Illustrations like William Blake's "Flagellation of a Female Samboe Slave" horrified British viewers and generated sentimental sympathy for antislavery (they also served to titillate and arouse). Abolitionists were especially worried that the exposure of women's bodies during whipping—either because they were stripped before being flogged or because the lash tore clothing as easily as it did flesh—prevented women from cultivating Christian purity and modesty.[26] The pressure that the Crown put on colonial legislatures to ban the flogging of enslaved women had as much to do with imposing bourgeois British gender norms on colonial subjects as it did with protecting them from violence.[27] "The system of [a]meliorating the condition of slaves," colonial secretary Henry Bathurst explained, required "making a distinction of treatment between the male and female slaves" in order to "restore to the female slaves that sense of shame which is at once the ornament and the protection of their sex, and which their present mode of punishment has tended unfortunately to weaken if not to obliterate."[28]

The 1826 slave code conceded to metropolitan pressure and banned the whipping of enslaved women, effectively denying enslavers one of their primary tools for controlling nearly half their labor force and the majority of field laborers. It did, however, allow girls (under twelve years old) to "be punished & corrected for any fault or misconduct . . . in such & the same manner, and in such & the same extent, as any child of free condition may be and usually punished and corrected in any school." Even then, the code stipulated that "such punishment shall be inflicted by a female and any indecent exposure of the person avoided." Officials were thus more concerned with what whipping women supposedly did to gender relations than they were with the physical damage done to women's bodies.[29] Most West Indian colonies, unlike Berbice, refused to outlaw the whipping of women until emancipation.[30]

At the same time reformers targeted whipping they were also promoting new or uncommon punishments, in effect exporting the technologies of discipline and control that had become popular in Britain in the decades after the American Revolution to the Caribbean. Berbice's 1826 code outlined several alternative punishments that could be used in lieu of whipping. These included solitary confinement (for up to three days), usually in plantation "hospitals" or in specially designed cells commonly known as "dark holes"; confinement in "public stocks" or "house stocks" where slaves could be locked by their hands, feet, or both; handcuffs; and the use of "distinguishing dress" and "distinguishing marks," such as metal collars padlocked to enslaved people's necks, to humiliate offenders.[31] These were punishments that could, penal reformers believed, cause discomfort, curtail mobility, and encourage penitent reflection while inflicting minimal physical damage on the body. The reality, of course, was that these punishments could be every bit as dangerous and terrifying as the whip, and in some cases, even worse. In complaint after complaint, Berbician slaves made their hatred of these new punishments known.

The most striking example of the new disciplinary regime during amelioration was the treadmill, a device that exemplified the goals and unintended consequences of penal reform in the West Indies. Devised in England in 1818 as a form of "hard labor" for prisoners, the treadmill or treadwheel was a large revolving cylinder—not unlike a paddle wheeler's propeller—with wide steps. Prisoners turned the wheel by walking or running while gripping a bar to keep from slipping and being mangled by the steps. Colloquially known as the "shin-scraper," the treadmill operated for ten hours a day in many British institutions, with prisoners walking for twenty-minute stretches interrupted by twenty-minute breaks. Endorsed by the British Society for the Improvement of Prison Discipline, the treadmill was adopted throughout England by the early 1820s before making its way to jails and workhouses in the British Caribbean.[32] In 1828 alone, the year the treadmill began operating "as a Legal Mode of Punishment" in Berbice's New Amsterdam jail, thirty-six slaves were sentenced to be "worked" on the treadmill.[33]

For a brief time, penal reformers and antislavery activists were united in their enthusiasm for the treadmill. One English justice lauded it as "the most tiresome, distressing, exemplary punishment that has ever been contrived by human ingenuity."[34] For abolitionists, the treadmill was a symbol of a new,

AN INTERIOR VIEW OF A JAMAICA HOUSE OF CORRECTION.

THE WHIPPING OF FEMALES you are restrained by me, officially. WAS IN PRACTICE, and I called upon you to make ducuments to put an end to
unless a repugnance to incapacity, and so CONTRARY IN LAW. So far from passing on Act to prevent the treatment of such cruelty
you have the same apprized your disapprobation of it. I communicated to you my opinion od that of the Secretary of State; —
the regulated of cutting off the hair of females, in the House of Correction previous to trial. I'm have paid no attention to the

Figure 5. Treadmill in Jamaica. *An Interior View of a Jamaica House of Correction*, engraving, ca. 1837. This image was included as a frontispiece in at least one edition of James Williams's *Narrative of Events, since the First of August, 1834, by James Williams, an Apprenticed Labourer in Jamaica* (London, 1837), a highly influential anti-apprenticeship pamphlet. It was circulated by British activists to dramatize the torturous effects of the treadmill—celebrated by reformers less than two decades earlier—and the continued prominence of flogging and other forms of violence during the period of apprenticeship (1834–38). The text at the bottom, an excerpt from an address given by Jamaican governor Lionel Smith, emphasizes the abuse of women in Jamaican workhouses, singling out the illegal and inhumane practices of flogging women and cutting their hair off before trial. © Michael Graham-Stewart Slavery Collection, National Maritime Museum, Greenwich, London.

more civilized penal regime, at least initially.[35] Unlike flogging, which was bloody and difficult to regulate because it usually happened on plantations and in private homes, the treadmill was public, conspicuous, and supposedly nonviolent. Installed in urban centers, it allowed colonial officials rather than plantation authorities to control punishment. Its mechanical operation, moreover, meant that its intensity could be standardized in a way that whipping could not (with the exception, perhaps, of Bentham's proposed whipping machine). People sentenced to the treadmill, which ran at a specified speed for a regulated period, would endure the same level of punishment.[36] The treadmill thus seemed to be the perfect solution to many of the problems that critics of slave punishment had long identified.

In practice, however, the treadmill was a brutal instrument of torture for British criminals and West Indian slaves alike. Pregnant women often miscarried on the wheel, and so many prisoners fell or jumped off that they had to be strapped to a bar above their heads and flogged by a driver to keep them running.[37] Missionary John Wray recalled the impression the treadmill made on the governor of British Guiana in 1833 when he visited the jail. "Going to the treadmill, [the governor] examined the 'cats' with which females as well as males were flogged (some poor women of late dreadfully so), and quite shocked with those instruments of punishment, ordered them to be discontinued."[38] It is unclear why the governor was surprised, since the official 1828 "Regulations for the Tread Mill" stipulated that drivers—armed with whips— were to be present "for the purpose of keeping the refractory and stubborn prisoners on the wheel."[39] Nevertheless, the governor was right to note that the treadmill had joined, not replaced, other forms of physical violence, and that the colonial jail could produce scenes of terror that rivaled those of any plantation. Reports like Wray's contributed to a rapid shift in metropolitan perceptions of the treadmill in colonial jails, especially during the post-slavery apprenticeship period (1834–38). Originally lauded as a symbol of progress, the treadmill instead became evidence of the persistence of physical violence in Britain's plantation colonies.[40]

The third leg of penal reform during amelioration is the least well known despite having had the largest impact on enslaved people's daily lives: the creation of a robust surveillance apparatus with the protector of slaves at its heart. The 1826 slave code contained a variety of ways for making the physical violence inflicted on slaves more visible. In addition to instituting punishment record books, it ordered that all punishments be administered "in the presence of one person of free condition, or of six slaves." The protector could then call on such witnesses when investigating slaves' complaints, asking if they recalled the precise number of lashes given, for instance, or if they knew what had happened to prompt a given punishment. The code also prohibited the use of the whip in the fields, and mandated that a medical practitioner approve the location of solitary confinement. The public stocks, moreover, were to be placed "under cover in some conspicuous place near the [plantation] buildings," presumably so that witnesses could more easily monitor punishment.[41] The protector of slaves was to enforce these regulations, advocate for enslaved people's welfare, and report on the progress of amelioration to the governor and his superiors across the Atlantic.

The rationale behind the stipulations for witnesses, the new types of record-keeping, and the appointment of a full-time protector of slaves was the same: to give officials, rather than individual overseers, managers, and planters, greater control of slave punishment and, by extension, colonial slavery itself. This move was consistent with the general shift in the way that the metropolitan government viewed enslaved people during the era of amelioration, as it began to incorporate them into the body politic by expanding their rights and restricting the arbitrary power of their owners. One of the major ways the Crown tried to accomplish this was by appropriating one of the fundamental "rights" masters had long claimed: the prerogative to inflict violence on the people they owned with impunity.

A consolidated slave code enacted by the Crown in 1831 further strengthened the imperial government's ability to monitor the treatment of slaves and enforcement of the law. It expanded the Crown's power to appoint assistant protectors of slaves, rather than allowing local authorities—most of whom were slaveowners—to appoint men disinclined to enforce the protective clauses of the law. It also gave protectors and their assistants greater powers to initiate criminal proceedings and conduct investigations. Anyone who obstructed their efforts to visit plantations and take evidence could be fined up to £500 or imprisoned for up to twelve months.[42] The 1831 code also reiterated enslaved people's right to legal redress, without which even the most protective laws were useless. "Each and every slave," the code specified, was allowed "at all times" to bring his or her complaint to the nearest protector, without having to request a pass, as was the case under the previous law in Berbice.[43]

By the time that the amelioration reforms were enacted in Berbice, metropolitan critics from James Ramsay to Edmund Burke and William Wilberforce had been arguing for more than half a century that the Crown needed to take a more active role in the management of colonial slavery. The prospect of reform seemed especially bright in Berbice, where the combination of Dutch legal tradition and Crown-sponsored reforms made it possible to enforce protections for slaves in ways that were unimaginable in most other colonies. Thanks to the presence of the fiscal and protector of slaves and the variety of records they were responsible for transmitting to the Colonial Office, from copies of their investigations of slaves' complaints to plantation punishment records, the Crown could reasonably expect to surveil slavery and monitor the treatment of enslaved people in Berbice. The system of supervision and record-keeping brought about by the 1826 and 1831 codes also generated a paper trail that shows enslaved people's efforts, successful and otherwise, to take advantage of imperial intervention to protest physical violence and other abuses. Enslaved people themselves, rather than their supposed protectors, were the most committed to the amelioration of slavery. For them, amelioration was not an experiment in whether slavery could be improved or modernized; it was a question of survival.

Slaves, Fiscals, and Protectors

For enslaved people, the laws and institutions created during amelioration expanded the possibilities for seeking redress. They were quick to use the legal protections granted to them to protest violence and especially to turn to colonial officials, who represented an imperial government increasingly seen by slaves as a potential ally in their battle for survival. As the Demerara fiscal wrote to the governor in 1824, slaves went to him "for what they term[ed] 'right'" because they considered the fiscal "their friend, at least during the investigation of complaints on estates."[44] Slaves in Berbice, like their brethren in Demerara, had a rich tradition of using the fiscal to protest abuses and claim customary rights well before the 1820s. Yet even after the 1826 slave code codified slaves' rights, offered new protections, and established a full-time protector of slaves, the process of complaining was fraught with obstacles at every stage.

Making a complaint with the fiscal, protector, or another official was dangerous and difficult. First, one had to weigh the advantages and disadvantages of complaining and decide whether a particular act of violence was worth protesting. Enslaved people were accustomed to violence, so recorded complaints represent only a small fraction of the punishments slaves endured, probably those that enslaved people saw as particularly excessive, unjustified, or illegal.[45] After deciding to complain, the next challenge was escaping one's plantation or owner. Traveling to town or to a nearby estate where an assistant protector could be found meant either asking plantation authorities for a pass to leave or leaving without permission and being considered a runaway.[46] Either option was risky, but most people who complained did so without a pass or while already away from their plantation on some other business. White authorities resented slaves' complaints as direct challenges to their authority and tried to prevent them.[47] Moreover, slaveowners suffered a financial loss when slaves complained, even when their complaints were dismissed. Owners incurred a twelve-guilder fine for every slave that went to the fiscal, and they were charged twenty-five guilders when the fiscal punished slaves for making "unfounded" complaints.

Plantation authorities did everything possible to keep enslaved people from making complaints. A man on plantation Philadelphia named Amsterdam told the fiscal in August 1821 that his decision to complain about a flogging "brought [the overseer] into such a passion that he sent all the negroes after him to catch him, but he escaped and came to town to complain." Amsterdam stripped to show his lacerated buttocks, the wounds confirming, the fiscal noted, that he "had of late a severe flogging."[48] In June 1825 a man named Donderdag, who complained to the fiscal about being overworked, underfed, and whipped every day, also told the fiscal that when his owner learned he was on his way to town he "had [him] caught & locked up in the stocks."[49] Three men from a different plantation reported in November 1823 that their manager, who frequently subjected them to "severe" and illegal floggings of some fifty lashes (sometimes "with a piece of mangrove"), also mocked them for complaining. They were "fools for going," he told them, since they would only be sent back and then flogged. "We are afraid to talk," one man explained, "because after going we get severely punished."[50] Punishment record books confirm such claims, listing regular punishments for "leaving the Estate to complain without cause," "having gone to the Protector with a groundless complaint," and "making a groundless & frivolous complaint."[51] Slaveowners and their representatives understood the political implications of enslaved people's complaints and consequently tried to keep slaves away from legal authorities.

When plantation authorities could not prevent slaves from exercising their right to seek redress, they often sought retribution after the fact. Many managers considered enslaved people who complained without cause guilty of committing a particularly serious offense—and responded with punishments that were often more severe than even punishments for acts like attempted murder or industrial sabotage.[52] A man named Cadet was one of many enslaved people punished for "leaving the estate without a pass and going to complain . . . without any cause."[53] Four years later, a teenager named Edward went to the protector with his "elderly" mother (she was in her early forties) and reported that the manager had him "flogged . . . for having complained" six weeks earlier.[54] As even the Colonial Office recognized, managers who discouraged enslaved people from complaining were undermining the spirit and letter of the amelioration reforms. As late as 1830, colonial secretary George Murray felt the need to remind the governor of Berbice that "the efficacy of the laws for the Protection of Slaves, must entirely depend upon their facility of access to the Protector and Assistant Protectors."[55] The consolidated slave code of 1831 similarly sought to remedy such problems by making it illegal for managers to punish enslaved people for making complaints and reiterating their right to complain, even without a pass.[56]

If an enslaved person managed to make it to the fiscal or protector—which could involve an arduous journey of a dozen miles or more—the next challenge was to persuade authorities he or she was telling the truth. This was difficult given the racial bias of colonial officials and especially the fiscal, who were skeptical of slave testimony and reluctant to prosecute their peers unless the evidence was overwhelming. Fiscal and slaveowner Michael Bennett believed that enslaved people were "in the habit of exaggerating their complaints and, indeed . . . very often [their complaints] are unfounded; nine times in ten they proceed from the most indolent and worthless negroes."[57]

The stakes were high when it came to convincing the protector or fiscal, since enslaved people who were suspected of lying not only had their complaint dismissed but also faced additional, state-sanctioned violence.[58] In 1819, for instance, a "very tall and stout" African field laborer named Scipio had his complaint dismissed after the fiscal determined he was lying. The fiscal then accompanied Scipio to his plantation and had him publicly flogged "as an example to the gang of that estate."[59] Four years later the acting fiscal had a group of men whose complaint was deemed "entirely groundless . . . flogged in the presence of the whole gang; who were all reprimanded for their disorderly behaviour."[60] The fiscal had the "unpleasant duty," he explained in an earlier letter to Berbice's governor, of "punishing slaves absconding from their work and preferring charges against their owners or managers which they could not substantiate."[61] Unpleasant or not, the fiscal regularly punished complainants he believed had lied. And on multiple occasions, officials criticized "the unnecessary severity with which [the fiscal] ha[d] usually punished the offence of making a groundless complaint."[62] The likelihood that colonial officials might punish rather than vindicate an enslaved person's complaint explains why more people did not go to the fiscal or protector.

To persuade officials that their grievances were legitimate—that they were telling the truth and that the law had been violated—enslaved people had to craft compelling narratives and be skilled plaintiffs. They had to demonstrate their knowledge of the colony's laws and produce sufficient evidence. Slaves would have learned from one another—and especially from friends and kin who had testified as complainants or witnesses—about the way the legal system worked, the kinds of questions they were likely to be asked, and the types of evidence they would need. They would have overheard managers and merchants, overseers and owners discussing cases they had been involved in. Enslaved people also learned about the law directly from colonial officials. When the 1826 slave code was enacted, for instance, the governor ordered civil magistrates to visit every plantation in their district, explain the new law, and record slaves' reactions.[63]

Enslaved complainants often coupled rights-based claims with charges that their enslavers had not honored customary obligations, that what historian Emília Viotti da Costa called the "unspoken contract" had been violated.[64] Central to the latter strategy was an effort to paint oneself as an obedient, hardworking slave who toiled under an unusually cruel master. Three people from plantation Beerenstein, for instance, claimed their manager was so violent, he often took "the whip out of the driver's hand, and flog[ged] us himself; his strokes are at random, and often very injurious, cutting away with the whip in all directions." They went on to say that the entire "gang is extremely dissatisfied on account of the bad behavior of the manager," and they were sure that "more people [would] come to complain." Their complaint was also long overdue; one man noted that "the manager is too hard against them, [they] cannot keep it out any longer."[65] People from other estates framed complaints in similar terms. Jeanette, from plantation Providence, told the protector: "We negroes like very well to work for *backra*, but we like to have a little time to eat and drink," too.[66] Tom, speaking for himself and three other men from a Corantine Coast sugar plantation, declared that they were "aware they [were] purchased to work," but maintained "that it [was] also necessary they should eat and drink."[67]

Some people tried to persuade officials that their complaints were symptoms of a larger problem: incompetent managers or owners who abused their authority. A man named Esterre told the fiscal in January 1821 that his new "master" assigned too much work and flogged slaves when they could not finish it. Their owner, Esterre noted, had "been but a short time in this colony, and never was on an estate before." So he "does not know how to deal with negroes, but lies always in trouble with them." Moreover, Esterre added, "his former masters were never dissatisfied with him." Samuel, an African driver who belonged to the same owner, agreed that their owner "knows very little of negro work and treatment." Their owner had also supposedly claimed the right to do whatever he wanted with his slaves, telling them "he has no fear of Fiscal or any one else, but that he will flog them when he finds it proper." Whether or not this was true, it was a rhetorical strategy that played into colonial notions of hierarchy and was designed to make the fiscal look unfavorably on an owner who disrespected the Crown's authority. Samuel's request that he and his family be sold to someone "who understands the working and treatment of slaves" underscored the fact that their complaint was aimed at not the slave system as a whole, but rather a particularly inept manager who was "always flogging them." Samuel assured the fiscal "that they would be able to please a reasonable master."[68]

Many slaves pursued a similar strategy. When Swift went to the fiscal in November 1823, he claimed "that whatever work he is put to he can do it, but the manager is too severe."[69] An African field laborer named Quassie told the fiscal in August 1821 that his "extremely severe" manager had subjected him to brutal floggings (one of 160 lashes, the other 230 lashes) and recently ordered him into the mud to catch crabs despite "the bad state of his feet." His manager did "not know how to manage negroes properly."[70] In July 1823 four women from a coffee plantation claimed that "for the most trifling offence" they were punished with the cart-whip, and that even though their workload was excessive, they did "not materially object to the work . . . but to the manager's exactness in examining the coffee after it is assorted." He flogged them if a single bean was bad, and "they consider[ed] it oppressive that for every such offence they should be punished." "Every negro is ready to come to town," they said, "so severe is the treatment of the manager."[71]

Some people who lodged complaints about violent punishments succeeded. In April 1824, Dundas, an African field laborer from plantation New Forest, complained that "the manager trouble me." "He beat me with a soldier's cutlass till [I] fell down, I said Massa you want to kill me he replied I don't care for Fiscal, or Governor or your own master." The manager then ordered the driver to give Dundas thirty-nine lashes—the legal limit—"with carracarra." The manager admitted he struck Dundas with a cutlass, but claimed it was warranted by Dundas's disrespect. Dundas "paid no attention to my orders, [and] on saying do you hear me, he turned round grinning and asked if I thought he was a black ass on this I struck him." The "few stripes" he ordered the driver to give Dundas, moreover, were for not finishing his work. The fiscal ruled that although "no injury was sustained" by the manager's assault, "the act itself however was most unlawful & unjustifiable & it being contrary to the court's ordinance directing the manner in which slaves were to be punished," fined Dundas's manager 300 guilders.[72]

Most successful complaints followed a similar pattern, with enslaved people persuading officials that the violence their enslavers inflicted was undeserved, illegal, and dangerous. Such complaints demonstrate the central role enslaved people themselves played in advancing amelioration by holding their enslavers legally accountable for abuse. An African "domestic" named Venus complained in May 1830 that her owner, a New Amsterdam liquor merchant, "beat her severely with a stick because he found fault with the manner in which she had boiled a ham." (Venus said she "boiled it as she usually does, and tried her best to cook it properly.") Her owner admitted that he had "on the irritation of the moment took a small stick with which he struck her three times." But he claimed that he had not done so "violently so as to injure her." He "requested to know if he could not accommodate the matter," but the deputy protector told him "that the Slave Law gave him no power to compromise, that the Offence was a serious one and bore the heaviest penalty," and that he would have to ask "a higher authority" for lenience. The lieutenant governor ordered Venus's owner to pay a £10 fine.[73]

The acting protector upheld a similar complaint from a man named Klaas in December 1832. Klaas said that the manager of plantation Nieuw Hoop had attacked him one night with a stick for not taking the manager's horse to the stable. Other witnesses explained that the manager lashed out at what he saw as Klaas's insolence. Klaas had refused to take the horse, "saying he was not the horse boy." The manager claimed he had only "laid hold of [Klass] to make him" obey his order, and "positively denie[d] having struck him." Moreover, he claimed, "he would not have used violent measures to get Klaas up if he had not been so insolent and set all authority at defiance." The acting protector ruled that "altho' he considered the conduct of the man Klaas most reprehensible . . . nothing could justify the violent measures [the manager] had resorted to." He also explained that "it was absolutely necessary to protect the negroes from such treatment, that [the manager] had violated the Law in doing so and that it would be the duty of the acting Protector to take proceedings against him for the assault."[74]

Complainants who knew that officials disapproved of spontaneous punishments provoked by rage had an advantage. One such man was Good-luck, who told the fiscal in 1824 that his owner "beat me with his fist all about my face struck me on my head . . . and reduced me to the state you now see me in." Goodluck's owner, aware that such outbursts were socially unaccept-able, "expressed his sincere regret for having allowed his passion to get the better of his reason," even as he justified his reaction by citing Goodluck's "negligence" in leaving a gate unlocked. The fiscal concluded that Goodluck's owner "had punished his servant in an unwarrantable manner and contrary to the Court's ordinance," and issued him a three-hundred-guilder fine, as "prescribed by the new ordinance."[75] As the fiscal explained in a different case later that year in which an enslaved man had been the victim of a "wanton and cruel attack" with an iron poker that almost ended his life, "the Law of the Land and the Ordinances of the legislation of this Colony made and pro-vided for the safety of the slave Population strictly prohibit the indulgence of wrath and anger towards slaves, or maiming and assaulting."[76] Slaves used this knowledge to their advantage, often describing managers, owners, and overseers who "flew in a passion" or punished them in "a terrible passion," hoping that this cultural script might improve their chances of success.[77]

The majority of complaints, however, either failed to persuade officials that a crime had been committed or led to an unsuccessful prosecution. By one measure, some 70 percent of complaints failed.[78] Enslaved people often lacked the evidence needed, and it did not take much for colonials to under-mine their complaints, often by simply undermining the character of the slaves who made them. John Cameron, for instance, claimed that his slave Philip—who complained of "being too much punished"—was "frequently drunk," a lazy worker, and that he bore "a very bad character amongst the negroes." The fiscal ruled that Philip's complaint was "frivolous and un-founded" and directed him to be punished for making a false complaint.[79] When Donderdag's owner told the fiscal that his slave was "a bad character" and a frequent runaway, the fiscal gave him fifty lashes for "false representa-tion."[80] The fiscal determined that another complaint from three men on plantation Cotton Tree was "without foundation" merely because it was "con-tradicted by the manager." And as he wrote to the slaves' owner, he "deemed it [his] duty to order the said three slaves to be exemplarily punished." He ordered each of them to receive seventy-five lashes in the public marketplace. While it was his "duty to attend to the complaints of negroes, and to cause redress in all cases of oppression," it was also his "duty to inflict punishment on slaves who prefer false and ungrounded complaints."[81]

When Princess, a creole "domestic" in her early twenties, complained in June 1822 that she had been horsewhipped "for nothing," her owner only had to explain that he beat her for "insolence, of which she is guilty," in order for the fiscal to reprimand her "for making this unnecessary complaint." Moreover, he threatened "that if her master complained of her conduct again, she would be punished."[82] Many enslaved people, like Princess, found that seeking help from colonial authorities backfired. The likelihood of failure must have discouraged all but the boldest—or the most desperate—people from lodging complaints. And yet, hundreds of slaves sought legal redress, and some of them, including Princess, would return to the fiscal even after their first complaint failed. Far more than the legal officials charged with protecting them, enslaved people were willing to use the law to limit the arbitrary power of their enslavers.

Even when colonial authorities determined that a punishment was excessive or unmerited, there was often little that could be done. Part of the problem, as officials and enslaved people knew all too well, was that under the laws that governed slavery, even during the era of amelioration, brutal violence was often legal. Before the 1826 code was adopted, things were especially bad. In February 1819, an enslaved woman named Minkie, a "stout" African "domestic" in her mid-forties, went to the fiscal. She said that her owner, after picking her up from the barracks (jail) where she had been confined for running away, ordered her to find someone else to purchase her. When Minkie told her owner, Thomas Jones, that she had been unable to find a buyer, he threatened that he would "put me down, and cut my ——, and would give me more than the law gives." Jones then had Minkie "laid down and tied to three stakes," and flogged by a driver with a cart whip, which tore her back and buttocks to pieces. When the fiscal examined Minkie's body, he noted that "her posteriors . . . [were] covered with a plaister by order of the doctor, and apparently lacerated to that degree, that the court judged it expedient to direct her not to uncover it."[83]

Jones admitted that he had flogged Minkie, but defended his actions as warranted by her behavior and, more importantly, perfectly legal. He explained that in the two years that he had owned Minkie she had run away repeatedly, and that she had not found anyone to purchase her. And when Minkie returned to his house, "she was so extremely insolent, that [he] was under the necessity of flogging her . . . for her insolence." When Jones told Minkie he would flog her, she allegedly replied: "You cannot flog me; I have been too long in the barracks; and if you flog me, it shall cost you plenty of money," presumably because she would go to the fiscal. Jones was thus "under the necessity of breaking her

mouth, previous to . . . having her tied town."[84] This was no admission of
wrongdoing: Berbician law permitted owners to strike slaves "guilty of insolence or impertinence in speaking or replying to a white or free person," provided that they only inflicted *"One Blow."*[85] Aware of the restrictions on
whipping, Jones said that he only ordered thirty-nine lashes, though he insisted
"that they should be well laid on." Nevertheless, the fiscal took the case before
the court of criminal justice. The court was "highly indignant at the treatment
of this female," but because "no evidence . . . could be obtained to convict the
proprietor of having inflicted severer punishment than that prescribed by law,"
the fiscal could only scold Minkie's owner. "Your conduct calls for redress," the
fiscal explained, but "unfortunately for the cause of humanity, sufficient evidence cannot be procured to inflict punishment on you." He warned Jones that
he would "vigilantly . . . watch over [his] behaviour to" Minkie.[86]

Princess, who had first complained in June 1822, returned to the fiscal less
than a year later only to find that the fiscal's ability to prosecute her new owner
hinged on the same technicality that let Jones escape conviction: the number of
lashes inflicted. Princess complained that her new owner, an Irish doctor
named Hugh McGee, had her staked down and then flogged with a cart whip
by his white "groom" or servant. Princess's brother had been ordered to hold a
candle so that the flogger could see his victim in the dark. "My clothes were
lifted up and I was flogged on my bare skin," Princess told the fiscal, hoping,
perhaps, that highlighting this physical exposure might improve her chances of
success. "Afterwards," she had been "scrubbed . . . with lime juice," and they
would have rubbed pepper into her wounds, too, but none could be found.
McGee said that he had ordered Princess to receive twelve lashes for "Insolence
and disobedience of orders." McGee had overheard Princess "muttering" and
"grumbling" after receiving his orders. Princess and other witnesses, however,
reported that she had merely been telling the groom that she knew he had been
using McGee's clothing when he was away and that she would report him.
McGee reasoned, like so many of his peers, that his "conduct toward the Negress Princess was solely in exercising the right of a Master to punish an insolent and insubordinate slave." Moreover, he had done so "far within the bounds
allowed by Law." Nevertheless, the fiscal prosecuted McGee "for excessive punishment by unusual means & at unreasonable hours."[87]

Princess and other witnesses told the fiscal that McGee had been upset by
Princess's refusal to submit to his sexual advances. McGee had only owned
Princess about a week, and, according to Princess's mother, "on the first eve-
ning of [their] arrival at the Doctor's House master called Princess to sleep

with him." Princess said that McGee "gave [her] mother & [herself] a glass of wine [and] afterwards the Doctor said [she] must come and sleep with him." She tried to rebuff McGee, telling him that she had "just come out of lying in, and that it was too soon to take a Husband," but she had little choice: McGee "said I must go and let the Boy shew me his room up stairs." Even then, Princess resisted. McGee "sent the Boy to call [her] three times but [she] would not go" until her mother said she "had better go or the Doctor would lick [whip] me." Upstairs, Princess repeated that it was too soon to "take Husband," and McGee ordered her to leave, threatening that "he had a great mind to get out of Bed and give [her] 39 lashes." But McGee soon called her back, "told the Boy to put out the light, and said [she] must sleep with him." So Princess "went into Bed with him," where McGee told her that she "must not think [she] was in Town," and that "he would soon make [her] pull off [her] petticoat and not wear a frock," threatening not only to rape her but to remove the garments that may have signified a degree of respectability. In dictating what Princess could wear, McGee further sought to assert his sexual dominance.[88]

Unfortunately for Princess, there was little that the fiscal could do, even though he concluded that she had been flogged "without any just cause or provocation." The problem was that she did not "know the number of lashes [she] received." Neither did her mother, who had been forced to watch the spectacle; she "had no heart to reckon" the number of lashes that tore her daughter's flesh. McGee claimed that he "ordered her to receive 12 stripes but she got twenty one," which was still under the legal limit. The court concluded "that the conduct of said Hugh R. McGee ha[d] been extremely improper, harsh and indelicate, and therefore deserving of reprehension." Yet "there [was] not sufficient Evidence to convict him . . . of any breach of established Law."[89]

Years after the 1826 reforms, officials' ability to regulate violence against enslaved people was limited. In August 1833, three "middle aged" men from plantation Rotterdam complained they had been flogged for cutting trees more slowly than their driver demanded. But the acting protector could not "interfere in this matter, the punishment not being contrary to Law." He could only recommend "in the strongest terms to give up corporal punishment except where it was found absolutely necessary, which he did not conceive it was on this occasion."[90]

Even in cases where a punishment was illegal, there was no guarantee that a prosecution would succeed. In March 1827, a woman named Catherine complained that her owner, a free colored woman named Cecilia Benjamin, had flogged her "because [she] did not come home every night to mind her

[Benjamin's] child, and make coffee in the morning" while she was hired out. Benjamin "tied [Catherine's] two hands with a hammock rope," then "threw the rope over a beam or rafter in the room." Catherine "was hauled up [so] that [her] feet did not touch the ground . . . and Misses [Benjamin] began to flog [her] with tamarind rods"—a horrific image much like those used by antislavery activists to represent slavery's inhumanity to women. When Catherine went to the fiscal's office, she "was much flogged," her "posteriors much marked with the stripes." The fiscal determined that Benjamin was "guilty of an act of Cruelty and had impugned the late slave Code," so he "instituted Criminal proceedings against the free black woman Cecilia Benjamin," and recommended that she be fined 1,400 guilders. But the court ruled that "it [was] not proven that she the said Cecilia Benjamin did commit the offence with which she stands charged," and acquitted her.[91] Officials may have felt the need in cases like this to bolster the authority of categorically weak masters, including women and free people of color.

Despite the support of the fiscal or protector, enslaved people's efforts to prosecute managers or owners often failed. John McDougald, manager of plantation Cotton Tree, stood accused of having a woman named Louisa flogged in November 1832, six years after the ban on flogging women went into effect. There was compelling evidence from Louisa and other witnesses, including the man who had flogged her at McDougald's insistence. Yet McDougald pled not guilty and was acquitted.[92] The manager of Goldstone Hall, James Beck, also escaped conviction in May 1832 for allegedly having resorted to an "illegal, cruel, and excessive mode of punishment": confining two enslaved women in the stocks and hanging them by their wrists for an hour, "to the great injury of the said slaves."[93]

Moreover, convictions often resulted in light penalties. When the fiscal fined Henry Bird 1,400 guilders for having flogged his slave, Phillis, with a "leathern strap" and a "chaise whip," for instance, Bird "presented a Petition to . . . the Lieutenant Governor praying to mitigate the fine." The lieutenant governor consented, reducing the fine by more than three-fourths to only 300 guilders.[94]

Slaveowners and other colonials accused of inflicting even the most grievous corporal punishments could escape official inquiry with little more than a slap on the wrist. Roosje, a creole field laborer in her mid-thirties, went to the fiscal in 1819 after a brutal flogging. The manager had ordered her to sort coffee, she said, although she was "too big" (too far advanced in pregnancy) to work. And when the manager discovered that Roosje and others had not sorted enough coffee by the midday break, he ordered the driver to flog them all. The driver hesitated when he came to Roosje, and pointed out that "this woman is rather big with child." The manager, indifferent, told him to "give it to her till the blood flies out."[95]

The following day, Roosje "told the driver [she] would not work as [she] had pains in [her] loins." The manager sent her to the hospital, where "the doctor examined [her], and said there was nothing the matter with [her], sitting down was not good." So Roosje was sent back to work, only to miscarry a few days later. "I was five months gone with child," she said. "The labour was hard. The midwife had to force it; the child was dead, one eye was out, the arm broken, and a stripe visible over the head, which must have been done with the double whip." The doctor came the next morning, but the stillborn child had already been buried.[96]

The driver and other witnesses corroborated Roosje's testimony and the fiscal prosecuted the manager. But the court ruled there was no evidence that he knew of Roosje's pregnancy when he ordered her flogged or, more importantly, that he had violated the regulations on whipping. It found him "not guilty of the charge of cruelty," although it did convict him of the less serious charge of "indiscretion and neglect of his duty," for which he only had to pay the court costs.[97] Here, then, was a legal regime in which beating a pregnant woman so severely that she miscarried and a fine of a few pounds sterling were considered morally equivalent.

Given the dangers involved in making a complaint and the unlikelihood that it would be upheld, one has to wonder why enslaved people continued to turn to the fiscal and protector year after year. One explanation is that enslaved people knew that even when their complaints failed, they still subjected their owners, managers, and overseers to external scrutiny. Any complaint, dismissed or upheld, was a reminder that the colonial government had the authority to monitor slave–master relationships, that the power overseers, managers, and owners had was not absolute, and that even across the Atlantic some people were paying attention to what happened to slaves in colonies like Berbice. In this regard, enslaved people understood very clearly the radical potential of amelioration, even though it fell short of actual emancipation. The mere act of complaining, of shining light on the atrocities of slavery and asserting one's legal or customary rights, was therefore itself a political act with transatlantic reverberations.

In March 1823, for example, nine women from plantation Port Mourant convinced the fiscal that their manager—who assigned too much work—relied on the whip indiscriminately and that, by extension, he was a poor manager. "Sometimes the whole of the women are flogged for the sake of two or three not finishing their task," one of the women explained. Last Saturday, she added, "the Manager went to the field, and found that they had not finished their row, and immediately ordered four women to be flogged." She "thought it very hard against those women, which were merely punished for nothing." The fiscal's investigation revealed that "the Manager was very severe upon them, and too frequently inflicted punishment without sufficient cause." He had not violated the law, so the fiscal could not issue a fine. But he did warn the manager "that his conduct would be vigilantly looked after in future; and if he continued the same system, the attorney of the estate would be recommended to discharge him from the management."[98] Such threats may have prevented future acts of violence against the slaves of Port Mourant and, however marginally, enabled their survival.

This Ungovernable Slave

Plantation authorities and slaveowners resented the intrusion of the Crown, the intervention of the fiscal and especially the protector, and the new laws of amelioration, all of which limited their autonomy. Yet they also took advantage of the government's increased interest in supervising the punishment of slaves for their own purposes. Through the same colonial authorities that might fine them for excessive violence, they could also reassert control through public displays of violence and terror that demonstrated the alliance of the plantocracy and the state. Even during the period of amelioration, the law continued to function more as an instrument of planter power than as a force for slaves' protection.

Owners and managers who turned to officials when enslaved people tested their authority sent a clear message to slaves that the law—and the Crown—was still largely on the side of enslavers. One such owner was Ann Bennett, who in August 1827 asked the protector for help with Mary Ann, a Barbados-born "domestic" Bennett had purchased in 1820. "I am under the necessity," Bennett explained, "of requesting you will inflict some punishment on this un-governable slave, her temper is so irritable and insupportable that I have no peace whatsoever." Mary Ann supposedly had a "comfortable house," and Bennett did "everything in [her] power to make her comfortable but her quarrel-some disposition is such that she will not let any of my people have a moment's rest." "At the most trifling occurrence," Mary Ann "flies out in so passionate a strain swearing she will kill, chop and beat out the brains of every one, that I am myself quite alarmed." When Bennett threatened that she would take Mary Ann to the protector, Mary Ann had supposedly replied: "do so and if the Protector can change my disposition get him to do it." The heart of the matter, as Bennett admitted, was that her "own authority [was] insufficient to control [Mary Ann]." When Mary Ann was questioned by the protector, she "appeared to be in a violent passion" and "merely remarked that no one had a right to trouble her." The protector, who may have taken the threat Mary Ann posed more seriously because her owner was a woman, sentenced her to five days' solitary confinement "on bread and water."[99]

The protector and fiscal routinely punished enslaved people at the request of owners and managers. When a civil magistrate told the fiscal that a woman named Sophia "was in the habit of absconding from the Estate for some days," and that previous punishments "appeared to have no effect on her," he asked the fiscal to "check such indolent conduct." The fiscal consented, sentencing Sophia to six days on the treadmill.[100] The attorney of plantation Rose Hall, John Alves, sought the protector's assistance in June 1828 with a man named Fraser, who "had for some time back behaved in a very unbecoming manner," and run away "for two or three weeks at a time" to avoid punishment. Alves had pardoned Fraser several times "on his promise of better behaviour," he said, but Fraser continued to disobey him, so he asked the protector "to interfere & prescribe such punishment as would make Fraser aware that such behaviour cannot be tolerated on an Estate." The protector sentenced Fraser to the treadmill.[101]

Indeed, such requests were so common that the deputy protector of slaves complained to the lieutenant governor in September 1827 about a widespread rumor that he was responsible for handling the complaints of free people *against* slaves—the exact opposite of the protector's role. The deputy protector realized that punishing enslaved people at the request of free people would discourage slaves from going to him. "When the complaint is made by the master, and where such decision might direct punishment for the slave," he explained, it "could not fail soon to excite universal distrust amongst the slaves toward the Protector, and make them shy in seeking his advice, or unfolding to him their grievances; in fact, they would view him merely in the light of a secondary Fiscal."[102] The colonial office also found this problematic. As the secretary of state reminded Berbice officials in 1829, "the Protector should be their guardian only and not their judge."[103]

Enslaved people were nevertheless right to see colonial officials as both potential allies and adversaries, in part because plantation authorities continued to turn to legal officials for help punishing slaves. Slaveowner William Grimes, for example, went to the fiscal in January 1829 because his slave, Betsey, was "so very bad his own authority [was] insufficient to keep her within bounds." She had used "gross and impertinent language," he claimed, and "on his remonstrating with Betsey on her bad behaviour she abused him." Betsey admitted in the fiscal's office that "her temper is so very high when roused, that she does not know what she says or does." The fiscal "reprimanded her for giving vent to such unwarrantable conduct and sentenced her to twelve days solitary confinement on plantains & water."[104]

In a similar case from May 1831, the fiscal was explicit about his obligation to punish enslaved people who challenged authorities. The manager of plantation Mary's Hope had asked the fiscal to punish a man named George, who had "liberated his mother [Bella] in defiance of my authority" from the stocks. The manager locked George up to punish him, but George's conduct, he told the fiscal, was "deserving of severer punishment than a Manager is authorised to inflict." The fiscal told George that interfering when the manager put his mother in the stocks "was unjustifiable, illegal & deserving of punishment." He was, he admitted, "inclined to make allowance for the feelings of a son witnessing the disgrace & punishment of a parent," but "the remedy to which he resolved, to afford her relief could not be sanctioned." Since George had disobeyed his manager, the fiscal sentenced him to ten days on the treadmill. It was his "duty," he told George, "to support the authority of Managers on Estates when they acted conformably to Law."[105] In the end, slaveowners found that the legal protections their slaves gained during amelioration did not weaken their authority nearly as much as they feared, even if they did lose some of their long-prized autonomy.

In retrospect, it is clear that no one was more committed to amelioration than enslaved people themselves. Unlike abolitionists or reformers, their very survival depended on making slavery less violent. And in taking advantage of the amelioration reforms that limited the violence enslavers could use against them, enslaved people also had the potential to undermine one of the key foundations of colonial slavery. Planters and their employees were right to worry that any effort to limit "the right of a master to punish" might jeopardize their control and empower slaves to challenge them in other ways.

Yet it is difficult to conclude that enslaved people, as a whole, succeeded in using the amelioration-era legal system to bring about significant improvements in the ways they were treated and punished, despite their courage and legal savvy. The evidence is mixed. The new laws did prohibit certain violent punishments, such as the flogging of women, and officials did sometimes prosecute enslavers found guilty of committing particularly egregious acts of violence or of punishing slaves without cause. Yet even during the era of amelioration, enslavers continued to exercise and defend their "right" to use physical violence, believing, as one Jamaican overseer argued, that "the stimulus to labor is decidedly the fear of the lash."[106] Moreover, continued complaints from slaves about brutal—and often illegal—punishments nearly a decade after the 1826 reforms were enacted should make us suspicious that the law was widely enforced. At the same time, the very punishments that officials wanted enslavers to use in place of flogging, such as solitary confinement in the stocks or "dancing" the treadmill, could be every bit as painful, dangerous, and traumatizing as the whip.

As enslaved people quickly realized, the imperial architects of amelioration policy and the colonial officials who enforced it were not opposed to coercive discipline or even slavery itself. They merely wanted to replace certain kinds of punishment with new ones. More importantly, they hoped to transition from a private disciplinary regime in which enslavers were responsible for deciding when and how to punish enslaved laborers to one where the state had the primary authority to regulate violence. Ultimately it was this shift that brought about the biggest changes during the era of amelioration, as plantation authorities and enslaved laborers struggled to adapt to a new landscape where the state asserted its power to intervene in the treatment of slaves.

Enslaved people were quick to embrace this newly interventionist government, recognizing that colonial officials could be powerful intermediaries in their efforts to negotiate a wide range of power relationships, including but not limited to those with their enslavers. But for most enslaved laborers, the problem of physical violence was one they encountered not primarily in their conflicts with overseers, managers, or planters, but with drivers—men who were on the frontline of plantation discipline and who, like colonial authorities, knew both how useful violence could be in asserting power and how quickly it could provoke resistance.

CHAPTER 3

The Slave Drivers' World

In the early morning hours one day in May 1833 on a sugar plantation with the ironic French name Ma Retraite (My Retirement), a group of slaves was preparing to plant sugarcane under the supervision of their driver. A punt loaded with cane shoots glided down the long canal that led to the field to be planted. The driver, an enslaved man named Frans, had ordered everyone in his gang to wait for the punt to reach them before taking their share of canes. Everyone obeyed except for Sam, who went to the punt before it reached the end of the canal, climbed aboard, and "refused to leave" when Frans told him to. Even worse, Sam "dared Frans to strike him" and threatened to hit back. Unfortunately for Sam, Frans prevailed in the struggle that ensued—a predictable outcome given drivers' reputation for physical strength. Humiliated, Sam declared that "Frans was not his master." Indeed, Frans was no one's "master," but as driver he expected other slaves to respect, or at least obey, him. He responded to Sam's challenge by reporting him to the plantation manager. The manager ordered Sam flogged and then reported him to the civil magistrate "for abusing the driver." Frans's fragile authority was thus reestablished—at least until the next conflict.[1]

Drivers like Frans played a crucial role on West Indian plantations, in part because colonial authority was so thinly spread. The head driver was, in the words of one West Indian planter, "the most important personage in the slave-population" and "the life and soul of an estate."[2] Drivers were especially important in black-majority colonies like Berbice, where few Europeans were willing to endure the discomforts and uncertainty of life on the frontier of the British Empire and where most planters were absentees who relied on a series of employees to run their plantations. On a typical Berbician coffee plantation, for example, the absentee owner lived in Europe and thus hired a local attorney, who lived in New Amsterdam, to represent his interests. The attorney, in turn, relied on a resident manager and an overseer to supervise day-to-day operations. On the plantation, the manager and overseer depended on a series of drivers to supervise field laborers, enforce their rules, and punish troublemakers.[3] On average, in Berbice there was roughly one driver for every thirty slaves. In total, there were more drivers throughout the colony than all white colonists combined.[4] If Caribbean plantations were "factories in the fields," as Sidney Mintz famously argued, then drivers were the foremen who made the agro-industrial slave system function through a combination of coercion, technical expertise, and managerial skill.[5] And just as the interests of capitalists and workers diverged, placing foremen in the difficult position of trying to simultaneously please their employers and the laborers they supervised, so, too, did drivers find themselves pulled in different directions by plantation authorities and enslaved workers. The conditions of plantation slavery, moreover, made the driver's predicament especially precarious: he was supposed to make a system run by extracting labor from people offered no incentive to work, people who lived on the brink of death. As such, these men—women were almost never appointed as drivers—occupied a crucial position in Atlantic slave societies.[6]

Despite drivers' crucial role as intermediaries, we know surprisingly little about how they tried to do their job. Popular images of drivers have been shaped by eighteenth- and nineteenth-century abolitionists, who depicted them as brutal, whip-wielding henchmen unfailingly loyal to their enslavers and feared by other slaves.[7] Since the late twentieth century, historians have challenged such simplistic images and have emphasized drivers' ambivalent political position: they could be both victimizers and victims, they simultaneously reinforced planter power and advocated for their fellow slaves, and they could lead rebellions as easily as they could thwart them.

Given the inherent challenge in trying to please both one's enslavers and other slaves, why would anyone want to be a driver? The most obvious answer, as anyone in a plantation society like Berbice knew, is that drivers lived significantly longer, better lives than other enslaved men. The head driver on the sugar plantation where Frans and Sam clashed, for instance, was in 1819 sixty-six years old.[8] In Berbice, drivers tended to be appointed in their twenties or thirties, and they could serve well into their fifties or even sixties. The average driver was about forty years old—about the age most enslaved men died.[9] Historian Richard Dunn's research on the occupational mortality differences of enslaved workers in Jamaica provides further evidence for drivers' greater longevity. Tracking the year-by-year work experience of the entire adult labor force (877 men and women) on Mesopotamia, a sugar plantation in western Jamaica, from 1762 to 1833, Dunn found that the seventeen male drivers—out of 485 enslaved men—lived longer than men in any other occupational category and much longer than field laborers. The average age of death for field laborers was only forty-two years, whereas the average age of death for drivers was slightly over sixty years.[10] Data from slave registration returns for multiple nineteenth-century British Caribbean slave societies suggest that the dynamics Dunn identified for Jamaica were typical. In general, drivers (as well as skilled laborers and domestics) had lower mortality rates than field laborers, especially on sugar plantations, and lived to advanced ages.[11]

Drivers outlived their peers because of the material advantages that came with their position. As supervisors valued more for their managerial skill and technical expertise than brute strength, drivers avoided the most physically demanding tasks associated with fieldwork, such as planting and cutting sugarcane. They also received better food and clothing—in larger quantities—from their enslavers, and they often had larger provision grounds and better housing, too.[12] Some drivers even hired other enslaved people to work for them, further reducing their labor burden.[13] Taken together, such perks helped drivers avoid or resist many of the illnesses that weakened and killed field laborers.[14] Drivers also had an advantage when it came to finding marital partners and forming families—major challenges in societies like Berbice, where men outnumbered women and competition for female partners could be fierce.[15] In sum, the advantages drivers enjoyed increased their chances of living longer, healthier lives than other enslaved men.

If being a driver was a strategy for making a viable life under the desperate conditions of plantation slavery, how, in practice, did one succeed in this demanding role? Histories of individual drivers like Frans, reconstructed from complaints enslaved people and white plantation officials made against drivers as well as complaints from drivers themselves, offer a rare look at the political maneuvering of drivers who struggled—and sometimes failed—to maintain legitimacy in the eyes of their enslavers or their fellow slaves. These records reveal that drivers relied on an array of tactics to project power, maintain authority, and juggle the competing interests of other slaves and their enslavers.

A driver's primary responsibility was to extract labor from other enslaved people and enforce discipline. And like their enslavers, drivers resorted to physical violence and intimidation, threatening, whipping, and beating other

slaves who caused problems. Yet even if they were empowered to inflict violence, drivers knew they could not do so indiscriminately. Excessive or unjustified acts of violence against other slaves could backfire, provoking
resistance from the very people drivers sought to control. The whip may have
been drivers' most obvious means of asserting power, but what other strategies did they use to get their subordinates to comply or cooperate with them?
The records of the fiscals and protectors of slaves offer glimpses of the less
obvious techniques drivers used to earn enslaved people's respect and trust,
such as negotiating with management for reduced workloads or increased
rations, or granting special privileges to the most cooperative enslaved laborers. To what extent did such acts allow drivers to fashion themselves as community leaders? And what happened when drivers' presumed responsibility
to take care of other slaves clashed with their obligations to enslavers?

As go-betweens, drivers had to interact closely not only with their subordinates but also with the overseers, managers, and planters above them. Drivers' relationships with their superiors were especially important when they
encountered other enslaved people who challenged them, as suggested by
Frans's decision to report Sam to his manager. When drivers found their authority called into question, how could they ask their enslavers for help without appearing to have failed at their job? How did white plantation authorities
respond to conflicts between drivers and other slaves?

Challenges from below were an inevitable problem for drivers, but it was
far more dangerous to lose the support or trust of white plantation authorities. What happened when enslavers decided that a driver was too close to
other slaves, too weak, or could not be counted on for some other reason?
How did managers handle the delicate task of disciplining or replacing a
driver? And how did drivers respond when they stood to lose their privileged
position?

With a Whip at Their Backs

Like white plantation officials, drivers relied on violence and intimidation to
control enslaved workers. Central to the "driving" system used on Caribbean
plantations—and, later, in North American and European industry—was
physical coercion.[16] As the men who actually inflicted most of the punishments other slaves endured, drivers were skilled with the whip, which was
both a weapon and an unmistakable symbol of power.[17] The whip was a

Figure 6. Enslaved woman and driver. *"The driver's whip unfolds its torturing coil. 'She only Sulks—go, lash her to her toil,'"* engraving by the Female Society for Birmingham, West-Bromwich, Wednesbury, Walsall, and Their Respective Neighborhoods, for the Relief of British Negro Slaves, in *Album for the Relief of British Negro Slaves* (Birmingham: Benjamin Hudson, 1828). The driver in this antislavery image orders an enslaved mother with a child on her lap back to the field, symbolizing one of the major arguments British activists made against slavery: that it prevented mothers from fulfilling their role as caretakers and therefore harmed families. In addition to his hat and coat, the driver is distinguished by his large whip, which represents his role in enforcing plantation discipline with physical violence. In the background, enslaved field laborers work with hoes while a second driver whips them. The image's title comes from a poem by James Beattie, *Minstrel* (book 1, stanza 29). Courtesy of the John Carter Brown Library at Brown University.

driver's most recognizable accessory, tucked into his belt or held in his hand as he supervised his gang. And, as their contemporaries noted, everyday shows of physical force were an important part of what made someone a driver. Drivers were especially likely to use violence against people who challenged them. Yet in some places, including Berbice, drivers' coercive power was limited by custom and law, and enslaved people protested when drivers exceeded established limits on physical violence or inflicted what they saw as unjustified violence.

Physical violence was so central to the driver's public persona that the lash-wielding driver often elicited comment in Caribbean travel narratives and abolitionist propaganda. British physician and traveler George Pinckard, for example, defined drivers in his *Notes on the West Indies* (1806) by their use of the whip: they were "slaves so termed from being promoted to the distinguished office of following their comrades, upon all occasions, with a whip at their backs, as an English carter attends his horses."[18] This tendency to associate drivers primarily with the violence they inflicted persisted at least into the mid-nineteenth century, with many writers, including Harriet Beecher Stowe, author of the widely read *Uncle Tom's Cabin* (1852), depicting drivers as violent, even savage.[19] Such one-dimensional caricatures exaggerated drivers' use of force and ignored their ambivalent position in plantation communities, but even in their excess they identified the connection between physical violence and power that permeated all relationships in slave society, including those between drivers and other enslaved people.

In Berbice, enslaved people who disobeyed orders or who questioned a driver's authority inevitably found themselves on the receiving end of a driver's whip. When Brandy, an enslaved man on plantation Woodlands, on Berbice's Atlantic coast, supposedly arrived late for work one morning in February 1827, the driver ordered another man to hold Brandy and then "flogged him with a cat [o' nine tails], which he carries in his pocket." And when Brandy told the driver, a man named Isaac, originally from Barbados and close to sixty years old, that "he would go complain to his master . . . the driver flogged him again," angry that Brandy dared challenge his authority. Undeterred, Brandy immediately went over the driver's head to their owner, John Rawlins. But Rawlins "saw no mark on Brandy, and therefore drove him away with the horsewhip," he told the fiscal.[20] Yet Brandy persisted in protesting the driver's violence, perhaps because he knew that drivers no longer had the right to carry their weapons into the field. Four months earlier the Berbice council of government had passed a new slave code—responding to metropolitan pressure to ameliorate slavery—which prohibited anyone from "carry[ing] a whip, or any other instrument of punishment, into the field or elsewhere, either as a badge of authority or a stimulus to labour."[21] Brandy and the other slaves on Woodlands would have remembered the day a civil magistrate visited their plantation and, in compliance with the colonial government's order, announced the new law.[22]

Unable to get any recourse from his owner, Brandy left the plantation without permission to complain to the assistant protector of slaves and civil magistrate, who lived nearby, but he "told [Brandy] to go to his master and get a pass to come and make a complaint." When Brandy returned to Woodlands and asked for the pass, "his master called the driver, had him tied down and flogged, and then gave him the pass." Only then did the assistant protector inspect Brandy's wounds, visit Woodlands to investigate, and, ultimately, forward the complaint to the protector of slaves, who referred the case to the fiscal.[23] Through complaints like Brandy's, enslaved people sought to set limits on the amount of violence drivers could get away with. But drivers and slaveowners were reluctant to give up the whip—despite the new law—because they recognized the central role physical coercion played in controlling enslaved people.

Plantation Highbury, a sugar estate some ten miles upriver from New Amsterdam, was another place where drivers apparently flaunted the new regulations on whipping.[24] Drivers on Highbury routinely whipped people who fell behind in their work as late as 1832—eight years after the new code was adopted. Secundo, an enslaved woman ordered to carry megass—the pulp or waste generated when cut canes were fed into the sugar mill's rollers—away from the mill, testified before the protector and, later, the court of criminal justice, that a driver there had flogged her and other women "with a leather strap." September, the driver in charge of the mill gang, admitted that when the manager "found fault with the gang for not doing their work properly," he "desired September to flog them with the strap," a weapon that was, he estimated, "about 2 feet long about an inch broad and tolerably thick." Secundo and some of the other megass carriers had also been flogged the following morning on their bare backs by another driver, Hussar. He explained to the protector "that he carried the strap to induce the women to work & makes use of it if they do not work properly." The Highbury drivers' testimony not only confirmed their continued reliance on flogging to assert power; it also highlighted the symbolic power of the whip in distinguishing drivers from other slaves. As September explained, "I walk with the leather whenever I am driver"—a fact that the other enslaved people there must have known all too well.[25]

If physical force helped drivers project power, it could also backfire. Indeed, physical violence was high on enslaved people's list of grievances against drivers.[26] Trim, for example, complained to the fiscal in March 1821 about the violent driver and unsympathetic manager on the Corantine Coast plantation where he lived. Carefully framing his complaint in terms of reciprocal obligations, like many slaves, Trim told the fiscal "that he knows very well that a negro is to work, he does his duty, but cannot please the manager." The manager flogged sick slaves instead of giving them the "physic" they requested and, probably worse, tolerated his driver's brutality. According to Trim, "the driver is continually finding fault with and licking him too much," and "when complaining about this to the manager, he gets for answer, 'It is your master's work.' "[27]

Hero, from Kilcoy, a cotton plantation on the Corantine Coast, also went to the fiscal to complain about the driver there after a particularly violent dispute in August 1825. "I have story [Berbician slang for conflict] with the driver," Hero began. "Driver trouble & lick [whip] me in the field. I had a pain in my stomach, driver told me to carry water for the negroes to drink." Hero had protested that he was too weak to carry the water, but the driver ignored him and "sent to call four negro men to hold [him] . . . down on the ground" while he whipped him "until the blood came out." Hero then "got up and wanted to take a hoe to work," but the "driver told [him] not to put [his] hand on that hoe." At that point Hero had had enough. Determining that the driver was being unreasonable, or perhaps that he had abused his authority to use physical force, Hero told the driver that he would "go to the massa in Town," the fiscal, "to go complain."[28] Like other enslaved people in Berbice, Hero knew that a driver's authority was not absolute. He also would have known, from other slaves on his plantation or neighboring estates, that the fiscal had the authority to regulate plantation staff, and that he could use this hierarchy to his advantage.

Drivers who were too harsh in other ways also lost the support of their enslaved subordinates. The driver Just, from the Rotterdam coffee plantation, found himself "abused" by three "middle aged" men for reporting their allegedly slow pace of work and disrespect to the manager. Just told the protector that he had found the men, who had been ordered to cut the large branches of the plantation's sandkoker trees, which provided shade for the coffee plants, sitting down and waiting for breakfast an hour before the designated break time. Even worse, "they had only finished [trimming] one tree since morning when the other [slaves] had done six," and they refused to return to work, which must have frustrated Just, who was ultimately responsible for his gang's daily output. So Just told the manager that they "had left their work and were sitting down," and when the manager confronted them in the field "they became so insolent to himself and the driver that he ordered them home and in the evening at six o'clock they were flogged." The next day the men complained about the driver and manager to the protector of slaves, which proved counterproductive when the protector dismissed their complaint because no law had been broken.[29] One wonders how the manager and driver dealt with the complainants when they returned to Rotterdam.

For Peter, an enslaved African sawyer and "old man . . . scarcely able to eat" the corn rations he received as part of his weekly allowance, the driver's mistake had been incriminating him for a petty theft that might have been overlooked. Peter, likely as malnourished as most Berbician slaves and weathered from years of abuse and hard labor, "went into his master's rice field, where he took a little rice." The driver, who had watched Peter, "reported this to his master, who searched his house and took all the corn away, which, as his allowance, he had lain up for a length of time." Eager to convince the fiscal—his only hope at this point—that this was not an isolated incident of callousness, Peter claimed "that the driver is so severe, the people are scarcely able to keep it out with him, he (the driver) often saying that he does not care whether the people hang or drown themselves, or whether they run away in the bush."[30]

Even though managers and other white authorities usually supported drivers—men selected for their trustworthiness and generally viewed as "sensible, well-behaved, negro[es]"—when other slaves complained against them, such complaints highlight the limitations of using physical violence to project power.[31] Drivers knew that they could not rule by brute force alone, that they could not distance themselves too far from "the people" with whom they worked and lived, and so they used the carrot as well as the stick.

The Driver Knows We Are in the Right

Politically savvy drivers fashioned themselves as community leaders or ombudsmen to earn other slaves' allegiance. Such drivers found ways large and small, public and private, of leveraging their authority and unique position to ease the burden of their subordinates. Most of these actions were never documented, which makes the most successful drivers—or at least the ones who were the most popular with other enslaved people—the most difficult to find in surviving documents. Still, the records from Berbice provide some important clues. A driver might, for example, negotiate with his manager for a reduced workload, decide to reward cooperative slaves with special privileges, or collaborate with obeah practitioners to heal the sick. Yet these tactics also had their risks, since drivers who were perceived by overseers or managers as being too sympathetic to other slaves jeopardized their relationships with the people who had appointed them and on whom they depended. Being too soft was as dangerous as being too severe.

A complaint from Adam, a fifty-year-old African-born "Bush Driver" on a woodcutting estate far up Berbice River, illustrates the risks drivers faced when they tried to help their subordinates. As Adam told the fiscal, he "had been deputed by the gang to represent to their mistress that they were not sufficiently fed and clothed." This was, from an enslaved person's perspective, Adam's responsibility as their leader. Adam agreed to talk to their owner, but "instead of affording redress . . . [she] directed him to be confined in the stocks" for overstepping his bounds. And when two men "stepped forward to expostulate" with their owner and stand up for Adam, their leader and advocate, "they were both flogged with the bush-rope."[32]

But Adam, who was "soon released from the stocks and sent to the Bush," where he was to supervise his gang as they harvested cassava and felled trees, continued to represent the other slaves on the estate. A few days after his failed attempt to negotiate with the owner, he traveled with eight other men downriver to New Amsterdam, where they made a long series of complaints to the fiscal, ranging from impossibly demanding tasks to a lack of food and clothing allowances and frequent, unmerited punishments. Here Adam publicly, and dangerously, identified himself as part of a community of slaves whose plight he empathized with, advocating for their welfare by subjecting his owner to the scrutiny of government officials.[33]

Other drivers ran into trouble with managers for arguing about the quantity or quality of work expected of a plantation's labor force. Unlike managers and slaveowners, who wanted to extract the maximum amount of labor from their enslaved workers in order to increase profits, drivers had good reasons to protest labor assignments that would be difficult to complete.[34] Lighter workloads not only eased slaves' burden, for which they might thank the driver. They also helped drivers avoid being held responsible, and punished, when their gang fell behind or did not complete their day's tasks. Slowing the pace of work or reducing tasks, however, was dangerous and difficult for drivers.

Such was the case on the coffee plantation Fredrick's Lust in July 1828. J. A. van Meurs, the exasperated manager, complained to the protector of slaves "that his gang had been very neglectful for the last week in performing their usual tasks," and "that he had reason to believe the Driver [Galant] had combined with the gang in trying to defeat his . . . authority over them." Moreover, Galant "had been very insolent in the morning," which prompted van Meurs to "secure" him and ask the protector for help. The protector took the situation seriously enough to travel to Frederick's Lust the next morning to investigate. There he ordered Galant "to state what had given rise to the Disobedience of the gang & his Insolence." Galant tried to minimize his responsibility by blaming the slaves he supervised for disobeying the manager's orders, which he claimed he had faithfully passed down. But instead of "clean[ing] the grass from 100 coffee trees or one row" each, as Galant had ordered, they insisted on working "two men on a row." The problems continued after the workday finished. When the manager ordered Galant to confine five men in the bedstocks for not finishing their work, Galant was "not able to catch the people that were to be confined." The manager then ordered Galant himself into confinement.[35]

When the protector questioned the other enslaved workers, however, they told a different story: Galant "had tried to put them up against the work by saying that had he to perform that task he would soon compel the manager to reduce the same." According to them, Galant apparently wanted their support to protest the manager's orders. Perhaps Galant thought he would have had a better chance persuading the manager to reduce the workload if he could claim that he was facing widespread resistance from below, casting himself as a mere messenger caught in between. Whatever the actual cause of the work shortfall, drivers like Galant, who used their authority against the interests of managers and plantation owners, took a serious risk. In Galant's case, the protector sided with the manager. He "severely reprimanded Galant & ordered him to receive Forty Lashes for attempting to bring insubordination & discontent amongst the gang over which he was placed in authority."[36]

Campaigning for less brutal working conditions for the slaves under one's charge was dangerous in part because drivers and managers had different notions about the amount of work to demand of slaves and about how it ought to be done. Enslaved laborers were quick to take advantage of this dynamic. When Caroline, a field laborer on the Everton sugar plantation, complained to the protector that she had been punished in late November 1830, she emphasized the discrepancy between the manager's and the driver's labor expectations. According to Caroline—and Grace, who testified on her behalf—the driver had ordered Caroline to weed grass on the estate's back dam with another woman, not far from where her daughter was working. But when the manager, a newcomer named Thomas Edgelow, found the two women working together, he "said it was a task for one, [and] removed the other woman." Grace protested that the driver "had put two women on each side of the parapet." He knew, Caroline claimed, that "the task was too great" for one person alone. Edgelow was not in the mood to negotiate; he "told [Caroline] to shut her mouth." And when she dared to "look round at the manager and he happened to see her," failing to bow her head—a physical display of deference Edgelow expected—he lashed out: "You d——d B——h what do you look at me for[?]" Undaunted, Caroline asked, "are people not to look any more[?]" Determined to assert his authority, Edgelow told Caroline, "I will confine you and cool you," and then ordered the driver to take Caroline to "the darkhouse" and, later, the public stocks, as punishment "for insolence."[37]

At least as troubling to the manager as Caroline's insubordination was his driver's failure to extract enough labor from his gang—his primary responsibility. On the day in question, he told the fiscal, "there appeared to be a combination among the gang, as the whole were far deficient in performing their day's work." The driver was not only unable or unwilling to compel Caroline and the other women to do the amount of work Edgelow demanded. Much worse, from the manager's perspective, was that he tolerated or perhaps even encouraged the work slowdown. The situation was so dangerous, the manager claimed, that "he was compelled to have the greater part of [the gang] alternately confined in the public stocks," taking over the driver's role in enforcing labor discipline.[38]

The struggle on Everton between manager, driver, and field laborers continued for several days, as evidenced by another complaint against Edgelow less than a week later. This time, fifteen women—including Grace, who had testified on Caroline's behalf when she first complained—went to the protector's office. Like many enslaved people who sought the protector's help, they framed their complaint in terms of impossible work requirements, unjustified punishments, and discrepancies in the amount of work expected by the manager and the driver. The women explained that they had been placed in the bedstocks for the past six nights because Edgelow remained unhappy with the amount of work they performed. The complainants claimed that the grass they were supposed to weed was "exceedingly high," and, more tellingly, that they were performing their daily tasks "to the satisfaction of the driver." Edgelow, however, remained convinced that there was "a conspiracy amongst the women, not to finish their work"—and that the driver was not doing what was necessary to restore order. When the protector questioned the driver, moreover, he sided with the women and second-guessed the manager's judgment. He told the protector that even though the women had only done about two-thirds of the work that the manager demanded, he thought "that what they [the women] finished might be taken as a day's work."[39] This time, instead of blaming the work shortfalls on the "combination," as he had done a few days earlier, the driver broke with the manager and supported the women in their labor dispute—a risky move that jeopardized his relationship with the manager but probably earned him the respect of his fellow slaves. The marginal position of drivers is perhaps best illustrated in moments such as this, when workplace disputes between field laborers and plantation management forced them to choose sides.

Drivers' success in reducing workloads or supporting other slaves' efforts at collective bargaining was limited, as the following complaint illustrates. Six men complained to the fiscal in December 1821 "that they [were] ill used" and, specifically, that they had recently been flogged because they damaged cotton that was too wet to have been ginned. The driver, an African man named Watson who had previously worked as a "domestick," carpenter, and probably field laborer, had tried to explain this to the manager. After all, he probably knew more about the actual work of ginning cotton than the man in charge of the plantation. But the "massa said, 'Never mind; I want the cotton ginned, and if they mash the seed I will cut their a— at flog-time.'" So the men ginned the wet cotton, and the manager followed through on his threat, ordering Watson to flog them.[40]

Yet even then Watson appears to have tried to spare them. When the fiscal performed a routine physical inspection of the complainants to determine how severely and how recently they had been flogged, he noticed that at least one of them lacked the telltale lacerations. When he asked "why the recent punishment did not appear," the man answered that "the driver knows we are in the right." The driver "therefore does not punish us by cutting us"— whipping severely—he explained.[41] Mitigating punishments allowed drivers to give the impression that they followed their managers' orders while also demonstrating to slaves that they did not condone them. This was also a means of distributing favors in a way that enhanced a driver's prestige and encouraged slaves to cooperate with drivers.

Another way drivers earned the allegiance and perhaps respect of other enslaved people was by participating in illicit spiritual practices like obeah and cooperating with obeah practitioners, especially when obeah was used to combat the ever-present diseases and malevolent powers enslaved people faced. When the enslaved people on plantations Demtichem and Op Hoop van Beter began to suspect that some malevolent force was responsible for an unusually high number of deaths and illnesses, for instance, it was the drivers who took the initiative and asked Hans and Willem, spiritual authorities from neighboring plantations who were identified by some of their peers as obeah practitioners, for help. The drivers also co-supervised the "Minje Mama" dances—divination and healing ceremonies meant to uncover the poison or "bad thing" and restore health—and they played the lead role in trying to keep white colonists from discovering their clandestine gatherings.[42]

Such drivers thus demonstrated an assumed responsibility for the health and well-being of the enslaved people they supervised, even at the risk of breaking well-known laws against the practice of obeah and jeopardizing their relationship with the managers who had appointed them. Indeed, the drivers on Demtichem and Op Hoop van Beter faced severe punishments, including branding, hundreds of lashes, and demotion, for having supervised obeah rituals and violating their managers' trust.[43] Yet by aligning themselves with obeah practitioners—powerful authorities in their own right—and participating in rituals often used to uncover the root cause of evil or determine one's guilt or innocence, drivers who escaped detection found another means of enhancing their prestige and power within their communities, taking advantage of the intersection of political and spiritual authority.[44]

The danger, of course, in relying on obeah and other unsanctioned means of enhancing one's authority was that these tactics could get drivers into serious trouble with their enslavers, the people on whom they ultimately relied for their power and their privileges. Drivers may have wanted other slaves to respect and obey them, but they *needed* the true rulers of the plantation system—white plantation authorities—to support them.

His Authority in the Field Would Be
Entirely Done Away With

Enlisting the support of the managers or planters who had appointed them was the drivers' best means of maintaining authority, as illustrated by the numerous cases in which drivers successfully turned to them for help. In many cases, moreover, drivers explicitly referenced their compromised "authority," speaking a language that overseers, managers, and slaveowners—men preoccupied if not obsessed with their need to project power and status—understood well. Such drivers displayed a canny understanding of plantation hierarchy and used the norms of that hierarchy to justify their own conduct and defend themselves. White plantation authorities, for their part, were usually eager to help embattled drivers reestablish control because they recognized that their own grip on power—not to mention their profits and physical safety—required that field laborers and other low-ranking slaves obeyed drivers, that the official hierarchy of the plantation be respected. As one planter wrote, a good driver should "suffer no freedoms from those under him, by conversation or trifling puerile conduct."[45] Or, as another planter, explained, "above all, [a driver] must be a man whose good character commands respect among his fellow labourers; and in this case, his influence and authority are truly valuable."[46]

Drivers knew that plantation officials were a reliable source of support when other slaves challenged their authority. One unnamed driver on plantation Niewen Hoop, for example, went to his manager after Woensdag, a field laborer disliked by the driver and several other slaves, had been, in the words of the plantation's attorney, "very abusive to the driver." The driver had found Woensdag taking a break without permission and scolded him. Woensdag, instead of begging forgiveness or returning to work without comment, countered that "when I feel hot & thirsty I must wash & drink, I then feel strong to finish my work." The driver, upset that Woensdag argued with him, replied, "oh, I know you, you are a lazy bugger & constantly going to the Fiscal to complain, and whether you are on, or off the Estate, we don't care." Woensdag "continued working," he claimed, even as the driver "kept on cursing" him.[47]

The driver knew that tolerating this kind of back talk, especially from a supposedly lazy worker, would cause him to lose face and set a dangerous precedent. So he went to the manager a few days later and told him that "if Woensdag was not punished for his conduct . . . towards him (the driver)

Figure 7. Manager or overseer and driver supervising slaves. Detail from William Hilhouse, *Map of British Guiana* (Demerary [Demerara]: 1827). This illustration of the three major crops cultivated in Britain's Guiana colonies—coffee, cotton, and sugar—appeared in a map of British Guiana. The artist highlighted the close working relationships between plantation managers or overseers and drivers, whose European-style dress helped distinguish them from the nearly-naked field slaves they supervised. The physical distance between the driver at the center of the image and the group of enslaved laborers cutting and loading canes into punts on the opposite bank of the river further underscores the distinctions many colonists made between drivers and other slaves. CO 700/British Guiana15, National Archives, Kew, London, UK.

that his authority in the field would be entirely done away with." Here the driver explicitly acknowledged his reliance on higher authorities. The manager, recognizing the need to confront challenges to the plantation hierarchy head-on, decided to confine Woensdag in the stocks for a day and planned to flog him later. But once Woensdag was released from the stocks and saw that "they were preparing to flog [him] with the carracarres & the whip," he protested this "double punishment," arguing with the manager and ultimately running away for more than a week before showing up in New Amsterdam at the fiscal's office.[48] Woensdag probably knew that his best hope was appealing to someone outside the plantation power structure, since the driver and manager were likely to remain allied against him.

"There are plenty of people who want negroes," Woensdag told the fiscal, "and as they say I am bad, let them put me up at Vendue." Woensdag thus displayed a savvy awareness of his market value, which he tried to leverage to improve his situation. "I cannot nor will not go back to the Estate," he continued. "If I go, I will go to the bush" (run away). This was no idle threat: Woensdag had run away before, which was one of the reasons that the driver disliked him. And, as the Niewen Hoop manager and attorney explained, Woensdag was "a healthy strong negro," but was nevertheless "always backward in his work" and "a bad character," which must have frustrated the driver even more. Drivers were no more willing than managers to tolerate troublemakers, like Woensdag, who jeopardized their status or disrespected them. Fortunately for drivers, they often found the support they needed by appealing to white authorities. In this case, for example, the fiscal "ordered Woensdag," who was "known to be a very bad character, . . . to receive 39 lashes for making a frivolous complaint."[49]

Enslaved people who fell out of favor with drivers could quickly wind up in trouble with white authorities, too, as a complaint from Welcome, a field laborer on the coffee plantation Vryburg, illustrates. Welcome told the fiscal that his manager had "called him to his door, and asked what was the matter with him, that he spoke so much for the last two or three days," and that some of the other slaves on the estate—including the drivers, probably—had told him that Welcome "was always speaking about him." Welcome told the manager "that [he] never said anything bad about him," and when "the manager said the negroes had told him [he] was a bad man," Welcome replied: "Well, master, if the driver don't like me, I cannot help it." According to Welcome, the manager told him to hold his tongue, and when Welcome told the manager that he "never saw an estate so bad as this," directly insulting his capacity to manage the plantation, the manager called two drivers to take him to the stocks. Welcome's complaint to the manager that the drivers "always gave [him] double the work [he was] able to do" suggests a mutual antipathy that had been brewing for some time. The next day, Welcome told the fiscal, he was flogged—104 lashes—and then put back in the stocks "for four days and four nights," not even "allowed to go to the privy house."[50]

The acting fiscal's investigation of Welcome's complaint, however, which "would have been a very serious one for the manager" if it had been true, he noted, revealed a competing narrative. In this telling, Welcome had been protesting the work he had been ordered to complete, defying the driver's authority and by extension the manager's. The acting fiscal accepted this version of events and concluded that "Welcome was a riotous insubordinate character, and was always the head man when anything was going on on the estate." In this case Welcome had been "endeavouring to persuade the other negroes that they had too much work given to them." The manager claimed that he put Welcome in the stocks (only for one night) for having been "very insolent" when he "endeavored to reason with him on the impropriety of his conduct" and then had him flogged (thirty-nine lashes, he claimed) the following morning. The acting fiscal noted his approval of Welcome's punishment, dismissed his complaint, and "severely reprimanded [him] for his misconduct."[51]

Similar cases confirm that white authorities, whether plantation supervisors or colonial officials, punished field laborers who disrespected drivers—and especially those who suggested drivers were incompetent. Moreover, colonial authorities usually took the driver's side in slave-driver conflicts.[52] The case of Mary from plantation Rotterdam, on the Berbice River, was typical. In May 1827 Mary complained to the protector that she had been confined in the stocks until she fainted after an altercation with the driver, Just. Mary had been picking coffee, she told the protector, when she began arguing with Just, an African man in his late twenties who had lived on Rotterdam for at least a decade. Just was upset that Mary returned late for work after the midday break. According to the manager, when Just and the overseer asked Mary why she was late to work, she "abused them, and said, that as the manager said nothing about it, they had no right to do so." According to Mary, Just had cursed her, probably as upset that Mary was undermining his authority as he was by her tardiness, which prompted her to go to the manager. But "instead of hearing what I had to say," Mary claimed, the manager "listened to the driver" and then put her into the hand and feet stocks for five hours.[53]

Going to the protector, however, backfired. The protector summoned Just and the manager, who said that Mary was "always in the habit of going late to the field; and that she had often been reprimanded on that account." Moreover, this was not the first time she had disrespected plantation authorities. Mary had "often been quarreling . . . with the overseer and driver," the manager testified, and "her former owner sold her to this estate on account of her insolence." Even the witnesses Mary called to testify on her behalf, who said they did not know whether she had fainted in the stocks, "gave her a very bad character, and said that she was very troublesome on the estate." The manager asked the protector to punish Mary for lying "and for repeated bad conduct on the estate," and the protector consented. He "reprimand[ed] her severely against using any insolence against the manager, or others put in authority over her," and threatened to send her to the treadmill—that dreaded new torture device—if she continued to cause problems.[54] The protector, like the manager, thus demonstrated his willingness to shore up a driver's authority in the face of challenges from below.

Colonial authorities in Berbice aimed to make other slaves show respect toward drivers. In July 1830, for example, the manager of plantation Demtichem ordered Francientje, a field laborer, to spend three agonizing nights in the bedstocks (she would escape after the second night and go to town to complain) for having been "extremely abusive" to a driver. Francientje had not finished her day's work, either, but the real problem was that she had disrespected the driver. As the manager explained, "other women had neglected their work on the same day but on expressing their contrition were pardoned." Francientje's behavior would have been, too, "had she not been abusive to the driver."[55] Five women from plantation Prospect told a similar tale two years later: the manager forced them to work all night in the sugar mill—after a full day in the field—"as punishment for having disobeyed the driver."[56] Indeed, punishment record books are full of people punished for challenging their drivers. Common "offences" meriting punishment included: "cursing the driver," "insolence to driver," "telling falsehood to driver," "obstinately persisting in disregarding the orders of the driver," "abusing driver & resisting [driver's] authority," "instigating the other negroes in the field to curse and abuse the driver," and "quarreling & fighting with the head driver."[57] Such offences suggest that officials were determined not only to punish enslaved laborers who disobeyed drivers in the workplace but also—perhaps especially—those who failed to show drivers deference or otherwise refused to recognize their authority.

The success of drivers in constructing authority by collaborating with their enslavers is perhaps best seen by looking at plantations where drivers became more powerful than the managers who were officially in charge. Sometimes managers apparently deferred to their drivers, ceding their own authority so long as the results tended to satisfy them. An enslaved woman who was "far advanced in pregnancy" from the cotton plantation Albion, for instance, claimed that her manager was intimidated by his driver. Her specific complaint, recorded by the fiscal in February 1825, was that the manager had allowed the driver to brutally flog her sister and then her. She intervened, she explained, when "the driver thought it proper to lay my sister down & flog her with the whip." When she "asked the driver why he flogged [her] sister," the driver "told [her] to go away and took his whip and flogged [her] also." The manager, having witnessed the entire scene, simply "got upon his horse and & rode away," unwilling to interfere.[58]

When the fiscal questioned the manager, he claimed that the driver had only given the woman's sister "a few stripes" for refusing to send her child, who had whooping cough (pertussis), home from the field for its own good. And when her pregnant sister had come to her defense, she was "very abusive" to the driver, who merely "threw his whip round her thigh once." Knowing she was pregnant and "fearful that she might induce the Driver by her passionate conduct to repeat the stripe," he told the driver to "let her alone," he claimed. Only then did he ride away. The woman, however, offered a different explanation for the manager's quick departure: "the manager," she claimed, did not stop the driver because he "is afraid of him"—an inversion of authority that would have alarmed officials. Lest there be any doubt about the extent of the driver's power, she reiterated: "the driver is too great a man."[59] With such complaints, enslaved laborers invoked plantation management values for their own purposes, framing specific complaints about abusive drivers as symptoms of a larger problem that colonial officials would be more likely to address: incompetent plantation management and irregularities in the official hierarchy that was supposed to govern colonial slavery.

Zealand, a driver on plantation Berenstein, seems to have possessed the same unrivaled authority, at least according to Rosetta, an enslaved woman there. The situation had become so bad by June 1819 that Rosetta made the long journey—some twenty miles—to New Amsterdam to complain to the fiscal about the driver who terrorized her. She told him that she had "nothing to say against the manager nor her owner, but that the driver Zealand [was] the person which made her go to town." Zealand was "continually licking and cursing her, and even cut her with a cutlass [machete] once in the arm . . . and once knocked her with a cutlass in her teeth." The most recent beating, moreover, was so bad that afterward "she hid herself a few days in the bush, [then] went to the colony hospital and miscarried there . . . which . . . she attributes to the several misbehaviors of Zealand against her." Objecting to the witnesses Zealand brought to defend himself—his son and his assistant driver—Rosetta claimed that "the remainder of the gang will substantiate her declaration." And she was probably right: one man testified that "he saw Zealand strike Rosetta with the bush-rope on her mouth, so that it made the blood come out and swelled her lips" (though he claimed he never saw Zealand strike her with a cutlass). The people who worked in the colony hospital also verified that Rosetta had indeed miscarried there.[60]

Zealand, when interrogated by the fiscal, admitted that he struck Rosetta during an argument about loading plantains (the good ones were to be sold, "the bad ones to be brought home for plantation use"), but he blamed Rosetta. Zealand gave her an order, but instead of complying, she "turned her head to him; upon which he, observing her to look very red in the eyes [angry], asked why she looked so; to which she gave him a very cross and disgusting answer." This disrespect "vex[ed]" Zealand, so "he went up to her with a thin piece of bush-rope, telling her not to be so insolent, and licking her at the same time with this said instrument of correction on her mouth, stating, that as her mouth was so bad the same only deserved to be punished." Like other drivers, Zealand saw physical violence as his prerogative. But why had the manager on Berenstein allowed Zealand to beat a pregnant woman so brutally that she miscarried? Why did Zealand think he could get away with it? Rosetta's explanation was unequivocal: "Zealand is the ruler of the estate." Even "the manager has less to say than he," she added. This was not, of course, how the plantation hierarchy was supposed to function, and Rosetta knew it. Her complaint, although explicitly against the driver, was also an indictment of the manager's weakness, an attempt to persuade the fiscal to intervene in a chaotic and potentially dangerous situation in which an enslaved man had more power than the free white man above him. As Rosetta reiterated, emphasizing the inversion of the proper plantation hierarchy, "the manager has not the least authority to hinder [Zealand] in his proceedings."[61] The danger that Zealand posed, Rosetta implied, was not that he abused the enslaved people below him, but rather that he had become the highest authority on the plantation.

Drivers like Zealand or the one on Albion, who brutalized other slaves with impunity and perhaps even intimidated overseers and managers, were indeed "rulers of the estate." Yet they did not necessarily pose a threat to the plantation regime. As long as they used their authority and violence to keep enslaved people at work and plantations productive, overseers and managers might tolerate, or even welcome, such power, allowing drivers to wield levels of authority not normally associated with enslaved people in plantation societies and dismissing the complaints of other enslaved laborers.[62] And when other drivers had trouble projecting power on their own, managers usually came to their rescue. Much more problematic for managers, however, were drivers that were irresponsible or leveraged their authority against the plantation system they were meant to uphold.

A Disgraced Driver

Drivers who lost the support of plantation managers were destined for failure. Trustworthy, competent drivers were critical to the smooth operation of a plantation, but "a bad or indifferent head driver," as Jamaican planter Thomas Roughley wrote, "sets almost every thing at variance; injures the negroes, and the culture of the land. He is like a cruel blast that pervades every thing, and spares nothing."[63] Managers placed a great deal of trust in their drivers, and when drivers lost that trust, whether through negligence or opposition, the consequences were severe. Some drivers found themselves on the receiving end of the lash, humiliated as they endured the kind of violence they were accustomed to doling out, and the least fortunate were "broke," or fired, from their coveted position. Demoted drivers lost not only their elite status but also what had probably been their best chance of forging a viable life under slavery. The severity with which managers dealt with drivers who caused problems and the ways that drivers reacted to punishment and demotion underscore the critical importance of the driver's role—for drivers themselves, for their families, and for the slave regime.

Managers punished drivers they saw as ineffective or uncooperative, as punishment record books make clear.[64] Bob, from plantation Alness, received twenty-five lashes for "great neglect as driver."[65] Horatio, from plantation Vryheid, spent thirty-six hours in solitary confinement for "allowing the negroes to do bad work in the field" and then, a week and a half later, whipped for "neglect of duty as Driver in the field."[66] Frank, also from Vryheid, was given thirty-six hours' solitary confinement for allowing enslaved women "to stray away from him in the field & not keeping them in proper control."[67] For "neglect of duty as Driver," London from Mary's Hope endured the same punishment.[68] Gallant, from Frederick's Lust, spent two and a half nights in the "darkroom" and then endured forty lashes for "neglecting his duty as Driver by giving wrong orders to the gang & putting the gang up against the manager."[69] Cicero, from Eliza and Mary, was flogged "for very great neglect of duty as driver in allowing the women gang under his charge to do their work in such a slovenly manner that they were obliged to go over it all again, by which there was a day's work of the whole gang lost."[70] Such punishments highlight the range of ways that drivers could run afoul of their managers.

Smart, a forty-year-old driver on the Friends sugar plantation, for example, complained to the acting protector of slaves in December 1830 that he was "punished whenever the gang of women under his charge fail to perform their tasks." Under the new manager, who had arrived just two months earlier, Smart had already been flogged twice for not getting the women he supervised to cut as much sugarcane as the manager ordered. Smart's "negligence," the manager explained to the acting protector, who investigated the complaint on site, was hurting the plantation's productivity. Smart had been "allowing the women to leave the canes uncut in the field." "Were it not for the Indolence of the cane cutting gang," the manager claimed, he could make twice as many hogsheads of sugar per day. So "in order to induce [Smart] to be more attentive," he explained, "he found it necessary to have him punished." The acting protector agreed and dismissed Smart's complaint.[71]

Managers also punished drivers caught turning a blind eye to minor infractions or granting slaves illicit privileges—which were of course the very actions that earned drivers credibility within their communities. The driver on one Canje River plantation, for instance, was "punished and locked in the stocks" when the manager found out that he had allowed Laura, an enslaved woman "with a child at the breast," to leave the field to nurse her infant.[72] In a similar case, when the driver on plantation Port Mourant "allowed the women to come to the house to get their breakfast," one woman testified, the manager flogged him for not keeping them at work all day without a break, as he ordered.[73] When the manager on plantation Waterloo found the slaves on his plantation dancing at night, supposedly with the driver's permission, he reported it to his employer, who sent word to the fiscal. When the fiscal went to Waterloo to investigate, and determined that the driver had supervised the illicit dance, he ordered the driver to endure fifty lashes.[74]

Indeed, drivers could be punished for almost anything other slaves did that displeased plantation officials.[75] This was an important difference between drivers and foremen, who were only responsible for employees' behavior during working hours. Plantations may have been factories, but they were also residential labor camps where workers were subjected to discipline and coercion outside of the workplace. Managers thus interpreted anything they saw as slave disobedience as evidence that their drivers had failed to exert the necessary authority. When an enslaved man named Thomas ran away from plantation Berenstein during the Christmas holidays in 1820, for example, the manager, a notoriously violent man (even by West Indian standards) named J. Deussen who prompted an unusually high number of complaints during his tenure, took it out on the driver, Primo. The manager, Primo explained, "locked him up in the stocks during the whole of the holidays," one of the rare occasions slaves were allowed to visit and celebrate with their friends and kin on other plantations. Thomas's escape, Primo protested, "was not his fault at all." But the manager disagreed: it was a sign that Primo was not doing his job. The manager "ill-treated [Primo] very much, tore his clothes and licked [whipped] him."[76]

By this point the manager-driver relationship had become so antagonistic that Primo—who himself had been accused by an enslaved woman on Berenstein of treating the others "very cruelly" just six weeks earlier—decided to seek the fiscal's help, effectively renouncing a position that had become unbearable and charging the manager with incompetence. A half dozen other slaves from Berenstein accompanied Primo and corroborated his account of an impossibly demanding and arbitrarily violent manager. Primo explained that "he never complained before, but is now compelled, hoping that he may get another manager to live with." Things had become so desperate that Primo refused to return to the estate after making his complaint "if the manager be allowed to remain there, preferring punishment in town to ill treatment on the estate." He asked the fiscal to remove the manager or transfer him to another plantation. The fiscal, however, did not have the authority to do either, and so whether Primo knew it or not, he was trying to extend the powers of the state and thus use the government's limited commitment to amelioration for his own purposes.[77]

Challenging a manager's authority could be even more dangerous for drivers than not maintaining order, as the following case from plantation Alness in August 1824 shows. When one of the plantation's attorneys visited the large cotton plantation, he was approached by a woman who had been "in confinement locked in the black hole," a punishment the manager had ordered. She asked the attorney to pardon her, and claimed that she had been confined "for some trifling fault." The manager, however, insisted that it was "highly necessary" that she be confined for her "impertinent language & insubordinate conduct." Before ordering her back to the "black hole," the manager asked her how she had escaped, and how she knew the attorney was there. She claimed that "Fielding the driver had let her out." According to Fielding, a stout "Ibo" man in his mid-thirties, the manager then became "vexed and ordered [him] to be confined" for having contradicted his orders, despite his insistence that he had not released the woman. Fielding then "became very violent," the attorney said, "and resisted being put in the stocks."[78]

When Fielding made the long journey to New Amsterdam and involved the fiscal, things went from bad to worse. The manager and attorney claimed that Fielding was "a bad character" and asked the fiscal "to adopt measures to quell the insubordinate conduct of this man to prevent others following his evil & dangerous example." Making an example out of Fielding was especially important because, as the attorney pointed out, "the estate [was] at a remote distance from town," on the Corantine Coast, where colonial authority was presumably weaker. The attorney and manager might have worried about the potential unrest that an embittered driver on a plantation of some three hundred and fifty slaves might cause. The fiscal agreed Fielding needed to be dealt with severely. He "recommended [Fielding] should be broke as a Driver of the Estate" after "receiv[ing] 39 lashes in presence of the whole gang & [then] to be confined for four weeks in solitary confinement." These punishments must have been humiliating for a man who was accustomed to being shown a measure of respect by enslaved people and white colonials alike. But the demotion itself was probably the worst, since Fielding had been a driver on Alness for at least seven years.[79] How, Fielding must have wondered, was he supposed to go back to being "a common negro"?[80]

The last resort for managers who were fed up with drivers like Fielding was to demote them. For drivers—men whose status and very survival depended on the many benefits they derived as supervisors—this was a crushing blow. Some drivers refused to accept demotion, clinging to a position they had grown accustomed to. But replacing a driver, especially a head driver, was rarely easy, and savvy managers avoided replacing drivers unless they determined that they had no other choice. As one Jamaican planter advised his peers, "it gives a great deal of vexation to an overseer when he changes his head driver," and "caprice should never have any hand in such a transaction."[81]

Managers sometimes found that convincing the very people who had been encouraged to respect, if not fear, their driver that he was no longer a legitimate authority was extremely difficult and sometimes impossible.

January was the head driver on Demtichem, a coffee plantation, who was publicly flogged and demoted for conspiring with an obeah practitioner, Hans, to combat an epidemic in 1819.[82] He had only recently been promoted from watchman, a position he held as late as 1817, and he never forgave the manager, Boas, for demoting him.[83] Indeed, ten years later January began a lengthy complaint to the fiscal with a bitter recollection of having been "flogged under the gallows" and then fired after he was convicted of having conspired with Hans. Yet despite not having been a driver for a decade, January, who was then in his late forties, still commanded significant political power among the estate's slaves, which made friction with Boas inevitable.[84]

According to January, their most recent confrontation came when a new attorney, Mr. Winter, arrived in 1829. As was customary, January and the others "beg[ged] that [they] may be allowed to drink a dram [of rum] at the door to welcome [him]." Boas's wife, meanwhile, told Boas that "the Gang are gone up to their Master's door to complain against you." Enraged, Boas confronted the slaves, who tried to explain that they were only asking for rum. But Boas ignored them, convinced that January was behind some conspiracy. He told Winter that "this man," indicating January, "has given me impudence." Boas then ordered January "taken and confined in the stocks."[85]

That might have been the end of it, were it not for the large group that stood up for January, their former driver and a man they continued to respect as a leader. "The whole gang," January claimed, "said if this man is locked up we must be locked up too." Boas confirmed that "the whole gang with the Exception of the [current] Drivers cried out, we must be put in confinement also." It took more than two hours, and the help of the drivers and "a few well disposed slaves," to get January's many supporters to disperse. By this point, January had apparently become too dangerous; a few days later Boas ordered January to board a schooner bound for a distant plantation on the Corantine Coast, where he would presumably pose less of a threat. When the ship reached New Amsterdam, however, January escaped and made his way to the fiscal to complain.[86]

When the fiscal questioned Boas, he also began with January's demotion ten years earlier. It remained a singular event in their antagonistic relationship. "Since that period," Boas told the fiscal, "this man has conducted himself whenever an opportunity occurred of treating me with the utmost disrespect." Boas's account of their most recent confrontation about the rum emphasized what he saw as January's insolence. When Boas pointed out that January was "not a Driver," for example, January countered that Boas was not his "master." According to Boas, "His answer was, do I belong to you? Is the rum yours? or are you able to buy me? and such other remarks in presence of Mr. Winter and the whole of the gang, which was intended of course to lessen me in their opinion."[87]

The struggle between Boas and January was, at its core, a decade-long battle over authority—its provenance, its legitimacy, and its limits—that had reached a boiling point. January had continued to challenge Boas's authority in ways large and small. As Boas told the fiscal, "the [current] driver has declared that this man January told the negroes not to call me 'Mr.' but plainly 'Boas,'" a calculated, effective blow to his status as a mere manager rather than planter. And one night, the manager claimed, an intoxicated January, "speaking Creole to me . . . asked me if I thought I would not be laid there (pointing to the Burial Ground)." Had January been an isolated, embittered slave, the situation might have been easy enough to control. But a significant number of people on the plantation continued to recognize January as an authority and leader—an indication that drivers' power derived at least as much from their peers' respect as it did from their official rank. On Demtichem, even the attorney, who described January as "a disgraced Driver," complained that he still "held an unfounded authority over the gang of slaves on Deutichem." Indeed, the flip side of choosing drivers from the most well respected slaves was that managers could never completely control such men, whose political power was not dependent on their enslavers' endorsement. What troubled Boas and the attorney was that January's authority came from his position within the slave community on Demtichem—a social world with its own structures of power and hierarchies that plantation managers and overseers could intervene in and disrupt but never completely control. Moreover, the very reason that January was fired—turning to a healer who could help the enslaved people on his plantation—may have been an act that the Demtichem slaves remembered as an example of his leadership and concern for their well-being. With this in mind, January's ability to sustain his authority ten years after his demotion is less surprising. The fiscal sympathized with the concerns of the attorney and manager, and told January "that his conduct appeared to be very reprehensible," that his "punishment was merited," and then sentenced him to another fifteen lashes.[88]

Managers and colonial authorities knew that firing a driver could be dangerous, and they took steps to minimize the disruption. The owner of plantation Broer's Lust, for instance, decided that it would be too dangerous to let La Rose, a tall, African man who had been his driver for more than five years, return to the estate after he complained to the fiscal about being flogged. According to La Rose, his owner, Dr. J. P. Broer, blamed him for the recent death of Hoop, an enslaved man on the estate. Broer blamed La Rose because other slaves on the estate said he was "bad" (meaning that he used obeah or harmful spiritual power), and at least two people—including Hoop's widow—told Broer that La Rose had given Hoop something to drink to combat "pain in the belly" that wound up instead killing him. La Rose denied having done anything other than offer Hoop some medical advice: that he should not eat yellow (ripe) plantains or "foefoe" (fufu) but instead cassava and toasted bread, and that a tea made from the leaves of the pigeon pea tree would help.[89] But Broer, La Rose testified, "said I was the cause of Hoop's death," for which he was given 120 lashes.[90]

Broer, however, countered that La Rose's "whole statement [was] false," that he did not hold La Rose accountable for Hoop's death. He admitted having punished La Rose several times, but claimed that it was for being "extremely impertinent to the manager in presence of the whole gang" and, more recently, for having given Hoop medicine against his orders. Broer decided that he needed to get rid of his now-dangerous driver, and he told the fiscal that "the return of La Rose immediately to the Estate would be attended with bad consequences in as much as he appeared to believe that I had obtained information from the two negroes mentioned by him" about treating Hoop's illness. Losing his status as driver was a devastating blow for La Rose, so Broer had good reason to fear retaliation. At Broer's request, the fiscal ordered La Rose "to be worked for a few days on the public works until [Broer] found an opportunity of hiring him out" to another plantation.[91]

For some drivers, the pain of losing their position and its corresponding rewards was simply too much to bear. A poignant example comes from the aptly named sugar plantation Canefield, where in April 1824 Philip, an African driver who had previously worked as a "doctor," as he was listed in slave registration returns, was demoted. According to the manager, Philip "was for some time back acting as a Driver to the Creoles [children] during which time lately he had been in the habit of neglecting his business and getting intoxicated."[92] Indeed, as early as 1819 Philip, then a hospital sick-nurse, had complained to the fiscal—unsuccessfully—"of being too much punished" for alleged drunkenness.[93] Now, five years later, the manager "put him in the stocks for the space of two days," and threatened to flog him if he continued to neglect his work. When Philip failed to show up for work a few days later, the manager sent him back to the stocks and, far worse, demoted him to field labor. The next morning, Philip was flogged and then sent to the field. But Philip refused to join the field gang, unwilling to relinquish the privileged position, and perhaps identity, he had held for at least seven years.[94]

Instead, Philip raced to the Canje River that bordered Canefield and dove in. The overseer thought Philip was trying to escape, but Philip had other plans. Soon after Philip splashed into the water, the overseer ordered nearby slaves to swim out and bring him back. But Philip was soon "about 50 feet from the Water Side," and "before they could reach him he disappeared" below the surface, where he drowned. Philip's wife of several years, Abaneba, later explained that her husband "never told her that he intended to drown himself," but she knew he was devastated by the demotion. As she put it, "his heart was turned." Philip committed suicide because "he was ashamed of being put into the field after so long a Headman."[95]

Drivers in Berbice and other plantation societies were crucial intermediaries who needed considerable political skills to maintain authority. Some drivers worked hard to earn the respect of their subordinates, negotiating with managers for reduced workloads or mitigating the punishments they were ordered to inflict on their fellow slaves in ways that made them seem more like community leaders than enforcers of planter power. And in some cases, drivers even leveraged the authority they had to directly undermine the plantation system their enslavers expected them to uphold, joining and sometimes leading acts of resistance that ranged from protests against specific injustices to large-scale, violent rebellions.[96] Yet even if the very qualities that made someone a good driver also made him a capable insurrectionary leader, very few drivers were rebels. Indeed, if they had been, the slave system could not have functioned. Drivers knew better than anyone that open resistance was likely to backfire, that challenging their enslavers might cost them their position if not their lives.

Ultimately, one of most effective strategies drivers used to maintain the authority they needed was cultivating the support of their enslavers—men who shared drivers' interest in promoting order and hierarchy. Drivers and white plantation authorities had their own distinct motivations, but they also needed each other and thus reinforced each other's authority. Trapped in a system designed to exploit and dehumanize them, men who became drivers knew that securing the resources they needed to carve out viable lives under slavery required them to cooperate with overseers, managers, and planters, even if that meant perpetuating the plantation regime. For people whose most urgent priority was surviving rather than escaping slavery, this was a compromise worth making.

If the ways that drivers navigated their world are surprising, it may be because they are not easily integrated into prevailing ways of writing about slavery, which privilege narratives of domination and resistance. What are we to make of drivers—men whose agency had little to do with resistance and who facilitated the exploitation of other enslaved people for their own gain? It is precisely in the drivers' politics, however, that one can glean the most useful insights. Understanding drivers' relationships with other slaves and with their enslavers—and their motivations—helps us see that surviving the plantation world and resisting slavery were not one and the same. And more importantly, for many enslaved people, survival took precedence. Yet being a driver was a survival strategy available only to men—a reminder that colonial slave societies were powerfully shaped by beliefs about gender and that men and women experienced slavery in markedly different ways. Such gender differences are even more visible in enslaved people's marriages and domestic lives, which could be scenes of intense and sometimes violent conflict between enslaved people, their enslavers, and enforcers of the law.

CHAPTER 4

Marital Discord and Domestic Struggles

An eighteen-year-old "domestic" named Betsy went to the protector of slaves one day in April 1827 to lodge a complaint against her ex-husband. Betsy, who was pregnant, told the protector that the day before she had run into her ex-husband, John William, while walking New Amsterdam's muddy streets. He was obviously drunk. When he noticed Betsy was pregnant, he became belligerent. Who, he demanded to know, was the father? She "told him it was not his business," or, as William recalled, "to kiss her a—e." He flew into a rage and a raucous struggle ensued. Both Betsy and William swore and screamed as he threw her to the ground and kicked her "under the belly." Having heard Betsy's story, the protector summoned William, who insisted he had done nothing wrong. He denied kicking her—aware that striking a pregnant woman in the belly was a particularly heinous act—but admitted giving her "three slaps." Such measured violence, he insisted, was a reasonable response to an insult from a woman he had until recently claimed as his wife. The protector, who knew "John William to be a bad character," sided with Betsy. Even though she was an enslaved woman and her ex-husband was a free man of color, the protector deemed the assault improper. As punishment, William was to be confined "in the dark room" during the upcoming Easter holidays.[1]

Betsy was one of many enslaved people in Berbice who appealed to colonial officials for assistance in resolving marital or domestic conflicts.[2] Doing so invited imperial intervention not only in slaves' disputes with managers and drivers about work and punishment, but into their most intimate relationships. Enslaved people dealt with a wide range of problems as husbands and wives, but they were most likely to reach out to authorities in moments of crisis, including cases of adultery, unwanted interference from outsiders, and extreme physical abuse.[3] Exploring these gendered conflicts—which have received little attention from historians—illuminates family life not only as a potential source of resilience against the many horrors of slavery, but also as the very terrain on which enslaved people negotiated power, dealt with violence, and struggled to survive.[4] Colonial officials, for their part, were willing to intervene in enslaved people's marital conflicts because the British imperial government had identified marriage and family as key targets of reform during amelioration. Promoting British models of marriage, family, and sex among slaves offered the promise of "civilizing" enslaved people while also promoting reproduction and thus the survival of a rapidly declining slave population. Focusing on enslaved people's marital conflicts, as documented and mediated by the colonial legal apparatus tasked with enforcing amelioration, thus reveals some of the major tensions—and accommodations—that occurred as Africans, Europeans, and West Indians confronted one another on the colonial Caribbean's shifting "gender frontier."[5] Marriage was simultaneously a barometer for the progress of amelioration, key to the fate of the slave population, and, most importantly, at the heart of the power relationships enslaved people negotiated as they struggled to survive.

It is easy to understand why imperial officials identified enslaved people's marriages and sexual practices as subjects of concern—antislavery activists had long criticized the slave trade and slavery for breaking apart families, and the end of the slave trade had made reproduction an urgent priority for the slave system's very survival. But how, exactly, did policy makers intend to regulate marriage, sex, and family? A variety of laws and regulations enacted in Berbice during the era of amelioration provides a window into the specific mechanisms officials used to coerce enslaved people into abandoning practices deemed inappropriate and embracing a narrow definition of marriage consistent with nineteenth-century British gender norms. Punishment records, meanwhile, allow us to gauge the extent to which slaveowners and their representatives cooperated with official policy. How invested were they in punishing official "offences" such as "fornication," wife-beating, polygyny, and infidelity, and more broadly in supervising enslaved people's domestic lives? What motivated their decisions to ignore or intervene in different kinds of conflicts between men and women? And what effect, if any, did official policy have on enslaved people's domestic lives?

The records of enslaved people's complaints to the protector and fiscal allow us to see what enslaved women and men themselves wanted when it came to marriage. Enslaved men wanted relationships with women for several reasons, but they faced a major problem given Berbice's uneven sex ratios. Women were scarce, and competition—between enslaved men and free men of color and white colonists—could be intense and violent. Given their demographic disadvantage, how did men try to attract women and prevent them from leaving? How did they deal with women who entered into relationships with other men against their wishes? How did they respond to male rivals? Finally, to what extent were they able to become patriarchs?

Enslaved women faced a different set of problems—both in their relationships with men and in getting help from colonial authorities. Berbice's uneven sex ratio may have given women like Betsy greater opportunities for finding new partners, but it also made them particularly vulnerable to enslaved men who sought to control them, often violently, or punish them for leaving.[6] How, in this context, did enslaved women try to construct marriages that suited them? To whom did they turn for protection from abusive men or support in escaping dangerous marriages? And to what extent did Berbice's patriarchal culture limit their options?

On the whole, enslaved men in Berbice were more likely than enslaved women to succeed in constructing the kind of marriages they wanted because their priorities and beliefs about gender were more closely aligned to the colony's laws, the men who administered them, and their enslavers. Men who sought help resolving marital conflicts took advantage of colonial authorities' beliefs about marriage—that wives should be subordinate to their husbands, that "promiscuousness" and extramarital sex among women was unacceptable, and that men were justified in using certain forms of violence to discipline their dependents—to shore up their own authority as would-be patriarchs.[7] Female subordination was central to the "sexual contract" that governed Berbician slave society, forcing women to rely primarily on their own informal networks to deal with marital conflicts.[8] For men and women alike, the problems they encountered in their marriages were central, not marginal, in their day-to-day lives.

Population Control and Marriage Policy

A major focus of the campaign for the amelioration of slavery was the fate of the slave family. Antislavery activists had long criticized the slave trade and slavery for separating families, degrading enslaved women's "virtue," and denying enslaved men the patriarchal authority to protect and control their families. They also criticized the low birth rates and high rates of infant mortality that—together with high death rates—prevented West Indian slave populations from reproducing themselves. By the 1820s, metropolitan reformers were actively promoting the kind of family structures, marriages, and gender relations they thought would create a stable, (re)productive slave population and prepare slaves for emancipation. In particular, they encouraged state-sanctioned, monogamous marriage and nuclear families headed by men.[9] These were, of course, the same domestic arrangements that reformers were championing in Britain at the same time, and efforts to bring slave families under state control mirrored domestic developments in population control. Proslavery politicians and some slaveowners, meanwhile, faced a severe labor crisis as slave populations rapidly declined once the ban on the British transatlantic slave trade went into effect (1808), and so they also began promoting marriage among slaves because they believed it would raise birthrates and create a self-sustaining labor force. As pro-natalism—a policy that encouraged childbearing—gained momentum during the era of amelioration, colonial governments and individual slaveowners developed a range of incentives to encourage men and women to marry and produce children. These ranged from better houses for married couples to cash payments for mothers. Reformers, politicians, and slaveowners thus came together, even if they had different motivations, in the early nineteenth century to surveil and regulate enslaved people's marriages, domestic arrangements, and sexual practices.[10]

Efforts to use marriage policy as a form of population control and especially as a strategy for promoting fertility are best illustrated, at least in terms of official policy, by several provisions in Berbice's first comprehensive slave code, adopted in 1826.[11] For the first time, slaves were granted the right to apply to the colonial government for marriage licenses.[12] Once "solemnized" by one of the colony's few ministers, as was also required in England, these marriages would be legally recognized and registered by colonial clerks (unlike the "reputed" or informal marriages enslaved people had long formed).[13] The 1826 slave code also offered new protections for married couples, including a provision preventing slaves from being sold away from their spouses or without children under age sixteen. Tellingly, the law extended the same protections against separation by sale to "reputed" husbands and wives—one indication that slaveowners recognized, to a degree, enslaved people's claims of kinship.[14] Another clause, aimed at promoting reproduction and monogamy, stipulated that every woman who had a child "while she preserve[d] her fidelity in marriage" was to be rewarded with a "gratuity" of twelve guilders once the child survived for six weeks—a timetable indicative of the colony's high rates of infant mortality, miscarriages, and stillbirths. For every subsequent child, mothers were to receive fifteen guilders; and if a woman gave birth to six children, on the youngest child's seventh birthday she was to be rewarded with an exemption from all other than "light" work.[15] Taken together, these policies were designed to pressure slaves to formalize their domestic bonds, embrace monogamy, and reproduce. The law reflected earlier arguments abolitionists made that promoting bourgeois British gender norms would not only be a benevolent civilizing policy for slaves but also benefit planters economically by increasing Afro-Caribbean women's reproductive capacity and thus reduce planters' reliance on the transatlantic slave trade and costly new purchases of slaves.[16]

The corollary to encouraging reproduction and monogamous marriage was an unprecedented criminalization of a range of sexual and marital behaviors that officials believed were immoral or threatened the stability of colonial slave society. Throughout the 1820s and 1830s the government and, to varying degrees, slaveowners, managers, and overseers, documented and punished everything from infidelity and "fornication" to polygamy and spousal abuse. Indeed, the punishment record books that the colonial government collected from slaveowners show that enslaved people could be punished for "lying with other men's wives," "seducing and attempting to seduce other men's wives," "infidelity to husbands," "committing fornication," and "ill-treating women and wives." These "offences" appeared alongside several dozen other behaviors that, according to the colonial government, needed to be monitored, quantified, and curtailed.[17] A civil magistrate who explained the 1826 amelioration reforms to slaves was explicit about the coercive purpose of punishment records in his report to the colonial government. "I made it a point," he wrote, "to impress upon their minds that the Punishment record book was meant not only as a check on the conduct of the managers towards the slaves, but also as a record . . . to know such of the Negroes whose characters are really bad and that such as appeared often in that book would be debarred of many of the benefits afforded to the slaves of good characters by the provisions of this code."[18]

Yet relatively few people were punished for sexual and marital offenses, especially when compared with other types of infractions, which suggests that plantation authorities and slaveowners did not normally concern themselves with enslaved people's domestic conflicts or sexual practices unless they threatened productivity or jeopardized managerial authority. A few comparisons from colony-wide punishment statistics are revealing. Between

July 1 and December 31, 1828, for example, six men were punished for "lying with other men's wives," two men were punished for "attempting to ravish" enslaved women, one man and three women were punished for "committing fornication," and eight men were punished for "ill-treating women and wives." These low levels of documented punishment stand in stark contrast to the high rates of documented punishment for many other offenses, such as "theft, petty larceny" (176 punishments), "refusing to work" (204 punishments), "disobedience" (413 punishments), "absconding and running away from work" (249 punishments), and "bad work and insufficient [work]" (1,813 punishments).[19] The results for the following six-month period were similar, with only five men punished for "lying with other mens' wives," six for "attempting to ravish" enslaved women, two for "seducing and attempting to seduce other men's wives," two for "infidelity to wives," eight for "ill-treating women or wives," five women punished for infidelity, and no punishments for "committing fornication."[20] Recorded punishments for sexual and marital offenses were thus extraordinarily low. Punishment record books from other colonies where such records were kept, including Demerara-Essequibo, St. Lucia, and Trinidad, reveal a similar pattern, suggesting that the situation in Berbice was typical of the nineteenth-century British West Indies.[21]

For most managers and slaveowners, then, promoting sexual morality or mediating domestic disputes among the enslaved people they supervised was a lower priority than defying the plantation work culture, at least when it came to involving the colonial government.[22] Nevertheless, the very existence of prohibitions for various sexual and marital offenses, combined with evidence that many enslaved people refused to conform to middle-class British notions of marriage, sex, and family, reminds us that the amelioration-era Caribbean was a "gender frontier" where multiple visions of marriage—African, European, and West Indian—existed and where official policy often bore little resemblance to social practice.[23]

Overall, the imperial government's effort to regulate enslaved people's domestic lives and use marriage to stabilize the population did not have the desired effect. Enslaved women in particular may have avoided formal marriage out of understandable fear that it would further limit their autonomy. As an Anglican missionary in Barbados observed in 1829, where there was similar pressure on slaves to formally marry, enslaved women "object[ed] to Christian matrimony, thinking that it gives them, as it were, a second master, and ties them for life to a man who may neglect or ill use them."[24] Enslaved people in Berbice who did want to legally marry, moreover, had to meet certain criteria and overcome several obstacles: they had to belong to the same owner, get their owner's written permission, travel to town and apply to the protector of slaves for a license, and then find a clergyman to solemnize the marriage.[25] They also had to be Christian, or at least pretend to be. An even more basic obstacle for enslaved men was finding a woman to marry—a difficult task given women's scarcity and the fact that many women had relationships with free men of color and white colonists as wives or concubines. Slaveowners' reluctance to allow their slaves to formalize their bonds, which would have limited their ability to separate married slaves by sale and threatened other claims they made on slaves as their property, especially insofar as it increased enslaved men's authority, probably also played a part in preventing some slaves from seeking marriage licenses.[26]

Among colonial officials, early optimism soon gave way to the realization that formal marriage was neither attractive nor easily attainable for most Berbician slaves. After all, they had long formed (and dissolved) their own relationships without the colonial government's acknowledgment and without a minister's blessing. In a January 1827 report to the governor, the protector of slaves claimed that "the aversion to marriage, which heretofore existed" among the Crown-owned or *winkel* slaves in New Amsterdam—those who had the most contact with missionaries, colonial administrators, and other colonials who might have pressured them to apply for marriage licenses— was "gradually disappearing." The protector praised the efforts of the *winkel* superintendent toward "increasing the comforts of the married families," and noted "the mental and religious improvement of the Winkel negroes . . . under [John Wray's] London Protestant Mission," one of the few places in the colony where slaves received formal instruction in Christianity.[27] But less than two years later, the protector admitted that the colony's slaves had not shown much interest in formal marriage. In September 1828 the protector noted that he had only granted five marriage licenses in the previous six months, and that on rural estates—where the vast majority of the colony's enslaved people lived—there were only twenty-nine "solemnized" marriages (in contrast to more than 3,100 couples living in "reputed marriages").[28] Two years later the number of official marriages had more than tripled, but ninety-seven "solemnized" marriages over four years in a population of more than 20,000 slaves was hardly evidence for widespread interest in formal marriage.[29] As late as 1832, the secretary of state for the colonies lamented that "the almost total absence of [formal] marriage amongst the slave population" in Berbice was "a subject of serious regret."[30]

Related efforts to increase birth rates enough to counteract population loss fared little better. Birth rates did increase significantly in the years immediately following the enactment of incentives for marriage and childbirth, from 28.7 births per 1,000 (1822–25) to 35.1 per 1,000 (1825–28), which coincided with the colony's short-lived period of population growth through self-reproduction (at an extremely modest rate of +0.8 per 1,000). But this trend did not last: by 1828–31 the birth rate had fallen to 31.8 per 1,000—only marginally higher than the birthrate before ameliorative legislation was enacted (30 per 1,000 between 1819 and 1822)—and Berbice's population was once again decreasing (at a rate of –4.8 per 1,000), as in almost all Caribbean sugar colonies. Even the highest recorded birth rate for Berbician slaves, moreover, was lower than the birth rates of many other West Indian colonies in the same period.[31] Any link between colonial marriage policy, birth rates, and population change, moreover, is tenuous at best.

On the whole, the new institutions and laws the imperial government created during the era of amelioration did relatively little to change the contours of enslaved people's domestic lives or increase Berbice's slave population. Yet official interest in slaves' sexual and marital practices did provide them new opportunities to negotiate—and terminate—their marriages through the colonial legal system. Thanks to enslaved people's legal activism, moreover, we have access to a remarkable archive that documents their struggles to construct viable domestic lives, rendered most clearly in moments of crisis.

Male Rivalry and Sexual Control

Enslaved men in Berbice, like their female counterparts, showed little interest in officially recognized marriage, but they did want relationships with women. Enslaved women provided men companionship, sex, and domestic labor, and, for African men—who came from societies where wealth, power, and prestige were measured in people (rather than land or other material resources)—wives were important dependents.[32] Yet enslaved men had to contend with a demographic landscape that made finding and keeping female partners difficult. Like other late-developing West Indian colonies (including Trinidad and Demerara-Essequibo), Berbice received a large number of captive Africans in the late eighteenth and early nineteenth centuries. And since slave ship cargoes contained many more men than women, in early nineteenth-century Berbice there were many more men than women. Berbice actually had the second highest male-to-female ratio in the West Indies.[33] Given the extreme scarcity of white women, moreover, many white men turned to enslaved women and free women of color not just for sex but also for quasi-marital relationships.[34] Whether or not enslaved women entered into such relationships voluntarily, this further reduced the number of women potentially available to enslaved men. Many enslaved men in Berbice, as in other slave societies with a preponderance of African men, thus had little hope of establishing exclusive claims to women.[35] Nevertheless, perhaps half of all adult men in Berbice managed to live with women (and sometimes children, too), whereas women rarely lived in households without men.[36] Some men, moreover, claimed multiple women as wives. Men had to work especially hard, however, to keep women, and the intensity of male conflict was high, especially when it seemed like women might shift their allegiances to other men. How did men attract and retain women? How did they compete with other men? And what happened when they failed to establish the kind of relationships they desired?

Among the things men had to offer women were material support and protection—critical responsibilities for any would-be patriarch, but problematic in a society where dire poverty and brutal violence were daily realities and where enslaved men lacked the legal and economic standing to compete with free men. Men who had enough resources to share, or exchange for sexual access to women or domestic labor, thus had an advantage when it came to finding partners.[37] The comparative ease with which high-ranking slaves, such as drivers and artisans, found wives and even formed polygynous families probably had as much to do with the material advantages they enjoyed as their social status.[38] Free men of color were apparently attractive partners, too, for similar reasons. The free black man George, for example, had enough money to hire his wife, Minkey, from her owner, as well as pay for the clothing and food that her owner did not supply.[39] Another free colored man, Richard Walsh, claimed that "he had spent a considerable sum of money" on his enslaved wife.[40] Men also gave women gifts while courting, such as England, who wooed a woman with "a root of sweet cassava."[41] Given that enslaved women were disproportionately field laborers and had virtually no chance of being employed as drivers or other high-status occupations—positions that brought some enslaved men greater opportunities for material gain—men who enjoyed some privileges took advantage of their relatively better economic position when looking for partners.

Even men with little in the way of material resources—that is, the overwhelming majority of slaves—sometimes shared their marginally better provisions with the women (and children) they were obligated to support. The enslaved man Conraad, for example, testified that the women on the remote woodcutting estate where he lived "never get any allowance, only occasionally a small piece of fish," and that "if they steal or secrete [*sic*] any of the roots of the cassavie, when preparing it, and detected, they get flogged, as was lately the case with his wife." As a result, Conraad "ha[d] to give [his wife] the half of his allowance," which totaled just six cassava cakes per week. William, who complained with Conraad, similarly testified "that his wife and children get no allowance whatever, that he is therefore obliged to give the greatest part of his allowance to them."[42] A complaint from a woman named Sankey, who protested her husband being sold without her and her children because she would be "unable to support" her "little child" without him, provides further evidence that material support, especially in the form of basic necessities like food, was one of the most important things men could offer their families.[43] They were able to do so both because they had greater access to skilled work than women, and thus more opportunities to barter or purchase goods, and because managers' distribution of weekly allowances favored men. Plantation authorities assumed that married men had an obligation to provide for their wives and sometimes even punished men who did not. The enslaved man Leander, for instance, was punished by his manager for being "unwilling to provide the necessities for his wife and child and to live with them because he wants a divorce without agreement from his wife."[44]

Men also offered women limited protection from physical abuse, even from white plantation authorities that were legally invested with the power to use violence against slaves. Fulfilling this patriarchal obligation, however, inevitably brought enslaved men into conflict with their enslavers, who viewed any attempt by slaves to limit their violence as threats to their mastery and masculinity. A man named Philip thus protested the way his wife and children were treated by "quitting his work without permission & presenting himself [to the manager] in a hostile manner armed with a cutlass, with his hat on his head," a symbolic refusal to assume the posture of deference the manager would have expected from an enslaved man. Philip's challenge resulted in "ninety lashes and a week's confinement in [the] dark room," brutal punishments meant to remind Philip of his subordinate status.[45] Other men went over the heads of plantation authorities and complained to colonial officials. Claas, a field laborer in his mid-thirties from the coffee plantation Op

Hoop van Beter, went to the fiscal in June 1824 after the plantation owner flogged his pregnant wife so brutally that she miscarried.[46] Earlier that year a man named Willem complained to the fiscal about "the manager punishing [his] wife . . . Kitty." Willem had tried reasoning with the manager, he explained, and even admitted that Kitty's "mouth was very bad and at times he himself did not know what to do with her," an apparent attempt at male bonding between Willem and his manager. Like white authorities, enslaved men like Willem expected a certain level of deference from women. The fiscal "regretted the Manager found it necessary to punish [Willem's] wife with the whip," but ruled that since Kitty's flogging was legal, Willem had no reason for "abscond[ing] from the Estate," and he would therefore be "confined for a fortnight."[47] We can only guess how the wives of men like Philip, Claas, and Willem felt about their husbands' risky efforts to protect them—acts that were also meant to assert men's masculinity—but it is likely that they made them attractive partners.

In addition to the challenges of attracting women and protecting them from other men, enslaved men also had to contend with women who left them for other men. Men who risked losing female partners sometimes turned to violence—against women and the men they perceived as threats. The investigation into the mysterious death of an enslaved man named Richmond, a "bow legged" African in his late forties, revealed that rivalries over women could be intense and, potentially, fatal.[48] According to Robert Kennedy, the manager of the sugar plantation where Richmond lived, "a considerable noise" woke him one night around 10:00. When Kennedy went to investigate, he "learnt that the negro Richmond . . . had attempted to cut England's throat." Richmond "suspected [that] the negro woman Olivia, formerly his wife" and nearly twenty years his junior, "had been connected with the negro England." So Richmond waited until nighttime, when England, a gray-haired African, began his shift as watchman to get revenge. But when Richmond ambushed England, knife in hand, England fought back, "wrestled with Richmond," and shouted for help. Fortunately for him, the drivers soon caught Richmond and put him in the stocks. Meanwhile, Kennedy, standing by, "received much abuse from Richmond, who threatened to bring him into trouble by taking him before the Fiscal."[49]

According to the manager, Richmond and Olivia's problems went back several months. When the manager took over the estate four months earlier, Richmond and Olivia, nurse to the plantation's children, "came up to him to declare they could not agree together." But he ignored them and, if they gave an explanation for their desire to separate, he did not mention it. After all, he had more than five hundred other slaves to worry about, and domestic quarrels were common. But when Richmond and Olivia approached him a few weeks later with the same story, he relented. "If you cannot live with and are satisfied to leave each other," he told them, "it is all good; but if I hear either of you disputing with any of the other negroes, in consequence of either of your taking up with some one else, I will punish you severely." Even if this was mere posturing for the fiscal—an attempt to portray himself as a competent, firm manager—it shows that plantation officials knew that when enslaved women left their partners and began new relationships there was a real potential for serious conflict.[50] Nevertheless, once Richmond and Olivia separated, following a model of "self-divorce" common among slaves, the manager claimed that he had had no problems with either of them until Richmond's foiled attempt to kill England. Olivia no longer lived with Richmond, but she continued cooking for him two or three times a week—a reminder of the material benefits married men enjoyed as a consequence of women's domestic labor. It was only when England began courting Olivia, the manager reasoned, that Richmond's "jealousy" prompted him to attack England.[51]

As it turned out, there was little time for the manager to get Richmond's side of the story. Just two days after England barely escaped with his life, a group of militiamen sent to investigate the disturbance noticed that Richmond appeared "drunk." Richmond then "immediately . . . seemed to reel, and fell on the ground apparently in a fit." He was brought into the manager's house, where two doctors "attempted to give him something" to help him, "but in a very few moments he expired." It is impossible to know what killed Richmond so suddenly, but it is conceivable that England or someone acting on his behalf (an obeah practitioner, perhaps?) poisoned Richmond in retaliation.[52] For men like Richmond and England, physical retaliation—even murder—was an acceptable, masculine response for dealing with challenges from other men.

A complaint from Bacchus, a twenty-eight-year-old driver on a plantation in neighboring Essequibo, provides further evidence of how disruptive male rivalries could be and also suggests that colonial authorities took pains to prevent such conflicts from escalating. Bacchus went to the protector of slaves in April 1830 and complained that the attorney of plantation Annandale, where he had lived, had sold him off the estate without his wife, Lydia. He admitted "that he was not lawfully married to Lydia," but added that he "has cohabited with her some years, and has two children by her," probably hoping these facts would strengthen his case. The attorney, however, told a different story: Lydia was not Bacchus's wife, but "the wife of another man, named Jonas," with whom she had three children. Moreover, Bacchus "took her away or cohabited with her unlawfully, which caused a great deal of commotion upon the estate between these two men; they were always quarreling." Lydia "made no complaint about Bacchus being sold," the attorney told the protector, and he decided to sell Bacchus "to prevent further disputes about this matter." Jonas confirmed the attorney's testimony, and added that Bacchus "took Lydia away from [Jonas] by force" after leaving his previous wife, and that he "often disputed with [Jonas] about Lydia." The protector, who did not bother to call Lydia herself as a witness, dismissed Bacchus's complaint. Bacchus had "unlawfully cohabited with Lydia," and "to enjoy the privileges conferred by the law in this respect upon husbands and wives, it is necessary that they should preserve their fidelity in marriage or reputed marriage to each other."[53]

Most marital disputes were undoubtedly handled among slaves themselves and thus not documented, but enslaved men in Berbice did occasionally appeal to colonial authorities for help protecting their marital claims to women. The irony in appealing to such men for help was that even when it worked, it highlighted the limits of enslaved men's patriarchal authority as subalterns. Plantation overseers and managers were often willing to help enslaved men, especially when they believed that intervening might prevent dangerous conflicts between men from escalating. In December 1826, for instance, a woman named Carolina was punished with fifteen hours in the bedstocks after her husband complained that she had "connexion with an other man."[54]

In May 1831, a man named Mark, a "well made" African field laborer on the sugar plantation Providence, was punished in the stocks and then flogged for repeatedly courting—and perhaps sexually assaulting—the wife of another man on a neighboring plantation.[55] As the manager of Providence told the protector, Mark had been "in the habit of going to Pl[antation] Everton and disturbing the man Hyacinth's wife," Hebe, so he had asked the manager of Everton to "secure [Mark] and send him home to be punished" if he continued. The manager of Everton obliged, prohibiting Mark from coming to his plantation "in consequence of his seducing Hyacinth's wife Hebe, who has five children by her husband." He also gave his drivers "orders to bring Mark to [him] whenever he should come in the negro yard, in consequence of former disturbances." So when an intoxicated Mark returned to the "negro yard" on Everton one day, a driver led the effort to apprehend him, which only succeeded after a protracted fight against Mark and his male friends, who came to his defense. The protector dismissed Mark's complaint, signaling his disapproval of Mark's having disobeyed the manager's order to leave Hyacinth's wife alone.[56] Yet again, the woman at the heart of this power struggle was not consulted, underscoring the fact that for colonial authorities, the problem men like Mark posed was not to married women themselves but to husbands whose exclusive sexual claims were jeopardized.

Punishment record books, though lacking the details and context of complaints to the fiscal and protector of slaves, offer other glimpses of the intensity of male rivalries and of the constant pressure—and outright sexual violence—women in Berbice faced at the hands of enslaved men. The 1828 punishment record book for plantation Goldstone Hall, a sugar estate on the Canje Creek, shows three men punished in a single month for what were probably attempted rapes of women who were claimed by other men. Yet in each case, the plantation officials who recorded the offense constructed rape as a crime against another man—challenging a husband's exclusive right to his wife's sexuality and violating the sanctity of his house—rather than an act of violence against women themselves. On October 1, Joe was whipped (twenty-five lashes) for "neglecting his night watch & going after another man's wife while asleep with an infant." Two weeks later, another man, Primus, was found "breaking in Swan's house . . . & trying to have carnal communication with his wife," for which he was given twenty-two lashes. Ten days later, Primus broke into another man's house and once again "tried to have carnal communication with his wife," and this time he was put in the "darkhouse" for fifty-four hours. Finally, on October 30, a man named Green was given twenty lashes "for breaking Josey's House & tr[ying] to have carnal communication with his wife" the night before. In describing enslaved couples' houses as belonging to men, rather than men and women together, and in identifying the female victims not by name but by their status as the dependents of other men, managers depicted enslaved people as arranged in patriarchal households. Goldstone Hall may have been unusual, either in terms of having an abnormally high level of male rivalry and sexual assault or in having a manager who was more inclined to punish and record such acts, but it is likely that other plantations and households were scenes of similar power struggles.[57]

Enslaved men also faced competition from the many white men who refused to respect their exclusive claims to women, which included sexually exploiting enslaved men's wives. Combating overseers, managers, and slave-owners, however, was more dangerous than fending off other enslaved men, not least of all because physical violence against white men was borderline suicidal. Perhaps the only feasible strategy in this situation, then, was to seek redress from the colonial government. And remarkably, this sometimes worked. In August 1822, for instance, a man from plantation Scotland named Felix went to the fiscal's office and complained that the manager was "always taking the negroes['] wives, particularly his wife" of two years, even though the manager "has a wife of his own." The manager even had a child with Felix's wife, and "since the child has been born, the manager is always punishing him and his wife without cause." The men on the estate had tried to solve the problem before, but to no avail. "Some time ago," Felix explained, "ten of the gang came to complain to their master [owner] . . . that the manager had connexion with their wives." Their owner, Dr. Broer, "promised to them that he would remove the manager from the estate," but never did. Dr. Broer may well have allowed his manager to have sex with—and perhaps rape—the enslaved women on the estate, so long as the manager ran a productive plantation. Felix and his wife were "daily punished, which has compelled them to come to your Honor for redress," he told the acting fiscal. When the acting fiscal, accompanied by Felix's owner, went to the plantation to investigate, he found that there was much truth to Felix's characterization of the manager. And though he determined that Felix had left the estate primarily to escape an impending punishment for not finishing the previous day's task, and punished him "for his misconduct," he also "severely reprimanded" the manager "for taking improper liberties with the women on the estate." Moreover, he "strongly recommended" that the owner "discharge [the manager] from his employ."[58] For men like Felix, going to colonial officials could be an effective strategy for defending their claims to women.

When men blamed their wives, instead of other men, for jeopardizing their patriarchal authority, they were likely to take out their anger on their wives' bodies. Men were particularly violent against women who left them for other men, a rejection that both deprived them of the many practical benefits married men enjoyed and diminished their male privilege. And in most cases, white plantation authorities and colonial officials alike sanctioned physical violence—what they understood as "correction" rather than "abuse"—as an acceptable means of disciplining social inferiors and dependents, including women.[59] Moreover, white colonists' own use of violence against enslaved women accused of supposedly deviant actions such as "infidelity to husbands" signaled their approval of enslaved men doing the same. When the manager on plantation Philadelphia found out that a woman named Sally had left her husband and begun "cohabiting with another man," for instance, he punished her with sixteen hours in solitary confinement.[60]

More commonly, enslaved men took it upon themselves to punish their wives for supposed transgressions, confident that plantation management and colonial officials were likely to condone and even support their violence. In May 1832, for instance, a free black man named Burnett beat his ex-wife, Rosaline, in the middle of a public street for having "slept with another man." When interrogated by the protector, Burnett tried to reframe Rosaline's complaint of abuse by downplaying the level of violence and emphasizing his wife's infidelity. He told the protector "he was very sorry for having raised his hand against Rosaline; but the circumstances which led to it, he hoped would be taken into consideration." Rosaline "had been his wife for a certain time," so when "he saw her coming out of the man's room, and being at the moment much irritated," he "struck her a blow." Burnett also pointed out that Rosaline had "return[ed] [the blow] and tore his shirt and other clothes from him," perhaps aware that white men would disapprove of such violent resistance by a woman and sympathize with the humiliation of having his clothing torn. Confronted with Burnett's testimony, Rosaline "acknowledged she was wrong in intriguing from her husband."[61] She may have gathered from the way other women were treated in Berbice that British officials came from a society where physical abuse was an acceptable response to a wife's infidelity.[62]

But Rosaline insisted she no longer wanted anything to do with Burnett and that she would not tolerate his abuse. She "requested that he (Burnett) might be cautioned not to molest her again; as she wished to separate from him—but at the same time that he might be punished for what had passed." Unfortunately for Rosaline, the protector instead "reprimanded both parties for their improper conduct, and dismissed the complaint."[63] More often than not, officials responded with little more than a slap on the wrist to men who used violence to avenge infidelity.

A similar case from September 1829 underscores men's reliance on violence as well as the extent to which enslaved men, plantation management, and colonial officials cooperated to circumscribe women's sexual mobility and reinforce marriage as an institution in which men had greater rights than women.[64] An African field laborer named Bella went to the protector to protest having been punished "in the hand and feet stocks" by her owner. This "old woman," as the clerk described her, had tried to protect her young daughter, Elizabeth, from a brutal beating at the hands of Elizabeth's rope-wielding husband, she said, but the owner punished her for interfering. The owner, however, claimed that Elizabeth was not innocent: a few weeks earlier, Elizabeth's husband, a carpenter named Barron, "went to him to complain that his wife was going off the estate to [plantation] No. 19, where she had an intrigue with another man."[65] Women like Elizabeth, who sought to take advantage of the colony's skewed sex ratio to refuse the constraints of their husbands' claims upon them, thus had to contend with men who wanted the exact opposite.

The owner, Andrew Ross, agreed to help Barron control his wife. He told Barron that if Elizabeth continued her "intrigue," Barron should bring her to him for punishment. So, when Barron reported a few weeks later that Elizabeth "had gone again to Plantation No. 19, and that he had just brought her back," Ross gave Barron permission to lock her up in the stocks (and perhaps more). It was at this point that Bella, no doubt concerned for Elizabeth's safety, "insisted on being locked up, too, to keep her daughter company," and Ross obliged. The following morning, moreover, Ross decided "that because [Bella] had encouraged and countenanced her daughter's infidelity," she would have to leave her job taking care of the plantation's children at the "Creole house" for more grueling work in the fields. When Bella refused "and was very saucy," the owner said, he placed her in the stocks a second time. The protector, after collecting testimony from several witnesses, dismissed Bella's complaint and reprimanded her for "promoting the licentious pursuit of her daughter," a decision that illustrated the challenges women in Berbice faced trying to negotiate their domestic relationships in the context of a patriarchal legal culture and a demographic environment that encouraged men to be especially vigilant about asserting their "right" to control the women they claimed as wives.[66]

That men in Berbice used violence and intimidation to control women is unsurprising. Indeed, male-on-female violence has been prevalent in societies across time and space, and until very recently, an accepted part of domestic life wherever patriarchy has been normative.[67] Rather than simply showing that enslaved men used violence as a strategy for controlling their wives, however, the evidence from Berbice can be historicized and contextualized by the extreme levels of violence that characterized colonial slavery. The plantation world's fragile hierarchies of race and status were enforced with violent acts both quotidian and extraordinary, and enslaved people would have regularly seen brute force used to control other people and reinforce divisions and differences—drivers flogging field laborers, plantation managers beating domestic slaves, and criminals sentenced to public tortures meant to terrorize others into submission. Enslaved men's violence against both women and men who challenged their exclusive sexual claims was thus part of this larger matrix of violence and terror.

Abuse, Infidelity, and Female Networks of Support

Rather than passively accept the implications of Berbice's patriarchal culture, enslaved women fought to shape the contours of their sex lives and marriages. Taking advantage of the uneven sex ratio, some women explored possible relationships with different men, trying to find the best arrangement. Within their relationships, moreover, they demanded certain minimum standards of treatment, even in a violent, exploitative society, even as women, and even as slaves. Yet they faced a number of obstacles—from their own partners, their neighbors, and other outsiders. And when problems arose that they could not solve on their own, which ranged from abusive husbands to competition from other women, they turned to colonial authorities and, more often, their own families.

Some of the most striking evidence for Berbician women's efforts to control their relationships with men comes from cases of polyandry. All but unheard of in the West and Central African societies from which enslaved Africans came (where polygyny, in contrast, was widespread), polyandry is usually thought of as very rare in Caribbean slave societies, too. It was thus the most extreme way that women in Berbice tried to take advantage of the colony's surplus of men to form the kind of relationships they wanted.[68] Though the extent of polyandry in Berbice is difficult to determine, at least some women were unwilling to yield to pressure from colonial officials, enslaved men, and plantation authorities to conform to monogamy.

A woman named Mary complained to the fiscal in May 1826 that her owner, L. F. Gallez, refused to allow her to keep two husbands. "I had a husband and a Abadika," which she defined as "a help mate or second husband." Mary claimed, "they quarreled about me[,] they wanted to fight with cutlasses." Eventually Gallez ordered her to choose one husband, but she refused, even when he threatened to lock her up. So Gallez sent one of her husbands to work on his remote woodcutting estate on the Canje River, but this did not solve the problem. When Mary's "help husband" died, she "took up with one belonging to the Estate," and then refused to go to the Canje estate where the other husband was unless her new help husband accompanied her. "I come to you," Mary told the fiscal, "to get my right." But the fiscal, in a ruling that was consistent with European views of polygamy as an immoral obstacle to civilization and provocative of dangerous male rivalries, "informed [Mary] that she could not be allowed to have two husbands. She must choose either the one or the other." Gallez had agreed to let her live with whichever husband she chose, as long as "she made a selection." But Mary refused to embrace monogamous marriage; "she knew it was the new Law," she admitted—referring to the not-yet-enacted 1826 slave code that was being discussed throughout Berbice in recent months—but "it was not right."[69] In explicitly rejecting pressure to conform to British gender conventions and abandon customary marriage practices that suited her, Mary may have represented many other Berbician slaves.

Though Mary's complaint is one of only two clear cases of polyandry in Berbice that I have found, the fact that she had a vocabulary to describe the practice ("Abadika," "help mate," "second husband") suggests that it may not have been as uncommon as historians have assumed, especially given Berbice's skewed sex ratios. When one considers the multiple cases of women punished for what their husbands constructed as extramarital sex, moreover, it is possible that many women in Berbice had two or more male partners at the same time, that plantation managers and overseers ignored or tolerated polyandry until it caused problems (as was the case for Gallez), and that the "licentiousness" and "promiscuity" colonials attributed to enslaved women might be better understood as evidence of polyandry. Might the behavior of women like Beata, punished on plantation De Standvastigheid in December 1826 for "neglecting her husband named William in *every* respect" and then again four days later for "continuation of neglect of her duties toward her husband," be evidence of women maintaining or testing out relationships with multiple men?[70]

Even when women did accept monogamy, they claimed the authority to begin and dissolve marriages on their own terms. In September 1825 a woman from plantation Rotterdam named Carolina complained to the fiscal that her manager, J. N. Lentz, locked "her up every evening on her coming from the Field in a dark room" because she refused to "take a Husband as the manager ordered." She would, she said, "take one of her own liking." Carolina had good reason to be selective, since a previous marriage to an anonymous white man had not worked out. "The person by whom she has a child (which is a mulatto child)," the fiscal noted, "does not mind her nor the child, she therefore does not wish lately to have another husband."[71] Yet because single adult women were in high demand, Carolina must have been under intense pressure to accept a new husband.

The attorney and manager countered Carolina's complaint with a classic strategy: undermining her character as a woman and in particular as a mother and wife. They claimed that she was "a very bad woman," that she "neglect[ed] [her] infant child to that degree that it nearly died," that she allowed another woman to care for the child for several years and "never troubled herself about the child but has constantly abused and ill treated the woman for her affectionate care of her infant which she stole away from the woman to bring to town." Carolina also, they claimed, "constantly create[d] disturbances on the Estate by cohabiting with other women's men," and her ex-husband had "left her on account of her making herself a common prostitute." The fiscal ordered Carolina confined "for a month at night and during the approaching holidays"—punishments that would have been unlikely for a man accused of the same behavior. Plantation managers and colonial officials, like enslaved men, did not approve of sexually unconstrained women.[72]

Women who faced physically abusive partners were in a particularly difficult situation because European colonists tended to tolerate men's violence. Even if colonials frowned on what they saw as excessive spousal abuse, they did little to prevent or punish it.[73] Plantation punishment records show only a handful of men punished in any given period for "ill-treating women and wives," and most of these were extreme cases that threatened women's lives or plantation order, such as when the slave Joe was punished for "having a cutlass in his hand & threatening to kill his wife."[74] Even then, punishments could be relatively moderate, especially when compared to the severe punishments meted out to slaves for "insolence" or poor work. For "outrageously attempting to stab his former wife," the enslaved man Apollo was punished with twenty-five lashes.[75] Phara received the same number of lashes for "threatening to poison his wife."[76] For "beating his wife in a brutal and merciless manner," Carl received twenty-one lashes.[77] A man on plantation Skeldon who "violently beat his wife Maria, causing her to be laid up in the Hospital," was given twenty-four lashes.[78] John received seventeen lashes for "beating his wife & persisting in the same," which suggests that the manager only intervened once a pattern of abuse was established.[79] The manager on the sugar plantation Herstelling described a man on his estate who "treated his former wife so ill that he broke her ribs" as "of notorious bad character," but it was

only after the wife's "repeated request" that the manger felt "obliged to separate them," perhaps afraid that he might soon have to explain a murder to his
employer. (The man continued to beat his new wife, too, the manager added,
"to that degree that the doctor has twice declared her case hopeless.")[80]

When plantation managers did intervene in cases of domestic violence,
they often punished both the man and the woman involved, wrongly choosing to believe that wives were as responsible as their husbands. In August
1828 a man named Floris, from the coffee plantation Overyssel, was flogged
"for fighting with his wife & for cutting a woman named Betye (who went to
separate them) very severely in the forehead." His wife Sarah, meanwhile, was
punished by two days' solitary confinement "for fighting with her man Floris." The same day, another couple, Johanna and Primo, were punished for
their own violent dispute the day before—Johanna "for fighting with Primo"
and he "for beating & fighting with the woman Johanna."[81] On a different
plantation a month later, Matthew and his wife, Sophia, were both put in
solitary confinement for fighting.[82] When the husband of Martha, an enslaved woman on plantation Bellevue, beat her for "adultery," instead of protecting Martha or punishing her husband, the manager sentenced Martha to
three days and nights of solitary confinement for "committing adultery &
striking her husband several times while correcting her."[83] A September 1828
entry in plantation Ma Retraite's punishment log was among the most explicit in assigning blame: Christian was flogged for "beating his wife Anna,"
while Anna was put in the stocks for "irritating her husband Christian to
strike her."[84] For colonial authorities, women who defended themselves
against husbands who used violence to uphold patriarchy deserved to be
punished.[85]

With few exceptions, plantation managers believed that it was a man's
right to use violence against his wife and that domestic violence was a private
matter. In choosing not to get involved, plantation officials signaled their approval of men's violence against women. In some cases, moreover, they even
punished bystanders for intervening. On plantation Nieuw Vigilantie in January 1830 the manager, Mr. Noteboom, punished an enslaved man, Ferdinand, for informing authorities that "his neighbor Dick beat his wife." As
Ferdinand explained, when he heard a commotion "he went to look what was
the matter." By the time he arrived at Dick's house, Dick was gone, and Ferdinand "found the woman lying on the ground crying," so "he went to the
driver and reported it." The driver told the overseer, who in turn told Noteboom; he asked Ferdinand "what business [he] had to interfere between Dick

and his wife," especially since "he was no driver." Noteboom, moreover, told the protector that Ferdinand "was a very quarrelsome and obstreperous character," and that "he was confined in the house stocks for quarreling at night with the negro Dick, [and] for insolence to the driver, when he ordered Ferdinand to desist."[86]

Despite this culture that condoned male-on-female violence, some women took the considerable risk of lodging formal complaints against abusive men. Such complaints—appeals to more powerful men for protection—probably represent only a small fraction of the actual domestic violence in Berbice, since most women probably did not report abuse and since most marital conflicts would have been resolved privately or by the "informal public" of neighbors, friends, and kin rather than the formal legal system.[87] A woman named Annatje, a thirty-five-year-old "domestic" from New Amsterdam, was one of a handful of women who turned to officials for protection and thus made it into the archival record.[88] Annatje told the acting protector in November 1830 that her husband, Frantz, had attacked her one night after she discovered him with another woman. When Annatje arrived home one night after work, her husband had gone out. She asked around at neighboring houses for him—perhaps suspecting that he was up to no good—and eventually "heard his voice" coming from one of the "outbuildings." So Annatje approached, and "the door being ajar, she pushed it open." There she "found Frantz in Criminal Connexion with a woman named Caroline." Frantz "rushed out at the door," but Annatje "got hold of Caroline & tore her clothes off" before she managed to escape. Annatje then went home and waited for Frantz. When he returned, "he beat [Annatje] with a stick," apparently angry that his wife had dared interrupt his affair and attack his mistress.[89]

At the protector's office, Frantz "admitted the charge laid against him by his wife to be correct." Unlike other abusive husbands, he made no attempt to justify having beaten his wife. However, the acting protector noted, Frantz "shewed much contrition and before Annatje begged forgiveness, assuring her and the Protector that he would not be guilty of such offence in future." The acting protector dismissed the case "at the recommendation of [Frantz's] wife," which suggests that Annatje may have gone to authorities to pressure Frantz into changing his behavior, hoping to return to a tolerable marital state and avoid retaliation. If this was the case, her strategy may have succeeded: the acting protector "reprimanded Frantz severely," and this was the only recorded complaint from Annatje against Frantz.[90]

For most women, turning to elite men outside the plantation community was a last resort when other strategies to protect themselves failed. A woman named Cecilia, who belonged to the *winkel* department, like Annatje, only sought the protector's help after her own efforts to escape a cheating, abusive husband had not worked. As Cecilia told the protector in 1830, she found herself in serious danger after leaving her husband. She "was living with the free man Richard Walsh as his wife," but when she "found out he had taken up with a free Woman," she decided to end their marriage. She "desired he would not come to [her] house again," and said she "would not on [her] part trouble or call on him for any thing." But Walsh was not prepared to let Cecilia go. One morning, shortly after Cecilia announced her intention to separate from him, Walsh went to her house, "and begged [her] to come to his, as he wished to speak to [her]." Perhaps afraid of Walsh, or simply unwilling to have anything more to do with him, Cecilia protested, "but he persuaded [her], and [she] promised to do so." So Cecilia went to Walsh's later that day, where she waited for him until it grew late and decided to return home.[91]

That evening Walsh went to Cecilia's house, where he argued with her over money and then lashed out in a violent rage. According to Cecilia, Walsh asked her to "lend him two dollars," which she did, and then he "began to quarrel with [her]," "destroy[ing] the cups, saucers, glasses &c in the House," terrorizing Cecilia in what was supposed to be the safe space of her home. He "would have destroyed [her] Bedstead," too, had Cecilia's brother not intervened and kicked Walsh out. But even the intervention of another man did not deter Walsh for long. He returned later that night on horseback, "tipsy and ma[king] a great noise." He quickly "became outrageous [and] swore he would break every thing in the house as it was his property." When Cecilia threatened to call the manager, Walsh "got more violent, and then began to cuff [her] about [her] face."[92]

Walsh, when summoned to the protector's office, "could not deny the correctness of [Cecilia's] statement." But he tried to justify his behavior, explaining that "he felt dissatisfied at [her] leaving him after he had spent a considerable sum of money on her." He had also "entrusted her with goods for sale which he could get no account of." Cecilia's efforts to see her abusive ex-husband held accountable were successful: the protector noted that Walsh had admitted assaulting Cecilia and sentenced him to six days' solitary confinement "on plantains & water." He also "seriously cautioned [Cecilia] not to have intercourse with him," as if she needed this condescending reminder.[93]

Cases like Cecilia's and Annatje's, where women asked colonial officials to intervene in conflicts with men, were rare, probably since women knew that male authorities were unlikely to support them and more likely to make their predicament worse. Many women who sought protection instead turned to their own kin- and gender-based networks of support.[94] And while brothers, like Cecilia's, and fathers sometimes tried to protect their sisters and daughters, it was more often mothers who stood up on behalf of their daughters. Yet even the most determined mothers regularly failed to protect their daughters from violence.

Susanna, an enslaved woman who belonged to the governor, went to the protector because James Walker, the *winkel* superintendent, was forcing her daughter, Elizabeth, "as well as other young women under his charge, to sleep every night in his house." Walker had hired Elizabeth out to another man, but still expected her to return "every evening to sleep at [his] house." The one night that Elizabeth failed to return to Walker's house, asserting her independence and perhaps hoping to have at least one night without being forced to have sex with Walker, he "arrested her" and then punished her by keeping "her the whole night in confinement, and sen[ding] her this morning with her hands tied, to the colony hospital, to put her in the stocks." As Susanna told the fiscal, "as a mother, the behaviour of Mr. Walker towards her daughter affects her very much." She added that "Mr. Walker [was] in the habit of locking up several young women," no doubt in an effort to restrict their sexual mobility.[95]

Some of the most vivid evidence of female support networks comes from instances where mothers complained on behalf of their daughters in cases of rape. In October 1830, a woman named Minkey went to the protector with a horrifying story: her fourteen-year-old daughter, Susannah, had been ambushed and gang raped by a group of "boys" and men, enslaved and free, in the middle of New Amsterdam. According to Minkey, Susannah was visiting family "at her Aunt's house in the Winkels" one evening when "the slave Boy John Quashie came there & told Susannah he was sent by Miss Brandes," Susannah's owner, to bring her home. Susannah left with Quashie, and when they "got opposite to the Market place, John Quashie whistled and immediately" a group of men "ran up," and held Susannah down. She "began to cry out," but one of the men "put his hands over her mouth & stifled her cries . . . Quashie then violated her person & was followed" by the others. "Susannah by struggling succeeded in getting loose & ran towards home, pursued by the slaves & free men" who had just raped her. They only gave up chase when a passerby intervened.[96]

The deputy protector, after listening to Minkey, had Susannah examined by Dr. Beresford, consistent with English beliefs that evidence collected by male experts, rather than the testimony of alleged victims, could best determine whether or not a rape had occurred.[97] He concluded that "the person of Susannah had been very much abused," so the deputy protector forwarded the case to the fiscal for prosecution. But Minkey's complaint ultimately failed because the fiscal determined, oddly, that "no evidence [could] be produced to convict . . . any of the parties accused by Susannah of having committed a Rape on her person."[98] Having been trained in England, the fiscal was likely following a decades-old legal precedent that rape required proof not only of non-consensual vaginal penetration and physical force but also ejaculation or emission.[99]

Mothers also defended their daughters against physical attacks from other women, including fights sparked by disputes over men. A particularly violent confrontation between two women from New Amsterdam, Jeanette, a nineteen-year-old domestic, and the "Sambo girl" Ellen in October 1829 highlights the important role that mothers played in such conflicts.[100] Ellen had apparently pursued Jeanette's husband for some time, and might have even had sex with him, but Jeanette reached her breaking point the day that her friend found Ellen making a shirt for her husband—a small act that reminds us of the material benefits women offered potential partners.[101]

Jeanette confronted Ellen about the shirt, but when Ellen "became very abusive" she went to Ellen's owner. "I am quiet at home Ma'am," she began, "and have been abused by Ellen without giving her the slightest provocation. . . . I am of a very hasty disposition, and if Ellen trouble me too much, and interferes with my business, I may take up something and chop her." Ellen's owner, however, refused to get involved, even after Jeanette's threat. She "told me, she had nothing to do with our nonsense, we must settle it amongst ourselves." Like most slaveowners, she preferred to stay out of such conflicts when possible. Ellen and Jeanette then traded gendered insults—Jeanette calling Ellen "a damned sow mouth b[itch]," and Ellen retorting that Jeanette was "a drunken b[itch]"—and challenged one another to a fight before going their separate ways.[102]

A few hours later, Jeanette ran into Ellen and Peggy (Ellen's "second"), both of them "half stripped (their Wrappers hauled down and tied tight round their Waists)," ready to fight. They exchanged words, and Jeanette's "mother hearing this came out." A crowd gathered and the women "began to fight." After "a considerable time," Jeanette "became quite faint" and left to get a drink of water. When Jeannette returned, Peggy came up with "a bit of rag" and "rubbed cayenne or stamped red pepper in [her] eyes." (Ellen and Peggy, in turn, accused Jeanette of throwing pepper.) Blinded, Jeanette struggled to fend off Peggy and Ellen at the same time. Her "mother seeing this interfered," she said, at which point Peggy began "to slap and cuff [her] mother." Jeanette's mother finally managed to free her daughter, who was in "the most dreadful agony," and take her "home to Master, who gave [her] brandy and water to wash [her] eyes and neck." Conflicting and confusing testimonies made it impossible for the fiscal to determine what exactly had happened, and he had little interest in exploring the root cause of the fight: Jeanette's husband's alleged relationship with Ellen. Instead he ruled that Jeanette, Ellen, and Peggy were all "guilty of breach of the Peace by fighting in the Street, and it appearing they had rubbed Pepper in each other's eyes" sentenced them to ten days' solitary confinement.[103]

Peggy, who fought alongside Ellen, knew from personal experience just how dangerous women could be in cases of adultery—and how important a mother's protection was. Two years earlier, when Peggy was only fourteen years old, she narrowly escaped a potentially fatal beating at the hands of a free black woman, Mrs. Gallez, who caught her in bed with Mr. Gallez. According to Peggy's statement to the deputy protector, she had been "shamefully beaten" by Mrs. Gallez "and her negroes" for allegedly having been "in the habit of sleeping with [Mr. Gallez] every night," a charge that she denied. Mrs. Gallez, however, described how she had caught Peggy and her husband red-handed. Returning home one evening she found "Mr. Gallez (my husband) lying with a girl (who I did not then know) on a mattress on the floor. As [Peggy] saw me she got up and hid behind a mosquito net. I locked the door to prevent her getting out. I then caught her, she bit and scratched my hands; I of course in return beat her." Meanwhile, "Mr. Gallez held my hands, and opened the door to let the girl out." Mrs. Gallez and some of her slaves then chased and caught Peggy, planning to take her to the "barracks" (jail) and presumably notify the fiscal.[104]

Meanwhile, Peggy's mother, Betsy, received word "that Mrs. Gallez was killing Peggy." Betsy raced to help her daughter, but Mrs. Gallez slapped her and told her she "should not attempt to take [Peggy] away by force, as she was not aware where I had found her." Betsy tried to free her daughter anyway, and when Gallez slapped her a second time, she "raised [her] hand to return the blow," she admitted, but a bystander (Mr. Mann) pulled her back, "and said I must not hit her, but go to complain, and I should receive satisfaction." Though Betsy would eventually follow this advice, like other slaves who recognized the potential advantage of going to colonial officials rather than fighting their battles alone, the immediate task remained freeing her daughter. Fortunately, her "master's negroes" soon came to her aid, Mrs. Gallez claimed, and "a large negro . . . pushed [Mrs. Gallez] on one side and loosed the rope from the girl."[105]

Forced to let Peggy go, Mrs. Gallez went to the home of Peggy's owner, Dr. Beresford, where she confronted Mrs. Beresford. "I told her I had found her girl with my husband," Mrs. Gallez explained to the protector, "and her negroes took away the girl form me, and the mother had beat me when I attempted to take her to the barracks." If Mrs. Gallez expected Mrs. Beresford to sympathize with her plight, one woman to another, she must have been sorely disappointed. Mrs. Beresford asked Mrs. Gallez why she was "coming to annoy" her. Mrs. Gallez replied, "whether I was a mulatto or white woman, that as I was married I had the same right."[106] In asserting her "right" to marry and to have her marriage respected, even as a free woman of color, Gallez revealed how important marital bonds were for some people in Berbice.

Peggy was fortunate that her mother intervened when she did because colonial authorities were sympathetic to Mrs. Gallez's violent reaction. The deputy protector, while acknowledging that "Mrs. Gallez acted intemperately," reasoned that "had she, in the irritation produced by finding [Peggy] and her husband in the situation described, attempted to destroy the lives of both, she would have been in some measure justified." So instead of punishing Mrs. Gallez for beating Peggy, he chastised Peggy—"in language that she could clearly understand"—for having "violated the marriage bed of Mrs. Gallez," a crime that earned her seven days in solitary confinement. "Let me hope this punishment," the deputy protector told Peggy, "will pave the way to a change in your character, which at present is extremely bad."[107]

But what about Mr. Gallez's "character"? Indeed, the severity of the punishment meted out to Peggy is made even more striking by the conspicuous absence of Mr. Gallez in these proceedings. He was, after all, hardly an innocent man seduced by Peggy. According to "the slave boy John," who belonged to Mr. Gallez, "on Sunday night [Mr. Gallez] said, I should look for a girl for him. I could not find one that night; but on Monday I got Peggy, and brought her to my master, who ordered me to open a bottle of wine, he gave her a glass of it, and then I went away."[108] Mr. Gallez was "grooming" Peggy, preparing her for sexual abuse and trying to minimize the possibility of resistance, much like contemporary sex offenders.[109] Yet neither Mr. Gallez nor John received so much as a scolding for coercing Peggy into having sex with a married man. Given the gendered double standards of Berbice's legal culture, which largely absolved men from any responsibility for extramarital sex— even when coerced—while justifying violence against the women involved, it is not surprising that women like Betsy took it upon themselves to protect their daughters.

A final case, from July 1829, underscores the gendered double standards and obstacles enslaved women faced. Nancy, who lived on plantation Alness, went to the deputy protector in the wake of a fight with another woman over the manager of plantation Waterloo, Mr. M'Donald. According to Nancy, "she was formerly in habits of intimacy with Mr. M'Donald," and was "in fact with child by him." But "last Friday she went to Plantation Waterloo, and found a slave, named Clarissa, in Mr. M'Donald's bed." Nancy immediately began "striking Clarissa with a yard measure," and the women fought until M'Donald drove Nancy out of the house with a horsewhip. Three days later, moreover, Clarissa's mother "beat Nancy with a shoe, because she had quarreled with her daughter."[110]

The deputy protector told Nancy that she had no grounds for complaint. Unlike Mrs. Gallez, a free woman who was justified in beating an enslaved woman she found in bed with her husband, Nancy was, after all, merely a slave and moreover a "concubine." She could not expect the manager or the colonial government to treat her like a legally married, free woman. The deputy protector therefore "reprobated, in strong terms, the conduct of the whole of the parties concerned in this disgraceful transaction," and dismissed the complaint. But he also took advantage of this opportunity to argue that the domestic problems women like Nancy faced could be solved if only they would embrace formal marriage. He "contrasted the rights enjoyed by a married woman, with the treatment to which a concubine is subject," and "pointed out and explained to Nancy the law recognizing the marriage of slaves, and the privileges that solemnity secured to them, the advantages she would derive from being lawfully married; and exhorted her to quit the immoral life she had hitherto pursued."[111] M'Donald, of course, was not subjected to a similar lecture.

What the deputy chose not to see was that some of the most serious domestic problems enslaved women faced, including adulterous, abusive husbands and physical attacks from female rivals, had less to do with whether their marriages were officially recognized than they did with the beliefs men in Berbice held about gender, sex, and power. Whether white or black, free or enslaved, men in Berbice agreed that women should be subordinate to men, that husbands should have authority over their wives, and that a patriarchal family was ideal. Enslaved women who challenged these gender conventions, which had deep roots in Old World Africa and Europe alike and which were sustained in the plantation societies of the West Indies, met with opposition from nearly every corner.

It is tempting to romanticize enslaved people's family lives, seeing the family as a protective force that insulated them from the horrors of slavery. And indeed many enslaved men and women in Berbice did turn to one another for companionship, sex, protection, and perhaps even love. Nevertheless, enslaved people's domestic lives could also be scenes of intense violence, terror, and power struggles. Even if the best evidence we have to examine enslaved people's marriages is skewed in favor of discord and turmoil—and it almost certainly is, since legal records rarely captured enslaved people's marriages when things were going well—it illustrates the gendered nature of power and authority at every level in West Indian slave society, including the most intimate relationships between men and women. Moreover, the problems enslaved men and women faced in their marriages were deeply connected to, rather than isolated from, the full range of power structures of Atlantic slavery. Slaveowners, plantation authorities, and colonial officials interfered in enslaved people's domestic lives not only by separating families by sale and sexually abusing enslaved women but also by mediating marital disputes, especially when enslaved people themselves asked for help.

When colonial authorities did intervene, they were guided by deeply patriarchal beliefs about marriage, family, and gender, which led them to favor enslaved men over women. Enslaved women's demographic advantage did little to increase their bargaining power and agency vis-à-vis enslaved men, who used violence, intimidation, and enforcers of the law to restrict women's social and sexual mobility. Enslaved women thus found themselves in a particularly vulnerable position because enslaved men, their enslavers, and colonial officials cooperated across lines of color and status to subordinate them. Despite the inherent danger of upholding enslaved men's masculine authority in a society where white men were supposed to be the only and unequivocal patriarchs, colonial officials and plantation authorities were often willing to do just that, both because it was consistent with their own gender ideology and because they believed that male-headed marriages and households would promote order. If white supremacy was one of the foundations of colonial slave societies, so, too, was male privilege.

More broadly, enslaved people's domestic conflicts remind us that they struggled not only as laborers to survive a violent plantation system and a hostile disease environment but also to navigate complex social worlds—as men and women, husbands and wives. Survival may have been their most urgent concern, but it was not their only one. For many slaves, marriage and family life were central strategies for making the best possible lives within the considerable constraints they faced. And despite the inherent instability of the society in which they lived, where slaveowners routinely broke family ties when they bought and sold slaves, enslaved people continued to marry and build families. Yet some problems were unavoidable—especially death. Indeed, for every marriage that ended in separation by sale or divorce, many more people lost their partners to the Grim Reaper.

CHAPTER 5

Spiritual Power and the "Bad Business" of Obeah

When the drivers on Op Hoop van Beter, a Berbice River coffee plantation, saw Madalon's bloodied, bruised body early one morning in August 1821, they knew that if knowledge about what had happened spread, their own lives might be in danger. Yet they were confident that others on the plantation of more than 170 slaves shared their interest in keeping the cause of the enslaved woman's death a secret. As the sun rose and the workday began, the drivers ordered a group of men to hide the body and then told the manager that Madalon had run away. While the manager initiated the search for Madalon, news of her disappearance spread. Within hours, a note had reached the nearby estate where her husband, Munro, lived. He traveled to Madalon's plantation to try to find out what had happened, but no one would tell him what they knew. Indeed, for more than a month the people on Op Hoop van Beter kept their secrets. Eventually, however, planter and militia officer William Sterk caught wind of a rumor that Madalon had been killed during a clandestine obeah ritual. Tracing the rumor to its source led Sterk to a slave named Vigilant, who reported that "Madalon was killed by the directions of a negro, named Willem," during the Minje Mama dance—a healing ritual also known as the Water Mama dance.[1]

Vigilant's admission set in motion a relentless investigation into Madalon's murder and the practice of obeah—an Afro-Caribbean spiritual complex of divination, healing, and harming—on the estate.[2] Within hours, Sterk apprehended Willem and took him two miles downriver to the New Amsterdam office of the fiscal. But the fiscal was not content with merely identifying Madalon's murderer. He was determined to uncover detailed information about the nature of the rituals that led to her death, about the people who participated in them, and, most of all, about the nature of Willem's authority. Over several months the fiscal interrogated some two dozen witnesses, most of them slaves who lived on or near Op Hoop van Beter. Finally, more than five months after Madalon's death, he brought formal charges against Willem and his collaborators for Madalon's murder and for facilitating the Minje Mama dance—a capital crime.[3] Meanwhile, onlookers like the London Missionary Society's John Wray, who lived in New Amsterdam and saw obeah as an obstacle to converting slaves, conducted their own informal investigations and commented on the case in letters sent across the Atlantic.[4] Two years before Madalon's death, in 1819, the fiscal had investigated a similar case involving an enslaved man named Hans who was accused of practicing "obiah" after he, like Willem, had organized the Minje Mama dance on a plantation not far from Op Hoop van Beter and denounced a suspected poisoner.[5] The fiscal dutifully sent records of both investigations to the Colonial Office, and Parliament published the proceedings of Willem's trial in 1823.[6] These records, taken together, reveal the central role that spiritual power, the Minje Mama dance, and obeah practitioners played in enslaved people's struggle to survive and, paradoxically, the dangers they presented and the social divisions they caused when things went wrong.[7]

Soon after the British took control of Berbice, they criminalized the "evil" that was obeah, following a pattern that began half a century earlier in Jamaica, where colonial authorities first constructed obeah as a distinct crime and linked it to slave rebellion and other attacks on whites.[8] Colonial legislatures—which usually defined obeah as "pretending to have communication with the devil" or "assuming the art of witchcraft"—regularly prosecuted enslaved people for obeah and sentenced those who were convicted to severe punishments, including "transportation" (deportation and sale into the overseas slave trade) and, less often, execution.[9] Yet, enslaved people throughout the British West Indies continued to use a variety of African and Afro-Caribbean practices that colonists lumped together as "obeah" for purposes that often had little to do with resisting slavery or harming whites. A weak missionary presence combined with massive importation of African captives allowed obeah to flourish well into the nineteenth century, as evidenced by continued efforts to curb it, such as the 1855 British Guiana "Ordinance to Repress the Commission of Obeah Practices"—the preamble to which claimed that "the practice of obeah ha[d] increased to a great extent in the colony."[10] Throughout the 1820s and 1830s, practicing obeah was one of several dozen offenses regularly recorded in Berbice's plantation punishment record

books (though a relatively small number of punishments for obeah were recorded in any given year), and the fiscal and protector of slaves investigated
several cases involving suspected obeah practitioners.[11] Enslaved people in
Berbice and elsewhere thus continued to turn to obeah despite its criminalization because they saw it as a powerful tool in their struggle to survive.

Obeah helped enslaved people solve problems and sustain life, as many
scholars have shown, but its practitioners and their techniques could also be
remarkably violent and dangerous—and not only for whites.[12] Even if we acknowledge that long-standing negative stereotypes of obeah reveal more
about white colonists' views of Afro-Caribbean spirituality than about enslaved people's beliefs and practices themselves, we must also grapple with
the very real risks involved in certain forms of obeah. The Minje Mama
dance, for instance, featured whippings, beatings, and other forms of physical
violence, much of it directed against people thought to be under the power of
malevolent spiritual forces or those who interfered with the dance or otherwise challenged obeah practitioners' authority. And sometimes, as the slaves
on Op Hoop van Beter learned, obeah proved fatal. Moreover, the Minje
Mama dance and other healing practices—even when they incorporated features of African cosmologies—came to include extreme violence when re-
configured in the plantation environments of the Americas, where physical
violence was central not only to masters' exercise of power but also in structuring power relationships among enslaved people themselves.

Obeah was always an ambivalent and ambiguous practice: it could be
used to heal or to harm, to preserve life or to destroy it, and was thus both
respected and feared by slaves.[13] The drivers on Op Hoop van Beter, for example, suspected that someone had used witchcraft, obeah, or some other
supernatural power to sicken and kill other slaves. To counteract her powers,
they called in an obeah specialist, Willem, who they thought could solve
their problems and help their community survive. The rituals Willem organized, however, resulted in much bloodshed, intensified social divisions on
the plantation, and created a new set of problems for the very people he was
supposed to help. Obeah practitioners like Willem and Hans were powerful
healers, skilled in channeling supernatural forces, but that same power also
made them threatening.

How did obeah practitioners construct themselves as authority figures
among people desperate to survive? How did they get others to cooperate
with them and accept the risks associated with illicit and sometimes violent
rituals? And what happened when they lost the allegiance of the people who

had turned to them or faced opposition? Focusing on the Minje Mama dance's role in Berbician slaves' battle for survival illustrates the complicated social politics of healing in a society where death and disease were daily realities and illuminates the various ways that obeah practitioners leveraged their skills and status to establish themselves as alternative authorities among slaves. As Willem and Hans knew, their authority was contested, contingent, and controversial. Above all, it rested on demonstrable success in practicing a dangerous craft.

They Could Bring Things on the Estate to Order

For the drivers on Op Hoop van Beter, the Minje Mama dance was a last resort. For weeks or months, they watched other slaves, many of them children, become incurably sick, and no one seemed to know why. Though they were accustomed to death, things seemed worse than normal. By early August the death toll was still rising, and the white-supervised medical treatment slaves received in the estate "hospital" proved useless. As the epidemic worsened, some people began to suspect that a malevolent spiritual force was the culprit. They needed someone with the requisite knowledge to identify and neutralize whatever was sickening and killing their friends, kin, shipmates, and neighbors. Lead drivers Primo and Mey realized they needed someone who could "put the estate to rights" or "bring things on the estate to order," as they understood it, by devising a solution to what they saw as a spiritual, not epidemiological, crisis.[14]

The drivers might have been motivated by compassion, but their desire to restore the spiritual and social order on the plantation stemmed from an urgent wish to maintain their own coveted positions of authority and respect. If people continued to die, there was a good chance they would be held accountable, and perhaps demoted, thus losing their best chance of surviving slavery. So the drivers turned to the illicit powers of an obeahman—an unsanctioned authority and outsider who had the potential, ironically, to help the drivers reinforce the plantation regime. Spiritual and political systems of authority—one based on Afro-Caribbean spiritual power, the other established by the official slaveholding power structure—thus converged on Op Hoop van Beter around the common goal of "putting the estate to rights," and saving the lives of the plantation's labor force.[15] Far from threatening the slave system, as one might assume, obeah in this case was called on to preserve it.

Africans and their descendants in the Americas often suspected malevolent spiritual forces when sickness, death, or misfortune struck. In the British Caribbean, even slaveholders knew that when someone died unexpectedly, slaves often accused one another of using spiritual powers like obeah. As Jamaican planter Bryan Edwards observed, "When, at any time, sudden or untimely death overtakes any of their companions . . . they never fail to impute it to the malicious contrivances and diabolical arts of some practitioner in Obeah."[16] John Wray similarly observed that slaves in Berbice "attribute[d] almost all their diseases to the Obeah-man or woman, and frequently also, the death of their friends; and [they] very frequently wore amulets to counteract their influence."[17]

Enslaved people turned to obeah practitioners for help, but they also viewed them with suspicion and fear. Though colonists probably exaggerated enslaved people's fear of obeah, grafting their own anxieties onto slaves, there is good evidence from Berbice and other colonies that enslaved people were concerned about the harm that at least some obeah practitioners could do. In 1822, when the slaves on plantation Friends became suspicious that Tobias had been "practising obeah on the estate," they went to the manager and pleaded with him to punish Tobias. The attorney, manager, and overseer all agreed that Tobias was "a very bad character, and disliked by all the other negroes on the estate." They had Tobias put in the stocks and later "sold at public vendue, and not allowed to return to the plantation."[18] Similar tensions between a suspected obeah practitioner and other slaves developed on Matthew Gregory "Monk" Lewis's Jamaican estate in 1816–18. In his *Journal* Lewis frequently complained of his problems with "a reputed Obeah-man," Adam, who was "a most dangerous fellow, and the terror of all his companions, with whom he live[d] in a constant state of warfare." Adam "was accused [by other slaves] of being an Obeah-man," was "strongly suspected of having poisoned more than twelve negroes," and had also "threatened the lives of many of the best negroes." By 1818 they had had enough: several "principal negroes" asked Lewis to remove Adam from the plantation, "as their lives were not safe while breathing the same air with Adam."[19]

When the drivers on Op Hoop van Beter decided to turn to Willem, they knew that bringing him to the plantation could help but would also expose them and other slaves to several dangers. Obeah and the Minje Mama dance were illegal, and the potential punishments were severe. And even if the drivers and Willem were able to avoid detection, the practice of obeah itself posed serious risks. Some obeah rituals involved whippings, beatings, and other forms of violence. Obeah practitioners themselves, moreover, could be violent and domineering, and their authority could just as easily challenge the drivers' grip on power as reinforce it. How, then, do we explain the drivers' decision to turn to Willem despite the risks?

Willem was no stranger to the people on Op Hoop van Beter. One of about one hundred slaves who lived on Buses Lust, a coffee plantation on the east bank of the Berbice River almost directly across from Op Hoop van Beter, Willem appears to have visited the plantation regularly, eventually developing a relationship with a woman, Johanna, who lived there. Born in Berbice at the end of the eighteenth century, Willem had developed a reputation as a healer by his early twenties, an impressive feat for a relatively young man.[20] Several witnesses testified that Willem (called Cuffey by some) was "Attetta Sara," "Monkesi Sara," "the Minje Mama," "Abdie Toboko" or "God Almighty's toboco," and "a real Obiah man (Confou man)"—terms used in recognition of his authority.[21] "Attetta Sara" meant "God's messenger" in Igbo. "Monkesi" was another name for the Minje Mama dance and was probably a variation of the Kongolese term *minkisi* (fetishes or charms). "Abdie Toboko," a term with Ijo roots, meant "God Almighty's child." "Confou" was likely a corruption of *comfa*, a Guyanese term (derived from the Akan word for spiritual healers, *komfo* or *O'komfo*) for a dance that featured spirit possession and, in some places, was a synonym for "obeah."[22] The multiplicity of terms used to describe Willem reflect the ethnic diversity of Berbice's slave population and reminds us that there were a variety of lenses through which Africans and Afro-Caribbeans interpreted spiritual power. And the fact that enslaved people used such terms more often than "obeah" in the trial record suggests that "obeah" might not yet have been the most significant term for spiritual power for all enslaved people in early nineteenth-century Berbice.[23]

When Willem learned of the epidemic, he first tried to treat sick people individually. The healing strategies he employed—what might be called everyday obeah—were relatively benign when compared with collective rituals such as the Minje Mama dance. Willem first obtained the permission of those he treated. Cornelia, the estate cook, explained, "Willem . . . came on the estate and asked if we were sick, if so, he could cure us? I said perhaps he could cure us; and as I was sick, he took three twigs of the cocoanut tree, and struck me on the head, and told me to go and wash myself." Willem "made her eyes turn," a common description for spirit possession or a trance state. Afterward, Cornelia recalled, "she found herself much better, and [believed] that this had helped to cure her." Fortuyn—who some witnesses claimed brought

Willem to the plantation in the first place—asked him to help one of his wives, who "had been two or three months with a sore on her foot." Willem also visited sick children in the plantation hospital. He "came to the hospital," one man explained, and "directed the children to be brought out," where they "were washed by Willem, who took off two bits [coins] that were tied round the neck of one of them" as payment for his services.[24]

These efforts to treat individual symptoms, however, could only do so much. Willem and the drivers realized that because they faced a widespread problem, a more systematic—and much more dangerous—divination and healing process was necessary. Willem needed to uncover and counteract the root cause of these different ailments if he was to put an end to the epidemic. It was time for the Minje Mama dance.

Unlike everyday obeah, the Minje Mama dance was a collective divination and healing ritual performed in moments of crisis. It was thus potentially more powerful and more dangerous than ordinary spiritual healing practices. Also known as the Water Mama dance and by other names, it was designed to identify the source of *maleficium*, or harmful spiritual practice. Africans and African-descended people throughout the Caribbean practiced variations of this ritual, characterized by dancing and trance-induced spirit possession. Similar rituals have also been practiced for centuries across West Africa, where the spirit is known as Mami Wata.[25] This ritual's primary goal in the Caribbean was identification of the person responsible for harming or killing others through spiritual powers or poison.

In the Guianas, the Minje Mama dance appears to have been widely practiced, perhaps because a healing and divination ritual organized around a water spirit was attractive to people who lived in a world surrounded by creeks, rivers, swamps, and an ocean, all inhabited by manatees or "mermaids."[26] It was thus extremely useful but also fraught with danger. The dance itself could be violent, and there was always the danger that an innocent participant or someone's friend or family member might be identified as the guilty party, which must have given some people pause before lending their support to this ritual. Yet as early as the eighteenth century, colonial observers recognized the central role the Minje Mama played in enslaved people's efforts to survive the daily threats of living and working in a brutal slave society. John Gabriel Stedman, who fought against the Maroons in Suriname in the 1770s and left a detailed account of his time there, wrote that "Several Old Negroes and Indians" told him that "Nothing was more Dreaded by their Wives and Children than the Watra Mama, Which Signifies the Mother of the Watters."[27]

Figure 8. Consulting the Water Mama. *La Mama-snekie, ou water-mama, faisant ses conjurations,* colored lithograph by Pierre Jacques Benoit, in *Voyage à Surinam: Description des possessions Néerlandaises dans la Guyane* (Brussels: Société des Beaux-Arts; Gérants, 1839), plate XVIII, fig. 36. This rare, firsthand representation of an Afro-Caribbean spiritual healing practice was produced by a Belgian artist who visited Suriname around 1831. In a lengthy description that accompanied the image, Benoit described his clandestine visit to a healer known as a Mama Snekie or Water Mama, accompanied by a woman who sought help healing her sick child. The Water Mama, who Benoit also identified as a sibyl and sorceress, kneels in front of an earthen pot full of snakes. At one point in the healing ritual, the Water Mama gave the mother water from the pot to drink and herbs for her child. The snakes in the pot as well as the large stuffed snake on the wall—likely a boa constrictor—suggest that the healing ritual was related to the Afro-Surinamese religion known today as Papa or Vodu, in which adherents believe spirits known as *papa gagu* inhabit the bodies of boa constrictors, known as *papa sineki*. Courtesy of the John Carter Brown Library at Brown University.

Central to the Watra Mama's authority was her reputation for helping those who worshipped her (for example, by locating poison) while harming or killing those who disobeyed her.[28] Stedman—who supplied one of the earliest descriptions of a Minje Mama or Watra Mama ritual, which he knew as "*Winty Play* or the Dance of the *Mairmaid*"—recognized the sway obeah practitioners had among their peers.[29] He described a class of "pretended *Loco-men* or *Prophets*" who took advantage of the "Superstitious . . . Common Class" of Afro-Surinamese by "Selling them *Obias*, or *Amulets* . . . with other charms." Stedman also described "a kind of *Sibils* . . . who deal in Oracles, these Sage

Matrons Dancing And Whirling Round in the Middle of an Audience, till Absolutely they froath at the mouth And drop down in the middle of them; Whatever She says to be done during this fit of Madness is Sacredly Performed by the Surrounding Multitude, which makes these meetings Exceedingly dangerous Amongst the Slaves, who are often told to murder their Masters or Desert to The Woods, & on which Account the Excessive of this piece of Fanatism, is forbid in the Colony of Surinam on Pain of the Most Rigorous Punishment." Nevertheless, Stedman wrote, "it is often Put in Execution in Private Places."[30] Legislators in Suriname had outlawed "watermama and similar African dances" in the 1770s, and British officials in Berbice similarly found the Minje Mama dance threatening enough to go to the trouble of having the legal prohibition of the ritual publicly "read and explained to the gangs of different estates on the river" in the early nineteenth century.[31]

Documents generated during the investigation and criminal trial of an enslaved healer named Hans, a fifty-six-year-old, half-blind field hand owned by the Crown, provide a rare opportunity to see the Minje Mama dance from the bottom up. In 1819 Hans organized the dance on Demtichem, a coffee plantation across the river from Op Hoop van Beter. The drivers on the plantation, January, Benjamin, and La Fleur, decided to contact an obeah practitioner when a series of unexplained, sudden deaths confounded them. As one of the drivers explained, "so many deaths had occurred that he had sent for a man to put every thing to rights." The driver "wished to have the bad people," meaning those who had used obeah, poison, or witchcraft to harm others, "off the estate."[32]

Hans, like Willem, enjoyed a reputation as a skilled healer. "Negroes in general," Hans boasted to John Wray, who interviewed him in jail after his arrest, "know that I possess the power of helping them if any thing is the matter with them and great numbers of negroes have applied to me and I have helped them." It was this reputation that gave the people on Demtichem confidence in Hans's abilities. "All the people and children got sick here," the lead driver, January, told him, "and we know that in other places you have helped them and therefore we have sent for you."[33]

When Hans arrived on the plantation, January explained to a large group gathered before his house that Hans had come "to put every thing to rights." Hans first needed to identify the "bad" person in their midst. He asked the children to "point out the persons who administered poison [on] the estate," and some people told him "they suspected there was poison in [head carpenter] Frederick's House."[34] Hans then sacrificed a pullet, placed the feathers in the children's hair, and washed them with a mixture of water and grass. He next "began to sing a country song," instructing everyone to "join in [the] chorus." Finally, Hans demanded payment for his services, as was customary among obeah practitioners.[35]

The next day Hans returned to continue the divination process. According to Venus, an enslaved woman born in Demerara who would soon play a key role in the dance, Hans declared that "he would pull off all the poison that was in the ground, which made the people on the estate die so suddenly." Hans washed everyone present and "sang the dance called Walter [Water] Mamma dans."[36] Hans made "all the negroes dance on one foot and clap their hands," according to Wray's letter, and some fell into a trance, possessed by the spirit of the Minje Mama. One man "became as tho' he was crazy, jumping high up from the ground and throwing himself down."[37] "My head began to turn," Venus told the fiscal, "as if I were mad." The plantation attorney thought "the minds of the negroes must have been greatly agitated, they having thrown themselves on the ground, biting the grass, tearing the earth with their hands, and conducting themselves like maniacs."[38]

Though potentially useful, this was a violent ritual. The slaves "that were the most turbulent," the head carpenter and suspected poisoner, Frederick, recalled, "were flogged with the wild canes . . . by order of Hans, and recovered; others more furious, and not recovering from the stripes [lashes], Hans struck with a bamboo, and they immediately recovered." According to Venus, Hans made sure that everyone was "flogged with the wild cane first; if not recovered he flogged them with a carracarra [vine], and put guinea pepper in their eyes which he had chewed. All of this was done to me, but I could not recover. . . . I could see and hear every thing, but was exactly as if I were crazy: I recovered a little after this last."[39]

As the dance continued, the results it produced sparked conflict, both about the poisoner's identity and about the extent of Hans's authority. "Venus went into the middle of the circle being apparently crazy" and "throwing herself upon the ground and rolling about." She then "burst out into Hysterical laughter and came up & struck [Frederick] again."[40] "Coming up to [him, she] said, [he] was the bad man on the estate." Venus told Frederick "that they want[ed] to remove [him]" from the plantation. She knew he was "the bad man" because she could "see it from the water that has been sprinkled over my face and eyes." She "ran out of the circle and said 'come, and I show you where the poison is hid,'" leading a group to Frederick's house.[41]

For Frederick, this may not have been the first time he had to defend himself against accusations that he had used poison against other slaves. According to John Wray, "the Negroes had frequently blamed Frederick as a poisoner" and even complained about him to the previous owner of the estate.[42] The fiscal believed that the others conspired to have Frederick identified as a poisoner in an effort to "rid themselves" of him because they were jealous of Frederick's relative wealth. As a head carpenter, Frederick had more opportunities than most other slaves to acquire cash and property, and his previous owner had left him "a joe every month" as a bequest for his loyalty. Frederick eventually accumulated enough money to purchase his own slave.[43] It is possible that other slaves were jealous, and that some people suspected Frederick had used illicit means to enrich himself. His unusual success in accumulating wealth would have made him a likely target for accusations of witchcraft, poisoning, and obeah.[44]

At Frederick's house, where his wife, Pompadour, let them in, Venus and the others "threw down two casks of water, broke down [the] kitchen and fowl-house, and dug up the earth with shovels," Frederick explained. But they could not find the poison. Venus claimed that she had made a mistake, that she had meant to accuse another man, and asked to be allowed to "go to Hans . . . to get my eyes properly washed." "No," Frederick protested, "I have been accused, and must insist, as my house has been broken, that this business shall be found out, or I know what to do."[45]

Frederick decided to tell the plantation overseer "that the negroes were breaking open his house, and digging up the ground, accusing him of being a poisoner." He had good reason to fear what might happen if the others believed Venus. The overseer put an end to the search for the poison and placed the drivers in the stocks, and the plantation attorney "reported the circumstance to the burgher officer and the Fiscal."[46] Meanwhile, Hans fled.

But the following evening Hans returned to locate the "bad thing" hidden somewhere in Frederick's house. He knew it was there "from the smell he had of it," and with the help of "the girl who had lost her mother" or a twin, he was sure he could find "the pot of obiah."[47] Two men brought Gabriel—a ten-year-old girl and a twin—to Frederick's house, where she was blindfolded and given a pot to hold over a hole that Hans had ordered two other men to dig in the dirt floor. Hans "made the people examine the Pot to see if there was any thing in it, but Water," and they all agreed that there was not.[48] But when Hans removed the cloth that covered the pot a moment later, it "appeared to contain a ram's horn, some fluid, and the bones of some animal."[49] The ram's horn was cut open, which exposed "blood, Negro hair, shavings of nails, the head of a snake," and other objects commonly associated with obeah and *minkisi*. "The stuff in the Horn," Hans explained, "was the bad thing which had destroyed the Children but it would do so no longer."[50]

Hans and the drivers might have been pleased that the Minje Mama dance had helped them locate the poisoner and his poison and, presumably, prevent more people from dying, but colonial authorities saw things differently. Hans was soon apprehended by the overseer, who found "numerous [obeah] articles . . . on his person" and "a handkerchief [with] *f.* 50 in money," and was brought to the New Amsterdam jail. Shortly thereafter the fiscal prosecuted him for practicing obeah and those who had cooperated with him, focusing on the drivers.[51] The fiscal recommended a death sentence for Hans, but the Court of Criminal Justice spared Hans's life, perhaps because it agreed with Hans's lawyer, who had argued that colonial authorities should take some responsibility for Hans's use of obeah because no real effort had been made in Berbice "to inform [Hans's] Mind in Christianity" and he had "been permitted to remain in that pagan state in which he had been brought from his own Country." The court sentenced Hans to be whipped under the gallows with his obeah materials around his neck, branded, imprisoned for a year, placed in the pillory four times, and forced to work in the colony's chain gang for the rest of his life. He was also to be publicly exposed with his obeah paraphernalia sixteen times over the next year, for an hour each time, when the Court of Criminal Justice met. Those who had helped Hans were to be whipped, and Venus, Wray wrote, "was stripped naked when she was flogged."[52] January was also demoted from his position as driver, a crushing blow to his status that he refused to accept even a decade later.[53]

As the people on Demtichem learned, the Minje Mama dance had exposed them to a host of dangers, including the colonial legal apparatus, their overseer and attorney, and significant physical violence at the hands of Hans himself. Nevertheless, the Minje Mama dance remained a vital tool in the struggle to restore physical and spiritual health in a world where disease and death were daily realities and malevolent powers abounded. Enslaved people needed obeah practitioners like Hans and Willem, especially in times of crisis.

Setting the Estate to Rights

When the drivers on Op Hoop van Beter allowed Willem to perform the Minje Mama dance on their plantation two years later, they were taking a serious, if calculated, risk. One Sunday afternoon in early August 1821, Willem slipped into "a small *coriaal*" (dugout canoe) after finishing his day's work at neighboring plantation Resolutie and paddled a short distance down the Berbice River to Op Hoop van Beter. When he arrived, "he inquired for the [head] driver's house," one man explained, "where he remained till the evening," no doubt consulting about the epidemic. Later that night, after visiting Johanna, Willem "made the people dance the Makisi [Minje Mama] dance," according to witnesses. "The man Cuffey [Willem] . . . was the Minje [Mama], and superintended the dance; if he was not there," one witness explained, "it could not be done."[54]

The dance evidently served its purpose: Willem returned to the plantation the next day and publicly denounced Madalon, an old, Central African (probably Kongolese) field laborer, as "a bad woman, and the cause of the healthy people on the estate becoming sick." Madalon appears to have had no family and few friends on the plantation, and this social isolation coupled with her advanced age and female gender could have made her vulnerable to accusations of witchcraft or poisoning. The person responsible had now been identified, but the healing process—and the real danger—had just begun. The challenge now, as Willem knew, was to "drive the bad story out of [Madalon's] head."[55]

The day after Willem accused Madalon, he returned to Op Hoop van Beter to continue what would turn out to be a brutally violent and socially divisive healing process. After the people finished their work in the coffee fields "and retired to the negro-houses," one witness explained, Willem called several people together, including Madalon and the drivers. That night, according to estate watchman Frederick (not the carpenter from Demtichem), "the woman Madalon was flogged by the negroes before the driver Primo's door, and at the same time pepper was rubbed into her private parts" to help purify her.[56]

Willem and the drivers tried to keep this gathering from attracting the attention of white authorities, but at some point the manager, J. Helmers, heard noises coming from the "negro-yard" and sent his overseer to investigate. "The first person the overseer met was Willem," one witness testified, "who took up some ashes from the fire and strewed them across the road, which prevented any body [from] seeing farther on." Meanwhile, Primo told the overseer that the commotion "was nothing but the people rejoicing in consequence of having finished weeding the last field of heavy grass."[57]

The overseer gone, Willem and the others finished whipping Madalon and then left her tied up by the wrists. Badly beaten and probably terrified, she might have spent the night there had it not been for Frederick, who untied her, covered her with a blanket, and took her to his house to recover and possibly to protect her from Willem. Willem soon found out what Frederick had done, however, and threatened to flog him for interfering.[58]

The centrality of violence in Willem's practice of obeah suggests that white colonists were not the only people who recognized the efficacy of violence and terror for projecting power. But how much and what kinds of violence were the people on Op Hoop van Beter willing to accept? Did Willem's recourse to physical force and intimidation bolster his authority or alienate others? Focusing on the specific types of violence Willem used and on others' reactions to them helps explain why enslaved people held ambivalent attitudes toward obeah practitioners.

The morning after Madalon's first beating, she went to work as usual. But with injuries still fresh from the night before, Frederick explained, she "was unable to get through her row" (her daily task). Quashee, "a temporary driver" who had some kind of sexual relationship with Madalon, completed her work for her.[59] "The driver asked her why she did not go to the hospital," another witness recalled, "seeing she was full of itch on her backside and a boil on her thigh," not to mention "some blood on her clothes."[60] Despite her injuries Madalon claimed she "preferred going to her work to going to the hospital, as there she got nothing but barley to eat."[61] Madalon had no shortage of reasons for avoiding the hospital, where she would have likely been locked in the stocks and subjected to painful, if not fatal, medical procedures.

Madalon also did not tell the manager what Willem and the others had done to her. Perhaps she thought that her ordeal was over and that speaking up would only provoke Willem and make matters worse. Or maybe she was afraid that the manager might side with Willem and the drivers and punish her for using obeah. To make sure that no one else went to the manager, Willem had "administered to the other negroes a drink," Frederick testified, "declaring that it would be the death of any one of them who should reveal what had taken place." Fear of Willem's physical violence was one reason that participants and observers kept quiet. When the fiscal asked Kees, the driver in charge of the *logie* (coffee storehouse), for example, why he did not go to the manager, he explained that "he was too much afraid of Willem, from the severe punishments he inflicted upon them." Lest the fiscal doubt him, Kees removed his clothes to reveal "the scars, or remains of flogging he had received from Willem."[62]

People also kept quiet because the beating that Madalon endured, at least at first, was not unusual. After all, enslaved people lived in a world ruled by violence, and this was not the first time they had seen ritual flogging used to heal or to deal with someone suspected of using supernatural forces to harm others. Indeed, Willem himself had previously performed the Minje Mama dance and other healing rituals on the plantation, and some people thought the efficacy of these treatments justified the pain they caused.

According to Vigilant, the Minje Mama dance was frequently "performed at plantation Op Hoop van Beter, on Sundays." He "was present on one occasion when it was danced, and saw a negro . . . denounced as a confoe [confou] man, and severely beat; the negro Willem . . . appeared to be the principal, and promoter of the dancing." Other witnesses corroborated Vigilant's account and identified the man beaten as David, who had confessed to William Sterk that he had been "flogged by the orders of the negro Willem" because the Op Hoop van Beter people "blamed him as being one of the Obii people on the estate." And according to Sterk, "after [David] was flogged he was ordered to give payment to . . . Willem for having flogged the Obeah work out of his head." The fact that Willem expected compensation, like most healers, suggests that at least some of the people on the estate did not see this violence as torture or "punishment," as the fiscal and other colonials did, but rather as an effective, if dangerous, healing strategy. David also knew, however, that sometimes Willem's violence had little to do with healing. When David offered Willem "three ells of Osnaburgh's," a coarse fabric, as payment, Willem became angry and "struck him with his own cutlass [machete] on the forehead, saying what he had sent him was not sufficient, and that Obeah people were not allowed to wear any thing of value."[63]

Violence and intimidation had also played a central role in the Minje Mama dance that Hans organized and in Hans's construction of authority. Hans beat everyone who participated in the dance; threatened to flog or kill Gabriel, the young girl who helped him find the poison in Frederick's house, if she cried; and rubbed "guinea pepper" in the eyes of participants in the dance. Though painful, these actions led to the Minje Mama dance's success: Venus was able to identify Frederick as the poisoner, and several witnesses testified that they were able to "recover," or emerge from the trance. Even after the dance, however, other slaves were afraid to approach or touch Hans, which suggests that his capacity for violence was not limited to the rituals he presided over.[64]

If violence was part of Willem's healing practice, it was also central to his efforts to maintain authority, stifle dissent, and coerce others into helping him. In addition to threatening to flog Frederick, Willem attacked one of the drivers for failing to take part in the Minje Mama dance. Willem "beat me the following morning for not being present at the dance," the driver told the fiscal. When the same driver admitted that he helped beat Madalon the following night, he claimed that he did so only because of "the influence of dread and fear under which he . . . as well as the rest of the negroes were, of the power possessed by the negro Willem . . . who was esteemed a great Obeah man, and the Minje Mama."[65] Indeed, colonists across the Caribbean noted the authority that obeah practitioners had among their contemporaries, and Berbice was no exception. As Wray observed, "It is impossible to describe the influence these men [obeah practitioners] obtain over the minds of the negroes."[66] Their authority stemmed from their ability to heal, of course, but also from their potential to harm.

On the third day, Willem returned to the plantation to finish what he had begun. He had Madalon tied up in front of the head driver's door that night, where she was flogged again, this time worse than before. Armed with branches from coconut and calabash trees, people took turns beating her, under Willem's command. Eventually, Madalon "acknowledged she had been guilty of the death of several persons."[67] But confessing did not bring an end to her ordeal. The physical abuse Willem and the others inflicted on Madalon, unlike the torture of suspected witches in early modern Europe, where witch-hunters generally operated with state and clerical support, was designed less to elicit a confession than to serve as a sort of exorcism.[68] And Madalon's admission of guilt did not mean that the "bad thing" had been neutralized.

So Willem and the others continued to beat and flog Madalon, so badly, in fact, that "she fainted from the excess of punishment," according to one witness. Willem "said it was only a sham" and ordered that the violence continue. His assistants dragged Madalon to a mango tree, where they "tied [her] up by the hands," one man explained, "so that her toes could just touch the ground." Frederick, who was hiding "in one of the negro-houses" to avoid Willem, told the fiscal that "the persons who surrounded and punished her were too numerous for him to distinguish the particular individuals who were striking her."[69]

Yet not everyone supported Willem. Only about a dozen people—a small fraction of the estate's slave population—appear in the trial record as participants, though many more probably witnessed it. Some people, like Frederick, disapproved of what was happening; others were apparently not welcome. One man, for instance, testified that "the negroes would not trust him . . . to be present at any of these transactions, in consequence of being hospital-mate," and thus perhaps too close to Anglo-American medicine. Another man explained that "Willem called him to go help flog the woman, but he did not go." "He saw the woman flogged," he admitted, "but did not help."[70] When Hans went to Demtichem—where some three hundred enslaved people lived—the situation was similar: only a small group took part in the Minje Mama dance.[71]

The types of physical violence that Hans and Willem used—floggings, beatings, and the application of hot peppers—were among the methods favored by slaveholders for torturing and punishing enslaved people. That most of these forms of violence were absent in African rituals designed to identify suspected witches and poisoners or combat their powers suggests that the Minje Mama dance was a creole, Caribbean phenomenon, not a watered-down African survival.[72] Its cosmological origins lay in various slave-exporting regions of Africa, but the brutal violence that characterized its practice had been learned on West Indian plantations.[73]

Obeah practitioners like Hans and Willem thus derived their authority from multiple sources: spiritual and physical, African and Caribbean. And they appropriated slaveowners' technology of control and terror to buttress their already impressive authority as spiritual experts and to stifle dissent. The Minje Mama dance therefore offers evidence for the persistence of African practices and cosmologies in New World slave societies as well as enslaved people's ability to adapt or modify such practices to cope with the unique challenges of plantation life.

Not long after Madalon confessed, one witness testified, Willem hit her with a shovel across the back, "which made her fall down, and exclaim she was dying." Madalon begged for her life. "You are killing me," she cried out. "No," Willem told her, "we are not killing you, but I will drive the bad story out of your head." Willem remained determined to complete the healing process, confident that it would succeed. He continued to flog her, and even claimed that he could bring Madalon back to life if she accidentally died.[74] At this point several participants began to worry that the violence had spun out of control—that Willem was abusing his authority and that he might cause yet another death in their community. As one man told lead driver Primo, "it was going too far." But those who tried to stop Willem failed. Frederick tried to intervene, but Willem drove him away and "said nothing could happen to the woman."[75] When Primo, the estate's highest-ranking slave and the one who had asked Willem to combat the epidemic in the first place, tried to end things himself, Willem struck him with a whip and continued to beat Madalon. Even the drivers had become powerless to stop him.[76]

When the beating was finished, Willem and the others left Madalon, unconscious, tied to a nearby tree for the night. Early the next morning, the people on Op Hoop van Beter discovered that she was dead.

An Authority No Longer

Madalon's death resulted in "the utter astonishment of many of the negroes," who saw it as proof that the obeah practitioner who was supposed to "bring things on the estate to order" had failed them.[77] As with all healers, Willem's authority had rested not only on his capacity for violence and intimidation but also on demonstrable success in practicing his craft. Madalon's death produced for Willem a sudden and almost complete loss of authority and therefore created a major crisis for him, for the drivers who had called him in, and for the other people on Op Hoop van Beter.

Far from helping, Willem had created a new set of dangers for everyone on the plantation, himself included. If word got out about the Minje Mama dance or about Madalon's death, anyone who had failed to alert authorities or helped Willem might face interrogation, torture, and severe punishment. The people on Op Hoop van Beter no doubt knew what had happened to Hans and the other people on Demtichem, and they knew that obeah and the Minje Mama dance—not to mention murder—were illegal. The ways that the various actors—Willem, the drivers, those who had participated in the rituals, Madalon's husband, and other bystanders—responded to Madalon's death reveal how complete Willem's loss of authority was and, paradoxically, how desperate most people were to keep the entire matter secret for as long as possible.

The immediate problem was getting rid of the corpse. The manager, Helmers, would soon notice Madalon's absence, and if he found the body, the numerous cuts, bruises, and welts it bore—the "marks of the punishment were very visible," one man observed—would prompt a threatening investigation. But even this urgent and seemingly simple task proved difficult for Willem. When he ordered a group of men to bury the body, they refused. They might have viewed the corpse as contaminated or spiritually dangerous, or maybe they were simply reluctant to get more involved in what was shaping up to be a major disaster. Willem "grew angry, and drove them away," one man recalled. "Willem said it was of no consequence whether they had buried the body or not, as he would do that," another witness testified. He boasted that "he was Minje Mama; he had plenty of people to assist him," but he soon realized that in fact no one was willing to help.[78]

Willem's encounter with Madalon's husband, Munro, who came looking for his wife a few days after she went missing, underscored just how little power Willem now had. When Munro went to Op Hoop van Beter, having received a note earlier that day saying that Madalon had run away, Fortuyn— the estate watchman—intercepted him on the bridge and "told him he was not to go to the negro-houses." Munro ignored Fortuyn and went to Madalon's house, where he found David and asked him what had happened to Madalon. But David "answered he did not know, as he was only stockkeeper, and knew nothing of what took place in the field." When Munro returned several days later, he went to the manager and asked "what had become of my wife?" Munro then went to the slave quarters, where he found Willem and a group of men who had supported him in the Minje Mama dance. Willem confronted Munro, asking, "How did you dare to go first to the manager's house?" Munro told him that he went to show his pass, as Berbician law and custom required, and, challenging Willem's claim to authority, insulted him: "I asked the Attetta Sara [Willem] if he thought I ought to have brought my pass first to him, or if he could read it?" Provoked to violence yet again, Willem ordered "several of the men . . . to beat [Munro]," but the others "interfered in his behalf." Fortuyn "said he had brought the Attetta Sara on the estate, and that he could not beat him, Munro, for nothing."[79]

As frustrating as it must have been to lose the support of the people on Op Hoop van Beter, things could have been even worse for Willem. Take, for instance, the case of Mamadoe, an alleged obeah practitioner or "doctor" who in 1824 wound up in trouble when he failed to find a permanent cure for a woman's ailment on plantation Nigg. According to plantation attorney Duncan Fraser, when the woman's husband became frustrated by Mamadoe's lack of attention to his wife, his "country man" Rhina (both were Kongolese) threatened Mamadoe: "I will give you this moon to cure her & if you do not do so in that time, I will know what to do to you." Fraser explained that "Rhina had been heard [by other slaves] to say that in his country, the way they treat Obiah men is to kill them, put them in their House & set fire to it." (An enslaved witness recalled Rhina telling him that in his country "dirty people" were locked in their house and burnt to death.) A few days later, Mamadoe's badly beaten body was found in his hut, which had been burned to the ground.[80] Rhina had apparently made good on his threat.

When Willem's authority collapsed, the drivers sought to take charge, reclaiming their role. But they, like Willem, found their authority tested when a group of men refused their order to dispose of Madalon's body. Baron explained that they had "told the driver *in Creole,* You have sent us five negroes to bury the body, and if afterwards it comes to the knowledge of the white people you will put us forward to bear the blame, and you will remain behind, concealed." The following afternoon the "driver said to [Baron], Yesterday you refused to bury that body, to-day we have done it ourselves." He explained "that they had buried the body without his assistance, and put the estate in order, or to rights again." They "had sunk the body in a small coriall with weights" in the river or some other body of water.[81] Taking responsibility for the conspiracy, the drivers thus showed others that they were not going to simply blame them for Madalon's death, as Baron feared.

Madalon's death and the crisis it provoked united people on Op Hoop van Beter, at least temporarily, around the shared goal of avoiding punishment for her murder and the practice of obeah. For several weeks, none of the dozens, if not hundreds, of people who knew about Madalon's death told colonial authorities what they had seen or heard. Part of the reason they kept quiet was that Willem and the drivers had threatened to kill them if they revealed what they knew. In addition to the loyalty oath some had taken earlier, the drivers told everyone "that if they revealed it to the Fiscal, or other white person, they should be hung." Such threats, some witnesses claimed, "prevented them at first from telling the truth."[82]

Helmers, however, might have known what had happened to Madalon long before Vigilant came forward in September and identified Willem as "the promoter of the said Minje Mama dance" and Madalon's murderer. When Sterk told Helmers what he had learned, Helmers admitted: "Something I have heard; but upon negro testimony I can make no dependence, as I have often experienced, without certain proof attached to the same." More revealing still, one of the drivers told the fiscal that "the manager himself knew" that the drivers had gone to Willem. The manager "said he must find some person capable of finding out who it was that was the cause of the death of so many Creoles [children] on the estate," the driver testified.[83] If this was true, the manager had good reason to feign ignorance. His tolerance of and perhaps even belief in obeah rituals and his inability to prevent the murder of one of his slaves would have been damning evidence of his failure to maintain adequate discipline and control on the plantation.

For months after Willem's arrest, the fiscal interrogated anyone he thought might have witnessed or participated in the Minje Mama dance. He

was troubled not so much by enslaved people's use of obeah but by the exceptional nature of what had happened on Op Hoop van Beter. As even the fiscal
knew, obeah did not ordinarily kill. Who was responsible for Madalon's
death, and why? How had an alleged obeah practitioner organized a violent,
collective divination and healing process without being discovered by plantation authorities? And why did other slaves cooperate with him? At one point
the fiscal questioned more than half a dozen enslaved people on the plantation itself, but, unfortunately for him, they had apparently "preconcerted and
agreed upon a certain statement, declaring their total ignorance of the subjects of inquiry." Eventually, however, several witnesses admitted that Madalon had died as a result of the Minje Mama dance and that Willem was, as
one man put it, "the cause of all the bad business."[84]

Many witnesses admitted that they had participated in the Minje Mama
dance but claimed that Willem and the drivers had coerced them. Willem
and the drivers, meanwhile, denied any knowledge of Madalon's death or the
Minje Mama dance. Willem told the fiscal that the only reason he went to Op
Hoop van Beter was "to see [his] wife Johanna" and that he had never organized the dance or practiced obeah.[85]

Willem could have pursued the strategy that Hans employed two years
earlier: admit to being a healer, distance his practice from "obeah," and try to
justify the rituals he organized. Hans told John Wray, who was able to speak
with him because he understood Berbice Dutch, that he saw himself as a
healer who provided badly needed services. He had, for example, administered ritual washings to pregnant women and children on multiple plantations (including Buses Lust, where Willem lived) to prevent the women from
miscarrying and the children from dying. "A Congo," Hans learned to heal in
his "own country," where his abilities set him apart. "Every one there is not
gifted with this power, but only a few which comes from God," he explained.
According to Wray, Hans had been "instructed in the Roman Catholic Religion" in Central Africa, where Portuguese missionaries had been converting
people for centuries. Hans "told me," Wray wrote, "that he always prayed to
God to bless the means he used for the recovery of people [and] that his act
consisted of doing good. I asked him to let me hear him pray in the African
language. He kneeled down and addressed God in his country name. When
concluding his prayer he made use of the name of Mary and Jesus Christ and
then made a cross on the ground with his fingers." Among Hans's powers was
the ability to locate poison: "If I go to any house where poison is hid I can
discover it from the smell."[86]

Hans insisted that he never used his powers to harm others, even whites. "Numerous applications have been made to me [to harm whites] but I have always rejected them. These applications," Hans claimed, "have been made to me by Negroes who have bad masters to cool their hearts—that is no part of my knowledge." Conscious of the stigma attached to the term obeah, Hans told Wray that he was "no Obiah man and [did] nothing that is bad." "All my Art," he explained, "consists in helping negroes that are sick."[87]

Willem, unlike Hans, denied being any sort of healer or spiritual authority. His only strategy of defense was to emphasize the fact that no one had found Madalon's body. Willem "denie[d] the whole of the circumstance; and in order to prove the whole is lie, he wishe[d] that the people should be taken to the estate, and made to point out where the body is buried."[88] Willem knew, of course, that Madalon's submerged remains would have been all but impossible to find.

After hearing testimony from more than a dozen witnesses, the fiscal aggressively prosecuted Willem and the people who assisted him, particularly the drivers. He was primarily concerned with the drivers' submission to an obeah practitioner—an illegitimate and dangerous authority in the fiscal's eyes—and with subversion of the plantation hierarchy. "Such conduct on the part of drivers having the charge of slaves," the fiscal explained, "cannot be tolerated, but on the contrary ought to be severely punished."[89]

The fiscal argued that Kees, the *logie* driver, should be taken to the plantation to "stand with a rope round his neck fastened to the mangoe-tree under which the woman Madalon was suspended," and then flogged "at the discretion of the honourable Court, and afterwards worked in chains . . . for the period of seven years." Kees begged for mercy on the grounds that he was "but a boy, and [had] only lately" been appointed as a driver. Young and inexperienced, he "had not the authority" to stand up to Willem, he argued (he was actually in his late twenties). He also claimed that because he did not "go to the field with the people" he had "no authority over them." Moreover, Kees added, "if not ordered by Willem, who also flogged me, I should not have beat the woman."[90] Unconvinced, the court sentenced Kees to one hundred lashes under the mango tree.[91]

Primo and Mey deserved more severe punishments, the fiscal argued, because they were the lead drivers, the men responsible for day-to-day discipline and order and the manager's most trusted slaves. In welcoming an obeah practitioner to their plantation, presiding over clandestine rituals, and covering up Madalon's death, they had done the exact opposite of what

drivers were supposed to do. The fiscal chastised them for "subjecting themselves (the drivers), in the presence of the gang of negroes over which they
were placed, to the implicit obedience of the orders and commands of . . .
Willem." They had failed to maintain "the authority confided to them, by enforcing due subordination on the estate" and had allowed the Minje Mama
dance to be performed despite its prohibition. The real crime, the fiscal implied, was not Madalon's murder but their failure to challenge Willem and
faithfully represent the plantation owner's interests. This was the same logic
the fiscal used when he prosecuted the head driver January in the case of
Hans. If January suspected "that any evil disposed person did reside" on
Demtichem, "it was his bounded duty to represent the same to his employer."
January's "offence"—collaborating with an obeah practitioner—"would be
rightly censured & severely punished if committed by any individual negro."
But in this case, it was "consequently far more deserving of the utmost rigour
of the law" because it had been "committed by the Head driver of [the] Estate,
in whom great trust & confidence is placed." As for Primo and Mey, the court
agreed that their actions were tantamount to treason and gave both a brutal
sentence: three hundred lashes each. They were also to be "brand-marked,
and degraded as drivers, afterwards to be worked in chains" for a year.[92]

Willem stood accused of murdering Madalon. Her death was only the
symptom of a larger problem, however: Willem's usurpation of planter authority, based on his ability to persuade people to acknowledge his authority and
obey his orders. The fiscal accused him "of treasonable practices, by deluding
the minds of the negroes belonging to plantation Op Hoop van Beter . . . from
their obedience to the laws of the land, and their proprietors, by instituting
and causing to be danced . . . the Minje Mama dance." Equally reprehensible
was the fact that Willem "proceeded to inflict corporal punishment on several
of the negroes, and even on the drivers of said estate, thereby confirming in the
minds of the gang his . . . extent of power." He had, in effect, acted more like a
master than a slave, fashioning himself as an authority and challenging the
plantocracy's monopoly on physical force. Willem had "used every means to
influence the minds of the gang on plantation Op Hoop van Beter, in the belief
of his possessing supernatural power," and had "taken it upon himself to rec-
tify abuses, presuming to judge and prescribe punishments." Because "the
power of taking away life is confided solely to regular constituted authorities;
and . . . all attempts to assert such power by any individual can only tend to the
subversion of all rule and subordination," the fiscal reasoned, Willem's crimes
needed to be punished with the utmost severity.[93] Colonials, Africans, and

African-descended people had different attitudes toward obeah, but they all recognized its political power and the potential dangers its practitioners posed—both to their bodies and to the plantation system itself.

On January 14, 1822—more than five months after Madalon had been killed—a unanimous court found Willem guilty of murder and of "dancing, or causing to be danced . . . the Minje or Water Mama dance."[94] It issued a sentence severe enough, it hoped, that in future people would think twice about practicing obeah. Willem was to be removed from the New Amsterdam jail where he had been confined for the previous four months and taken upriver to Op Hoop van Beter. There he would be "delivered into the hands of the public executioner, and in the presence of this Court . . . be hung by the neck on the Mangoe tree under which the negress Madalon was suspended during her aforesaid punishment, until . . . dead." Afterward Willem was to have "his head . . . severed from his body, and stuck on a pole . . . there to remain until destroyed by the elements, or birds of prey."[95] This gruesome execution and decapitation—standard practice for leaders of slave rebellions in the Caribbean—were designed to do more than punish Willem. In British legal tradition, such aggravated capital punishments were reserved for traitors.[96] Willem was thus marked not merely as a murderer or a practitioner of an outlawed spiritual practice, but as a rebel, a man who had used an illegitimate source of power to subvert the social hierarchy and gain political power over the slaves of Op Hoop van Beter.[97] Slaveholders and colonial authorities hoped this "spiritual terror" and "symbolics of mutilation" would send a clear message to other slaves: this is what happens when you break our laws and challenge our authority.[98] Willem's decapitated body would be buried under the same mango tree, an effort to reclaim the space for the plantation regime and to imprint a haunted memory of violence and terror on the landscape.[99]

Four days after Willem's conviction, the fiscal and other officials accompanied Willem and the other prisoners to the plantation to witness the spectacle. According to John Wray, "the scene on the Estate was most solemn. The Governor, the Fiscal, and all the Members of the Court were present—also the Militia, and 400 or 500 Negroes and a great number of White people." After Willem listened to his sentence, Wray recalled, he "walked firmly to the Tree, and told the Executioner to fasten the rope well." Willem "walked up the Ladder," and Wray "offered up an earnest prayer." A moment later, Willem "was launched into an awful Eternity."[100]

Here was the irony of the Minje Mama dance, a healing ritual meant to

Figure 9. Executed slaves. *Five of the culprits in chains, as they appeared on the 20th of September, 1823*, engraving by Joshua Bryant, in *Account of an Insurrection of the Negro Slaves in the colony of Demerara, Which Broke Out on the 18th of August, 1823* (Georgetown, Demerara: A. Stevenson, 1824), fold-out plate 12; following p. 88. This engraving depicts two phases in the capital punishment of three men convicted of participating in the 1823 rebellion in Demerara. Like the corpses of the men seen here, Willem was sentenced to be hanged and then decapitated. His severed head was then placed on a post in a prominent place to terrorize other slaves and deter them from disobeying colonial authorities. Such spectacular punishments were common in the British Caribbean, where enslaved people who subverted the plantation regime were marked not only as criminals but as traitors. Courtesy of the John Carter Brown Library at Brown University.

"set the estate to rights" that instead led to the violent and public deaths of two enslaved people—one beaten to death by an obeah practitioner and his accomplices, the other executed and mutilated by order of colonial officials. The spiritual powers enslaved people relied on to protect and heal them could just as easily endanger them, especially when practitioners like Willem abused their authority, deviated from community expectations, or failed.

Alongside the largely unseen spiritual forces that tied enslaved people together and also brought them into conflict were much more tangible things—food and property, money and land—that were just as important to their everyday struggle for survival. And like the unwritten rules that governed spiritual healing, those that regulated enslaved people's economic relationships with their enslavers and one another were complex and frequently contested.

CHAPTER 6

The Moral Economy of Survival

In May 1819, the enslaved people on one of the coffee plantations along the Berbice River gathered for an annual ritual. Consistent with the custom of the colony, the overseer distributed a mix of items during the Whitsunday holidays, a rare period of rest and celebration for enslaved people and a time of year when they expected basic necessities and small luxuries. The overseer laid out beef, "stockfish," barley, tobacco and pipes, salt, and a coarse fabric known as osnaburgs used to make clothing—about four yards for the men, a bit more for the women, and even more for the "house people." But rather than graciously accepting what their overseer saw as generous gifts, the enslaved people rejected the allowances as insufficient. The clothing in particular was less than they had come to expect, and, they claimed, less than they needed.[1]

An enslaved African man named August was the first to protest his allowance. According to his owner, A. J. Glasius, when it was August's turn to take his allowance, he picked up the fabric, examined it briefly, and then "exclaimed, 'Is this the osnaburgs we are to receive?'" confronting the overseer. "I will not have it," August declared. His defiance started a wave of protest, as other people refused their allowance, too. Glasius ordered the drivers and overseer to apprehend August before the protest escalated. But August "cried out, 'Come, my lads, let us be off.'" Twenty-five other people followed him "off the estate towards the back," only returning after nightfall.[2]

Testimony gathered by the fiscal, who investigated after Glasius complained to him, revealed that August and the other "ringleaders" were fed up with an owner who had long violated their hard-won customary rights, especially their right to receive the basic necessities to survive. As Conraad, one of the first to follow August's lead, explained, "they have had no clothing for years, and therefore seeing the quantity of three ells [a bit less than four yards] put out for them last Sunday after so many years disappointment, he with others had refused to take the osnaburgs." Jenny "refused to take the five ells of osnaburgs because it was not sufficient for a coat." Another man told the fiscal "he took his osnaburgs, but seeing his mattys [friends or work-mates] refuse to take it, he threw it down also." In the end, their bold protest backfired: August and Conraad were flogged on the fiscal's orders for having "create[d] much uneasiness, and evince[d] a spirit of disobedience which ought to be checked, to prevent a recurrence of such conduct."[3]

The protest August sparked was one battle in a much larger war that enslaved people throughout the West Indies had been fighting for centuries. Even under the desperate conditions of Caribbean slavery, or perhaps because of them, enslaved people came to believe that they had certain basic rights that they were entitled to assert. Not unlike peasants or other laborers in non-slave societies, they set limits on the amount of exploitation their enslavers could get away with and demanded various concessions from those who profited from their labor, including the right to subsistence. They also claimed the right to control and trade certain kinds of property on their own. Taken together, enslaved people's customary economic rights were part of a fragile moral economy—a bundle of constantly renegotiated, unwritten rules about economic fairness and material welfare—that was increasingly supported by statute law and enforced through litigation during the era of amelioration.[4]

In nineteenth-century Berbice, enslaved people claimed three broad economic rights. First, and most essential, was the right to be provided with sufficient quantities of basic necessities like clothing and especially food—a claim to subsistence. They also fought to control private property such as small livestock and produce, and to access the land they needed to raise their own animals and crops. Finally, enslaved people claimed the right to make and enforce bargains—to exchange goods and small sums of cash, barter services for payment, and claim damages for stolen or destroyed property—with other slaves and free colonists. Defending these rights was central to enslaved people's struggle for survival.

Until the early nineteenth century, such rights rested on custom rather than law and, therefore, were inherently fragile. Enslaved people had negotiated, bargained, and fought to establish and defend them for generations, but they faced resistance at every turn from slaveowners and others who tried to limit the claims they could make.[5] During the era of amelioration, however, customary rights—or privileges, as enslavers preferred to see them—were placed on a more solid footing. New laws enacted during amelioration recognized and codified the customary obligations of enslaved laborers and their enslavers, thereby providing enslaved people new ground for protecting their rights.

Even during amelioration, however, enslaved people's rights were constantly under threat. Slaveowners, managers, and overseers scrimped on allowances or withheld them as punishment, trying to reduce their obligation to provide subsistence. Enslaved people also had to contend with plantation authorities and other slaves who stole their possessions and refused to recognize property claims. Colonists refused to settle their debts, and slaveowners failed to pay slaves for work in excess of customary limits. What options did enslaved people have, in such situations, for securing their rights? If slavery was always a negotiated relationship, what did the process of negotiation look like during the era of amelioration?

As August's protest shows, direct confrontation with plantation authorities remained an option for securing customary rights, but it was a dangerous tactic. Collective bargaining and strikes could easily backfire. Another option, more dangerous still, was simply taking what one felt entitled to—an action that could be severely punished. Therefore, many enslaved people instead went to colonial officials to protest violations of their economic rights, taking advantage of the fact that the laws of amelioration were designed, in part, to codify some of the very economic rights that they had long fought for, such as the right to receive enough food and clothing, or protect private property. The process of lodging a complaint, moreover, was itself a tactic for establishing and securing rights. And as administrators of imperial policy, the fiscal and protector of slaves were charged with enforcing laws designed to guarantee slaves a minimum standard of treatment and encourage them to be industrious (the "savings bank" for slaves established by the colonial government is a particularly striking example of policy makers' belief in the virtue of extending private property rights to enslaved people).[6] Such overlap between the priorities of colonial officials and those of enslaved people themselves made it much easier to defend certain economic rights.

At the same time, the claims enslaved people made—and especially their appeals to the fiscal or protector of slaves—also pushed amelioration farther than it was intended to go. In particular, by asserting the right to negotiate market relations much like free people were empowered to do, slaves claimed a measure of economic independence and legal standing that their enslavers had long tried to prevent them from attaining. The impact of enslaved people's grassroots activism on amelioration policy was made clear when the Colonial Office passed a "Small Debt Enactment," just three years after the 1826 slave code, in response to enslaved people's efforts to collect payment.

Understanding enslaved people's always-contested claims to "fair" economic treatment shows how enslaved laborers, white plantation authorities, and other free people negotiated their multiple relationships as employers and workers, producers and consumers, in an especially brutal and impoverished society during the final years of slavery. In asserting their rights through hardscrabble negotiation and legal activism, enslaved people fought to improve their material conditions while also leveraging the power of the colonial government to challenge what it meant legally and customarily to be enslaved. Although most enslaved people in Berbice would not escape slavery until they died, in their day-to-day struggles to limit their economic exploitation and especially to access the material goods they needed to survive, they helped shape the world of Atlantic slavery.

A Reasonable Allowance

Slaveowners were expected to provide enslaved people the basic necessities needed to survive, including clothing and food. In Berbice, this customary obligation to provide enslaved people's subsistence was made explicit in the 1826 slave code, which stipulated that slaves were to receive "a reasonable weekly allowance, according to the custom of the colony and as may be best obtained."[7] The right to receive enough food to stay alive, however, was one that routinely brought enslaved people and their enslavers into conflict, before and after the 1826 reforms.

When allowances of food (or clothing) fell below what enslaved people expected or claimed they deserved, they felt aggrieved. Sometimes they went so far as to openly protest, engaging in a range of individual and collective labor actions much like industrial workers who were dissatisfied with the wages they received.[8] Their options, however, were limited, and every strategy they used to pressure overseers, managers, and owners to provide them the material goods they were entitled to came with its own risks. Slaves could try negotiating with white plantation authorities directly, as the slaves on Recumzigt who withheld their labor had done. If that did not work, they could travel to New Amsterdam and lay their case before the fiscal or protector of slaves, hoping for a sympathetic hearing. A third option was both the simplest and most dangerous: taking the food they felt they deserved.

Underlying all of these actions was the notion that the customary and in some cases legal rules governing enslaved people's relationships with their enslavers—what historian Emília Viotti da Costa called the "unspoken contract"—had been violated.[9] Enslaved people framed their claims in terms of reciprocal obligations and responsibilities: if they fulfilled their duties—to show deference, to be obedient, and most importantly to work—then the people who profited from their labor had a responsibility to provide for their material welfare. In essence, slaves demanded payment in kind for their labor. When possible, they also made claims based on the colony's laws. This was particularly true of that most basic necessity: food.

According to the fiscal, the customary weekly allowance for adult slaves in 1826 was two bunches of plantains—the staple energy source for Berbician slaves—or seven to nine pounds of another starch (rice, corn flour, or wheat flour).[10] Enslaved people were also customarily entitled to two pounds of salt fish (dried cod)—a crucial source of protein in an otherwise starchy, monotonous diet.[11] Supplying slaves with food was an obligation most owners accepted, at least in the abstract, out of self-interest. There was a limit beyond which they could not starve people and still expect them to live, let alone work. Disputes over allowances thus usually revolved around the specific quantity and quality of food and, in some cases, whether slaves had forfeited their right to their allowance for negligence or some other reason. In practice, there was often a large gap between enslavers' and slaves' definitions of just what constituted "a reasonable weekly allowance."

Some enslaved people who felt shortchanged directly confronted plantation authorities. Such was the case with ten men from plantation Niew Vigilantie, who in January 1825 claimed they had not received the quantity of rations they deserved at Christmas, an important holiday for slaves and a rare period of rest and celebration.[12] After Christmas they refused to return to work, in part because they felt entitled to "a day of rest" after celebrating. "This is our day," they declared, "it is not a day of work." They underscored their dissatisfaction by leaving to "walk on neighboring plantations." When they returned, the attorney-manager tried to put them in the stocks, but they resisted, and "made use of the most insolent and abusive language," he said.[13]

The next day the three "ringleaders" led a delegation to the fiscal's office, where they defended their protest as a reasonable response to an attorney-manager who did not reward their efforts as custom dictated. As one of the men explained, they had "been in the habit of drinking before the door on Holidays," when they generally received about twelve flasks of rum. But this Christmas, they claimed, the attorney-manager reduced the quantity of rum and food that he distributed. They had done nothing to deserve this reduction. "We are a large gang and good people we worked well and therefore on Holidays we reasonably expect to enjoy ourselves & get a good supply of Rum, Fish, & Pork." But they had only received "a piece of salt fish & a small Piece of Pork and a head of Tobacco."[14] This rhetorical strategy—portraying themselves as obedient workers wronged by a miserly master—was one that many complainants used. A man from plantation Goedland, for instance, began an April 1827 complaint to the protector by stating, "from the time my master bought me, I have always tried to please him as much as possible." But his owner did not reciprocate: two months earlier he had ordered the men on Goedland to work "on *our* Sunday," promising to pay them a guilder each, as custom dictated, but he never paid them anything. Moreover, they "never get any allowance of clothes."[15]

Despite their best effort, the people from Niew Vigilantie failed to convince the fiscal, probably because the attorney-manager produced a detailed account of the generous rations he claimed to have distributed on Christmas Eve. The fiscal, satisfied that the people on Niew Vigilantie were sufficiently rewarded for their labor, concluded their "conduct . . . was reprehensible, & their complaint ungrounded." It was his "duty," he reasoned, "to inflict punishment on them," an outcome that illustrates the obstacles enslaved people faced in securing their customary rights.[16]

As the Niew Vigilantie case also shows, when direct negotiations between enslaved workers and plantation management broke down, slaves sometimes went to colonial officials. And some of them succeeded in leveraging the power of the fiscal or protector to obtain the food they demanded. Even when their complaints failed to produce any tangible change, moreover, they were powerful rebukes of managerial authority and reminders that enslaved people were willing to use the colonial legal system to secure their rights. The fiscal and protector, interested in mediating disputes with an eye toward compromises that promoted order and stability, therefore played a crucial role in establishing and clarifying the rights slaves could claim.

In September 1832, two men from La Fraternite coffee estate succeeded where the Niew Vigilantie complainants had failed. Hendrik, a Berbice-born slave in his early twenties, and Figo, an African man with "country marks" on his face and arms who was nearly forty years old, complained to the protector that they had not received "their grog as usual." When they brought this to the attention of the manager, moreover, he locked them "in the darkroom." They emphasized that this was a deviation from custom (both had lived on the estate for more than a decade), and that their manager had not kept his word. The manager had told them Saturday night, when they normally received their rum, that he would distribute it the following morning. So when Sunday came, Figo and Hendrik "went to cut firewood & grass, which is the custom on the Estate to bring to the Manager, before the weekly allowance is given out." But when some people did not bring wood or grass, or "did not come so soon," the manager decided that everyone "should have no rum at all" as punishment. Figo and Hendrik refused to pay the price for other people's negligence. Having completed their task, they expected the customary reward. They "abused" the manager, according to the driver, "and made a great disturbance in the yard." For being "very insolent," the manager explained, "they were punished."[17]

The protector dismissed Figo and Hendrik's complaint, which might have otherwise been upheld, because they were "insolent." He reminded them "it was their duty to be civil and obedient to those placed in authority over them." But he also chastised the manager for "having stopt the rum of those who brought home what was required of them," since "it was giving but poor encouragement to those who were willing to work to place them on a footing with those of an opposite disposition"—an admission that Figo and Hendrik's demand was not so unmerited after all, even if their means of protest was unacceptable.[18]

Nearly a decade earlier, seven women from plantation Prospect—all African field laborers—had similarly gone to the fiscal after negotiations with their overseer and manager failed. Their grievances were many: they were overworked, they did not have enough time to eat, they were "too much punished," and they never received their allowance. And while the attorney or owner regularly sent plenty of plantains, tobacco, and other items, they never received them, presumably because the manager hoarded or sold the provisions. Going to the fiscal was a last resort. When "the men" complained to the owner some time earlier, they were flogged. The women portrayed themselves as loyal slaves who were "badly treated, which ma[de] them come to complain instead of going in the bush"—running away.[19] The mere mention of "going in the bush," however, was also an implicit threat that if they could not get redress through the formal complaint they would run away and withdraw their labor, a relatively common strategy for enslaved people in Berbice and elsewhere commonly known as *petit marronage*.[20] Whether the threat worked in this case is unknown, since the fiscal did not record his decision, but the complaint shows that enslaved people believed that invoking a manager's violation of the moral economy was one way they might improve their living conditions, however marginally.[21]

Other cases indicate that colonial officials found it unacceptable for enslavers to withhold food, even as punishment. Take, for instance, a complaint lodged by a woodcutter named Klaas against his owner, J. V. Mittleholzer, in January 1823. Klaas told the fiscal that in November 1822 Mittleholzer sent him and others "in the bush to square wood"—lonely, brutal work—under a driver's supervision. Mittleholzer gave them "two bunches of plantains and a little salt-fish for each man." But a month later, when he went to check their progress, he was upset "that they had not done as much work as they ought to." So Mittleholzer left them in the bush without additional rations and ordered the driver to keep them there through Christmas if they did not finish their work. Klaas and the other woodcutters "remained in the bush until the holidays were over, without any thing to eat."[22]

After Christmas, Klaas and the others "all agreed to go home, and went to their master, and asked him what was the reason he kept them in the bush without anything to eat, and without giving them their holidays." Mittleholzer ignored them, and when the driver "asked him to give something to eat for the negroes; for they had nothing," Mittleholzer claimed he had "nothing to give them." So Klaas decided to "seek redress" with the fiscal, who ruled in Klaas's favor. Mittleholzer "had acted incorrectly," he explained, "in keeping the negroes in the woods during the holidays" without food. "If they had neglected their work," the fiscal reasoned, Mittleholzer "should have punished them in some other way." He also threatened that if any of Mittleholzer's slaves "again complained of not receiving their regular rations he would be fined."[23]

Bristol, "an elderly and sickly man" who lived on plantation New Forest, also found appealing to the fiscal could be an effective means of securing his allowance. In June 1822 Bristol complained that his manager had withheld his rations for several weeks to punish him. Bristol claimed, moreover, "the manager never found fault with him" until the previous week, when he told Bristol "that he should get a good flogging." Bristol had "done nothing wrong," he insisted, so he refused to submit to the whipping. But when he went for his allowance on Sunday, the manager was still determined to punish him. "So, boy," the manager told him, "you did not come in on Friday to get flogged but you come to-day for your rations." The manager withheld Bristol's allowance, and when Bristol demanded it again the next day the manager called a driver to flog him. "I don't know what kind of work you do," the manager told Bristol, "that you come here to claim your allowance." Unable to get his rations for several weeks, even after he went to the plantation attorney, Bristol "made [his] escape to town" to see the fiscal.[24]

The manager and driver, when questioned by the fiscal, claimed the right to withhold Bristol's allowance as punishment. Bristol had "neglected the light duty assigned to him," and refused to submit to the lash. Worse still, Bristol had run away for two days, and "on Sunday morning, when the gang were receiving their allowance, he made his appearance, and demanded his." Nevertheless, the fiscal ordered the manager to give Bristol his allowance and "warned [Bristol] to be more attentive in future to his duty."[25]

Clothing was also a part of the plantation's moral economy, as the following complaint from a group of men on the Foulis sugar plantation in May 1822 illustrates. Quashy, who spoke for the group, began by emphasizing how patiently they had endured years of harsh treatment—including shifts of up to twenty hours in the boiling house—without complaining or rebelling. They had "suffered this for many years, but at present . . . cannot suffer it any longer." The time had come to "declare before his Honor the Fiscal the way they are treated and clothed by their owner." Their chief complaint concerned the quantity and quality of food and clothing their owner, William Munro, provided. They claimed that "before Dr. Munro went home [to England], four years ago, he gave them a round jacket for their clothing; and since that time until today they never received anything else." Their food was also inadequate. They only received "a small bunch of plantains" each week, and never "any salt fish," a source of much needed protein.[26]

The acting fiscal, accompanied by a burgher officer, traveled some twenty-five miles to Foulis, on Berbice's western Atlantic coast, to investigate, underscoring the seriousness with which colonial officials sometimes handled complaints of material neglect. They dismissed many of the slaves' complaints but found that "some irregularities were certainly chargeable against the overseers for not personally attending to see the allowance dealt out to the gang at a proper time, and in a proper manner." As a result, "they were according[ly] admonished." The acting fiscal also gave Munro "a copy of the ordinance respecting the clothing and feeding of negroes" along with a warning "that penalties would be rigidly enforced if the enactments were not strictly complied with." But this victory came at a price: "two of the complainants, who it was proved, were guilty of insolence and disobedience of orders, were punished in presence of the whole gang."[27]

As with food, there was no general agreement as to how much or what type of clothing enslaved people were entitled to. The 1826 slave code, for example, only stipulated that every owner or manager "shall provide such slave or slaves with proper clothing according to the custom of the colony," a standard as difficult to enforce as it was vague.[28] The most generous owners gave male field laborers (as opposed to drivers and artisans) about thirteen ells of cloth and a jacket, and female field laborers about eleven ells and a jacket. Less generous owners gave men two "laps" (loincloths) and a jacket and women a wrapper and two petticoats.[29] Clothing regulations were so vague, however, that as late as 1830 the deputy protector of slaves observed that "the consequence is that scarcely two Estates, if they belong to different proprietors, receive the same" allowance. There was, he conceded, "much difficulty in arriving at any degree of accuracy on this subject."[30]

The other consequence of not having a more specific requirement was that the quality and quantity of clothing slaves expected were worked out over years of negotiation and compromise. Customary entitlements were inherently unstable and subject to continual renegotiation. Some enslaved people looked to their neighbors, or to people who belonged to the same owner but lived on other plantations, when determining the amount of clothing they thought they could demand. Seven people from the cotton plantation Rosehall, for example, told the fiscal that they were unhappy with their allowance—"a small blue salempores cap, a jacket, a blanket, and a hat"—because the people on estate "No. 1, belonging to the same proprietor, had checks and osnaburgs added to their allowance." The owner had apparently provided them, but "the manager disposed of the same for his private use and benefit."[31]

When owners or managers withheld clothing or gave enslaved people less than they had come to expect, turning to the fiscal or protector could be an effective means of protest. In June 1830, twenty-five enslaved people from plantation Waterloo—a group large enough to signal collective support and get officials' attention—complained to the protector that they had not received clothing for a year. They also said that their mistress, who had hired them out against their wishes to a distant plantation on the Corantine Coast, had "told them that their clothing was on board the schooner that was to convey them to Corantine, which they did not believe." The deputy protector said he was powerless to prevent their owner from uprooting them, but promised to intervene if she did not supply the clothing. "If they . . . experienced any injustice," moreover, they were welcome "to come to Town & inform him of it."[32]

Juno, an enslaved woman who lived in New Amsterdam, complained in July 1833 that "neither she nor her children receive any regular allowance of food or clothing from their owner." They "had received a few things but not to the extent directed by Law," a claim that displayed her familiarity with the colony's slave code. Juno's owner claimed Juno and her children had "been fed from his own table and they never complained to him of want of food," but he admitted "that they had not been supplied with clothing as specified in the Law." The acting protector therefore ruled that he was required to distribute double the amount of clothing as specified by law. He also told Juno and her children "what they were entitled to, and desired if they did not receive it, to return to his office."[33] Successes such as these must have increased enslaved people's confidence in claiming customary entitlements.

A woodcutter named John complained in January 1834 "that his owner does not supply him with the lawful quantity of provisions or clothing." John was specific: "last year he only received a jacket, a hat, 1 Ell of Osnaburg, & 1 pair of trowsers." He also showed the protector a canister used to measure cornmeal rations. John's manager said he had given John "1 lined jacket, 1 hat, 1 razor, 2 yards Osnaburg, [and] 1 pair trowsers." The protector dismissed the complaint about the lack of food, since "the ten canisters of cornmeal [John said he received] were found to contain more than the law directed," but upheld the charge of insufficient clothing. John's manager was fined and "directed to give [John] twice the quantity prescribed by Law."[34] For every person like John or Juno, who turned to colonial officials to claim the goods they were entitled to, there were undoubtedly many more who used the possibility of making a formal complaint as leverage in their undocumented negotiations with plantation management.

Though colonial officials could be powerful allies in enslaved people's battle to secure badly needed food and clothing, slaves sometimes took a more direct—and more dangerous—route: taking what they wanted or needed. To colonial authorities, these were indefensible thefts, and plantation punishment record books are full of accounts of slaves punished for "offences" such as "sheep, hog, and poultry stealing" and "killing and destroying stock." But reducing such actions to "stealing" adopts the slaveowner's point of view and fails to account for enslaved people's moral reasoning for taking basic necessities. For enslaved people, who were chronically malnourished and poor, there was nothing unethical about taking things from the people who forced them to work without pay, especially when it came to food.[35] As observers like British traveler George Pinckard noted, enslaved people who "robb[ed] their masters" did "not even consider this a theft, as is too evident by an expression very common among them, viz. *'Me no tief him: me take him from Massa.'*"[36] Therefore "thefts," as colonial authorities saw them, are better viewed as political acts designed to redistribute the profits of plantation labor and compensate enslaved people for their work. Enslaved people's own explanations for taking plantation produce reveal their notions of economic fairness and politics of survival.

When an enslaved woman named Peggy from plantation Port Mourant was locked in the stocks for allegedly having taken plantains without permission, she went to the protector in protest. Peggy explained that taking the plantains was a response to hunger brought on by insufficient rations. She "only gets one calabash of rice a week," she said, "which is not sufficient." So Peggy "and others planted a few plantain trees on the dam" to supplement their allowance, only to be put in the stocks when they "went to cut a few branches for their own use." The manager, however, claimed that Peggy and the others received plenty of "American Corn meal & rice," and that the plantains they took "were stolen out of the Estate's plantain walk and taken by main force from the watchman after maltreating him and not out of their own provision grounds." Siding with the manager, the acting protector dismissed Peggy's complaint.[37]

When Jupiter, an enslaved African field laborer in his mid-forties on the sugar plantation Mary's Hope, was whipped for taking plantains from one of the estate's "walks," he was also adamant that he had "been flogged by the Manager for nothing." He was hungry and had only taken a bit of food he desperately needed. "I did not think there was any harm in so doing," he declared. The manager, however, told the fiscal that the plantain walks were off-limits because they were recently replanted and needed time to mature. Jupiter was, moreover, "a very worthless character." The fiscal, unconvinced by Jupiter's justification, agreed with the manager that "the crime of theft should be punished."[38]

In rare cases, however, enslaved people actually persuaded officials that taking food was justified. On plantation Goldenfleece in February 1825, for instance, Prudence and her husband grew tired of "seeing the[ir] child grow thin" as a result of the "scanty allowance" the manager provided. So they resolved to steal some plantains one night. But the watchman caught them and told the manager, who ordered Prudence's husband locked up at night for four weeks. Even the watchman, according to Prudence, recognized the root cause of what was apparently an ongoing problem: "the watchman . . . said Massa if you give the creoles [children] each their allowance you would put a stop to this." The manager still did not increase the amount of food he provided, so Prudence escalated her protest. She took the small bunch of plantains she received as her weekly allowance and dropped them at the manager's door, and then refused to go to the field. If she could not get the amount of food she needed, she would not work. The manager then ordered two men to flog her "with a cow skin." As soon as Prudence was "let loose," she traveled nearly thirty miles to the fiscal's office, having determined that she could not secure the resources her family needed alone. She noted that she had never complained before but was "now under the necessity" of doing so to ensure her family's survival. She had given birth to ten children, but five of them had already died, and she was not willing to bury any more children. After a lengthy investigation and hearing the manager's testimony, the fiscal upheld Prudence's complaint. He also recommended that the manager increase the allowances, and the manager agreed.[39]

Many enslaved complainants, like Prudence, asserted their right to be supplied with regular rations of clothing and food—the bare minimum their enslavers owed them in exchange for their labor. Rations were especially important in colonies like Berbice, where enslaved people depended on them as their primary means of subsistence, and when white plantation authorities did not honor their customary obligations, enslaved people protested.[40] Some negotiated with plantation officials directly. Others simply appropriated what they wanted or needed. And sometimes they sought help from the protector and fiscal, knowing that the law supported some of their customary entitlements. Every strategy was fraught with its own dangers, however, and disputes over allowances were only one part of a broader battle for economic fairness, material welfare, and survival.

To Acquire, Hold, and Enjoy Property

In July 1832, an enslaved man named Jacob, in his early forties though years of brutal work made him look over sixty, complained to the protector that his manager searched his house without permission. While Jacob was out cutting wood, the manager had gone to his house, "opened his packall [basket], and took . . . a bottle of crab oil," a natural insect repellent. Upset that the manager had violated the privacy of a home that he considered his own and rifled through his possessions, Jacob went to the manager the next day and asked "the reason of opening & examining his packall."[41]

According to the manager, Jacob went to him "in a most insolent manner & demanded of him what right he had to open his packall." The manager said he saw Jacob's housemate "putting away something in haste, that he suspected it was rum and seeing a packall under the bed, it occurred to him that the rum might be secreted therein." When he saw that it was only crab oil, he had returned it before Jacob even came home. But Jacob remained angry. He told the manager, "Sir, you are not a Buckra [master] Gentleman," an insult made worse by the fact that it "was said before the gang," the manager noted. Jacob also declared that "it is no gentleman way to open negroes' packall." For this "extreme insolence," as the manager saw it, Jacob received twelve lashes.[42]

Jacob failed to convince the protector that he had been wronged. The protector ruled that "Jacob deserved correction for his Insolence."[43] Yet his complaint nevertheless suggests other important economic rights that enslaved people in Berbice claimed in addition to their right to be provided with food and clothing by their enslavers. Jacob's grievance may have been primarily about the manager's intrusion into his personal space, but his anger at the search and seizure of his crab oil—however temporary—illustrates slaves' determination to assert their right to accumulate, control, and use various material items without interference. Despite being treated like property themselves, there were certain things that enslaved people believed belonged to them and no one else. Fiercely guarding these items, whether a bottle of crab oil, a chicken, or a pair of pants, was a way of claiming a measure of economic and social autonomy. More importantly, it was also a pragmatic survival strategy in a society where poverty was the norm and where opportunities to accumulate material goods were rare. Enslaved people therefore fought to establish and protect their rights to raise crops and animals, to sell and exchange their produce, and to prevent other people—including managers, owners, and other slaves—from taking or destroying the things they claimed.

By 1826, the colonial government had officially recognized enslaved people's hard-won right "to acquire, hold, and enjoy property free from controul." It was the "usage of this colony," according to the law's framers, and it was "expedient that the said custom should be recognized and as far as need be established by law." Unlike the U.S. South, where property ownership among enslaved people was widespread but not legally recognized, after 1826 slaves in Berbice slaves could use the law to protect their property.[44] Enslaved people could own a wide variety of things, including "lands . . . , money, cattle, implements, or utensils of husbandry, or household furniture." The only excluded items were boats, "fire arms, [and] ammunition"—prohibitions designed to limit enslaved people's mobility and reduce the possibility of armed resistance—and "such colonial produce as is prohibited to be sold or bartered by the existing law," a clause meant to prevent enslaved people from competing with slaveowners in selling export crops and make slaves' possession of such crops prima facie evidence of theft.[45]

Among the most important things enslaved people claimed the right to use, if not own outright, were provision grounds. These plots of land were generally smaller in Berbice than in many other large Caribbean colonies, such as Jamaica, where slaves were expected to subsist solely or primarily on their own produce instead of on planter-provided rations. In Berbice, protecting low-lying land from flooding was time and labor intensive, so planters devoted almost all the land they controlled to the cultivation of staple crops for export, preferring to provide enslaved people with weekly rations.[46] Nevertheless, provision grounds and garden plots were common sights in Berbice, and the items enslaved people cultivated on them—rice, corn, root crops such as yams and cassava, poultry, pigs, herbs, and various vegetables and fruits—served two crucial functions. First, they supplemented a diet that was monotonous and nutritionally deficient, potentially increasing slaves' health and chances of survival by providing much-needed nutrients and calories.[47] Second, exchanging foodstuffs and livestock, whether with one another, itinerant "hucksters," or at Sunday markets in town, offered a measure of economic autonomy.[48] Enslaved people in Berbice therefore had good reasons to defend their rights to access and cultivate their own land and to protect the crops and animals they raised, even if they were not "proto-peasants," like some other Caribbean slaves.[49]

Most managers granted enslaved people access to provision land, if not adequate time to cultivate it, so disputes usually hinged on particulars. Some disputes, moreover, suggest that the land slaves claimed held importance beyond its economic value. In January 1825 on plantation Augsburg, a coffee estate owned by the Lutheran church, an African field laborer in his mid-thirties named Baron complained that his manager denied him access to a provision ground inherited from his brother, who had left "his wife and two children under [Baron's] care." "This piece of ground," Baron told the fiscal, "was taken some time afterwards by another negro," Kees, which "caused a dispute between this negro and myself." The manager, however, decided that Kees could keep the land because Baron "had neglected to plant this ground" and only claimed it once "the produce of the ground was about ripe." He offered to give Baron another piece of land, but Baron objected, perhaps because for Baron the land had a cultural, as well as economic, value. Such intrafamily land transfers were, for many Africans and their descendants, crucial links to their ancestors, who were sometimes buried on provision grounds.[50] Baron and his wife continued to claim the ground as their own, stretching customary use rights into quasi-possession. Baron's wife was especially confrontational, according to the manager. "She not only continued to express her discontent," he said, "but spoke disrespectfully," and when he threatened, "you had better be quiet or you will have to sleep in the stocks," she became "more unruly," leading the manager to put her in the stocks. The fiscal, unfortunately for Baron, reinforced the manager's decision, sentencing Baron to thirty-nine lashes and dismissing his complaint.[51]

The right to use planation provision grounds was not itself a major point of contention between enslaved people and managers. It was, after all, a legal requirement (after 1826) that all plantations set aside land for provision grounds, and shifting the burden of subsistence to slaves also saved slaveowners money.[52] Far more common were complaints that enslaved people were unable to profitably use provision grounds because other people took their produce or livestock. Especially common were complaints that poultry or pigs had been stolen or slaughtered without permission or compensation.[53]

Two men from plantation Bestendigheid, artisans in their early fifties, lodged a complaint against their manager in 1821 for killing their hogs, likely the most valuable things they owned. One of the men alone had lost ten hogs. Worse still, the men claimed, the manager had refused to allow them to sell or exchange their hogs in town instead of slaughtering them. Complaining to the manager, however, only earned them confinement in the stocks, which explains why they went to the fiscal.[54]

Protecting one's property from managers, as the men from Bestendigheid knew, could be dangerous and difficult. In February 1819, a man named Bethune, a "Mandingo" in his mid-thirties, complained that his manager had taken his "Guinea-bird eggs." Bethune told the fiscal that the manager "broke the doors of the negro-house open in search of Guinea-bird eggs, which he said had been stolen from him." Like Jacob, Bethune resented the manager's intrusion into his personal dwelling. The manager thought the eggs at

Bethune's house were the ones that had been stolen—even though Bethune pointed out that "the eggs in his house were old and nearly hatched" whereas the missing eggs "were fresh lain ones"—so he confiscated them. The manager then had Bethune locked up for three nights before giving him fifty lashes.[55]

Two and a half years later, fifteen slaves from plantation Plegt Ankar faced a similar problem: their owner, John Quarles, routinely helped himself to the chickens and ducks they raised. As Mourant, an African field laborer who had "belonged to Quarles about 30 months," told the fiscal, "while the gang are at work in the field, Mr. Quarles goes to the negro-houses, and if he sees any fowls or ducks belonging to the negroes, he will take them and kill them for his dinner, and if the negroes speak about it, Mr. Quarles says the ground belongs to him, and not to the negroes." These constant thefts made it impossible, or at the very least, unprofitable, for the Plegt Ankar slaves to raise livestock. Their complaint was a rejection of Quarles's logic that everything on his plantation was ultimately his and that even as slaves they had economic claims that free people, including their enslavers, were obliged to respect.[56]

The acting fiscal, who traveled to Plegt Ankar to investigate, concluded that "the negroes were very hard-worked" and that Quarles "frequently kill[ed] their ducks and fowls without paying for them at the time he takes them." He agreed with the slaves that they had a right to protect their property and to be compensated for their losses. He also threatened Quarles "that if any more complaints were made against him by his negroes for such treatment, he would be criminally prosecuted," and ordered Quarles "to pay them the full value for any of their ducks or fowls that he had ordered to be killed."[57] This was a victory at once concrete and symbolic: the Plegt Ankar people were reimbursed for their stolen property and they also showed their owner that they had the wherewithal to use the legal system to uphold their rights.

Some of the most compelling evidence for the importance of provision grounds and other personal property comes from plantations Catharinasburg and Ithaca, where large numbers of slaves were to be removed and protested by striking. Such forced removals were not uncommon, since Berbice's economic decline left many slaveowners unable to pay their debts and resulted in sales of entire estates. When the people on Catharinasburg learned in November 1828 that their owner had mortgaged many of them and that they were to be sold, they were determined to avoid being uprooted—from one another, from their property, and from the very land they knew as home.

Their first strategy was to stage a symbolic exodus or walkout. On November 7, as the protector noted, "two hundred and twenty-six" people—a number guaranteed to cause alarm—"had retired from the estate into the bush, determined not to be sold separately."[58]

The protector accompanied the fiscal to Catharinasburg, at the governor's request, and his account of their investigation highlighted enslaved people's attachment to their plantation. They protested a move that would be socially and economically traumatic, and even the protector and fiscal recognized the hardships they would soon endure. They "regret[ted] that the [financial] embarrassments of their proprietor, had led to a separation from the other negroes of the estate and from the houses and gardens, to which they were naturally attached." But "wherever the British flag flew," the protector explained "its laws must be obeyed." He added, "if they were not disposed to come down with [the fiscal], willingly, he had the means of compelling him."[59]

The people on Catharinasburg emphasized the material losses they would suffer if they left, perhaps thinking this was their best strategy. According to the protector, they "admitted the necessity of obedience, [but] dwelt upon the hardship of their condition, with a sincerity to which every humane mind must have responded." When they were first sent to Catharinasburg, a plantation far from New Amsterdam, "it was felt by them as a banishment," but "time had reconciled them to a separation from every other part of the Colony." Moreover, "they had erected comfortable negro houses, and cultivated extensive provision fields," which "were now in bearing." They had, in short, "become a comfortable and contented negro community."[60]

The colonial government, however, had no authority to interfere. Mortgaging slaves and separating them from their homes, kin, and property were frowned on, but not illegal. So the protector and fiscal ordered the Catharinasburg people to prepare to leave. The slaves asked for two months, but the fiscal and protector refused to grant them more than a fortnight. When the departure day came, the protector and fiscal accompanied the slaves downriver, floating away from the plantation "amidst . . . the moanings and lamentations as well of the negroes that accompanied us, as those that remained on the estate."[61]

The protector of slaves, David Power, included in his report to the governor an account of the "strong impression . . . this scene left upon my mind" and a critique of the laws that allowed it. "I consider this forcible expulsion," he wrote, "by the inexorable hand of the law, of improved and contented negroes, satisfied with their master and satisfied with their condition . . . to be more pregnant with cruelty—to give a greater shock to the best feelings of our nature—to make the negroes themselves more hostile to White ascendance, than all the abominations of African piracy over the brute natives of that continent, or even the aggravated horrors of the middle passage." Until "this right of mortgaging the persons of negroes be made illegal," Power continued, "by the attachment of the cultivator to the soil, little indeed, in my humble judgment, can be done in the way of effective negro amelioration. What value, may I take the liberty of asking, can attach to the legal right of the negro to hold lands and to cultivate them, if it is in the power of any remorseless mortgagee, or an insolvent owner, to drag him from that soil and fix him for the rest of his life hundreds of miles, probably, from the very spot which was the entire object of his regard?"[62]

On plantation Ithaca, the removal of some enslaved laborers to another estate was also a bitter point of contention between the owner and his slaves. In February 1828, more than fifty people traveled to the fiscal's office to complain that their owner, L. F. Gallez, planned to move them across the river, to Frederickslust. Their spokesman, the "elderly man" Midas, an African who had lived on Ithaca since at least 1819 (well before Gallez), charged that Gallez had violated an old agreement between them. When Mr. Gallez "returned from England some time ago he came here, called up the gang and asked if we would like to have him for an owner. We replied Yes if you take good care of us." Gallez had "promised to do so," Midas claimed, but he did not. Now, when they tried to "expostulate with Mr. Gallez," "he drove us away like dogs." And when they "insisted to be heard," Gallez told them "to go to the fiscal."[63]

And so Midas and the others went to the fiscal and persuaded him to visit Ithaca. There Gallez, his attorney, his manager, and other slaves confirmed that the Ithaca people regularly worked on Frederickslust. As the manager explained, "the negroes from here work there some times for two months sometimes for shorter periods." The reason, according to the managers of both plantations, was that Ithaca was "an old cultivated estate," where the "land [was] exhausted," unlike Frederickslust. This practice had long upset the Ithaca slaves, but the breaking point came when a rumor spread—which Gallez denied—that they would soon be moved permanently. But even temporary displacements had serious social and economic consequences for the people on Ithaca.[64]

As they explained, they routinely returned after weeks or months away to find their provision grounds, stock, and homes damaged or stolen. As Midas said, "we objected [to being worked on Frederickslust] pointing out the many hardships we suffer. . . . We are removed without any notice. We therefore have to leave our Stock, and provision grounds, and on our return we find we have been plundered during our absence, as every bad disposed negro in the neighborhood, and passers by, has it in their power to deprive us of our little property."[65]

Losing their "little property," they said, was all the more painful because selling their surplus was the only means they had to supply themselves with goods that Gallez should have provided. As one man explained, "by these constant removals all our poultry and provisions out of our own ground is Stolen and we are thereby deprived of the means of buying anything whatever. Since we belong to Mr. Gallez, he has given us clothing but once, and we would not complain of this now, if we were allowed to work the Estate as formerly and raise our Stock and ground provisions, which we sold and were able to supply our own wants but we have lost everything."[66]

The people on Ithaca were determined not to be sent to Frederickslust, and certainly not permanently. Midas was adamant: "Here we have lived all our lives, have made ourselves comfortable, and if [Gallez] intends to abandon this property we desire to be sold. We cannot go to Frederickslust." For Midas and the others, there was much more than the economic value of the land they cultivated at stake. Moving across the river would be particularly bad since the people on Ithaca "cannot agree with the negroes" on Frederickslust, according to two witnesses. The Ithaca slaves' complaint failed, however, when the fiscal explained he did "not deem himself authorised to Prohibit such occasional removals from the Estate." The silver lining in this case was that the fiscal found their accusation that they "were not furnished with clothing . . . fully and satisfactorily proven." He threatened to fine Gallez unless he supplied the clothing.[67]

Though the complaints of the enslaved people on Ithaca were primarily aimed at their owner, the charge that "bad disposed negro[es]" stole from them reminds us that enslaved people could threaten each other's economic rights, too. Theft within enslaved communities was a predictable reaction to intense competition for scarce resources in a highly stratified society. A small minority of enslaved people, especially "domestics," artisans, and drivers, were significantly better off, at least materially, than their peers.[68] At one extreme were people like Frederick, the head carpenter on Demtichem (accused of using poison against other slaves in 1817 and identified during the Minje Mama dance), who amassed enough money to buy his own slave and, upon his death, bequeath him to his daughter.[69] At the other end of the spectrum were people like Quaces, shunned by other enslaved people, the manager claimed, because he was "a notoriously idle and abandoned character, possessed of not the smallest property on earth beyond his annual allowance [of] clothing." He was known for "prowling about the estate at night or during his leisure hours," the manager claimed, and was "an annoyance to the industrious and well disposed negroes who attend to rearing ground provisions and fowls. No careful negro will allow him to spend a night in his house and he is known and distinguished from his rascality on the estate invariably by the name of Quaces s[on] of a w[hor]e."[70]

These differences in wealth and status fed social tensions and created prime conditions for theft. And while the objects enslaved people took from one another might seem trivial—a pair of pants, a chicken—the seriousness with which they sought to reclaim them and the violence that often followed accusations of theft are understandable given the small amounts of property most enslaved people had.[71] Stealing from slaveowners or their employees could easily be construed as appropriating what was rightfully one's own, but taking things from one another was a different matter and a violation of the moral economy.[72]

Most property disputes between enslaved people, like other conflicts, were probably settled privately or mediated within the slave community and thus never documented. Punishment records, however, reveal that some allegations of theft came to the attention of plantation authorities, who likely knew that they could spark serious conflicts. Frans, from plantation Demtichem, was given twenty-five lashes for "stealing out of the woman Annatye's house a basket containing beads, scissors, Thimble, &ca."[73] On plantation Eliza and Mary, Hannibal was sent to the stocks "for breaking open one of the negroes's chambers & stealing there from several articles of clothing." Two and a half months earlier, the manager noted, Hannibal had been punished "for stealing a jacket & waistcoat belonging to one of the overseers."[74] On plantation Albion, Toby was punished by solitary confinement for "killing the negroes fowls."[75] For stealing a turkey from another slave, Major, on plantation Vryheid, was sentenced to "3 days & 3 nights in solitary conf[inement] & four Sundays in public stocks three hours each time."[76]

Property conflicts between enslaved people could lead to significant violence. The people on plantations No. 5 and No. 7 saw firsthand how quickly an apparently minor dispute between Sampson and Mercy, African field laborers in their early sixties and fifties, respectively, became a nearly fatal fight. According to the manager, Peter McCulloch, the previous Saturday "a boy" told him "that the man Sampson was fighting with a woman named Mercy in the negro yard." Sampson and Mercy were "wrestling and then laying on the ground," and "Sampson had a knife in his hand, with which he attempted to stab Mercy." When the two were separated, McCulloch "reprimanded [Sampson] for fighting & directed the [other] men . . . to take the knife from him and to try to get him in the hospital," where he could be locked in the stocks. But no one could capture Sampson.[77]

When Sampson "saw the woman Mercy at some distance & being in a very great passion," McCulloch continued, "he made towards her with a knife in his hand." One man tried to knock the knife out of Sampson's hand with a bayonet, but Sampson seized it, "brandish[ed] it about," and then ran after McCulloch, "no doubt with intention to do [him] some serous injury." Sampson "cried out he would not rest unless he killed Mercy; some member of her family or me," McCulloch said. McCulloch retrieved a gun from the house, which prompted Sampson, pursued by the "whole of the men Gang," to run to the water's edge. Only there did Sampson, still "holding the bayonet in one hand, and the knife in the other," surrender when he "stuck fast in the mud." The fiscal sentenced Sampson to forty-five lashes in the marketplace and "to work on the Estate . . . with a light chain round his ancle [sic] for three months as a mark of disgrace."[78]

The fight that nearly ended Mercy's life began, the manager explained, as a seemingly minor dispute "about some fowls." Sampson was the plantation's "stock-keeper" and had accused Mercy of stealing two of McCulloch's chickens—a serious accusation that might have led to a severe punishment for theft. Mercy retaliated by taking three of Sampson's own fowls, and Mercy and Sampson "began to quarrel about this story." Mercy "asked him how he liked somebody to take away his property," she said, and Sampson "gave [her] a slap in [the] face." Mercy "said [she] would not take it & on his giving [her] another [slap she] closed in and threw him on the ground."[79] The way the fight then escalated underscored how easily thefts could produce violence.

Some enslaved people turned to colonials for help recovering property taken by other slaves—a strategy that facilitated their survival even as it reinforced the power structures that made slavery function and divided enslaved people against one another. In a process that had parallels in other colonial societies, using the legal system to claim entitlements as individuals made collective resistance more difficult by perpetuating internal conflicts and reifying the political authority of the colonial state as protector.[80]

Complainants usually had two goals. First, they wanted to recover their property (if they had not already done so) or receive some kind of compensation. Second, they wanted to see the alleged thief punished. In August 1822, a man named James, a forty-year-old African field laborer, complained that his owner's housekeeper stole his chickens and eggs. They were his only means of earning money to buy the things he needed to survive. In the four years since his owner had bought him, he claimed, "his master never gave him allowance of any kind for food or clothing." He was "obliged to find himself in every thing," which was only possible if his property rights were respected. But recently, the housekeeper "was in the habit of every day killing a fowl belonging to him; and whenever she wanted any eggs, she would go to the fowl's nest and take what she wanted." James's owner, however, claimed that only "once or twice while he was ill" his housekeeper had taken "some eggs and chickens" from James, and that "he had been paid the full price he had demanded for them."[81] Even if James's owner was lying, his defense was an implicit acknowledgment that enslaved people had a right to be compensated when they were victims of theft and, more broadly, that they had recognizable claims to property.

Part of the reason enslaved people went to authorities is that trying to recover stolen property on one's own could be frustrating and dangerous, as Harry, a teenage *winkel* slave and boatbuilder, discovered in October 1820. Harry told the fiscal that while he and Quaco, an African field laborer in his late thirties, were hired out to the "market-master," Quaco had stolen his goat. When Quaco learned that Harry had accused him of theft, he confronted Harry with "a bamboo stick," giving him "four blows on his side." The "licking" Harry had endured was so bad, he claimed, that he had been in the hospital with a pain in his side for the past three or four months.[82]

Leander had an equally difficult time recovering a pair of turkeys he claimed a man named Quashee stole. Leander first reported the theft to the manager of Quashee's plantation, who said "he would see the complainant paid, knowing that Quashee was a thief." Meanwhile, Leander found his turkeys at a woman's house, but she refused to return them because "she had purchased them from a country negro." She offered to return the turkeys if Leander reimbursed her. But Leander was not inclined to purchase his own livestock, so he appealed to the protector. The protector, however, dismissed the complaint and recommended Leander "avail himself of the promise made by [Quashee's] manager."[83]

Baron, an African field laborer on the Herstelling sugar plantation, wanted the manager to punish the man who had stolen his "cutlass" (machete). Baron "knew" that Mathias, also an African field laborer, "had done so but he denied it." Baron first went to the driver, but "when questioned by the Driver [Mathias] continued to deny it." Fortunately, Baron soon had the proof he needed: "Mathias's wife called me showed me my cutlass & said her husband had brought it here," he explained.[84]

The following day Baron went to the manager. He "said Massa I told you Mathias had stolen my cutlass, he denied it he cursed & wanted to fight with me for accusing him. You inquired about it & he denied it, but here the cutlass is his wife showed it to me & I took it away." Baron had already recovered the cutlass; his goal was retribution. And he was explicit: Mathias "must be flogged." Baron entered the manager's house, as the manager described it, "in a most violent passion with his cutlass in his hand brandishing it about & speaking very loud," and declaring he would "not go away until you have Mathias flogged." Instead, the manager whipped Baron "with a carracarra he had in his hand, & beat [him] all over [his] head, directed [him] to be confined in the stocks," and then "confined [him] a whole week in the dark house." The manager saw Baron's impassioned plea as an insolent demand from someone who was supposed to take orders, not give them. The fiscal ruled that Baron had been "extremely impetuous, impertinent, and disrespectful," failing to show the deference whites expected from blacks, and so he sentenced him to an additional thirty-nine lashes.[85]

Other complainants had better luck persuading the fiscal to use his power to punish thieves. Among them was Trim, an African in his early thirties who lived in New Amsterdam and whose house was broken into during the 1825 Christmas holidays by a man named Smart. Returning in the early morning hours on December 24, after having gone "out with the rest of [his] master's people to a dance," Trim found that someone had taken his blankets, trousers, shirts, and a nightgown. "Massa heard about it," Trim explained, but "told me not to make too much noise about it but as the two next nights were dancing nights all people were to look out well wherever they went" for the stolen items.[86]

Sure enough, at a Christmas Eve dance, Trim saw "the negro Smart . . . with [his] night gown on." Trim "took hold of him," he told the fiscal, and a fight was narrowly avoided when another man intervened, took the nightgown, and told Trim not to "make a disturbance here," promising to hold onto the gown until morning. The next day Trim's manager and the undersheriff, who had been summoned to investigate, confiscated two blankets and a pair of trousers from Smart's house, which they returned to Trim. Like Baron, who wanted Mathias flogged, Trim went to the fiscal to see Smart punished. And he got what he wanted: the fiscal sentenced Smart to fifty lashes. Smart's owner, moreover, told the fiscal that "amongst my own people [Smart] is not considered Honest & frequently accused of stealing their things." Apparently fed up with problems caused by Smart's thefts, his owner declared his "intention to dispose of [Smart]" immediately."[87]

White plantation authorities punished slaves who stole from one another because they recognized the social turmoil that unpunished thefts could generate. In January 1830, the manager of the *winkel* slaves in New Amsterdam told the fiscal that an enslaved cooper named Paul had stolen two turkeys from Toetoe, an "elderly" (sixty-two-year-old) and "very stout" midwife.[88] Toetoe and her husband suspected the turkeys had been taken one night, so Toetoe went looking for them at nearby Fort St. Andrews the next morning. There she found the turkeys "in possession of . . . the mess man," who told her that he had "bought them from a man whose name he did not know, but who was to come at 11 o'clock for payment." So Toetoe waited to catch the thief red-handed. When "Paul came for the money," she "claimed the Turkies, accused him of stealing them, and reported the circumstance to the manager." The manager then wrote the fiscal, who investigated Toetoe's complaint and sentenced Paul to ten days of brutal "work" on the treadmill.[89]

Michael, an African carpenter in his early twenties from plantation Providence, endured a harsh punishment when the manager concluded that he had taken "some money, cloth and coral" from the trunk of Jenny, an African in her early forties. The manager "inspected the chest that had been broken open, and discovered that it was forced with a carpenter's chisel." Michael's chisel "was evidently the one which had forced the chest," he concluded, which was "sufficient proof for Michael's guilt." More important, probably, was Michael's reputation for stealing. He "had committed similar offences before," the manager explained, "and almost all of the negroes of the estate believed he was the person who had robbed Jenny." To satisfy those who suspected Michael, the manager ordered the driver to give him thirty-nine lashes (Michael claimed he endured one hundred) and then confined him in the stocks at night for a week.[90]

Some managers recognized the devastating effect that even small property losses could have on enslaved people. William Cort, the manager of plantation Hampshire, for example, contacted a civil magistrate after a woman from the neighboring estate attacked two women on Hampshire and damaged their clothing and jewelry. "The aggressor Bella," Cort complained, "has been allowed to go as yet unpunished." And when Maria, one of Bella's victims, had complained to Bella's owner, he "most harshly and illegally, on Sunday, ordered her into the dark house, without any inquiry into the cause of the disturbance." Cort was at least as concerned with the damage done to Maria's clothing and jewelry as the harm done to her body. "My woman Maria," he told the civil magistrate, "has not only been severely beaten, but has suffered a serious loss to her in the destruction of her Christmas finery, ear-ring, necklace &c." For a woman who probably had very little in the way of "finery," this was a significant injury indeed. Cort demanded "restitution of the value of the articles destroyed, and the aggressor to undergo such punishment" as the civil magistrate saw fit.[91]

The protector of slaves, who investigated Cort's complaint, determined that the fight between Bella and Maria was the symptom of a long-standing hostility between the gangs of Hampshire and Albion, where Bella lived. This tension had been caused, at least in part, by Maria's relationship with Bella's brother, which Bella disapproved of. To diffuse a rapidly escalating conflict, the protector "recommended . . . an amicable arrangement, not only between the slaves of two such neighboring properties, but also between those who were in authority over them, as an evil of that kind was calculated to extend itself into various tumultuous factions throughout the whole range of the coast." His solution acknowledged the central role that property played in the slaves' moral economy and social system. "As Mr. Cort's negresses had suffered a loss of property," he explained, "he was of opinion that they should receive a full compensation from the attorney of Albion."[92]

Enslaved people in Berbice asserted their right to use and control various types of personal property, from provision grounds to livestock. Their claims are most visible in moments where they were contested. When enslavers or other slaves tried to deprive enslaved people of their property, arguments and violence often followed. And when enslaved people could not recover their property or secure compensation on their own, they sometimes turned to managers, owners, and the colonial government for help. Their complaints, moreover, highlight the extent to which the rights they claimed relied at least as much on vigilant litigation and knowledge of the law as they did on customary entitlements. Property ownership itself, however, was only part of a broader claim enslaved people made to be able to participate in the market economy—to trade their goods and receive compensation for certain kinds of labor.

Enforcing Bargains

In May 1819, seven men from the cotton plantation Rosehall—most of them Africans in their thirties—went to the fiscal because their manager refused to honor an agreement he made to pay them for working Sundays, a day they were supposed to be exempt from plantation labor. Nelson, speaking for the group, explained that "they were all engaged by the manager to gin cotton for himself on Sundays, for which he promised each f.3 a day." They worked three Sundays in a row in good faith, but never received the payment they were due. So, they showed their dissatisfaction by refusing to work. Their strike attracted the manager's attention, but did not prompt him to settle the debt. When the men again approached him to "demand the payment," he refused to recognize the legitimacy of their claim. Instead, he called the driver and gave them a "d—— good payment" with his whip.[93]

The claim that the men from Rosehall made—the right to enforce a bargain they had made with their manager—was part of a broader economic right enslaved people fought for: the ability to make deals and enforce them. In other kinds of bargains as well, slaves claimed the right to enforce explicit agreements and sometimes even implicit obligations. They demanded the right to trade and sell their goods, to hire themselves and their services, and to collect payments from people with whom they had made agreements. In short, enslaved people sought to make others recognize their legal personhood, respect their claims of ownership, and compensate them for certain kinds of labor or property losses.[94] Given that these rights directly challenged the logic of slavery, in which slaves were chattels with no property claims and no right to make contracts, much less enforce them against free people, it is understandable how difficult it was for slaves to uphold them. If a manager could pay his slaves with a flogging in lieu of cash, how could enslaved people deal with people who stole or damaged their property, or bought goods from them and then refused to pay for them?

A major help for slaves in this regard were the new laws passed during amelioration. Seven years after the conflict on plantation Rosehall, the 1826 slave code explicitly recognized enslaved people's customary right to participate in the colonial economy. The law made it illegal, for example, to employ slaves on Sundays without paying them "wages" in cash, not kind (the rates of which were established by the protector and approved by the lieutenant governor).[95] The law also recognized enslaved people's property claims and right to be compensated for any goods they sold, stipulating that fines and imprisonment could be imposed on anyone who "defrauded" slaves, "unjustly appropriate[d]" their "land, money, or property of any kind," or "disturb[ed] any such slave in the possession or free use and enjoyment" of their property.[96]

Like the men from Rosehall, many enslaved people turned to colonial authorities for help collecting payment or recovering debts.[97] When Zondag wanted to collect a debt of some eleven guilders from John Blank in April 1827, he went to the protector, who wrote Blank and "recommended that he settle without delay." The next day, Zondag returned to the protector and reported that "Blank had settled with him to his satisfaction, thanking the Protector for his interference."[98] Even before 1826, slaves claimed the right to be paid for goods and services they provided on their own time, but doing so was never easy. In February 1819, for example, an enslaved man named London went to the fiscal after Napier, a black soldier or "pioneer," refused to pay him for taking him to the fort in his small boat. London had repeatedly asked Napier to pay, but Napier always refused. The last time he tried to collect the debt, moreover, Napier "seized him tore his jacket and cut him in two places with a knife." Napier, on the other hand, claimed that London owed *him* money, and that London had initiated the fight when Napier demanded payment.[99]

As London's complaint suggests, collecting payment on one's own was fraught with danger. When Nelly, a New Amsterdam huckster hired out to Mary Jane Campbell, was beaten by a man who owed her money, Campbell complained to the fiscal on Nelly's behalf. Nelly explained that the slave August had "bought calico from [her] for eleven guilders." But when she "went to him two or three times for the money . . . he drove [her] away said he would not pay [her]." Determined to get her money, Nelly confronted August again: "I said you have bought my calico & you got money & refused to pay me to day you & I will have it. I won't go away without it." Nelly thought August had money in his jacket or hat, so she grabbed him and told him that she would "not let [him] go unless [he] pa[id]." August tried to persuade Nelly to leave him alone lest the fiscal, who was dining nearby, see the fight, but Nelly claimed she responded, "that is what I want. The fiscal is a Gentleman & he won't let you cheat me out of my money."[100]

The "scuffle" continued, and Nelly soon heard someone "run down stairs & at once [she] felt blows all over [her neck]." It was John Cotton, a cooper who had hired August. Cotton beat Nelly with a stick "all over [her] head & shoulders," then ordered her out of his yard. Whether the fiscal forced August to settle his debt is unknown, but he did rule that Cotton had violated regulations "respecting the mode & treatment of punishments to be inflicted on slaves," for which Cotton would be prosecuted before the court of criminal justice.[101] The prosecution was for the assault, but it was also an implicit recognition that people like Nelly had a right to collect payment and that Cotton's interference was illegal.

Most enslaved people, like Nelly, only went to the fiscal or protector after their own efforts to collect money owed them failed. And they were careful to point out that they had exhausted other means before turning to the government. Telemachus, for example, sought the protector's help collecting payment for a hog he sold John Taylor because he "ha[d] not yet been able to receive the amount, although he made repeated applications." The deputy protector wrote Taylor, "requesting an immediate settlement of the above claim," and Taylor agreed to pay as soon as he could get the money.[102]

A woman named Fanny, a fifty-year-old African domestic, similarly claimed that "Johannes de Vry owe[d] [her] one bit for one month," and that when she went to recover the debt a few days earlier, de Vry threatened "that if she did not go, he would give her what she would not like." De Vry then "pushed her out of doors, and slashed her with a rope several times," only stopping when "the neighbours interfered." The protector wrote the fiscal and asked him to punish de Vry, who had ruined his chances of mounting a successful defense by showing up several times at the protector's office when it was closed, often drunk. The fiscal sentenced de Vry to a week in jail, hoping that it would "be an example to this worthless class of persons."[103]

John Clark also went to the protector, he claimed, when all else had failed. He "held a claim for six guilders against one F Schmidt," he said, "and although his master tried all his means to recover this sum for complainant he has not been able to do so." The protector contacted Schmidt, who "promised to settle the amount as soon as he should have it in his power." If the debt was not settled soon, the protector added, he would take Schmidt to court.[104] A woman named Jessy also found the protector sympathetic to her complaint against a goldsmith, who had lost a pair of earrings Jessy had given him to repair a couple of years earlier. Jessy had, she claimed, "agreed to pay three guilders for the repairs, and has often called at Mr. Burmester's [the gold-smith] for the ear-rings and tendered the money, but cannot get them." The protector "thought Jessy was perfectly right in making the present applica-tion," and told Burmester he "was to pay for [the earrings], to which he agreed."[105]

Responding to these problems, the Berbice government passed a "Small Debt Enactment" in October 1829 designed to make it easier for enslaved people to enforce bargains. This law was a direct response to enslaved peo-ple's protests and complaints and, more broadly, one example of how enslaved people influenced the amelioration campaign. The ordinance, which was en-thusiastically supported by Britain's colonial office, was the brainchild of the protector of slaves, who hailed its passage as "a great and most important advance" that allowed an enslaved person "to enter a court of law, and re-cover without any expense whatever a small sum of money which may have been unjustly withheld from him."[106] Before 1829, the problem was not that enslaved people lacked access to the court system. The problem was that going to court was prohibitively expensive—and the protector's ability to help the enslaved people who went to him was minimal.

Previously, as the protector complained to the governor as early as 1827, "considerable inconvenience ha[d] been experienced from the want of some judicial court for the recovery of trivial debts at small expense." The "ineffi-cacy" of his "attempts to recover [slaves'] outstanding claims for the sale of pigs, poultry, &c.," the protector lamented, was becoming "each day more perplexing." The problem was that "few slaves, if any, [were] prepared to en-counter the present heavy expense of attending a suit before the Court of Criminal justice," so the protector's authority was "limited chiefly to threats," which he claimed were "almost disregarded."[107] As with other amelioration reforms, enforcement was key. The following year the protector repeated his complaint that his "power" to compel "persons indebted to Slaves in small sums" to "discharge their debt by installment . . . had become inoperative."[108] The 1829 ordinance, in contrast, gave the protector of slaves as well as civil magistrates throughout the colony the authority to summarily "hear, try, and determine . . . all cases and complaints brought before them . . . concerning the recovery of any Debt" of one hundred guilders or less.[109]

Despite the new law, many complainants still failed to recover debts, usu-ally because of conflicting testimony or lack of evidence. Susette, a field la-borer who lived in the *winkel* village, for example, complained that "Cumba

White a free Woman assaulted & beat her this morning for asking her payment for ironing clothes." Susette claimed four witnesses had seen the fight, and they admitted that Cumba and Susette "were quarreling about money matters." But Cumba claimed that she had paid Susette the two guilders she owed. Since she only had a dollar, she asked Susette to give her one guilder back in change, she said. "Susette was not pleased with this and became insolent," Cumba claimed, so she "laid hold of her and thought of sending her to the Fiscal." The men who witnessed the fight, moreover, "changed the money," broke up the fight, and "took Susette away," they claimed. The protector dismissed Susette's complaint.[110]

A complaint in November 1830 from John Hardman, a domestic from New Amsterdam, fared no better. Hardman complained that "C. Kraan tore his coat last Easter at a dance, for which he promised to pay him, that Kraan had never done so, and therefore request[ed] the Protector to compel Kraan to pay the damage done to his coat." Kraan, however, claimed that John had attacked *him*, and that John "gave him several blows, & was going to throw him down stairs, when luckily for him he caught hold of John's coat, which may thereby be damaged." He denied that he ever promised to pay John, and when John did not show up with the witnesses he claimed would corroborate his account, the protector dismissed the case.[111]

Other complainants were more fortunate, in part because the protector now had the authority to compel debtors to pay. When Sally Kitty told the protector in January 1830 that "R. Akers owe[d] her eighteen guilders, for which she [held] his acceptance," the protector summoned Akers, presented Kitty's evidence, and forced Akers to settle his debt.[112] Four months later, a cook named Hannibal turned to the protector for help collecting a debt from Charles Ross. Hannibal claimed he had sold two sheep to Ross for thirty-three guilders each, but Ross instead "offer[ed] his acceptance payable at the end of this year at the rate of thirty guilders." Ross admitted that he owed Hannibal, but not thirty-three guilders. "It was at Hannibal's particular request," he said, "that he took the sheep at f.30," which he would "prove by a certificate of Mr. Oldfield, who was present when the bargain was struck." Oldfield's certificate corroborated Ross's account, and Hannibal accepted his "acknowledgment for sixty guilders payable in three months."[113]

These efforts to recover debts and collect payment are illustrative of the broader effort enslaved people in Berbice made to participate in the colonial economy in order to improve their material welfare and chances of survival. Although enslaved people could not avoid working for their enslavers

without pay most of the time, they demanded a measure of economic autonomy, including the right to sell or barter their labor and goods during their
own time, as well as the right to enforce contracts and bargains, that would
help them get by. Enslaved people's claims, moreover, laid the foundation for
many of the reforms introduced during the era of amelioration, which in
many ways represented a codification of practices and implicit agreements
that had already been established by custom and on-the-ground negotiation.
The imperial government, for its part, endorsed enslaved people's efforts to
enforce bargains because it saw this basic economic right as one of the keys to
beginning the transition to wage labor and transforming owner-slave relationships into employer-employee ones.[114] Yet even as the colonial government took steps to officially recognize enslaved people's economic rights and
make it easier to enforce them during the era of amelioration, enslaved people had a difficult and dangerous time protecting them.

Berbician slaves constantly struggled to claim economic rights that were central to their daily struggle for material welfare. Understanding the rights they
fought for and their strategies for securing them helps us understand what
enslaved people valued and how they tried to make viable lives under extraordinary conditions. It also allows us see the extent to which their priorities overlapped with those of an imperial government officially committed to
ameliorating their living conditions. Enslaved people took advantage of
whatever opportunities were available to them to claim rights that had previously rested only on custom—the right to be provided with at least a minimum of food and clothing; the right to access, control, and exchange different
kinds of personal property without interference; and the right to negotiate
market relations. Yet even once these rights were given explicit legal protection, slaveowners and plantation authorities contested them, not least of all
because they challenged some of the central fictions of West Indian slavery:
that slaves had no legal claims their owners were bound to respect, that enslaved laborers would never be compensated for their time or work, and that
as chattel, rather than people, slaves had no claims of ownership.

   In the end, however, asserting these economic rights was less threatening
to the slave system than it might first appear. Many of the economic claims
enslaved people made did limit their enslavers' autonomy and improve enslaved people's living conditions, however marginally, but the impetus behind them had less to do with resisting slavery than with simply finding a
way to stay alive.[115] Asserting one's property rights was, at the most basic

level, a means of trying to survive extreme conditions of poverty and deprivation, rather than a struggle for equality or economic justice. Enslaved people's conservative politics of survival thus bore a disconcerting similarity to the politics of amelioration, a failed experiment based on the flawed premise that an exploitative system that relied on violence and white supremacy could ever be fair.

Epilogue

By January 1831, the enslaved man Fortuin was desperate. As a last resort, he went to Berbice's fiscal and asked to be sold to a new owner. Fortuin blamed the man who purchased him the previous year, Andrew Ross, for the recent deaths of his daughter, Sarah, and infant grandson, Edward, and he was worried that he and his surviving family members would soon meet the same end. "Seeing my children die in this manner," Fortuin told the fiscal, "I went to Mr. Ross and told him I could not stand it, he must sell us, or we would all die." Fortuin had confronted Ross twice after Edward's death, telling him he "had brought him and his family to die here and that they must be sold." Ross had refused, so Fortuin's last resort was to "beg" the fiscal to intervene. But even though Ross admitted to the fiscal that Sarah had indeed "taken ill and died of worms," and dysentery had killed Edward, the fiscal could not help Fortuin. "Although the loss he had sustained must weigh heavily," the fiscal told him, "he ought to endeavour to submit thereto with resignation."[1]

Fortuin may not have been willing to simply accept that death was imminent—his complaint instead testifies to a tenacious will to protect his family and survive—but this was the world in which enslaved people throughout the Americas lived, worked, and died. In Berbice, at the core of enslaved people's world was the struggle to simply stay alive. When they asked officials to protect them from sadistic managers, collaborated with drivers to negotiate workloads, sought protection from violent husbands, turned to obeah practitioners to combat disease, or defended their right to be fed and clothed by their enslavers, they were trying first and foremost to survive. Understanding how the problem of survival shaped enslaved people's actions and relationships is thus central to understanding their experience.

If we look past the distinctive features of nineteenth-century Berbice—its riverine ecology and the omnipresence of water, the legacy of Dutch colonialism and especially Dutch legal institutions like the fiscal, and an interventionist British imperial government that imposed new regulations to ameliorate and ultimately replace slavery—it looks very similar to other

Atlantic slave societies. Most plantation societies in the Americas had a similarly horrific demographic landscape: high death rates, low birth rates, and slave populations that could only be sustained or increased by new arrivals of African captives to replace the dead. The Hobbesian world that Berbician slaves inhabited—a world of unrelenting labor, brutal violence, poor nutrition, and an unforgiving disease environment—was at its core very much like other American slave societies. The 1782 complaint of a colonist in Saint Domingue that enslaved people were "always dying" could have been made of any number of Atlantic slave societies, including Berbice, where slaveowners worked their slaves to death.[2] Understanding the slave society that developed in Berbice, especially from the vantage point of the enslaved people who struggled to survive it, can therefore illuminate some of the most important features of Atlantic slavery writ large.

The most obvious similarity between Berbice and other Atlantic slave societies is that all were death traps. Wherever sugar was king, and even in some slave societies where sugar was not the primary crop, extraordinary death tolls and pitiful birth rates created an insatiable demand for African captives. Major slave societies such as Jamaica and Saint Domingue, where half of all newly arrived African captives died within a few years, or northeastern Brazil, where mortality rates were even higher, differed more in scale than in kind from Berbice.[3] For enslaved people themselves, the central concern everywhere was finding a way to live while surrounded by death. The emphasis in many histories of slavery, however, on the power struggles between masters and slaves, on enslaved people's efforts to win some measure of autonomy if not outright freedom, has made it surprisingly difficult to acknowledge this basic condition of slave life and even harder to grapple with its implications.

The demographic catastrophe that typified Berbice and most Atlantic slave societies stands in marked contrast to the history of slavery in North America and especially the southern United States. The U.S. South was one of the only large slave societies in the Americas where slave population increase quickly led to the emergence of a creole slave population.[4] While early African arrivals to the Chesapeake and Lowcountry had much in common with their counterparts who were taken to Brazil and the Caribbean, by the mid-eighteenth century North American slave populations were self-sustaining and growing quickly, a shift that occurred first in the Chesapeake. Moreover, rather than declining after the transatlantic slave trade ended, as happened almost everywhere else in the Americas, the slave population of the South increased exponentially during the nineteenth century.[5] U.S. slaveowners on the Atlantic coast with surplus slaves and declining yields of tobacco and rice sold some one million men and women to the rapidly expanding "Cotton Kingdom" of the lower South.[6] This "Second Middle Passage" gave new birth to American slavery—and American capitalism—at the same time slavery was increasingly under attack throughout the Americas and seemingly in decline everywhere except Brazil and Cuba.[7] It was also the central event for enslaved people themselves in the antebellum South, where perhaps one in three marriages were broken by sale and forced separation, and where slaves likely saw the challenge of keeping their families together as a more pressing concern than sheer survival.[8]

The history of slavery in Berbice also reveals that the power relationships of Atlantic slave societies were remarkably broad and complex. If we uncritically adapt models developed for the study of slavery in North America to other slave societies, we can be easily misled into focusing too intently on the master-slave binary. Focusing too narrowly on the ways that enslaved people resisted their enslavers exaggerates enslaved people's agency and also, paradoxically, the importance of slaveowners in enslaved people's day-to-day lives. Nowhere did slaveowners have as much unrestricted power over the people they enslaved as in the antebellum United States. In Berbice and other West Indian colonies, including Jamaica, most "planters" were in fact absentees who lived an ocean away and delegated authority to a series of employees, typically attorneys, who managed their estates.[9] The overseers and managers hired to handle day-to-day operations, moreover, were subject to the authority of different government officials—magistrates, fiscals, protectors of slaves, judges, and, farther away but no less important, metropolitan politicians—who claimed the prerogative to supervise their management of plantations and treatment of slaves. At the same time, enslaved people in most Atlantic slave societies, especially those established by Spain and France, had limited legal rights and access to third parties, judicial and ecclesiastical, who offered the possibility, however remote, of protection and redress.[10] Enslaved people from Lima, Quito, and Colombia to Cuba, Mexico, and Saint Domingue regularly used the law and the Catholic church to protest especially brutal treatment, denounce owners who violated colonial laws on the treatment of slaves, and in some cases sue for their freedom.[11] The multiple layers of power that Berbician slaves navigated had multiple parallels throughout the Atlantic world, where slavery was rarely about masters and slaves alone.

Recognizing the role third parties played in enslaved people's relationships with their enslavers and each other challenges us to reconsider the politics of Atlantic slavery. Slaveowners in the U.S. South, for example, who were
usually resident owners in close contact with the relatively small number of
slaves they owned, were much more successful than their West Indian and
Latin American counterparts in constructing slavery as a relation of private
property, largely exempt from government intervention. And even when
Southern slaveowners enacted state laws that supposedly offered enslaved
people protection from the same kinds of abuse British reformers sought to
curtail in the West Indies through parliamentary action, they did everything
in their power to make such laws meaningless. In contrast to enslaved people
in much of the Atlantic world, where government officials asserted their right
to regulate the treatment of slaves, Southern slaves lived in a society where
they had virtually no means of enforcing the limited rights they were supposed to have, as underscored by the fact that Southern courts did not accept
their testimony against whites.[12] When viewed in the comparative perspective provided by Berbice, Southern slaveowners' ability to prevent enslaved
people from using the law to seek redress—a common means of negotiating
and resisting slavery in other Atlantic slave societies—is a striking anomaly
that should be explained rather than taken for granted.

Yet even in the South, where slaveowners' insistence on self-regulation
was extreme, enslaved people's lives were never determined solely by their
relationships or conflicts with the people who owned them.[13] On even the
smallest plantations and farms, enslaved people navigated a range of relationships with other people on and off the estate. The master-slave binary, which
was always more of a planter fantasy than a reality, is thus as limiting for the
study of slavery in the United States as it is for more typical Atlantic slave
societies like Berbice.

Perhaps the most important lesson, then, to take from Berbician slaves'
struggle to survive is that the relationships they navigated with one another—
and the fragile communities they built—were at least as important as their
relationships with enslavers. Enslaved people's lives were powerfully shaped
by the constraints of enslavement, but their experiences cannot be reduced to
their legal status as slaves or their inherent opposition to the people who
owned and supervised them. Plantations in Berbice and other Atlantic slave
societies were not only sites of exploitation but complex social worlds inhabited not by hundreds of anonymous "slaves" but by Kongolese, Igbo, and Cor-
omantee immigrants, husbands and wives, drivers, carpenters, sugar-boilers

and "domestics," parents, children, and shipmates, obeah practitioners and clients—in short, communities of individuals and groups from diverse backgrounds who had a range of concerns and faced different challenges. Keeping such differences and the divisions they sometimes caused in the foreground allows us to better appreciate enslaved people's world on its own terms and especially to understand why concerted resistance against slavery was not inevitable or even easily achievable on most plantations.

In prioritizing survival rather than freedom, enslaved Africans and their descendants competed not only with their enslavers but also with one another for the resources they needed to endure, if not escape, enslavement. Their struggles to navigate the unforgiving world of Atlantic slavery revealed human nature at its worst and best. Theirs was a world of horror and catastrophe, competition and conflict, but also one of courage, hope, and perseverance. It was, in the end, a world at once utterly foreign and disconcertingly similar to our own.

Abstract of Offenses Committed by
Male and Female Plantation Slaves,
January 1–May 14, 1830

| NATURE OF OFFENCES | Male offenders | Female offenders | Males flogged | Males and females in stocks, and otherwise | TOTAL | Punishments inflicted by managers | | | |
| | | | | | | Males | | Females | |
						Maximum	Minimum	Maximum	Minimum
Attempting to poison	–	–	–	–	–	–	–	–	–
Attempting to ravish	–	–	–	–	–	–	–	–	–
Attempting to murder	–	–	–	–	–	–	–	–	–
Attempting to commit suicide	–	–	–	–	–	–	–	–	–
Cutting others with cutlasses	2	–	2	–	2	25 lashes	17 lashes	–	–
Incendiaries	2	–	2	–	2	25 lashes	15 lashes	–	–
Killing and destroying stock	1	–	1	–	1	25 lashes	–	–	–
Cruelty to animals	3	–	2	1	3	25 lashes	3 days' confinement	–	–
Housebreaking and stealing	8	–	4	4	8	25 lashes	1 hour public stocks	–	–
Theft, petty larceny	131	11	69	73	142	25 lashes	1/2 hour ditto	3 days' and nights' solitary confinement	10 minutes' public stocks

Offence									
Sheep, hog and poultry stealing	4	—	2	2	4	25 lashes	1 night bed-stocks	—	—
Encouraging others to steal	—	—	—	—	—	—	—	—	—
Conniving at theft, and attempting to steal	8	1	6	3	9	25 lashes	3 days' solitary confinement	1 night bed-stocks	—
Receiving stolen goods, knowing them to be such	1	—	1	—	1	10 lashes	—	—	—
Striking manager	—	—	—	—	—	—	—	—	—
Biting overseer	—	—	—	—	—	—	—	—	—
Striking overseer	—	—	—	—	—	—	—	—	—
Striking driver	2	1	2	1	3	25 lashes	3 lashes	1 night bed-stocks	—
Biting driver	—	—	—	—	—	—	—	—	—
Holding and tearing driver's shirt	—	—	—	—	—	—	—	—	—
Raising cutlass against driver	—	—	—	—	—	—	—	—	—
Resisting manager in discharge of duty	1	—	1	—	1	19 lashes	—	—	—
Breaking stocks	—	—	—	—	—	—	—	—	—
Refusing to work	44	41	21	64	85	25 lashes	1/2 hour confinement	3 days' and 3 nights' confinement	1/4 hour public stocks

| NATURE OF OFFENCES | Male offenders | Female offenders | Males flogged | Males and females in stocks, and otherwise | TOTAL | Punishments inflicted by managers | | | |
| | | | | | | Males | | Females | |
						Maximum	Minimum	Maximum	Minimum
Disobedience	168	77	54	191	245	25 lashes	1/2 hour public stocks	4 hours' house-stocks	1 night solitary confinement
Insolence	123	107	53	177	230	25 lashes	1/4 hour ditto	3 days' and nights' solitary confinement	5 minutes' public stocks
Insubordination	35	44	23	56	79	25 lashes	47 hours' confinement	6 hours' house-stocks	1 night bed-stocks
Abusive language to owners	–	6	–	6	6	–	–	2 days' confinement	1 night bed-stocks
Absconding from work	123	16	78	61	139	25 lashes	30 minutes' public-stocks	2 nights' confinement	10 minutes' public stocks
Encouraging others to abscond	4	–	4	–	4	18 lashes	24 hours' solitary confinement	–	–
Inducing gang to turn out late	–	–	–	–	–	–	–	–	–
Contemptuous behaviour and language	7	2	2	7	9	20 lashes	15 minutes' public stocks	3 days' confinement	1 night bed-stocks
Mutinous language	1	–	1	–	1	25 lashes	–	–	–

Quarrelling	8	13	1	20	21	20 lashes	5 minutes' public stocks	1 night bed stocks	5 minutes' pub. Stocks
Ditto and fighting	21	46	6	61	67	25 lashes	2 1/2 hours' public stocks	3 days' and nights' solitary confinement	1 hour public stocks
Scalding others	–	–	–	–	–	–	–	–	–
Beating others	12	5	8	9	17	25 lashes	3 lashes	6 hours' house-stocks	1 night bed-stocks
Biting others	–	2	–	2	2	–	–	3 days' confinement	1 hour pub. stocks
Maltreating children	1	3	–	4	4	10 lashes	–	1 night bed-stocks	1 hour ditto
Attempting to strike a white man	1	–	1	–	1	25 lashes	–	–	–
Lying with other men's wives	3	–	3	–	3	25 lashes	16 lashes	–	–
Seducing and attempting to seduce other men's wives	2	–	2	–	2	22 lashes	10 lashes	–	–
Committing fornication	1	1	1	1	2	15 lashes	–	1 night bed-stocks	–
Infidelity to husbands	–	3	–	3	3	–	–	1 night bed-stocks	1/2 hour pub. stocks
Father selling daughter to prostitution	–	–	–	–	–	–	–	–	–

NATURE OF OFFENCES	Male offenders	Female offenders	Males flogged	Males and females in stocks, and otherwise	TOTAL	Punishments inflicted by managers			
						Males		Females	
						Maximum	Minimum	Maximum	Minimum
Drunkenness	40	3	19	24	43	25 lashes	1 night bed-stocks	6 hours' solitary confinement	–
Bad work, and not finishing task	480	451	171	760	931	25 lashes	1/2 hour pub-lic stocks	1 night and day solitary confinement	1 night bed-stocks
Neglect of duty	528	298	216	610	826	25 lashes	1 night bed-stocks	3 nights' and days' solitary confinement	5 minutes' pub. stocks
Neglecting stock	26	–	14	12	26	15 lashes	1 hour public stocks	–	–
Neglecting to throw grass	7	–	–	7	7	3 days' and nights' solitary confinement	1 night bed-stocks	–	–
Not coming to work in proper time	58	106	12	152	164	24 lashes	1/2 hour pub-lic stocks	1 night bed-stocks	1/2 hour's pub. stocks
Neglecting prayers	–	–	–	–	–	–	–	–	–
Introducing rum on estate	–	–	–	–	–	–	–	–	–
Refusing to keep Sabbath-day	–	–	–	–	–	–	–	–	–

Offense									
Riding mules at night	–	–	–	–	–	–	–	–	–
Idleness, laziness and indolence	167	100	39	228	267	25 lashes	1/2 hour public stocks	1 night bed-stocks	1/4 hour pub. stocks
Leaving estate at night	22	17	7	32	39	25 lashes	1 hour public stocks	2 days' confinement	1 night bed-stocks
Absenting from hospital	9	4	1	12	13	6 lashes	3 days' confinement	1 night bed-stocks	–
Neglecting sores	6	1	3	4	7	3 days' and nights' solitary confinement	1 night bed-stocks	3 days' confinement	1 day confined
Refusing to take medicine	2	1	2	1	3	20 lashes	1 night ditto	1 night bed-stocks	–
Eating dirt, charcoal, &c.	–	–	–	–	–	–	–	–	–
Neglecting person	–	3	–	3	3	–	–	3 days' solitary confinement	1 night bed-stocks
Neglecting gardens	–	–	–	–	–	–	–	–	–
Setting bad example to children	–	–	–	–	–	–	–	–	–
Selling and destroying clothes furnished by owners	3	–	2	1	3	25 lashes	1 hour public stocks	–	–

| NATURE OF OFFENCES | Male offenders | Female offenders | Males flogged | Males and females in stocks, and otherwise | TOTAL | Punishments inflicted by managers | | | |
| | | | | | | Males | | Females | |
						Maximum	Minimum	Maximum	Minimum
Selling working utensils	1	–	–	1	1	1 night bed-stocks	–	–	–
Riotous conduct	8	17	1	24	25	25 lashes	1 hour public stocks	3 days' and nights' solitary confinement	20 minutes' public stocks
Breaking carts and punts	2	–	–	2	2	2 hours' house-stocks	1 night bed-stocks	–	–
Harbouring runaways	2	–	2	–	2	25 lashes	18 lashes	–	–
Preventing others from working	4	–	4	–	4	25 lashes	1 night bed-stocks	–	–
Breaking hospital, and aiding others to get out of stocks	4	1	4	1	5	25 lashes	7 lashes	1 night bed-stocks	–
Cutting and stealing canes	2	2	1	3	4	22 lashes	1 1/2 days' solitary confinement	30 hours' solitary confinement	1/2 hour public stocks
Practising obeah	1	–	1	–	1	25 lashes	–	–	–
Lying and false swearing	3	3	2	4	6	18 lashes	1 hour public stocks	1 night bed-stocks	10 minutes pub. stocks

False complaints	8	9	5	12	17	25 lashes	1 day and night solitary confinement	3 days' solitary confinement	1 night bed-stocks
Indecent language and behaviour	3	9	–	12	12	2 days' solitary confinement	1/2 hour public stocks	2 hours' public stocks	1 night confined
False pretense of sickness	5	1	3	3	6	15 lashes	1 hour ditto	1 night bed-stocks	–
Cutting and eating dead cattle	2	1	–	3	3	3 days' and nights' solitary confinement	1/2 hour ditto	ditto	–
Carelessness in not guarding against fire	–	–	–	–	–	–	–	–	–
Ill-treating women and wives	8	–	7	1	8	25 lashes	1 hour public stocks	1 night bed-stocks	–
TOTAL	2,118	1,406	866	2,658	3,524				

Reprinted from CO 116/145,266–67.

NOTES

Introduction

1. "In Relation to proceedings of the Fiscal R.O. Versus Richard Bell On a complaint of the Negro Billy," Sept. 19–Oct. 10, 1825, Colonial Office series (hereafter CO) 116/140, National Archives, Kew, London, United Kingdom, 338–73 ("he swelled," "sick house," 343; "hung down," "not good," "put in the coffin," 344; "frothing," 351); "Return of Slaves . . . attached to Plant^n Den Arend . . . ," March 28, 1825, Treasury series (hereafter T) 71/442, 185–86, National Archives, Kew, London, United Kingdom. Missionary John Wray, who lived in Demerara and then Berbice in the early nineteenth century, observed that enslaved people's burial practices included ritual washing of the corpse; the emptying of rum glasses, food, and tobacco into the coffin; and a procession of drumming and dancing mourners that lasted the entire night. See Emília Viotti da Costa, *Crowns of Glory, Tears of Blood: The Demerara Slave Rebellion of 1823* (New York: Oxford University Press, 1994), 105–6, 339n61.

2. "Fiscal R.O. Versus Richard Bell," 344 ("bad negro"), 347 ("finding"), 358 ("a very lazy").

3. Ibid., 338–45 (quotations, 342).

4. I borrow the "over the shoulder" metaphor from Daniel K. Richter, *Facing East from Indian Country: A Native History of Early America* (Cambridge, Mass.: Harvard University Press, 2001), 8–9.

5. Estimates for pre-boarding mortality in Africa vary widely. For conflicting estimates, see Joseph Miller, *Way of Death: Merchant Capitalism and the Angolan Slave Trade, 1730–1830* (Madison: University of Wisconsin Press, 1988), 384–85; Patrick Manning, *The African Diaspora: A History Through Culture* (New York: Columbia University Press, 2009), 121, 131; Paul Lovejoy, *Transformations in Slavery: A History of Slavery in Africa*, 2nd ed., (Cambridge: Cambridge University Press, 2000), 63. Between 1787 and 1807, the peak years of the slave trade to Berbice, an average of 10.1 percent of African captives died aboard slave ships that sailed from Africa to the Caribbean. *Voyages: The Trans-Atlantic Slave Trade Database*, www.slavevoyages.org, accessed Feb. 3, 2015. For causes of death in Berbice, see B. W. Higman, *Slave Populations of the British Caribbean, 1807–1834* (Baltimore: Johns Hopkins University Press, 1984), 343–46.

6. Higman, *Slave Populations*, 27–30.

7. The mean age at death for field laborers in Berbice ranged from a low of 23.7 years, for creole men, to a high of 37 for African-born men. See Higman, *Slave Populations*, Table S9.27, "Mean Age of Slaves at Death, by Sex, Birthplace, and Occupation, Berbice, 1819–22," 666.

8. Stephanie E. Smallwood, *Saltwater Slavery: A Middle Passage from Africa to American Diaspora* (Cambridge, Mass.: Harvard University Press, 2007); Vincent Brown, *The Reaper's*

Garden: Death and Power in the World of Atlantic Slavery (Cambridge, Mass.: Harvard University Press, 2008).

9. For the problems of using Western notions of "freedom" and "slavery" to understand African societies, see Suzanne Miers and Igor Kopytoff, "African 'Slavery' as an Institution of Marginality," in *Slavery in Africa: Historical and Anthropological Perspectives* (Madison: University of Wisconsin Press, 1977): 3–81.

10. Sidney Mintz, "Slave Life on Caribbean Sugar Plantations: Some Unanswered Questions," in Stephan Palmié, ed., *Slave Cultures and the Cultures of Slavery* (Knoxville: University of Tennessee Press, 1995), 13.

11. For a widely cited critique of agency as the "master trope of new social history," see Walter Johnson, "On Agency," *Journal of Social History* 37, no. 1 (2003): 113–24. Other critiques of the domination and resistance framework include Dylan C. Penningroth, "My People, My People: The Dynamics of Community in Southern Slavery," in *New Studies in the History of American Slavery*, ed. Edward E. Baptist and Stephanie M. H. Camp (Athens: University of Georgia Press, 2006), 166–78; Vincent Brown, "Social Death and Political Life in the Study of Slavery," *American Historical Review* 114, no. 5 (2009): 1231–49; Joseph Miller, *The Problem of Slavery as History* (New Haven: Yale University Press, 2012), 19–23; Justin Roberts, *Slavery and the Enlightenment in the British Atlantic, 1750–1807* (New York: Cambridge University Press, 2013), 2–3; and Marjoleine Kars, "Dodging Rebellion: Politics and Gender in the Berbice Slave Uprising of 1763," *American Historical Review* 121, no. 1 (2016): 39–69.

12. Brown, "Social Death and Political Life," 1246.

13. For an introduction to these records, see Trevor Burnard and John Lean, "Hearing Slave Voices: The Fiscal's Reports of Berbice and Demerara-Essequebo," *Archives* 27, no. 107 (2002): 120–33.

14. As a "conquered" colony, Berbice did not have the same political rights as older West Indian colonies such as Jamaica, where local assemblies had greater autonomy under the old representative system. By the early nineteenth century, Britain had instituted a new form of government known as "crown colony rule," intended, as Barry Higman has explained, "to put control firmly in the hands of governors and the newly emerged Colonial Office in London. Rather than an assembly made up of rich white men elected by their equals, the governor of a crown colony needed only the support of a Council, the members of which he nominated and most of whom were officials appointed ex officio. The governor, in turn, was under the thumb of the Colonial Office." B. W. Higman, *A Concise History of the Caribbean* (New York: Cambridge University Press, 2011), 191. The crown colony system would replace the old representative system throughout the British Caribbean over the course of the nineteenth century, including British Guiana in 1831. However, between the Dutch surrender of Berbice in 1814 and the enactment of crown colony rule, Berbice's government retained a Court of Policy with limited legislative powers and can "best described as a hybrid between the West Indian legislative and a Crown Colony government," with the Colonial Office having the authority to enact new laws through Orders-in-Council (Gordon Eton Gill, "Labor, Material Welfare, and Culture in Hydrologic Plantation Enterprises: A Study of Slavery in the British Colony of Berbice [Guyana]" [Ph.D. diss., Howard University, 2004, 356–57]). See also Hume Wrong, *Government of the West Indies* (Oxford: Clarendon Press, 1923); D. J. Murray, *The West Indies and the Development of Colonial Government, 1801–1834* (Oxford: Clarendon Press, 1965), 47–66 (esp. 59–65); and Higman, *Slave Populations*, 45.

15. As Da Costa observed, "Grievances always presuppose a notion of entitlement, thus, a close reading of the slaves' complaints uncovers their notions of 'rights.' Conversely, the

complaints also reveal the world they wished to create within the limits imposed on them by their masters. But it is important to remember that such complaints involved negotiations with masters and public authorities, and thus a search for common ground, a sort of compromise. The plaintiffs invoked norms that they thought whites in positions of authority might find acceptable. It is thus a 'public transcript' that we find in the records of the fiscals and protectors of slaves." *Crowns of Glory*, 72–73. For enslaved people's use of the law in Latin America (and especially Cuba), where colonial authorities offered protections that were much less common in most British and North American slave societies, see Alejandro de la Fuente, "Slave Law and Claims-Making in Cuba: The Tannenbaum Debate Revisited," *Law and History Review* 22, no. 2 (2004): 339–69. For a different example of subaltern engagement with colonial law to claim rights and protection, see Steve J. Stern, *Peru's Indian Peoples and the Challenge of Spanish Conquest: Huamanga to 1640* (Madison: University of Wisconsin Press, 1982), esp. ch. 5.

16. J. H. Lean, "The Secret Lives of Slaves: Berbice, 1819–1827" (Ph.D. diss., University of Canterbury, 2002), 30–33.

17. For "public" and "hidden" transcripts, see James Scott, *Domination and the Arts of Resistance: Hidden Transcripts* (New Haven: Yale University Press, 1990).

18. Rachel Sarah O'Toole described the process of reading judicial records involving enslaved Africans (and indigenous people) in colonial Peru "with the grain" as the search not for what the actors "really" wanted but how "Andeans and Africans were also presenting themselves (or being presented) as witnesses, plaintiffs, and defendants in a legal context that many of them were versed in the logistics of or would quickly learn." O'Toole, *Bound Lives: Africans, Indians, and the Making of Race in Colonial Peru* (Pittsburgh: University of Pittsburgh Press, 2012), 12. See also Ann Laura Stoler, *Along the Archival Grain: Epistemic Anxieties and Colonial Common Sense* (Princeton, N.J.: Princeton University Press, 2009), whom O'Toole cited.

19. For the rapid development of the often overlooked British colonies in the southern Caribbean in the late eighteenth and early nineteenth centuries, see Kit Candlin, *The Last Caribbean Frontier, 1795–1815* (New York: Palgrave Macmillan, 2012).

20. For Atlantic Creoles, see Ira Berlin, *Many Thousands Gone: The First Two Centuries of Slavery in North America* (Cambridge, Mass.: Harvard University Press, 1998); Jane G. Landers, *Atlantic Creoles in the Age of Revolutions* (Cambridge, Mass.: Harvard University Press, 2010).

Chapter 1. Slavery and Empire on the Wild Coast

1. *Voyages: The Trans-Atlantic Slave Trade Database*, www.slavevoyages.org, voyage 80435, accessed Nov. 4, 2014. Grand Mesurado was never a major slaving port, exporting only 5,375 documented captives over the entire slave trade. *Voyages*, accessed Nov. 6, 2014. For slave ship revolts on the Windward Coast, see David Richardson, "Shipboard Revolts, African Authority, and the Atlantic Slave Trade," *William and Mary Quarterly* 58, no. 1 (2001): 69–92 (esp. 77, 81); Eric Robert Taylor, *If We Must Die: Shipboard Insurrections in the Era of the Atlantic Slave Trade* (Baton Rouge: Louisiana State University Press, 2006), 63–64. For the slave trade on the Windward Coast, which exported fewer captives than any other Atlantic African region, see Adam Jones and Marion Johnson, "Slaves from the Windward Coast," *Journal of African History* 21, no. 1 (1980): 17–34; Marcus Rediker, *The Slave Ship: A Human History* (New York: Viking, 2007), 82–84; Jelmer Vos, "The Slave Trade from the Windward Coast: The Case of the Dutch, 1740–1805," *African Economic History* 38 (2010): 29–51. Alexander Geddes described slave ships as "portable prisons," and James Stanfield called the slave ship a "floating dungeon." Geddes, *An Apology for Slavery: or Six Cogent Arguments against the Immediate Abolition of the Slave Trade*

(London: J. Johnson and R. Faulder, 1792), 45; Stanfield, *The Guinea Voyage, A Poem in Three Books* (London: James Phillips, 1789), 26. See also Rediker, *Slave Ship*, 45, 370n12.

2. Alvin O. Thompson, *Colonialism and Underdevelopment in Guyana, 1580–1803* (Bridgetown, Barbados: Carib Research & Publications, 1987), 2; Gordon Eton Gill, "Labor, Material Welfare, and Culture in Hydrologic Plantation Enterprises: A Study of Slavery in the British Colony of Berbice (Guyana)" (Ph.D. diss., Howard University, 2004), 18; Alvin O. Thompson, *Unprofitable Servants: Crown Slaves in Berbice, Guyana, 1803–1831* (Kingston: University of the West Indies Press, 2002), 16.

3. Thomas Staunton St. Clair, *A Residence in the West Indies and America . . .* (London, 1834), 84–85.

4. "Remarks and Observations on the Coast of Guyana by Cap^{tn} Thompson," in "The Coast of Guyana . . ." (London, 1783), Colonial Office (hereafter CO) 700/ BritishGuiana2, National Archives, Kew, London, United Kingdom.

5. George Pinckard, *Notes on the West Indies . . .* (London: Longman, Hurst, Rees, and Orme, 1806), 2:335; Henry Bolingbroke, *A Voyage to the Demerary . . .* (London: Richard Phillips, 1807), 11–12; Thompson, *Colonialism and Underdevelopment*, 2.

6. Bird also captained earlier voyages to the Guianas, St. Barthélemy and Trinidad. *Voyages*, voyages 81322, 84058, 28208, 80744, accessed Nov. 4, 2014.

7. Bolingbroke, *A Voyage to the Demerary*, 168–70.

8. For the sharks that followed slave ships, see Marcus Rediker, "History from Below the Water Line: Sharks and the Atlantic Slave Trade," *Atlantic Studies* 5, no. 2 (2008): 285–97.

9. Buyers normally traveled to Demerara, where many more slave ships landed, to purchase slaves or received them via transshipment. See Bolingbroke, *Voyage to Demerary*, 163–64; Thompson, *Unprofitable Servants*, 18–20; Gill, "Labor, Material Welfare, and Culture," 18–19, 110. Berbice was the principal place of slave landing for only fifteen slave ships between 1790 and 1808, whereas Demerara was the principal place of slave landing for 265 slave ships in the same period. *Voyages*, accessed July 28, 2016.

10. Pinckard, *Notes on the West Indies*, 2:326–27.

11. St. Clair, *Residence in the West Indies*, 195. For the process of preparing captives for sale, see Stephanie E. Smallwood, *Saltwater Slavery: A Middle Passage from Africa to American Diaspora* (Cambridge, Mass: Harvard University Press, 2007), 153–81.

12. St. Clair, *Residence in the West Indies*, 190. In August 1805 the British government issued an Order in Council that restricted the transatlantic slave trade to Berbice and the other "conquered colonies" Britain occupied during the Napoleonic Wars (Demerara, Trinidad, Tobago, St. Lucia, and Suriname). The complete ban on British transatlantic slave trading was passed in March 1807 and went into effect in January 1808.

13. Pinckard, *Notes on the West Indies*, 2:326.

14. St. Clair, *Residence in the West Indies*, 221.

15. Berbice Dutch was based largely on the language spoken by Ịjọ people from the Niger River delta. See Norval S. H. Smith, Ian E. Robertson, and Kay Williamson, "The Ijo Element in Berbice Dutch," *Language in Society* 16, no. 1 (1987): 49–89; J. H. Lean, "The Secret Lives of Slaves: Berbice, 1819 to 1827" (Ph.D. diss., University of Canterbury, 2002), 31–32; Gill, "Labor, Material Welfare, and Culture," 317–22; and Silvia Kouwenberg, "The Invisible Hand in Creole Genesis: Reanalysis in the Formation of Berbice Dutch," in *Complex Processes in New Languages*, ed. Enoch Aboh and Norval Smith (Amsterdam: John Benjamins, 2009), 115–58.

16. About 30 percent of slaves in Berbice were registered as having country marks or

scarification tattoos in 1819. B. W. Higman, *Slave Populations of the British Caribbean, 1807–1834* (Baltimore: Johns Hopkins University Press, 1984), 128.

17. For "shipmates" and fictive kinship, see Sidney W. Mintz and Richard Price, *The Birth of African-American Culture: An Anthropological Perspective* (Boston: Beacon Press, 1976), 43–44; Rediker, *Slave Ship*, 305–6.

18. For the expansion of slavery in the southern Caribbean and the contrast with declining slavery in older West Indian colonies, see Seymour Drescher, *Econocide: British Slavery in the Era of Abolition*, 2nd ed. (Chapel Hill: University of North Carolina Press, 2010), esp. 92–112. As Drescher noted, the "decline thesis" for West Indian slavery largely ignored "British slavery's enormous new frontier at the beginning of the nineteenth century." Ibid., xxiii. See also Kit Candlin, *The Last Caribbean Frontier, 1795–1815* (London: Palgrave Macmillan, 2012).

19. Rik Van Welie, "Slave Trading and Slavery in the Dutch Colonial Empire: A Global Comparison," *New West Indian Guide* 82, nos. 1–2 (2008): 66; Gert Oostindie, " 'British Capital, Industry and Perseverance' Versus Dutch 'Old School'?: The Dutch Atlantic and the Takeover of Berbice, Demerara and Essequibo, 1750–1815," *BMGN-Low Countries Historical Review* 127, no. 4 (2012): 50; *Voyages*, accessed Nov. 13, 2016.

20. David Eltis, "The Traffic in Slaves Between the British West Indian Colonies, 1807–1833," *Economic History Review* 25, no. 1 (1972): 55–56. According to Bolingbroke, the colonies were "daily getting more negroes from the West Indian islands" (*Voyage to Demerary*, 177).

21. Oostindie, "British Capital," 50; Gill, "Labor, Material Welfare, and Culture," 44. As Nicholas Draper has shown, the disproportionate emphasis on Jamaica has obscured the importance of Britain's southern Caribbean colonies. See Draper, "The Rise of a New Planter Class? Some Countercurrents from British Guiana and Trinidad, 1807–33," *Atlantic Studies* 9, no. 1 (2012): 65–83.

22. For Ralegh's voyage and the subsequent explorations it inspired, see Joyce Lorimer, ed., *Sir Walter Ralegh's Discoverie of Guiana* (Hants, Eng.: Ashgate, 2006). See also Thompson, *Colonialism and Underdevelopment*, 16–19.

23. For early Dutch colonization, see Cornelis Christiaan Goslinga, *The Dutch in the Caribbean and in the Guianas, 1680–1791* (Dover, N.H.: Van Gorcum, 1985); Thompson, *Colonialism and Underdevelopment*; Marjoleine Kars, " 'Cleansing the Land': Dutch-Amerindian Cooperation in the Suppression of the 1763 Slave Rebellion in Berbice," in *Empires and Indigenes: Intercultural Alliance, Imperial Expansion, and Warfare in the Early Modern World*, ed. Wayne Lee (New York: New York University Press, 2011), 252–54, 264. For native peoples, see Neil Whitehead, "Native Peoples Confront Colonial Regimes in Northeastern South America (c. 1500–1900)," in *The Cambridge History of the Native Peoples of the Americas*, vol. 3, *South America*, part 2, ed. Frank Salomon and Stuart B. Schwartz (New York: Cambridge University Press, 1999), 382–442.

24. For the early colonization of Berbice, see Thompson, *Colonialism and Underdevelopment*, 25–26, 34–35; Marjoleine Kars, "Policing and Transgressing Borders: Soldiers, Slave Rebels, and the Early Modern Atlantic," *New West Indian Guide* 83, nos. 3–4 (2009): 189; Kars, "Adventures in Research: Chasing the Past in Guyana," *Uncommon Sense*, no. 124 (2007); Kars, " 'Cleansing the Land,' " 252–54. According to David Eltis, "in the Guianas, two-thirds of all arrivals before 1750 came from the adjacent Gold Coast and Bight of Benin," with West Central Africa becoming predominant in the third quarter of the eighteenth century. Eltis, "The Volume and Structure of the Transatlantic Slave Trade: A Reassessment," *William and Mary Quarterly* 58, no. 1 (2001): 39. Of the 5,349 captives who disembarked in Berbice between 1620 and 1750,

2,742 were purchased on the Gold Coast. *Voyages*, accessed Nov. 13, 2016. See also Van Welie, "Slave Trading and Slavery," 66.

25. For the 1763 rebellion, see Kars, "'Cleansing the Land'"; Kars, "Policing and Transgressing"; and Kars, "Dodging Rebellion: Politics and Gender in the Berbice Slave Uprising of 1763," *American Historical Review* 121, no. 1 (2016): 39–69.

26. Thompson, *Colonialism and Underdevelopment*, 153–74; Kars, "Policing and Transgressing," 191; Kars, "'Cleansing the Land,'" 251–75.

27. Thompson, *Colonialism and Underdevelopment*, 43.

28. For the 1772 Rule on the Treatment of Servants and Slaves, see Emília Viotti da Costa, *Crowns of Glory, Tears of Blood: The Demerara Slave Rebellion of 1823* (New York: Oxford University Press, 1994), 44–45.

29. For the Dutch slave trade, see Johannes Postma, *The Dutch in the Atlantic Slave Trade, 1600–1815* (Cambridge: Cambridge University Press, 1990); Van Welie, "Slave Trading and Slavery"; Postma, "A Reassessment of the Dutch Atlantic Slave Trade," in *Riches from Atlantic Commerce: Dutch Transatlantic Trade and Shipping, 1585–1817*, ed. Johannes Postma and Victor Enthoven (Leiden: Brill, 2003), 115–38.

30. Thompson, *Colonialism and Underdevelopment*, 38.

31. Ibid., 92.

32. *Voyages*, accessed Nov. 6, 2014. This figure is based on documented slave voyages and therefore the actual number of captives is probably higher. Under the Second WIC, 12,904 slaves were imported to Berbice and Essequibo together between 1674 and 1740. See Van Welie, "Slave Trading and Slavery," 63.

33. Van Welie, "Slave Trading and Slavery," 65.

34. Kars, "Policing and Transgressing," 189; Oostindie, "British Capital," 31.

35. *Voyages*, accessed Nov. 25, 2014.

36. Oostindie, "British Capital," 35–38.

37. Ibid., 35–36; Thompson, *Colonialism and Underdevelopment*, 44–45.

38. Quoted in Oostindie, "British Capital," 36.

39. Pinckard, *Notes on the West Indies*, 2:314.

40. Higman, *Slave Populations*, 91–92.

41. Berbice had two wet seasons, a short one from December to early February and a longer one from late April to mid-August. See Bolingbroke, *Voyage to Demerary*, 86; Thompson, *Unprofitable Servants*, 20; Gill, "Labor, Material Welfare, and Culture," 26.

42. Pinckard, *Notes on the West Indies*, 2:198.

43. St. Clair, *Residence in the West Indies*, 139, 122.

44. Pinckard, *Notes on the West Indies*, 2:185.

45. Ibid., 210.

46. St. Clair, *Residence in the West Indies*, 98.

47. Da Costa, *Crowns of Glory*, 141–42.

48. Pinckard, *Notes on the West Indies*, 2:183 ("singularly unhealthy"); Thompson, *Unprofitable Servants*, 20–21. For Berbice's disease environment, see Gill, "Labor, Material Welfare, and Culture," chapter 6, 227–61.

49. *Copy of the Report of the Commissioners appointed for the management of The Crown Estates in the colony of Berbice . . .* , Parliamentary Papers, House of Commons (hereafter PP), May 20, 1816, 3.

50. Higman, *Slave Populations*, 344–45, Table S8.13, "Causes of Slave Deaths: Berbice,

1819–22," 630–35; Gill, "Labor, Material Welfare, and Culture," 231. Field laborers were in near constant contact with water and were therefore the most likely to die of diarrhea, which accounted for 16.6 percent of deaths among male field workers and 19.2 percent of deaths among women field workers. Higman, *Slave Populations*, Table S9.40, "Causes of Adult Slave Deaths by Sex and Occupation: Berbice, 1819–22 (Slaves Aged 20–50 Years)," 678.

51. Gill, "Labor, Material Welfare, and Culture," 233–39; J. R. McNeill, *Mosquito Empires: Ecology and War in the Greater Caribbean, 1620–1914* (Cambridge: Cambridge University Press, 2010), 196.

52. Higman, *Slave Populations*, 298.

53. Gill emphasized the importance of Berbice's ecology in "Labor, Material Welfare, and Culture." For similar environmental factors in Suriname, see Gert Oostindie and Alex van Stipriaan, "Slavery and Slave Cultures in a Hydraulic Society: Suriname," in *Slave Cultures and the Cultures of Slavery*, ed. Stephan Palmié (Knoxville: University of Tennessee Press, 1995), 78–99.

54. Lean, "Secret Lives of Slaves," 27.

55. Bolingbroke, *Voyage to Demerary*, 30; Oostindie and van Stipriaan, "Slavery and Slave Cultures," 87.

56. Thompson, *Colonialism and Underdevelopment*, 110; Da Costa, *Crowns of Glory*, 44; Oostindie and van Stipriaan, "Slavery and Slave Cultures," 87; Gill, "Labor, Material Welfare, and Culture," 142–45.

57. In 1781, British forces occupied Berbice. The French recaptured the colony in 1782 and returned it to their Dutch allies in 1783. Britain recaptured Berbice in 1796 and maintained possession until 1802, when it restored the colony to the revolutionary Batavian Republic. In September 1803 the British occupied Berbice, Demerara, and Essequibo yet again. The colonies were formally ceded to Britain in 1814 and united in 1831 as British Guiana, which remained part of the British Empire until 1966, when the independent Co-operative Republic of Guyana was founded.

58. Drescher, *Econocide*, 76.

59. Da Costa, *Crowns of Glory*, 20; Drescher, *Econocide*, 95–96.

60. Bolingbroke, *Voyage to Demerary*, 177.

61. Thompson, *Colonialism and Underdevelopment*, 92.

62. "A Statement of the Population in the Colony of Berbice . . . ," Jan. 1799, CO 111/73, 10 (thanks to Marjoleine Kars, Han Jordaan, and Victor Enthoven for this citation); Thompson, *Colonialism and Underdevelopment*, 64–65; Higman, *Slave Populations*, Table S1.2, "Estimated Annual Slave Populations by Colony, 1807–34," 417–18; Thompson, *Unprofitable Servants*, 25; Gill, "Labor, Material Welfare, and Culture," 44.

63. Drescher, *Econocide*, 96.

64. Bolingbroke, *Voyage to Demerary*. See also Da Costa, *Crowns of Glory*, 40–41; Oostindie, "British Capital" (esp. 51).

65. Bolingbroke, *Voyage to Demerary*, 178.

66. Ibid., 183.

67. Drescher, *Econocide*, 94.

68. Higman, *Slave Populations*, 63.

69. Da Costa, *Crowns of Glory*, 28. See also Thompson, *Colonialism and Underdevelopment*, 64.

70. Quoted in Drescher, *Econocide*, 97.

71. Draper, "Rise of a New Planter Class?" 68.

72. Alvin O. Thompson, *A Documentary History of Slavery in Berbice, 1796–1834*

(Georgetown, Guyana: Free Press, 2002), 2; Gill, "Labor, Material Welfare, and Culture," 38–39; Drescher, *Econocide*, 83.

73. Da Costa, *Crowns of Glory*, 28.

74. Higman, *Slave Populations*, 63; Klaas Kramer, "Plantation Development in Berbice from 1753 to 1779: The Shift from the Interior to the Coast," *New West Indian Guide* 65, nos. 1–2 (1991), 53–56; Thompson, *Unprofitable Servants*, 24; Gill, "Labor, Material Welfare, and Culture," 41–42.

75. Higman, *Slave Populations*, 63; Gill, "Labor, Material Welfare, and Culture," 226.

76. Adamson, *Sugar Without Slaves*, 24; Da Costa, *Crowns of Glory*, 40–43.

77. Berbice's slave population peaked in 1807. See Higman, *Slave Populations*, 417–19; Thompson, *Unprofitable Servants*, 53.

78. Of West Indian sugar colonies, only Barbados had a self-reproducing population in the nineteenth century. See Higman, *Slave Populations*, 307–14.

79. Bolingbroke, *Voyage to Demerary*, 176.

80. Eltis, "Traffic in Slaves," 59–60. Between 1822 and 1830, slaves in British Guiana sold for average of £114 11s (shillings) 5d (pence), compared with just £44 15s 2d in Jamaica in the same period. See Draper, "Rise of a New Planter Class?" 68.

81. Demerara imported about 6,000 slaves from other colonies between 1809 and 1820. See Eltis, "Traffic in Slaves," 55, 57–58; Draper, "Rise of a New Planter Class?" 68; Drescher, *Econocide*, 173.

82. Drescher, *Econocide*, 84–87. For the U.S. cotton kingdom, see Walter Johnson, *River of Dark Dreams: Slavery and Empire in the Cotton Kingdom* (Cambridge, Mass.: Harvard University Press, 2013).

83. Da Costa, *Crowns of Glory*, 28.

84. Adamson, *Sugar Without Slaves*, 25; Gill, "Labor, Material Welfare, and Culture," 125.

85. Da Costa, *Crowns of Glory*, 28; Adamson, *Sugar Without Slaves*, 26.

86. Between 1813 and 1815 alone about one-eighth of Berbice's slave population was transferred to Demerara. See Gill, "Labor, Material Welfare, and Culture," 50. For more on the movement of enslaved people from Berbice to Demerara, see Eltis, "Traffic in Slaves," 59; Thompson, *Documentary History*, 1; and Thompson, *Unprofitable Servants*, 24–25.

87. Higman, *Slave Populations*, 72, 76.

88. "Third-phase" colonies were those that Britain acquired from other European powers during the French Revolutionary and Napoleonic Wars. The last colonies that Britain established in the Caribbean, they included Trinidad, St. Lucia, Demerara, Essequibo, and Berbice. See Higman, *Slave Populations*, 44–45, 58–64.

89. Ibid., Table S1.2, "Estimated Annual Slave Populations by Colony, 1807–34," 417–18. Figures are for 1807.

90. Ibid.

91. Ibid., Table 5.7, "Slave Sex Ratios and Percentages African and Colored by Colony, c. 1817 and c. 1832," 116, 122–23.

92. Ibid. In 1817, only 7.1 percent of slaves in Barbados and 37 percent of those in Jamaica were African.

93. Ibid., Table 5.10, "Birthplaces of African Slaves: St. Kitts, St. Lucia, Trinidad, Berbice, and Anguilla, 1813–27," 127, Table S3.4, "Birthplaces of Slaves: Berbice, 1819," 454–55 (these figures are based on only 9.6 percent of all enslaved people in the colony).

94. Philip D. Morgan, "The Cultural Implications of the Atlantic Slave Trade: African

Regional Origins, American Destinations and New World Developments," *Slavery and Abolition* 18, no. 1 (1997), 128.

95. Higman, *Slave Populations*, Table S3.4, "Birthplaces of Slaves: Berbice," 454–56.

96. Sex ratios became more even as the population became more creolized, but men outnumbered women throughout the period of slavery. See Higman, *Slave Populations*, Table 5.7, "Slave Sex Ratios and Percentages of African and Colored by Colony, c. 1817 and c. 1832," 116, fig. 5.1, "Slave Sex Ratios, 1616–34," 117.

97. For the lack of urban development, see Thompson, *Colonialism and Underdevelopment*, 76.

98. Pinckard, *Notes on the West Indies*, 2:316–17.

99. Higman, *Slave Populations*, 256.

100. Pinckard, *Notes on the West Indies*, 2:314.

101. Bolingbroke, *Voyage to Demerary*, 168–70.

102. For *winkel* slaves, see Thompson, *Unprofitable Servants*.

103. Population statistics for New Amsterdam vary considerably. See Higman, *Slave Populations*, Table 4.4, "Major Town Slave Populations, 1813–34," 94; Thompson, *Unprofitable Servants*, 107.

104. Thompson, *Unprofitable Servants*, 103 (quote), 104–5 .

105. Thompson, *Colonialism and Underdevelopment*, 70.

106. Lean, "Secret Lives of Slaves," 27, Table 7.6, "Punishments 1826 & 1827: Absentee vs Local Landlords," 318.

107. Peter Kolchin, *American Slavery, 1619–1877* (New York: Hill and Wang, 2003 [1993]), 30. "In the [antebellum] South as a whole," Kolchin writes, "slaves formed about one-third of the population," and "like their colonial forebears, antebellum Southern slaves did not generally live in the kind of overwhelmingly black world that prevailed in much of the Caribbean." Ibid., 100.

108. "A Statement of the Population," Jan. 1799.

109. Thompson, *Colonialism and Underdevelopment*, 112; Thompson, *Unprofitable Servants*, 26.

110. Higman, *Slave Populations*, Table S.2.1, "White and Freedman Populations by Sex and Colony, c. 1830," 433.

111. Thompson, *Colonialism and Underdevelopment*, 112–13; Thompson, *Unprofitable Servants*, 107. Absentee-owned plantations usually had larger slave populations (180 slaves, on average) than those with resident planters. See Lean, "Secret Lives of Slaves," 162, 324. "The great majority" of enslaved people in North America "lived on holdings of under fifty" people, and only 2.7 percent of Southern slaveholders owned fifty or more slaves in 1860. Only about one-quarter of American slaves lived on estates of fifty or more people. See Kolchin, *American Slavery*, 30 (quote), 100–101.

112. For intensifying work regimes and deteriorating living conditions under British rule, see Da Costa, *Crowns of Glory*, 40–43, 54–55. The dynamics Da Costa identified for Demerara were even more pronounced in Berbice since Demerara siphoned off much of Berbice's slave population.

113. Henry Bentinck to Earl Bathurst, April 29, 1814, CO 111/81, quoted in Thompson, *Documentary History*, 134.

114. Ibid.

115. Ibid.

116. Minutes of the Court of Policy and Criminal Justice, June 6, 1814, Guyana National Archives [Walter Rodney Archives], in Thompson, *Documentary History*, 136.

117. Gill, "Labor, Material Welfare, and Culture," 296.

118. Minutes of the Court of Policy and Criminal Justice, May 14, 1814, Guyana National Archives [Walter Rodney Archives], in Thompson, *Documentary History*, 137–38.

119. Thompson, *Documentary History*, 17–18.

120. For currencies used in Demerara (and Berbice), see Da Costa, *Crowns of Glory*, 137.

121. In 1819, about 35 percent of all registered slaveowners had Dutch surnames. Many overseers and managers were also Dutch. See Higman, *Slave Populations*, 109.

122. Da Costa, *Crowns of Glory*, 21; Lean, "Secret Lives of Slaves," 22.

123. M. Shahabuddeen, *The Legal System of Guyana* (Georgetown, Guyana: Guyana Printers, 1973); Lean, "Secret Lives of Slaves," 22. For the different legal regimes of American slave societies, see Alan Watson, *Slave Law in the Americas* (Athens: University of Georgia Press, 1989). For Dutch slave laws in neighboring Suriname, see Natalie Zemon Davis, "Judges, Masters, Diviners: Slaves' Experience of Criminal Justice in Colonial Suriname," *Law and History Review* 29, no. 4 (2011): 925–84 (esp. 941–43, 959–60). It was not unusual in the British Empire for conquered colonies to be governed by a mix of local and British laws. See Lauren Benton, *Law and Colonial Cultures: Legal Regimes in World History, 1400–1900* (Cambridge: Cambridge University Press, 2002).

124. South Africa's Cape Colony—which Britain also seized from the Dutch during the French Revolutionary Wars—had a fiscal as well. See Robert John Ross, *Cape of Torments: Slavery and Resistance in South Africa* (London: Routledge & Kegan Paul, 1983), and John Edwin Mason, *Social Death and Resurrection: Slavery and Emancipation in South Africa* (Charlottesville: University of Virginia Press, 2003).

125. Bolingbroke, *Voyage to Demerary*, 78.

126. Henry G. Dalton, *History of British Guiana* . . . (London: Longman, Brown, Green, and Longmans, 1855), 1:273–75; Da Costa, *Crowns of Glory*, 44–46. For a brief history of the fiscal and his responsibilities, see Appendix 1, "Office of the Fiscal," CO 116/155.

127. Da Costa, *Crowns of Glory*, 46; Lean, "Secret Lives of Slaves," 38.

128. Shahabuddeen, *Legal System of Guyana*, 373–78.

129. Ibid., 375. Owners incurred a twelve-guilder fine for every slave that went to the fiscal and were charged twenty-five guilders when the fiscal punished enslaved people for making "unfounded" complaints.

130. Lean, "Secret Lives of Slaves," 38–39; Trevor Burnard, *Hearing Slaves Speak* (Georgetown, Guyana: Caribbean Press, 2010), xiii.

131. As Mary Turner observed, the fiscal "combined in his person every level of authority over slaves" ("The 11 O'Clock Flog: Women, Work and Labour Law in the British Caribbean," *Slavery and Abolition* 20, no. 1 [1999], 41).

132. Gill, "Labor, Material Welfare, and Culture," 54; Turner, "11 O'Clock Flog," 41.

133. "EXTRACT of a Letter addressed to Sir B. D'Urban, by Mr. M. S. Bennett, Fiscal of Berbice . . . ," Jan. 21, 1826, in *Further papers relating to slaves in the West Indies . . . copies of the record of the proceedings of the fiscals of Demerara and Berbice, in their capacity of guardians and protectors of the slaves,* Parliamentary Papers 401 (1826), 4.

134. Da Costa, *Crowns of Glory*, 33.

135. For abolitionists' hopes that ending the slave trade would lead to better conditions for slaves, see Claudius K. Fergus, *Revolutionary Emancipation: Slavery and Abolitionism in the British West Indies* (Baton Rouge: Louisiana State University Press, 2013), chapter 3.

136. Robin Blackburn, *The Overthrow of Colonial Slavery, 1776–1848* (London: Verso, 1988), 421–22.

137. D. J. Murray, *The West Indies and the Development of Colonial Government, 1801–1834* (Oxford: Clarendon Press, 1965), 106, 127; David Lambert, *White Creole Culture, Politics and Identity During the Age of Abolition* (Cambridge: Cambridge University Press, 2005), 143.

138. For the connections between abolitionism and other reform efforts, see David Turley, *The Culture of English Antislavery, 1780–1860* (New York: Routledge, 1991), 104–49. For the overlap of penal reform and antislavery, see Diana Paton, *No Bond but the Law: Punishment, Race, and Gender in Jamaican State Formation, 1780–1870* (Durham, N.C.: Duke University Press, 2004). See also Margaret Abruzzo, *Polemical Pain: Slavery, Cruelty, and the Rise of Humanitarianism* (Baltimore: Johns Hopkins University Press, 2011). For resident planters who promoted agricultural "improvement" and amelioration, see David Collins, *Practical Rules for the Management and Medical Treatment of Negro Slaves . . .* (London: Printed by J. Barfield, 1803); Joshua Steele, *Mitigation of Slavery, in Two Parts* (London: R. and A. Taylor, 1814); Lambert, *White Creole Culture*, 41–72 (esp. 44–47); Justin Roberts, *Slavery and the Enlightenment in the British Atlantic, 1750–1807* (New York: Cambridge University Press, 2013), 26–79.

139. For representative planter opposition to amelioration, see James M'Queen, *The West India Colonies . . .* (London: Baldwin, Cradock, and Joy, 1824); Alexander M'Donnell, *Considerations on Negro Slavery* (London: Longman, Hurst, Rees, Orme, Brown, and Green, 1824). For the intellectual history of amelioration, see Christa Dierksheide, *Amelioration and Empire: Progress and Slavery in the Plantation Americas* (Charlottesville: University of Virginia Press, 2014).

140. Murray, *West Indies*, 127–30.

141. David Brion Davis, *Slavery and Human Progress* (New York: Oxford University Press, 1984), 192–94; Blackburn, *Overthrow of Colonial Slavery*, 421–22; Murray, *West Indies*, 128–29; Lambert, *White Creole Culture*, 146–47. For the Colonial Office's recommendations, see Circulars, May 28 and July 9, 1824, CO 29/20, 246–64, 265–91.

142. Michael Craton, *Testing the Chains: Resistance to Slavery in the British West Indies* (Ithaca, N.Y.: Cornell University Press, 1982), 254–66; Mary Turner, "The British Caribbean, 1823–1838: The Transition from Slave to Free Legal Status," in *Masters, Servants, and Magistrates in Britain and the Empire, 1562–1955*, ed. Douglas Hay and Paul Craven (Chapel Hill: University of North Carolina Press, 2004), 305–9; Lambert, *White Creole Culture*, 147–48;

143. Lambert, *White Creole Culture*, 105–39 (esp. 112–15).

144. Da Costa, *Crowns of Glory*, esp. 177–79, 182. As Da Costa noted, it is unclear "whether the slaves thought the 'new laws' made them free, or whether they just expected to have two or three days a week for themselves" (172). For other revolts sparked by similar rumors, see David Patrick Geggus, "Slavery, War, and Revolution in the Greater Caribbean, 1789–1815," in *A Turbulent Time: The French Revolution and the Greater Caribbean*, ed. David Barry Gaspar and David Patrick Geggus (Bloomington: Indiana University Press, 1997), 1–50 (esp. 7–8); Wim Klooster, "Slave Revolts, Royal Justice, and a Ubiquitous Rumor in the Age of Revolutions," *William and Mary Quarterly* 71, no. 3 (2014): 401–24.

145. Da Costa, *Crowns of Glory*, 178–85, 197 (quotation); Klooster, "Slave Revolts," 421.

146. Murray, *West Indies*, 130; J. R. Ward, *British West Indian Slavery, 1750–1834: The Process of Amelioration* (Oxford: Clarendon Press, 1988), 275; Caroline Quarrier Spence, "Ameliorating Empire: Slavery and Protection in the British Colonies, 1783–1865" (Ph.D. diss., Harvard University, 2014), 195–96. For the impact of the rebellion on British antislavery, see Gelien Matthews, *Caribbean Slave Revolts and the British Abolitionist Movement* (Baton Rouge: Louisiana State University Press, 2006), esp. 38–57.

147. The Crown granted Smith a royal reprieve after intense public outrage at the death

sentence, but Smith died in prison before the news arrived. For the burning of Wray's chapel and his harassment after the Demerara rebellion, see Da Costa, *Crowns of Glory*, 247–49.

148. Murray, *West Indies*, 133. For amelioration in Trinidad, see Claudius Fergus, "Centering the City in the Amelioration of Slavery in Trinidad, 1824–1834," *Journal of Caribbean History* 40, no. 1 (2006): 117–39; Fergus, *Revolutionary Emancipation*, 142–60; Spence, "Ameliorating Empire."

149. The full text of the 1826 code was published in *The Berbice Royal Gazette*, Sept. 30, 1826 (reprinted in Thompson, *Documentary History*, 206–228) (hereafter 1826 slave code). For the differences between the slave codes of Demerara and Berbice, see *Papers in Explanation of the Measures Adopted by His Majesty's Government for the Melioration of the Condition of the Slave Population . . . Part II*, PP 008 (1826–27), 202–22. For the debate over reform in Demerara and Berbice, see Murray, *West Indies*, 134–38; Da Costa, *Crowns of Glory*, 178; Spence, "Ameliorating Empire," 203–11.

150. Thompson, *Documentary History*, 23–36.

151. Edward Trelawny to Earl of Bedford, April 14, 1750, quoted in James Robertson, "A 1748 'Petition of Negro Slaves' and the Local Politics of Slavery in Jamaica," *William and Mary Quarterly* 67, no. 2 (2010): 339.

152. Burke did not share his proposed code until 1792, when he sent a copy to home secretary Henry Dundas as the metropolitan government debated the slave trade. Jamaican planter and politician Edward Long, who drafted a plan for the amelioration of slavery in 1774, had similarly argued that the protective measures of the 1685 French *Code Noir*—which he generally praised—were insufficient because there was no way of enforcing them. Long proposed that European officers be appointed to inspect plantations throughout the island and report violations. See Long, *The History of Jamaica . . .* (London, 1774), 2:440–41; Fergus, *Revolutionary Emancipation*, 40–41; Spence, "Ameliorating Empire," 55–57.

153. "A Letter to the Right Hon. Hendry Dundas . . . with the Sketch of a Negro Code," in *The Writings and Speeches of Edmund Burke*, ed. P. J. Marshall (Oxford: Oxford University Press, 1991), 6:257–89 ("be under the sole guardianship," 276; "protector of negroes," 276–77; "Inspectors," "the state and condition," 277; "cruelly and inhumanly," "particular malice," 288; "blows," "stripes," 287). See also Robert Worthington Smith, "The Attempt of British Humanitarianism to Modify Chattel Slavery," in *British Humanitarianism: Essays Honoring Frank J. Klingberg . . .* , ed. Samuel Clyde McCulloch (Philadelphia: Church Historical Society, 1950), 169–70; Fergus, *Revolutionary Emancipation*, 52–54; and Spence, "Ameliorating Empire," 52–54.

154. In Berbice, the office of protector of slaves was established in 1817, though the position was initially staffed by the fiscal. See Thompson, *Unprofitable Servants*, 29. For Spanish and French antecedents, see Spence, "Ameliorating Empire."

155. Earl Bathurst to David Power, June 3, 1826, in *Parliamentary Papers* 008 (1826–1827), 192–93.

156. 1826 slave code, clauses 15, 16, 17.

157. "Reports of the Civil Magistrates in the Several Districts On the Promulgation of the New Code of the 25th September 1826," CO 111/102, 302–3.

158. For abolitionists' use of the fiscals' and protectors of slaves' records to criticize amelioration, see Diana Fung-Shing Lee, "Signs of the Hour: The Final Years of Slavery in British Colonial Berbice" (honors thesis, Bowdoin College, 2014).

159. *Anti-Slavery Monthly Reporter* 1, no. 5 (October 1825): 33.

160. For the treadmill in England, see Robin Evans, *The Fabrication of Virtue: English Prison*

Architecture, 1750–1840 (Cambridge: Cambridge University Press, 1982), 295–309; and Michael Ignatieff, *A Just Measure of Pain: The Penitentiary in the Industrial Revolution, 1750–1850* (New York: Pantheon Books, 1978), 177–79. For treadmills in the West Indies, see Higman, *Slave Populations*, 201, 243–44; Paton, *No Bond*, 44–45, 88; Thompson, *Unprofitable Servants*, 40–41.

161. "Regulations for the Tread Mill, Erected in The Colonial Jail of Berbice, for a Legal Mode of Correctional Punishment," encl. in Shanks to Earl Bathurst, July 29, 1828, CO 111/107, 5–7; "To His Excellency the Governor, Monthly Return of Slaves Worked on the Treadmill in August 1828," CO 111/107, 11.

162. As Lisa Ford argued, "the anti-slavery project was a legal one as well as a moral one" that constituted an attack on slaveowners' "rights in private property by investing slaves with tempered legal subjecthood" and "interposing imperial law between and over masters and slaves." Ford, "Anti-Slavery and the Reconstitution of Empire," *Australian Historical Studies* 45, no. 1 (2014): 72–73. See also Mason, *Social Death and Resurrection*, 50; Spence, "Ameliorating Empire."

163. As Caroline Spence observed in her discussion of the Crown's decision to maintain Spanish law in Trinidad and govern it as Crown Colony rather than grant it a legislative assembly, "Parliament recognized that protecting the interests of the slaves and the free people of color meant curbing the authority of white planters, even when it came to traditions and liberties that many whites had come to regard as fundamental to the British constitution" (Spence, "Ameliorating Empire," 131).

164. Turner, "11 O'Clock Flog," 49.

165. The recording of enslaved people's complaints to the fiscal only began in February 1819, after the newly arrived president of the courts of criminal and civil justice, Henry Beard, instructed fiscal Michael Samuel Bennett to keep written records. Henry Beard to Earl Bathurst, Feb. 19, 1825, CO 116/138; M. S. Bennett to Henry Beard, Feb. 19, 1825, CO 116/138. See also Lean, "Secret Lives of Slaves," 9–11.

166. "Complaint of the Woman Named Mary Belonging to L. F. Gallez," May 19, 1826, CO 116/141.

167. For an introduction to these records, see John Lean and Trevor Burnard, "Hearing Slave Voices: The Fiscal's Reports of Berbice and Demerara-Essequebo," *Archives* 27, no. 107 (2002): 120–33.

Chapter 2. Challenging the "Right of a Master to Punish"

1. "No. 23," Nov. 9, 1827, Colonial Office series (hereafter CO) 116/144, 39–40 ("a month"), 40 (all other quotations), National Archives, Kew, London, United Kingdom.

2. Ibid., 41 ("other wrist"), 42 ("yesterday was"), 43 ("Me see"), 44 ("one or two").

3. For the connections between abolitionism and other reform efforts, see David Turley, *The Culture of English Antislavery, 1780–1860* (New York: Routledge, 1991), 108–54. For the overlap of penal reform and antislavery, see Diana Paton, *No Bond but the Law: Punishment, Race, and Gender in Jamaican State Formation, 1780–1870* (Durham, N.C.: Duke University Press, 2004). For amelioration, see Justin Roberts, *Slavery and the Enlightenment in the British Atlantic, 1750–1807* (New York: Cambridge University Press, 2013); and Christa Dierksheide, *Amelioration and Empire: Progress and Slavery in the Plantation Americas* (Charlottesville: University of Virginia Press, 2014). See also Margaret Abruzzo, *Polemical Pain: Slavery, Cruelty, and the Rise of Humanitarianism* (Baltimore: Johns Hopkins University Press, 2011).

4. Trinidad planter and pro-slavery activist William Burnley, for example, argued that a

master's "domestic jurisdiction" over his slaves and especially his ability to use violence were critical to maintaining order. "If taken away totally, or even partially repealed by the enactment of regulations prohibiting several corporal punishments," Burnley claimed, "the fabric of slavery is virtually destroyed, and the negro, tho' not free, will cease to be of any value to his master." Quoted in Caroline Quarrier Spence, "Ameliorating Empire: Slavery and Protection in the British Colonies, 1783–1865" (Ph.D. diss., Harvard University, 2014), 187.

5. The full text of the 1826 code was published in *The Berbice Royal Gazette*, Sept. 30, 1826 (reprinted in Alvin O. Thompson, *A Documentary History of Slavery in Berbice, 1796–1834* [Georgetown, Guyana: Free Press, 2002], 206–28) (hereafter 1826 slave code). In 1831, a revised, consolidated slave code that repealed and replaced all slave laws passed since 1824 was enacted by Order in Council. See Order in Council, Nov. 5, 1831, *Papers in Explanation of Measures Adopted for the Melioration of the Condition of the Slave Population in the West Indies*, Parliamentary Papers, House of Commons (hereafter PP), 1830–31 (230), 93–138. See also Mary Turner, "'The British Caribbean, 1823–1838: The Transition from Slave to Free Legal Status," in *Masters, Servants, and Magistrates in Britain and the Empire, 1562–1955*, ed. Douglas Hay and Paul Craven (Chapel Hill: University of North Carolina Press, 2004), 310–13.

6. The classic work on this transformation is Michel Foucault, *Discipline and Punish: The Birth of the Prison*, trans. Alan Sheridan (New York: Vintage, 1977). See also James Heath, *Eighteenth Century Penal Theory* (Oxford: Oxford University Press, 1963); Michael Ignatieff, *A Just Measure of Pain: The Penitentiary in the Industrial Revolution, 1750–1850* (New York: Pantheon Books, 1978); and David J. Bentley, *English Criminal Justice in the Nineteenth Century* (London: Hambledon Press, 1998).

7. Branding was abolished in England in 1779, and whipping became much less common toward the end of the eighteenth century (declining from 17 to 11 percent of verdicts issued at the Old Bailey, England's central criminal court, between 1775 and 1790). By 1805, the first year national punishment statistics became available, whipping accounted for less than 5 percent of sentences at assize and sessions courts. See Ignatieff, *Just Measure of Pain*, 90; Bentley, *English Criminal Justice*, 11–12. Sailors also faced much greater levels of violence than other Britons and Anglo-Americans. See Marcus Rediker, *Between the Devil and the Deep Blue Sea: Merchant Seamen, Pirates, and the Anglo-American Maritime World, 1700–1750* (Cambridge: Cambridge University Press, 1987), 207–27.

8. Diana Paton, "Punishment, Crime, and the Bodies of Slaves in Eighteenth-Century Jamaica," *Journal of Social History* 34, no. 4 (2001): 923–54; Kirsten Fischer, *Suspect Relations: Sex, Race, and Resistance in Colonial North Carolina* (Ithaca, N.Y.: Cornell University Press, 2002), 179–80; Alvin Thompson, *Colonialism and Underdevelopment in Guyana, 1580–1803* (Bridgetown, Barbados: Carib Research & Publications, 1987), 118–19; Vincent Brown, *The Reaper's Garden: Death and Power in the World of Atlantic Slavery* (Cambridge, Mass.: Harvard University Press, 2008), 129–44; Russell Smandych, "'To Soften the Extreme Rigor of Their Bondage': James Stephen's Attempt to Reform the Criminal Slave Laws of the West Indies, 1813–1833," *Law and History Review* 23, no. 3 (2005): 568–70.

9. J. R. Ward, *British West Indian Slavery, 1750–1834: The Process of Amelioration* (Oxford: Clarendon Press, 1988), 204–5.

10. As the Jamaican planter and politician Bryan Edwards wrote, "In countries where slavery is established, the leading principle on which government is supported, is fear." *The History, Civil and Commercial, of the British Colonies in the West Indies* (London: John Stockdale, 1801), 3:13.

11. Ward, *West Indian Slavery*; Roberts, *Slavery and the Enlightenment*.

12. For Gladstone's experiments in amelioration, see Dierksheide, *Amelioration and Empire*, 180–209.

13. Joshua Steele, *Mitigation of Slavery, in Two Parts* (London: R. and A. Taylor, 1814). See also David Lambert, *White Creole Culture, Politics and Identity During the Age of Abolition* (Cambridge: Cambridge University Press, 2005), 41–72 (esp. 44–47); Roberts, *Slavery and the Enlightenment*, 47–49.

14. David Collins, *Practical Rules for the Management and Medical Treatment of Negro Slaves . . .* (London: J. Barfield, 1803), 23–26 (quotation, 23). See also Roberts, *Slavery and the Enlightenment*, esp. 238–78

15. Henry Bolingbroke, *A Voyage to the Demerary . . .* (London: Richard Phillips, 1807), 106.

16. For pre-amelioration slave laws, see Elsa Goveia, "The West Indian Slave Laws of the Eighteenth Century," in *Caribbean Slave Society and Economy: A Student Reader*, ed. Hilary Beckles and Verene A. Shepherd (Kingston: Ian Randle, 1991), 346–62. For early legal reforms, see David Barry Gaspar, "Ameliorating Slavery: The Leeward Islands Slave Act of 1798," in *The Lesser Antilles in the Age of European Expansion*, ed. Robert L. Paquette, and Stanley L. Engerman (Gainesville: University Press of Florida, 1996), 241–58. In Berbice, the British colonial government did not make "the murder or . . . maiming or wounding of a Slave . . . , whether the Same is caused by Excessive punishment or otherwise," a criminal offense until 1811, although the Dutch colonial government enacted a law in 1768 that made punishments that led to death within twenty-four hours punishable by a fine. For the British law, see Minutes of the Court of Policy and Criminal Justice, July 1, 1811, Walter Rodney Archives (Guyana National Archives), Georgetown, Guyana; Thompson, *Documentary History*, 196–97. For the Dutch law, see "Verbod slaven zo zwaar straffen dat ze binnen 24 uur overlijden," July 4, 1768, *Plakaatboek Guyana (Guyana Ordinance book), 1670–1816*, ed. J. Th. de Smidt, T. van der Lee, and H. J. M. van Dapperen (The Hague: Huygens Institute for the History of the Netherlands, 2014), at http://resources.huygens .knaw.nl/retroboeken/guyana/#page=185&accessor=search_in_text&view=transcriptiePane& source=berbice, accessed June 28, 2016. Thanks to Marjoleine Kars for this reference.

17. 1826 slave code, clause 12.

18. Ibid., clause 14. An 1810 law in Berbice stipulated that private citizens (e.g., managers, drivers) could not administer more than thirty-nine lashes—the biblical standard—"on One Day or at One Time." This was an increase from a Dutch law that set the limit at twenty-five lashes. For the Dutch "Rule on the Treatment of Servants and Slaves," enacted in 1772, see Emília Viotti da Costa, *Crowns of Glory, Tears of Blood: The Demerara Slave Rebellion of 1823* (New York: Oxford University Press, 1994), 44–45.

19. Ibid., clauses 15–16. Punishment records were not entirely without precedent in the British Caribbean. Beginning in the middle of the eighteenth century, some slaveowners introduced work logs to better regulate plantation labor and discipline. These records were intended for private use, however, and not for government officials. For the evolution of plantation record-keeping, see Roberts, *Slavery and the Enlightenment*.

20. 1826 slave code, clause 41.

21. "Proclamation of Acting-Governor Dalrymple," Nov. 14, 1810, reissued by Lieutenant-Governor Bentinck on Oct. 4, 1814, *Berbice Gazette*, cited in Thompson, *Documentary History*, 197–98 ("hands and feets," 198; all other quotations, 197). These rules did not apply to members of the colonial government, who could exceed thirty-nine lashes as they saw fit. The framers of the law believed that some slaves "merit[ed] a more severe and public punishment," and

managers and owners were instructed to take such slaves to the nearest burgher (local militia) officer or captain, who were authorized to supervise floggings of up to one hundred lashes (ibid., 197). "Carracarra" was a vine native to the Guianas often referred to as "bush rope." See Alvin Thompson, *Unprofitable Servants: Crown Slaves in Berbice, Guyana, 1803–1831* (Kingston: University of the West Indies Press, 2002), 39; and Thompson, *Colonialism and Underdevelopment*, 116. Exchange rates varied from about f10 to £1 up to f14 to £1 during the first three decades of the nineteenth century. See Bolingbroke, *Voyage to Demerary*, 71; James Walker, *Letters on the West Indies* (London: Rest Fenner, 1818), 266; "Evidence of Charles Kyte," Aug. 23, 1825, and "Evidence of Henry White," June 6, 1825, both in "Report of the Commissioners appointed to inquire into the State of the Winkel Establishment in the Colony of Berbice," T1/3483/1; Da Costa, *Crowns of Glory*, 345n28; Thompson, *Unprofitable Servants*, 56–57; Markus A. Denzel, *Handbook of World Exchange Rates, 1590–1914* (Farnham, England: Ashgate, 2010), 5. Thanks to Alvin Thompson for the T1 citation.

22. Paton, *No Bond*, 86.

23. Jeremy Bentham, *The Rationale of Punishment* (London: Robert Heward, 1830), 81–82; Ignatieff, *Just Measure of Pain*, 75–76. A Louisiana slaveowner purportedly used a similar whipping machine. See Edward E. Baptist, *The Half Has Never Been Told: Slavery and the Making of American Capitalism* (New York: Basic Books, 2014), 141–42. For similar efforts to standardize flogging in post-emancipation Jamaica, see Paton, *No Bond*, 144.

24. Minute Book of the Barbados Agricultural Society, Nov. 14, 1812, cited in B. W. Higman, *Slave Populations of the British Caribbean, 1807–1834* (Baltimore: Johns Hopkins University Press, 1984), 199–200.

25. 1826 slave code, clause 13.

26. Diana Paton, "Decency, Dependence and the Lash: Gender and the British Debate over Slave Emancipation, 1830–34," *Slavery and Abolition* 17, no. 3 (1996): 163–84; Pamela Scully, *Liberating the Family? Gender and British Slave Emancipation in the Rural Western Cape, South Africa, 1823–1853* (Portsmouth, N.H.: Heinemann, 1997); Henrice Altink, "'An Outrage on All Decency': Abolitionist Reactions to Flogging Jamaican Slave Women, 1780–1834," *Slavery and Abolition* 23, no. 2 (2002): 107–22. For the pornographic and voyeuristic qualities of these images, see Mary A. Favret, "Flogging: The Anti-Slavery Movement Writes Pornography," in *Romanticism and Gender*, ed. Anne Janowitz (Cambridge: D.S. Brewer, 1998), 19–43; Colette Colligan, "Anti-Abolition Writes Obscenity: The English Vice, Transatlantic Slavery, and England's Obscene Print Culture," in *International Exposure: Perspectives on Modern European Pornography, 1800–2000*, ed. Lisa Z. Sigel (New Brunswick, N.J.: Rutgers University Press, 2005), 67–99. See also Marcus Wood, *Blind Memory: Visual Representations of Slavery in England and America, 1780–1865* (Manchester: Manchester University Press, 2000), 234–39; and Wood, *Slavery, Empathy, and Pornography* (Oxford: Oxford University Press, 2002). For gender and amelioration, see Melanie Newton, "'New Ideas of Correctness': Gender, Amelioration and Emancipation in Barbados, 1810s–50s," *Slavery and Abolition* 21, no. 3 (2000): 94–124.

27. See Chapter 4.

28. Bathurst to Governors of Colonies Having Local Legislatures, May 28, 1823, quoted in Paton, *No Bond*, 6–7.

29. 1826 slave code, clause 14.

30. Altink, "Outrage on All Decency," 108.

31. 1826 slave code, clause 14.

32. For the treadmill in England, see Ignatieff, *Just Measure of Pain*, 177–79; Robin Evans,

The Fabrication of Virtue: English Prison Architecture, 1750–1840 (Cambridge: Cambridge University Press, 1982), 295–309. For the first treadmills in the West Indies, see Higman, *Slave Populations*, 243–44; Paton, *No Bond*, 44–45, 88; and Thompson, *Unprofitable Servants*, 40–41.

33. *Berbice Gazette*, May 14, 1828 (quotations); Thompson, *Unprofitable Servants*, 40.

34. Quoted in Ignatieff, *Just Measure of Pain*, 177.

35. Paton, *No Bond*, 88.

36. In Berbice, slaves could be "worked" on the treadmill up to twelve intervals per day, totaling nearly three hours. See "Regulations for the Tread Mill, Erected in the Colonial Jail of Berbice, for a Legal Mode of Correctional Punishment," encl. in Shanks to Earl Bathurst, July 29, 1828, CO 111/107, 5–7.

37. Ignatieff, *Just Measure of Pain*, 177; Paton, *No Bond*, 105–6, 112.

38. Quoted in Thomas Rain, *The Life and Labours of John Wray . . .* (London: John Snow & Co., 1892), 301.

39. "Regulations for the Tread Mill."

40. Henrice Altink, *Representations of Slave Women in Discourses on Slavery and Abolition, 1780–1838* (New York: Routledge, 2007), 149–53; Paton, *No Bond*, 83, 106–7.

41. 1826 slave code, clause 14.

42. Turner, "British Caribbean," 310–11.

43. 1831 slave code, quoted in ibid., 312–13.

44. Charles Herbert to Benjamin D'Urban, Sept. 17, 1824, in *Papers Relating to the Manumission, Government, and Population of Slaves in the West Indies, 1822–1824*, PP (1825), 18.

45. John Edwin Mason reached a similar conclusion in his analysis of the records of the fiscals and protectors from Cape Colony (South Africa), another site of British experiments in amelioration. Cape Colony slaves, Mason argued, "developed a moral code by which to judge the physical punishment to which they were subject. In this 'moral economy,' slaves acknowledged that some beatings were inevitable, if not legitimate. But their code set rules governing the distribution of the violence," and "when the punishments that they received did violate both the law and the moral economy, they did not hesitate to turn to the law." See Mason, *Social Death and Resurrection: Slavery and Emancipation in South Africa* (Charlottesville: University of Virginia Press, 2003), 158–59.

46. Enslaved people legally needed written permission to travel off their plantations. See *Berbice Gazette*, July 16, 1814; Thompson, *Colonialism and Underdevelopment*, 114.

47. A sample of 231 complaints from 1824–25 revealed that 84 percent of complaints were made by slaves without passes and only 3 percent of complainants had passes (the other 13 percent of complaints do not have sufficient information). See J. H. Lean, "The Secret Lives of Slaves: Berbice, 1819 to 1827" (Ph.D. diss., University of Canterbury, 2002), 283–84.

48. Simon, who complained with Amsterdam, also said that their overseer was "a very severe man" who sometimes ordered floggings of one hundred lashes. "Examination of a complaint preferred by the negroes *Amsterdam* and *Simon*," Aug. 28, 1821, CO 116/138, 87.

49. "Complaint of Donderdag . . . ," June 13, 1825, CO 116/140.

50. "Complaint of the negroes *Wallace, Swift,* and *Pompey*," Nov. 10, 1823, CO 116/138, 115–16 (quotations, 116).

51. July 1, 1828, entry, "Punishment record book of plantation Allness . . . ," CO 116/145, 48–49 ("leaving the Estate"); July 17, 1828, entry, "Punishment record book of Ross & Barnstedt's Task Gang . . . ," CO 116/145, 81–82 ("having gone"); July 7, 1828, entry, "Punishment record book of plantation Reliance . . . ," CO 116/145, 82–83 ("making a groundless").

52. "Secret Lives of Slaves," 65.

53. May 2, 1826(?), entry, "Punishment record book of plantation De Standvastigheid," CO 116/143.

54. Aug. 28, 1830, CO 116/146, 190; "Return of Slaves, attached to Plantation Karel & Willemshoop . . . ," Feb. 14, 1819, T 71/438, 321–22.

55. In the same letter, Murray criticized a manager who had refused to give one of his slaves a pass to complain. George Murray to Henry Beard, Oct. 6, 1830, CO 116/145, 249.

56. Turner, "British Caribbean," 313.

57. *Further papers relating to slaves in the West Indies . . . copies of the record of the proceedings of the fiscals of Demerara and Berbice, in their capacity of guardians and protectors of the slaves,* PP 401 (1826), 4.

58. Michael Samuel Bennett to Benjamin D'Urban, Jan. 21, 1826, CO 116/138.

59. "Complaint of the Negro Scipio . . . ," Feb. 10, 1819, CO 116/138, 34–36 ("as an example," 36); "Return of Slaves attached to Plantation Friends . . . ," Feb. 19, 1819, Treasury series (hereafter T) 71/438, 681–82 ("very tall," 682), National Archives, Kew, London, United Kingdom.

60. "Examination of a Complaint preferred by the negroes *Caesar, Duncan, Hero, Bacchus, Watt, Hector, Jeffery, Welcome* and *Smith* . . . ," June 11, 1822, CO 116/138, 120–21 (quotation, 121).

61. Michael Bennett to Henry Beard, March 15, 1819, CO 116/138, 42.

62. Benjamin D'Urban to Henry Beard, March 16, 1831, CO 116/142.

63. "Reports of the Civil Magistrates . . . on the promulgation of the New Code," 1826, CO 111/ 102, 300–306.

64. Da Costa argued that "slaves perceived slavery as a system of reciprocal obligations. They assumed that between masters and slaves there was an unspoken contract, an invisible text that defined rules and obligations, a text they used to assess any violations of their 'rights.'" Da Costa, *Crowns of Glory,* 73.

65. "Examination of the coloured girl *Magdaleentje,* and the negroes *Andries* and *Michael* . . . ," June 15, 1821, CO 116/138, 83.

66. "*Complaint No.* 13," Feb. 9, 1827, CO 116/143, 184.

67. "Complaint of the negroes *Tom, Joe, Hercules and Matross* . . . ," Aug. 4, 1823, CO 116/138, 104.

68. "EXAMINATION of a complaint preferred by the negro *Esterre* . . . ," Jan. 2, 1821, CO 116/138, 73–74 ("been but a short time," "does not know," "his former," 73; all other quotations, 74). Their owner, F. Alidus Spangeberg, purchased Esterre in February 1820 and Samuel in May 1820. See "Return of Slaves the Property of F. Alidus Spangeberg . . . ," Feb. 27, 1822, T 71/440, 637–38.

69. "Complaint of the negroes *Wallace, Swift,* and *Pompey,*" 116.

70. "Complaint of *Quassie* . . . ," Aug. 31, 1821, CO 116/138, 88–89 ("the bad state," 88; "extremely severe," "not know how," 89); "Return of Slaves, attached to Plantation Vrow Johanna . . . ," Feb. 18, 1819, T 71/438, 447–48.

71. "Complaint of the negro women *Dina, Amba, Lena,* and *Zemire* . . . ," July 18, 1823, CO 116/138, 102; "Return of Slaves, attached to Plantation Recumzigt . . . ," March 12, 1819, T 71/438, 295–96.

72. "Complaint of the Negro Dundas . . . ," April 30, 1824, CO 116/140 (quotations); "Return of Slaves attached to Pln New Forest . . . ," Feb. 27, 1819, T 71/438, 585–86.

73. May 31, 1830, CO 116/146, 106–9 ("beat her severely," "boiled it," 106; "on the irritation," "violently," "requested to know," 108; "that the Slave Law," 109); "Return of Slaves the Property of Petrus Koulen," Jan. 28, 1831, T 71/444, 309.

74. Dec. 11, 1832, CO 116/151, 193–96 ("saying he was," 194; "laid hold of," "he would not," 195; "altho' he considered," "it was absolutely necessary," 196).

75. "Complaint of the negro Goodluck . . . ," March 30, 1824, CO 116/140. It is unclear what law the fiscal was referring to.

76. "Demand and conclusion . . . in a case of Criminal proceedings instituted by M.S. Bennett . . . versus Robert Risk . . . ," CO 116/139, 504 ("wanton and cruel attack"), 505 ("the Law").

77. "Complaint of the sambo girl *Betsey* . . . ," May 8, 1819, CO 116/138, 46 ("flew in a passion"); "Complaint of the negro [blank] . . . " Oct. 20, 1823, CO 116/138, 113. See also Lean, "Secret Lives of Slaves," 139–40.

78. Lean calculated that out of nearly 2,000 complaints made to the fiscal and protector of slaves between 1819 and 1827, only about 30 percent "were officially upheld and the defendant punished or admonished" (Lean, "Secret Lives of Slaves," 69).

79. "Complaint of negro *Philip* . . . ," June 14, 1819, CO 116/138, 53–54 ("being too much," "frequently drunk," 53; "a very bad," "frivolous and unfounded," 54).

80. "Complaint of Donderdag."

81. "Investigation of a Complaint preferred by the Negroes *Brutus, Goodluck,* and *Ambrose* . . . ," CO 116/138, appx. 14–15 ("without foundation," "contradicted," 14; "deemed it," 14–15; "duty to attend," 15).

82. "Examination of a Complaint by the negress *Princess* . . . ," June 11, 1822, CO 116/138, 121 (all quotations); "Return of Slaves the Property of Robert Semple," Feb. 27, 1819, T 71/438, 615.

83. "Return of Slaves, the Property of Tho⁵ C. Jones," Feb. 26, 1819, T 71/438, 359–60 ("stout," 360); "Investigation of a complaint preferred by the Negress *Minkie* . . . ," CO 116/138 appx. 9–10 ("put me down," "laid down," 9; "her posteriors," 10); "Complaint of the woman *Minkie* . . . ," CO 116/138, 39.

84. "Investigation of a complaint preferred by the Negress *Minkie*," 10.

85. "Proclamation of Acting-Governor Dalrymple," Nov. 14, 1810.

86. "Investigation of a complaint preferred by the Negress *Minkie*," 10.

87. "In Relation to the proceedings The Fiscal R.O. versus H. R. McGee . . . ," May–July, 1823, CO 116/140, 1–38; "In relation to the Complaint of the Negress Princess against H. McGee," May 9–July 10, 1823, CO 116/139, 973–1020 ("Afterwards," 995; "for excessive punishment," 978; "Insolence and disobedience," 986; "My clothes," 1009–10; "conduct towards," 1016, "muttering," "grumbling," 988).

88. "In relation to the Complaint of the Negress Princess," 1005 ("on the first," "gave her,"), 1006 ("just come out," "take Husband," "said I must," "had better," "he had,"), 1007 ("told the boy," "went into Bed," "must not think").

89. "The Fiscal R.O. versus H. R. McGee," 7 ("without any"); "Complaint of the Negress Princess," 979 ("that the conduct," "there [was]"), 993 ("had no heart"), 986 ("ordered her"), 1005 ("on the first evening"), 1011 ("know the number").

90. Aug. 10, 1833, CO 116/146, 221–24 ("middle aged," 221; "interfere in," "in the strongest terms," 223).

91. "Complaint of the negress Catherine . . . ," March 9, 1827, CO 116/141.

92. Nov. 14, 1832, CO 116/151, 169–71, 273–78; "Charles Herbert First Fiscal R.O. versus John McDougald," Jan. 31, 1833, CO 116/152, 261–64.

93. "William Furlonge and David Power vs. James Beck," April 1832, CO 116/150, 268–71

(quotations, 269). For the complaint that initiated the prosecution, see Sept. 3, 1831, CO 116/149, 113–15.

94. Oct. 2, 1829, CO 116/142, 67–71 ("leathern strap," "chaise whip," 69; "presented a Petition," 70).

95. "Investigation of a Complaint preferred by the Negress *Roosje* . . . ," CO 116/138, appx. 15–16 ("too big," 15); "Complaint *Jonas* versus *Grade*, manager," June 10, 1819, CO 116/138, 56–60 ("this woman," "give it to her," 57); "In relation to the Complaint of The Woman *Roosje* against C. T. Grade," CO 116/139, 113–89; "Return of Slaves . . . attached to Pl^n L'Esperance . . . ," Feb. 26, 1819, T 71/438, 341. Three years earlier John Wray commented on a similar case with a very different outcome because of the extreme formalism that characterized laws on physical violence in Berbice. A pregnant woman, America, had been "cart-whipped in a most brutal manner," receiving "at least 150 lashes" at the hands of two drivers because she had been "insolent" to the manager's wife. The manager had smoked a pipe and watched casually while the drivers took turns flogging her before putting her in the stocks for several days. The major difference in this case, however, was that the number of lashes exceeded the limit by more than one hundred, and the manager was therefore convicted of "excessive cruelty," issued a 300-guilder fine, and sentenced to three months in jail. See John Wray to Zachary Macaulay, Nov. 1816, enc. in Lieutenant-Governor Bentinck to Lord Bathurst, May 26, 1817, in PP 433 (1818), 229–30; and "Sentence of the Court of Criminal Justice on Jacobus Overeem, manager of Sandvoort," in ibid., 236–38. See also Thompson, *Unprofitable Servants*, 29–30.

96. "Complaint *Jonas* versus *Grade*, manager," 57.

97. "In relation to the Complaint of the Woman *Roosje*," 121–22.

98. "Examination of a Complaint preferred by the negroes *Maria, Jane, Fanny, Marianne, Polly, Bella, Caroline, Betsy* and *Nancy* . . . ," March 3, 1823, CO 116/138, 136.

99. "Mrs. Ann Bennett prefers a Complaint against her slave Mary Ann," Aug. 2, 1827, CO 116/141, 52–54 ("I am under," "comfortable house," "everything in," 52; "At the most trifling," "do so," "own authority," 53; "appeared to be," "merely remarked," "on bread," 54); "Return of Slaves the property of Ann Bennett . . . ," April 26, 1822, T 71/440, 359–60 ("domestic," 360).

100. "No. 16," April 19, 1831, CO 116/142, 122–23 ("was in the habit," 122; "appeared to," 123).

101. "No. 25," June 16, 1828, CO 116/144.

102. Charles Bird to Henry Beard, Sept. 1, 1827, CO 116/143, 247–48.

103. The secretary of state explained that "when a slave prefers complaints against his master from an improper motive and without sufficient grounds he should incur punishment but for this offence he should be brought to trial before some regular tribunal which should investigate the specific charge of groundless frivolous accusation and award such punishment as the law may have previously prescribed." Feb. 4, 1829, CO 114/5, quoted in Gordon Eton Gill, "Labor, Material Welfare, and Culture in Hydrologic Plantation Enterprises: A Study of Slavery in the British Colony of Berbice (Guyana)" (Ph.D. diss., Howard University, 2004), 62.

104. "William Grimes Owner of the Slave Betsey Complains," Jan. 21, 1829, CO 116/142, 6.

105. "No. 20," May 9, 1831, CO 116/142, 143–52 ("liberated his," 144; "deserving of," 145; "was unjustifiable," "inclined," "the remedy," 148; "duty to support," 149).

106. PP 721 (1832), 12, cited in Higman, *Slave Populations*, 200.

Chapter 3. The Slave Drivers' World

1. May 8, 1833, Colonial Office series (hereafter CO) 116/152, 127–29 ("refused to leave," "dared Frans," "Frans was not," 128; "for abusing," 127), National Archives, Kew, London, United

Kingdom. Managers commonly punished slaves for "insolence" toward drivers. See, for example, "Complaint of the Negro Peter," Aug. 2, 1823, CO 116/138, 103; Aug. 12, 1823, in *Copies of the Records of the Proceedings of the Fiscals of Demerara and Berbice* . . . , Parliamentary Papers, House of Commons (hereafter PP), 476 (1825), 57; and Nov. 21, 1833, CO 116/153, 158–61.

2. Thomas Roughley, *The Jamaica Planter's Guide: or, A System for Planting and Managing a Sugar Estate, or Other Plantations on That Island, and Throughout the British West Indies in General* . . . (London: Longman, Hurst, Rees, Orme, and Brown, 1823), 79 ("most important"), 81 ("life and soul"). British planter P. J. Laborie also described drivers as "the soul of a plantation" (Laborie, *The Coffee Planter of Saint Domingo; With an Appendix, Containing a View of the Constitution, Government, Laws, and State of That Colony, Previous to the Year 1789. To Which Are Added, Some Hints on the Present State of the Island, Under the British Government* [London: T. Cadell and W. Davies, 1798], 164). Drivers were often, literally, the most valued slaves on the plantation, reflecting slaveowners' recognition of their agricultural expertise and managerial skill. In Berbice, the colonial government set the official compensation rate for slaveowners whose drivers were executed or transported at 1,500 guilders, which was 300 guilders more than the rate for ordinary field slaves. *Berbice Gazette*, Jan. 11, 1814. See also Robert L. Paquette, "The Drivers Shall Lead Them: Image and Reality in Slave Resistance," in *Slavery, Secession, and Southern History*, ed. Robert L. Paquette and Lou Ferleger (Charlottesville: University of Virginia Press, 2000), 50; Laurent Dubois, *Avengers of the New World: The Story of the Haitian Revolution* (Cambridge, Mass.: Harvard University Press, 2004), 32.

3. This managerial structure is based on plantation Op Hoop van Beter and draws on *Trial of a Slave in Berbice, for the Crime of Obeah and Murder: Return to an Address to His Majesty, by The Honorable House of Commons, dated 29th of July 1822; for, Copy of any Information which may have been received concerning the Trial of a Slave, for the Crime of Obeah, in the Colony of Berbice*, PP 348 (1823); and "Return of Slaves, attached to Plantation Op Hoop van Beter . . . ," Feb. 1, 1819, Treasury series (hereafter T) 71/438, 119–24, National Archives, Kew, London, United Kingdom.

4. B. W. Higman calculated that on typical Berbician plantations (those with more than fifty slaves), drivers accounted for between 2 and 2.9 percent of the registered occupations for enslaved men. Slave registration returns from 1834 reveal that the 812 registered "head people" accounted for about 4.2 percent of the entire registered enslaved population (19,201) in Berbice. See Higman, *Slave Populations of the British Caribbean, 1807–1834* (Baltimore: Johns Hopkins University Press, 1984), Table S7.1, "Occupational Distribution of Slaves, 1834," 551; Table S7.5, "Occupations of Slaves by Sex: Berbice, 1819," 571; Table S7.13, "Occupations of Slaves by Sex and Slave-holding Size Group: Berbice, 1819," 589. The white or European population was well below 600 people throughout the 1820s (estimates include 556 Europeans in 1822, 570 in 1827, and 552 in 1829, for example). See Higman, *Slave Populations*, Table S2.1, "White and Freedman Populations by Sex and Colony, c. 1830," 433; and Alvin O. Thompson, *Unprofitable Servants: Crown Slaves in Berbice, Guyana, 1803–1831* (Kingston: University of the West Indies Press, 2002), 26.

5. For the Caribbean sugar plantation as synthesis of field and factory, see Sidney W. Mintz, *Caribbean Transformations* (Chicago: Aldine, 1974); Mintz, *Sweetness and Power: The Place of Sugar in Modern History* (New York: Viking, 1985). The dilemma that foremen faced was similar to that of drivers—how to satisfy employers and enforce their orders while maintaining good relations with the employees they supervised—although both foremen and other employees had a range of options enslaved people did not, including the freedom to leave their jobs. See Richard Price, *Masters, Unions, and Men: Work Control in Building and the Rise of Labour, 1830–1914*

(Cambridge: Cambridge University Press, 1980), 38–39; Joseph Melling, "Men in the Middle or Men on the Margin? The Historical Development of Relations Between Employers and Supervisors in British industry," in *The International Yearbook of Organization Studies*, ed. David Dunkerly and Graeme Salaman (London: Routledge, 1982), 242–70. For the lack of scholarship on foremen, see Patricia Van den Eeckhout, "Foremen in American and Western European Industry Before the First World War," in *Supervision and Authority in Industry: Western European Experiences, 1830–1939*, ed. Van den Eeckhout (New York: Berghahn Books, 2009), 1.

6. According to 1819 slave registration returns, only 7 out of 325 drivers—slightly more than 2 percent—were women. No women were listed as first or head drivers, which was typical for most British colonies. See Higman, *Slave Populations*, Table S7.5, "Occupations of Slaves by Sex: Berbice, 1819," 571, 192–93. Female drivers were common, in contrast, in Barbados and Martinique, where they regularly supervised the second and third gangs, where young children and weaker slaves predominated. See Dale W. Tomich, *Slavery in the Circuit of Sugar: Martinique and the World Economy, 1830–1848* (Baltimore: Johns Hopkins University Press, 1990), 220; Bernard Moitt, *Women and Slavery in the French Antilles, 1635–1848* (Bloomington: Indiana University Press, 2001), 42–43; Justin Roberts, *Slavery and the Enlightenment in the British Atlantic, 1750–1807* (New York: Cambridge University Press, 2013), 141, 155–56. When British traveler George Pinckard visited Demerara in the late eighteenth century, he observed the "novelty" of field laborers "employed at their labour, with female drivers carrying the whip at their backs." Though Pinckard thought women might be too weak to inflict the violence he thought necessary, his companion, "a gentleman of the colony," told him "that it was by no means uncommon" to appoint women as drivers and that he was "much mistaken" about their supposed weakness, "for, on the contrary, the '*women drivers*' were sometimes peculiarly severe, and often corrected the stoutest slaves with no feeble arm." Pinckard, *Notes on the West Indies . . .* (London: Longman, Hurst, Rees, and Orme, 1806), 3:179.

7. For the historiography of drivers, see Paquette, "The Drivers Shall Lead Them," 38–43. As Paquette noted, French historian Gabriel Debien produced some of the most nuanced analyses of Caribbean drivers. See Debien, *Les Escalves aux Antilles françaises (XVIIème-XVIIIème siècles)* (Gourbeyre [Basse-Terre], Guadeloupe, 1974), 105–17; Debien, "Sur les plantations Mauger à l'Artibonite (Saint Domingue 1763–1803)," in *Enquêtes et documents: Nantes, Afrique, Amérique* (Nantes: Centre de Recherches sur l'Histoire de la France Atlantique, 1981), 219–314.

8. "Return of Slaves, attached to Plantation Ma Retraite . . . ," July 27, 1819, T 71/438, 333–34. Only 5.3 percent of slaves in 1819 in Berbice were fifty years old or older, and just 1.9 percent were sixty or older. See Higman, *Slave Populations*, Table S4.1, "Age Structure of Slaves by Sex, Birthplace, and Colony," 468.

9. My analysis of the one hundred male drivers listed on 1817 slave registration returns from forty-five plantations of different sizes and crop types revealed an average age of 39.4 years, with fifty-five drivers at least 40 years old and fourteen drivers aged 50 or above. Average age varied very little according to birthplace, with African drivers aged 39 years on average and Creole drivers aged 40.6 years on average. The youngest drivers were 24 and the oldest was 69. See T 71/437. The mean age at death for enslaved men in Berbice was 39 years old (for Africans) and 16.0 years old (for Creoles). See Higman, *Slave Populations*, Table S9.42, "Mean Age of Slaves at Death, by Sex, Birthplace and Cause of Death: Berbice, 1819–22," 680.

10. This difference in longevity cannot be explained, moreover, only by the fact that drivers tended to be appointed to their position in their twenties or thirties and were therefore selected

from a population that had already survived well into adulthood. Indeed, even after being promoted, drivers often had remarkably long working lives, with the average Mesopotamia driver
serving for 12.6 years—in addition to 11.5 years in other jobs, for a total working life of 24.1 years.
Field laborers, in contrast, had an average working life of just 17.7 years. Richard S. Dunn, *A Tale
of Two Plantations: Slave Life and Labor in Jamaica and Virginia* (Cambridge, Mass.: Harvard
University Press, 2014), 143, 432, Appendix 16, "The Occupation, Health, and Longevity of Mesopotamia Adult Slaves, 1762–1833." Thanks to Richard Dunn for discussing these demographics
with me.

   11. According to Higman, "the most important occupational mortality differential was that
between field laborers and 'privileged' drivers, skilled tradespeople, and domestics" (*Slave Populations*, 333). Using data from St. Lucia, the only location where Higman analyzed occupational
mortality differences by age, sex, birthplace, and crop type, he found that for "creole males attached to sugar estates, the death rates of field laborers were more than double those of the privileged group at all ages over 30 years, and 50 percent higher among younger slaves." On non-sugar
plantations, "the differential was less consistent, creole male field laborers under 40 years of age
having much higher death rates than the privileged, but in the older age groups (when the sample
became small) there was little difference between the two groups." See Higman, *Slave Populations*, 333 (quotes), Table S9.28, "Slave Age-Specific Death Rates by Sex, Birthplace, Occupation,
and Crop-Type: St. Lucia, 1815–1819," 667. Puzzlingly, Higman's data for Berbice, where occupational groups cannot be distinguished by crop types, shows that "skilled tradesmen [and drivers]
had lower death rates than male field laborers only to about 40 years," with "skilled tradespeople
& drivers" actually having higher mortality rates, as a group, than field laborers between ages 40
and 59. See Higman, *Slave Populations*, 334 (quote), Table S9.31, "Slave Age-specific Death Rates
by Sex and Occupation: Berbice, 1819–22," 670. It is difficult to interpret this data—which is not
consistent with evidence from other locations—without disaggregating drivers and skilled
tradespeople. Moreover, when small occupational groups such as drivers are broken down by age
and crop type, the sample size is quite small and thus the results may reflect minor perturbations
rather than general patterns. Thanks to Barry Higman for discussing this data with me.

   12. The driver Zealand, for example, had "the use of the milk of the cows," an invaluable
source of nutrition undoubtedly denied to the estate's other slaves. "Examination of the negro
woman *Rosetta*, belonging to plantation Beerenstein," June 4, 1819, CO 116/138, 54. See also
Alvin O. Thompson, *A Documentary History of Slavery in Berbice, 1796–1834* (Georgetown,
Guyana: Free Press, 2002), 10–11; and Thompson, *Unprofitable Servants*, 160–61. Drivers in other
slave societies received similar perks. See Robert S. Starobin, "Privileged Bondsmen and the
Process of Accommodation: The Role of Houseservants and Drivers as Seen in Their Own Let-
ters," *Journal of Social History* 5, no. 1 (1971): 61–62, 65–67; Eugene Genovese, *Roll, Jordan, Roll:
The World the Slaves Made* (New York: Vintage, 1972), 370–71; Higman, *Slave Populations*, 207,
209, 221–22, 224; Carolyn E. Fick, *The Making of Haiti: The Saint Domingue Revolution from
Below* (Knoxville: University of Tennessee Press, 1990), 30; Michael Mullin, *Africa in America:
Slave Acculturation and Resistance in the American South and the British Caribbean, 1736–1831*
(Urbana: University of Illinois Press, 1992), 147–8; Paquette, "The Drivers Shall Lead Them," 32–
33; Roberts, *Slavery and the Enlightenment*, 202; and Justin Roberts, "The 'Better Sort' and the
'Poorer Sort': Wealth Inequalities, Family Formation and the Economy of Energy on British
Caribbean Sugar Plantations, 1750–1800," *Slavery & Abolition* 35, no. 3 (2014): 458–73.

   13. Zealand had his own "washerwoman." See "Examination of the negro woman *Rosetta*,"

54. A driver's wife on plantation Vryberg was able to afford to hire a carpenter, whom he paid with rum. See "Complaint of the Negro Gasper Belonging to Pln. Vryberg," Nov. 20, 1825, CO 116/140.

14. Higman, *Slave Populations*, 345–46; Dunn, *Two Plantations*, 432, Appendix 16, "The Occupation, Health, and Longevity of Mesopotamia Adult Slaves, 1762–1833."

15. Drivers were more likely than field laborers to have wives and had some of the largest families among enslaved people. Some drivers, moreover, had multiple wives or partners, an impressive measure of their status and ability to attract women despite demographic obstacles. An extreme example was the head driver April, "Father and Grandfather to upwards of seventy negroes"—a quantity of offspring that suggests April had many different sexual partners, if not wives. See "Complaint of twenty two negro men the property of L. F. Gallez in Upper Canje . . . ," Sept. 21, 1824, CO 116/140. See also Genovese, *Roll, Jordan, Roll*, 371; Higman, *Slave Populations*, 370–71; Philip D. Morgan, *Slave Counterpoint: Black Culture in the Eighteenth-Century Chesapeake and Lowcountry* (Chapel Hill: University of North Carolina Press, 1998), 223; Anthony E. Kaye, *Joining Places: Slave Neighborhoods in the Old South* (Chapel Hill: University of North Carolina Press, 2007), 79; and Roberts, *Slavery and the Enlightenment*, 251–53. For Berbice's sexual demography and slaves' marriages, see Chapter 4.

16. For a good discussion of gang labor, see Roberts, *Slavery and the Enlightenment*, 131–60. For the "driving" method of supervision in factory work as "a combination of authoritarian rule and physical compulsion," see Daniel Nelson, *Managers and Workers: Origins of the Twentieth-Century Factory System in the United States, 1880–1920* (Madison: University of Wisconsin Press, 1996), 44.

17. Much, if not most, of the violence drivers inflicted was in the form of punishments they were ordered to administer.

18. Pinckard, *Notes on the West Indies*, 2:201. Pinckard's analogy was part of a widespread process of "animalization" in describing Africans and people of African descent in New World slave societies. See David Brion Davis, *The Problem of Slavery in the Age of Emancipation* (New York: Knopf, 2014), 3–44.

19. For literary portrayals of drivers, see Paquette, "The Drivers Shall Lead Them," 34–38.

20. "Complaint No. 14—*Plantation Woodlands, West Coast, Berbice*," Feb. 1, 1827, CO 116/143, 185–86 ("flogged him with a cat," "he would go," 185), ("saw no mark," 186); "Return of Slaves attached to Plantation Woodlands . . . ," Dec. 29, 1817, T 71/437, 287–88. For similar cases, see "Complaint *Jonas* versus *Grade*, manager [Plantation L'Espérance], Jun. 10, 1819," in *Further Papers Relating to Slaves in the West Indies; (Demerara and Berbice:) VIZ Further Return to an Address of The Honourable House of Commons, dated the 13th of April 1824; for Copies of the Record of the Proceedings of the Fiscals of Demerara and Berbice . . .*, PP 476 (1825), 25–28; and "Complaint, No. 14," April 30, in *Protectors of Slaves Reports. Return to an Address to His Majesty, dated 15 December 1830; for, Copy of Any Reports Which May Have Been Received From the Protectors of Slaves in the Colonies of Demerara, Berbice, Trinidad, St. Lucia, the Cape of Good Hope and Mauritius . . .*, PP 262 (1831), 115.

21. 1826 Berbice slave code, clause 12, *The Berbice Royal Gazette*, Sept. 30, 1826, CO 111/102 (reprinted in Alvin O. Thompson, *A Documentary History of Slavery in Berbice, 1796–1834* [Georgetown, Guyana: Free Press, 2002]). In an 1823 letter to the lieutenant-governors of Berbice and Demerara, Henry Bathurst, secretary of state for war and the colonies, asked that local officials take steps to end "the practice of driving slaves to their work by the sound of the whip, and . . . the arbitrary infliction of it by the driver as a stimulus to labour," which was "repugnant

to the feelings of every individual in this country." Bathurst urged that "the whip should no longer be carried into the field, and there displayed by the driver as the emblem of his authority, or employed as the ready instrument of his displeasure." Bathurst, "Copy of a Letter addressed to the Governors of Demerara and Berbice," May 28, 1823, in *Papers presented to Parliament by His Majesty's Command, in Explanation of the Measures Adopted by His Majesty's Government, for the Melioration of the Condition of the Slave Population in His Majesty's Possessions in the West Indies, and on the Continent of South America,* PP 003 (1824), 4.

22. H. Downie reported to lieutenant-governor Henry Beard on October 25, 1826, that he had visited Woodlands and other plantations in the West Coast district to deliver the new slave code, as Beard had instructed earlier that month. H. Downie to Henry Beard, Oct. 25, 1826, in "Reports of the Civil Magistrates in the several districts in the Colony of Berbice on the promulgation of the New Code of the 25th September 1826 for improving the condition of the slave population therein," 1826, CO 111/102, 300.

23. "Complaint No. 14," Feb. 1, 1827, CO 116/143, 185–86 (quotations, 185).

24. The original (Dutch) name of Highbury, one of the oldest sugar plantations in Berbice, was Dankbaarheid. It was one of a handful of plantations owned by the Berbice Association of Holland and, later, the British Crown. By 1827, if not before, the Crown had sold the plantation to private owners. See "*Complaint No. 3*," Jan. 2, 1827, CO 116/143, 177; and Thompson, *Unprofitable Servants,* 47–48.

25. Dec. 22, 1832, CO 116/151, 200–03 ("with a leather strap," 200; "found fault," "he desired," "about 2 feet," 201; "that he carried the strap," 202); "Charles Herbert First Fiscal R.O. versus John Junor," Jan. 21, 1833, CO 116/151, 261–72 ("walk with the leather," 264).

26. Official complaints from enslaved people specifically against drivers were quite rare, accounting for less than 1 percent of all complaints to the fiscal and protector between 1819 and 1827, for example. See J. H. Lean, "The Secret Lives of Slaves: Berbice, 1819 to 1827" (Ph.D. diss., University of Canterbury, 2002), Table 2.13, 106. Most slave-driver disputes were likely dealt with on plantations, without legal officials' intervention.

27. "Examination of a Complaint Preferred by the Negroes *Trim* and *Rose,* belonging to plantation No 49, Courantyn Coast," March 30, 1821, CO 116/138, 80.

28. "Complaint of the Negro Hero Belonging to Pln. Kilcoy," Aug. 25, 1825, CO 116/140.

29. Aug. 10, 1833, CO 116/146, 221–24 ("abused," "they had only finished," "had left," "they became," 223; "middle aged," 221).

30. "Examination of the negro *Peter,* belonging to J. A. Delinert [Dehnert]," Aug. 29, 1820, CO 116/138, 68. In 1817 Peter [Pieter] was fifty years old—one of the oldest slaves his master owned. "Return of Slaves the property of Dehnert & Johannes Zimmerman . . . ," Oct. 18, 1817, T 71/437, 95.

31. See, for example, the description of Bob, "a sensible, well-behaved negro," in "Examination of the Negro *John,* belonging to William Ross, Corentine Coast," Aug. 12, 1822, CO 116/138, 129–30 (quotation, 130). Jamaican planter Alexander Barclay's description of the typical driver as "the only responsible negro [on the plantation] . . . selected in consideration of his good conduct, intelligence, and established character for sobriety, attention, and honesty, and the influence he possesses among the other slaves" is representative of planters' views toward drivers. Barclay, *A Practical View of the Present State of Slavery the West Indies . . .* (London: Smith, Elder, & Co., 1826), 39–40.

32. "INVESTIGATION Complaint of Nine Negro Men, belonging to Mrs. Ibon Sanders, residing in *Upper Berbice . . . ,*" Feb. 1, 1819, CO 116/138, 26–31 ("had been deputed," "instead of

affording," "stepped forward," "they were both," 28); "Return of Slaves attached to Plantn. Bien Content . . . ," Dec. 22, 1817, T 71/437, 316–17 ("Bush Driver," 316).

33. "INVESTIGATION Complaint of Nine Negro Men," 28.

34. Managers in Demerara were given a 2 to 10 percent commission on the production of the estates they managed. Berbician managers were likely compensated similarly. Emília Viotti da Costa, *Crowns of Glory, Tears of Blood: The Demerara Slave Rebellion of 1823* (New York: Oxford University Press, 1994), 58.

35. "No. 31," July 15, 1828, CO 116/144.

36. Ibid. For a similar case, see "Examination of *Will*, belonging to M'Lear, of Demerara, in Mr. Forbes's task-gang," Oct. 9, 1823, in *Copies of the Records of the Proceedings of the Fiscals of Demerara and Berbice . . . ,* PP 476 (1825), 62.

37. Nov. 26, 1830, CO 116/147, 130–33 ("said it was," "had put two women," "are not people," 131; "the task was too great," "told [Caroline] to shut," "look round," "You d——d," "are people," "I will confine," 130).

38. Ibid. (quotations, 133).

39. Dec. 2, 1830, CO 116/147, 148–51 ("exceedingly high," "to the satisfaction of the driver," 148; "a conspiracy," 149; "that what they," 150).

40. "Complains [sic] of *Jack, Boast, Jem, Tancra, Trim, Harry,* and *Peter,* property of M. Jeffray," Dec. 24, 1821, CO 116/138, 93–94 (quotations, 93). In 1817 Watson was listed in a slave registration return as a twenty-four-year-old African "domestick." See "Return of Slaves attached to Pl. Nigg . . . ," Dec. 22, 1817, T 71/437, 173. An 1819 return listed his job as carpenter and described him as having a "pleasant countenance & well made." See "Return of Slaves attached to Plantation Nigg . . . ," Feb. 22, 1819, T 71/437, 355–56.

41. "Complains [sic] of *Jack, Boast, Jem, Tancra, Trim, Harry,* and *Peter . . . ,*" 93. Watson denied that "he did not cut them in consequence of knowing they were in the right," and said that the reason the recent floggings had not left more severe scars was "that on a former occasion he received orders from his master when he was vexed, and directed a negro to be flogged, that they should be burnt, but not cut." Ibid., 94. See also "Complaint of the Negro *Tommy*, belonging to William Fraser," Feb. 9–10, 1819, CO 116/138, 32–34; and "Complaint of the negro Scipio, belonging to plantation Friends," Feb. 10, 1819, CO 116/138, 34–36. Solomon Northup, a free black man from New York who was kidnapped and then enslaved in Louisiana, where he eventually became a driver, recounted how he faked whippings and collaborated with the slaves he supervised. "During my eight years' experience as a driver," Northup wrote, "I learned to handle the whip with marvelous dexterity and precision, throwing the lash within a hair's breadth of the back, the ear, the nose, without, however, touching either of them. If Epps [Northup's owner] was observed at a distance, or we had reason to apprehend he was sneaking somewhere in the vicinity, I would commence plying the lash vigorously, when, according to arrangement, they would squirm and screech as if in agony, although not one of them had in fact been even grazed." Northup, *Twelve Years a Slave: Narrative of Solomon Northup* (Auburn: Derby and Miller, 1853), 226–27.

42. See Chapter 5. See also Randy M. Browne, "The 'Bad Business' of Obeah: Power, Authority, and the Politics of Slave Culture in the British Caribbean," *William and Mary Quarterly* 68, no. 3 (2011): 451–80.

43. Ibid.

44. Vincent Brown, "Spiritual Terror and Sacred Authority: The Power of the Supernatural in Jamaican Slave Society," in *New Studies in the History of American Slavery*, ed. Stephanie M. H. Camp and Edward E. Baptist (Athens: University of Georgia Press, 2006), 196–97.

45. Roughley, *Jamaica Planter's Guide*, 81.

46. Barclay, *A Practical View*, 40.

47. Woensdag's poor standing in his community is illustrated by his experience on Christmas. When the day's work was finished and the manager distributed rum to the estate's slaves, a holiday custom throughout the colony, Woensdag refused to join them, he explained, "as the negroes said they did not care about me." Later, "when they began to dance," Woensdag tried to participate, only to be "pushed out of the dance finding I was a poor fellow without a mother or family." "Complaint of the Negro Woensdag the Property of Plan. Niewen Hoop," Jan. 7, 1825, CO 116/140. In other documents this plantation's name is rendered as "Niewenhoop" or "Nieuw Hoop."

48. Ibid. For a similar case see "Complaint, No. 17," Oct. 23, 1829, in *Protectors of Slaves Reports*, PP 262 (1831), 82. Woensdag's decision to leave the plantation for several days before making his complaint was typical of many slaves in Berbice and other West Indian colonies, where *petit marronage*—running away for a few days or weeks without the intention of permanently abandoning one's plantation—was fairly common.

49. "Complaint of the Negro Woensdag."

50. "Examination of a Complaint preferred by the negro *Welcome*, belonging to plantation Vryburg . . . ," June 28, 1822, CO 116/138, 123–24 (quotations, 123).

51. Ibid., 124.

52. Explicitly labeled "offences" on punishment records included "striking driver," "biting driver," "holding and tearing drivers' clothes," "raising cutlass against driver," "fighting the driver, and insubordination," and "threatening violence to drivers, overseers, &c. in the discharge of their duty." See, for example, "Abstract of Offences committed by Male and Female Plantation Slaves in the Colony Berbice . . . from 1st July to 31st December 1828 . . . ," in *Protectors of Slaves Reports*, PP 262 (1831), 19–20.

53. "Complaint No. 16," May 24, 1827, CO 116/143, 223–24 (quotations, 223); "Return of Slaves attached to Plantation Rotterdam . . . ," Dec. 30, 1817, T 71/437, 323–25.

54. "Complaint No. 16," May 24, 1827, CO 116/143, 223–24 (quotations, 224).

55. July 9, 1830, CO 116/146, 138–41 (quotations, 139).

56. Feb. 24, 1832, CO 116/150, 127–29 (quotation, 127). For similar cases, see "Complaint of *Jack*, belonging to plantation Lochaber," Sept. 19, 1823, and "Reply of *Mr. Tush*, manager of plantation Lochaber, on the complaints of Jack and Jonathan, of said estate," Sept. 30, 1823, CO 116/138, 110–11; "No. 10," March 1, 1831, CO 116/142, 92–98.

57. Oct. 20, 1828, entry, "Punishment Record Book of Plantn. Allness . . . ," CO 116/145, 49–50 ("cursing the driver"); Nov. 10, 1828, entry, "Punishment Record Book of Plantn. Allness . . . ," CO 116/145, 49–50 ("insolence to driver"); July 23, 1828, entry, "Punishment Record Book of Plant Sandvoort & Goed Bananaland . . . ," CO 1161/145, 59–60 ("telling falsehood"); July 29, 1828, entry, 59–60 ("obstinately persisting"); Oct. 24, 1828 entry, "Punishment Record Book of Ross & Barnstedt's Task Gang . . . ," CO 116/145, 81–82 ("abusing driver & resisting his authority"); July 13, 1828 entry, "Punishment Record Book of Plantation Reliance . . . ," CO 116/145, 82–83 ("instigating the other negroes"); Nov. 20, 1828 entry, "Punishment record Book of Pln. Bestendigheid . . . ," CO 116/145, 102–3 ("quarreling & fighting").

58. "Complaint of the Negress Named [blank] Belonging to Pln. Albion Corentine Coast," Feb. 8, 1825, CO 116/140.

59. Ibid.

60. "Examination of the negro woman *Rosetta*," 54–56 (quotations, 54). The Berbice

Association purchased Berenstein (sometimes spelled "Beerenstein") in 1817 with the intent of using the estate to grow food for their *winkel* slaves. Berenstein was so far from New Amsterdam, according to James Walker, superintendent of the *winkel* department, that enslaved people considered it "a remote & disagreeable banishment." Quoted in Thompson, *Unprofitable Servants*, 154.

61. "Examination of the negro woman *Rosetta*," 54. A year and a half later Rosetta complained again, this time about an "extremely severe" manager, J. Deussen, and against another driver, "Primo, who, instigated by Duessen, treats them very cruelly." See "Examination of a complaint made by the negro woman *Rosetta*, belonging to plantation Beerenstein," Nov. 15, 1820, CO 116/138, 69.

62. Labor historians have similarly observed that employers or managers generally supported foremen when employees complained about them so long as production was not jeopardized. See Price, *Masters, Unions, and Men*, 36–39; Nelson, *Managers and Workers*, 45.

63. Roughley, *Jamaica Planter's Guide*, 80.

64. "Driver not co-operating" was a specific "offence" on Berbician punishment records.

65. Nov. 20, 1828, entry, "Punishment Record Book of Plant. Allness . . . ," CO 116/145, 49–50.

66. July 7 and 16, 1828, entries, "Punishment Record Book of Plantn Vryheid . . . ," CO 116/145, 54–55.

67. Oct. 10, 1828, entry, ibid., 54–55.

68. Nov. 12, 1828, entry, "Punishment Record Book of Plantn. Mary's Hope . . . ," CO 116/145, 112–13.

69. July 17, 1828, entry, "Punishment Record Book of Plantn. Frederick's Lust . . . ," CO 116/145, 140–41.

70. Aug. 13, 1827, entry, "Punishment Record Book of Plant. Eliza & Mary . . . ," CO 116/144.

71. Dec. 1, 1830, CO 116/147, 144–47 ("punished whenever," 144; all other quotations, 146). For a similar case, see "Complaint, No. 9," Sept. 30, 1829, in *Protectors of Slaves Reports*, PP 262 (1831), 75.

72. "Examination of the negro woman *Laura*, belonging to plantation No. 6, Cauje [*sic*] Creek," June 4, 1819, CO 116/138, 55. The manager denied that the driver was punished.

73. "Examination of a Complaint Preferred by the Negroes *Maria, Jane, Fanny, Marianne, Polly, Bella, Caroline, Betsy and Nancy*, belonging to plantation Port Mourant, against the Manager of said estate," March 3, 1823, CO 116/138, 136.

74. "The complaint of Hector Downie[?] proprietor of Plant. Waterloo against two of his slaves named Tom and Adam for having a dance at night contrary to the Court's ordinance and the repeated prohibition of the said proprietor," Sept. 23, 1824, CO 116/140; M. S. Bennett to Henry Beard, Sept. 29, 1824, CO 116/140. An ordinance passed by the court of policy and criminal justice on March 8, 1814, prohibited "Any and all Dancing, on any Estates, or in any place within the jurisdiction of this Government, from henceforth until the year 1815, or until our further pleasure and license be made known." Reprinted in *Berbice Gazette*, April 2, 1814. In 1827 the fiscal referred to an 1817 ordinance stipulating that slaves were allowed to dance from 8:00 p.m. on December 24 until 8:00 p.m. on December 26 to celebrate Christmas, one of the few times a year slaves were allowed to celebrate. *Berbice Gazette*, Dec. 19, 1827. For holidays or "dancing days," see Thompson, *Unprofitable Servants*, 193–96.

75. Thomas Roughley's description of the consequences of having a "bad head driver" suggests the range of problems attributed to drivers. With an "ill disposed" driver, Roughley wrote,

"the work will not be carried on agreeable to [the overseer's] dictates; things suffer in general; the slaves run away, or are inclined to be turbulent; he and they cabal; bad sugar is made; and perhaps the horrid and abominable practice of Obea is carried on, dismembering and disabling one another; even aiming at the existence of the white people. The root, then, of this evil must be struck at, and the head driver and his abettors sent to public punishment." Roughley, *Jamaica Planter's Guide*, 82–83.

76. "Examination of a complaint preferred by the negro *Primo*, driver of plantation Beerenstein," Dec. 29, 1820, CO 116/138, 72–73 (quotations, 72). For J. Deussen's management and complaints about him, see Thompson, *Unprofitable Servants*, 155–56, 187, 192, 201, 219–22, 225–26, 233.

77. "Examination of a complaint preferred by the negro *Primo*," 72–73 (quotation, 73). For the complaint against Primo, see "Examination of a complaint made by the negro woman *Rosetta*."

78. "Complaint of the Negro Fielding Belonging to Plantation Alness Corentine Coast," Aug. 18, 1824, CO 116/140; "Return of Slaves attached to Plantation Alness . . . ," Dec. 2, 1817, T 71/437, 253; "Return of Slaves . . . of Plantation Alness . . . ," Jan. 1, 1819, T 71/438, 475–76. In 1825 there were 356 slaves registered on Alness (a slight decrease from the 1822 registration return, which listed 367 slaves). See "Return of Slaves . . . attached to Plantation Alness . . . ," Jan. 1, 1825, T 71/442, 529–32.

79. "Complaint of the Negro Fielding." The earliest slave registration return for plantation Alness—from 1817—lists Fielding as one of four field drivers. See "Return of Slaves attached to Plantation Alness . . . ," Dec. 2, 1817, 253.

80. Dec. 29, 1826, entry, "Extract Punishment Record Book of Plantation Vryheid . . . ," CO 116/143, 4–5.

81. Roughley, *Jamaica Planter's Guide*, 82.

82. "Complaint Against the Negro Hans," June 17, 1819, CO 116/138, 60–63; "Declaration and demand in a Criminal Case presented[?] to the Honorable Court of Criminal Justice of the Colony Berbice at the Instance of M.S. Bennett Fiscal of the Colony R.O. Plaintiff Versus the Negroe January head driver of Plant. Deutichem on the East Bank of the River Berbice," Aug. 4, 1819, Court of Policy and Court of Civil and Criminal Justice, AB6, 11–14, Walter Rodney Archives, Georgetown, Guyana; Browne, "The 'Bad Business' of Obeah," 451–80. The name of the plantation where January was enslaved is spelled various ways in different documents, including Demtichem, Dentichem, Duidichim, Deutichem—all variations on a Dutch town named Doetinchem.

83. January was listed as "watchman" in "Return of Slaves, attached to Plantation Deutichem . . . ," Dec. 30, 1817, T 71/437, 383.

84. "Complaint of the Slave January Belonging to Plant. Deutichem," March 9, 1829, CO 116/142, 76–97 ("flogged under the gallows," 76). January's age was recorded as thirty-six in 1817 and thirty-seven in 1819. See "Return of Slaves, attached to Plantation Deutichem," Dec. 30, 1817; and "Return of Slaves attached to Plantation Deutichem . . . ," Jan. 1, 1819, T 71/438, 669. See also Browne, " 'Bad Business' of Obeah," 465–68.

85. "Complaint of the Slave January," 76–79 ("beg[ged] that," "the Gang are gone," 77; "this man," "taken and confined," 78).

86. Ibid., 77–86 ("whole gang," 78; "a few well disposed," 86).

87. Ibid., 81–84 ("Since that period," 81; "not a Driver," "His answer," 84).

88. Ibid., 94–96 ("the [current] driver," "a disgraced Driver," "held an unfounded," 95; "speaking Creole," 94; "that his conduct," "punishment was merited," 96).

89. Fufu is a dough-like food made from mashed plantains, yams, or cassava. Pigeon peas, also known as Congo peas or gungo peas, were widely cultivated in the Caribbean.

90. "Complaint of the Negro La Rose, belonging to pl. Broer's lust property of J. P. Broer," July 10, 1826, CO 116/141. La Rose was registered in 1819 as a tall, twenty-eight-year-old African driver with "country marks on both sides of the head." See "Return of Slaves, the Property of J. P. Broer . . . ," Feb. 22, 1819, T 71/438, 31–32.

91. "Complaint of the Negro La Rose."

92. "Copies of the Quarterly Returns of the Burgher Officers to the Council of Government Berbice From 1st January 1824 to 6th April 1826," Report of Captain K[eith] Cooper, CO 116/140 (quotation); "Return of Slaves, attached to Plantation Canefield . . . ," Feb. 19, 1819, T 71/438, 125; "Return of Slaves . . . attached to Plant. Canefield," March 26, 1825, T/71, 211–12.

93. The fiscal dismissed Philip's complaint as unfounded and ordered him to be punished. John Cameron, the manager of Canefield, said that "Philip has been often put in the stocks, on account of his being frequently drunk, and his very great neglect of the sick." Philip also had "a very bad character amongst the negroes, who accuse him of taking their fowls to procure rum." See "Complaint of negro *Philip*, the property of plantation Canefield Carye," June 14, 1819, CO 116/138, 53–54 ("of being too much punished," "Philip has been," 53).

94. "Copies of the Quarterly Returns of the Burgher Officers."

95. Ibid. For suicide among slaves in Berbice, see Lean, "Secret Lives," 270–80.

96. For drivers (*commandeurs*) in the Haitian Revolution, for example, see Fick, *Making of Haiti,* 91–92, 94–95, 241, 244. In his study of slave resistance in nineteenth-century Cuba, Manuel Barcia concluded that "slaves in the position of contramayoral [driver] often used their post to launch some of the most daunting African-led rebellions in the Cuban countryside," and that they were regular participants and leaders in plots and rebellions. He also noted, however, that drivers were sometimes "as hated as overseers or owners, and thus . . . they were frequently victims of slave uprisings." Barcia, *Seeds of Insurrection: Domination and Resistance on Western Cuban Plantations, 1808–1848* (Baton Rouge: Louisiana State University Press, 2008), 43 ("slaves in the position"), 96 ("as hated"). For a summary of the rebellions drivers appear to have supported or led, see Paquette, "The Drivers Shall Lead Them," 44–50.

Chapter 4. Marital Discord and Domestic Struggles

1. "*Complaint No. 4*," April 9, 1827, Colonial Office series (hereafter CO) 116/143, 215–16 ("told him," "to kiss," "under the," "three slaps," 215; "John William," "in the dark," 216), National Archives, Kew, London, United Kingdom; "Return of Slaves made by La Rose, his property," Nov. 1, 1817, Treasury series (hereafter T) 71/437, 207, National Archives, Kew, London, United Kingdom. Three months later William was convicted of attacking another woman, Rebecca, "in a violent and ruffian-like manner" after her mother complained to the deputy protector of slaves. He was sentenced to be whipped "in the jail-yard, in presence of the Fiscal." See "*Complaint No. 5*," July 11, 1827, CO 116/143, 250; and "No. 3, fiscal's Report on Result of Cases referred to him by the Deputy Protector of Slaves," Feb. 29, 1828, CO 116/144, 23. The fiscal's decision may have been influenced by the fact that in (early modern) England "targeting a married woman's belly was understood to be a symbolic act of denigration and destruction" that was particularly unacceptable. Garthine Walker, *Crime, Gender and Social Order in Early Modern England* (Cambridge: Cambridge University Press, 2003), 60, 61 (quotation).

2. My broad conception of marital relationships includes not only couples that were legally married (which was only possible after 1826) but also people who self-identified as husbands

and wives—what colonials described as "reputed marriages" and what historians have called "self-marriages" or common-law marriages.

3. The types of conflicts explored in this chapter reflect the sources that documented them and do not represent the full range of marital or domestic problems enslaved people faced. It is worth reflecting on the silences of the archival record and considering the range of issues not documented by colonial authorities, such as same-sex relationships. "Sodomy" was listed on Demerara and Essequibo punishment records (under the category of "Serious and aggravated Offences"), but very few punishments were recorded. For a persuasive argument that historians know little about homosexuality and slavery because they have assumed that sexuality can be understood in terms of contemporary heterosexual norms, see Clarence Walker, "Sexuality: The Secret Everyone Already Knows" (presentation, University of North Carolina at Chapel Hill, March 24, 2011). James H. Sweet has also argued that "ample evidence exists of same-sex behaviors in early Africa and the diaspora, including among ritually powerful men who took on the social roles of women in places such as Angola, Nigeria, Portugal, and Brazil. Unfortunately, scholars and activists have tended to rely on Western categories such as 'sodomy,' 'pederasty,' 'homosexuality,' and 'gay' to represent these behaviors. None of these categories accurately represents the social histories of most of these men." Sweet, "Defying Social Death: The Multiple Configurations of African Slave Family in the Atlantic World," *William and Mary Quarterly* 70, no. 2 (2013): 254n6. See also Sweet, "Mutual Misunderstandings: Gesture, Gender and Healing in the African Portuguese World," *Past and Present*, no. 203, suppl. 4 (2009): 128–43.

4. Historians of slavery have done much to explore sexual relationships between enslaved people and colonials or whites but very little to understand how gender shaped relationships between enslaved men and women themselves. Also, as historian Henrice Altink observed, "Caribbean historians have not yet explored in great detail the nature of slave marriage" due to a "lack of sources that provide an insight into the slaves' intimate world" as well as historians' greater interest "in dispelling the myth instigated by contemporary observers that the slave family was overwhelmingly matrifocal and unstable than in the quality of the slaves' intimate relationships" (Altink, *Representations of Slave Women in Discourses on Slavery & Abolition, 1780–1838* [New York: Routledge, 2007], 210n5). Feminist scholars, however, have long urged historians to pay greater attention to the way gender shaped relationships between enslaved men and women and to domestic violence in slave families. See bell hooks, *Ain't I a Woman: Black Women and Feminism* (Boston: South End Press, 1981), 15–49; Barbara Bush, *Slave Women in Caribbean Society, 1650–1832* (Bloomington: Indiana University Press, 1990), 8; Claire Robertson, "Africa into the Americas? Slavery and Women, the Family, and the Gender Division of Labor," in *More Than Chattel: Black Women and Slavery in the Americas*, ed. David Barry Gaspar and Darlene Clark Hine (Bloomington: Indiana University Press, 1996), 3–40; Nell Irvin Painter, "Soul Murder and Slavery: Toward a Fully Loaded Cost Accounting," in *Southern History Across the Color Line* (Chapel Hill: University of North Carolina Press, 2002), 15–39; and Jennifer L. Morgan, *Laboring Women: Reproduction and Gender in New World Slavery* (Philadelphia: University of Pennsylvania Press, 2004). For enslaved people's domestic conflicts in the antebellum U.S. South, see Brenda Stevenson, "Distress and Discord in Virginia Slave Families, 1830–1860," in *In Joy and in Sorrow: Women, Family, and Marriage in the Victorian South, 1830–1900*, ed. Carol K. Bleser (New York: Oxford University Press, 1991), 103–24; Ann Patton Malone, *Sweet Chariot: Slave Family and Household Structure in Nineteenth-Century Louisiana* (Chapel Hill: University of North Carolina Press, 1992), 228–29; Christopher Morris, "Within the Slave Cabin: Violence in Mississippi Slave Families," in *Over the Threshold: Intimate Violence in Early*

America, ed. Christine Daniels and Michael V. Kennedy (New York: Routledge, 1999), 268–81; and Emily West, *Chains of Love: Slave Couples in Antebellum South Carolina* (Urbana: University of Illinois Press, 2004), 43–79.

5. In her analysis of Anglo-Native American encounters in colonial Virginia, Kathleen Brown coined the term "gender frontier" to describe "the meeting of two or more culturally specific systems of knowledge about gender and nature" (Brown, *Good Wives, Nasty Wenches, and Anxious Patriarchs: Gender, Race, and Power in Colonial Virginia* [Chapel Hill: University of North Carolina Press, 1996], 33). See also Brown, "Brave New Worlds: Women's and Gender History," *William and Mary Quarterly* 50, no. 2 (1993): 317–22; and Jane T. Merritt, "Cultural Encounters Along a Gender Frontier: Mahican, Delaware, and German Women in Eighteenth-Century Pennsylvania," *Pennsylvania History* 67, no. 4 (2000): 502–31.

6. Lois Green Carr and Lorena S. Walsh found that the shortage of white women in the seventeenth-century Chesapeake, where men significantly outnumbered women, afforded them greater sexual freedom, choice of marital partners, and bargaining power in their relationships than they would have otherwise had in England, where sex ratios were more balanced. See Carr and Walsh, "The Planter's Wife: The Experience of White Women in Seventeenth-Century Maryland," *William and Mary Quarterly* 34, no. 4 (1977): 542–71.

7. I am sensitive to critiques that using "patriarchal" to describe enslaved men's authority can be problematic, given that the laws and logic of slavery undermined some of the central features of patriarchy: that husbands were supposed to have exclusive control of their wives' bodies and a responsibility to protect them from other men's violence. Enslaved men were certainly not able to fulfill these obligations to the degree that free men in many societies were, nor did they establish the kind of patriarchal dominance that characterized African family structures during the era of the slave trade. Nevertheless, enslaved men in Berbice were more successful than one might assume in shaping the contours of their sexual relationships with women, in large part because there was broad agreement among African-, European-, and Caribbean-born men that women should be subordinate to men. Similar beliefs about gender did not, of course, erase the significant differences in power and status between enslaved men and their enslavers, but patriarchy is not predicated on male egalitarianism. To consider the relationship between the gendered authority of enslaved men as compared with that of white colonials, Steve Stern's understanding of patriarchy as a system that "acknowledges gendered ranking and tension, as well as alliance, among men and among women, rather than limiting gender status to an alliance of men to subordinate women," is particularly helpful. Steve J. Stern, *The Secret History of Gender: Women, Men, and Power in Late Colonial Mexico* (Chapel Hill: University of North Carolina Press, 1995), 21. For patriarchy in Africa and the Diaspora, see Robertson, "Africa into the Americas?"

8. Prabhu P. Mohapatra, drawing on the work of Carole Pateman, described the "sexual contract" as "primarily a compact amongst men to ensure orderly access to women's bodies, and [a contract that] establishes male sex rights." Mohapatra, "'Restoring the Family': Wife Murders and the Making of a Sexual Contract for Indian Immigrant Labour in the British Caribbean Colonies, 1860–1920," *Studies in History* 11, no. 2 (1995): 229. See also Carol Pateman, *The Sexual Contract* (Stanford: Stanford University Press, 1988).

9. Cecilia A. Green, "'A Civil Inconvenience'? The Vexed Question of Slave Marriage in the British West Indies," *Law and History Review* 25, no. 1 (2007), 13.

10. For gender in British antislavery and amelioration, see Diana Paton, "Decency, Dependence and the Lash: Gender and the British Debate over Slave Emancipation, 1830–34," *Slavery*

& *Abolition* 17, no. 3 (1996): 163–84; Pamela Scully, *Liberating the Family?: Gender and British Slave Emancipation in the Rural Western Cape, S. Africa, 1823–1853* (Portsmouth, N.H.: Heinemann, 1997); Hilary McD. Beckles, "Female Enslavement and Gender Ideologies in the Caribbean," in *Identity in the Shadow of Slavery*, ed. Paul E. Lovejoy (London: Continuum, 2000), 177–79; and Altink, *Representations of Slave Women*. For pro-natalism, see Michael Craton, "Changing Patterns of Slave Families in the British West Indies," *Journal of Interdisciplinary History* 10, no. 1 (1979): 30–31; B. W. Higman, *Slave Populations of the British Caribbean, 1807–1834* (Baltimore: Johns Hopkins University Press, 1984), 348–54; and Katherine Paugh, "The Politics of Childbearing in the British Caribbean and the Atlantic World During the Age of Abolition, 1776–1838," *Past and Present* 221, no. 1 (2013): 119–60. As Paugh argued, the overly stark distinctions many historians make between abolitionists and "anti-abolitionists" has obscured "widespread agreement on the importance of encouraging reproduction in order to achieve economic stability in the Caribbean" (ibid., 136).

11. The full text of the law was reprinted in *The Berbice Royal Gazette*, Sept. 30, 1826 (reprinted in Alvin O. Thompson, *A Documentary History of Slavery in Berbice, 1796–1834* [Georgetown, Guyana: Free Press, 2002]; hereafter 1826 slave code). Michel Foucault described a range of governmental strategies that focused on disciplining individual bodies ("an anatomo-politics of the human body") and on regulating biological processes as a means of population control ("a bio-politics of the population") as "bio-power." In the late early modern period, he argued, "there was an explosion of numerous and diverse techniques for achieving the subjugation of bodies and the control of populations, marking a beginning of an era of 'bio-power.'" Foucault, *The History of Sexuality*, vol. 1: *An Introduction*, trans. Robert Hurley (New York: Pantheon, 1978), 139–40. Though Foucault focused on state responses to rapidly expanding European populations—a very different situation than the declining slave populations of the nineteenth-century British Caribbean—his concept is still helpful in understanding the ways policy makers tried to simultaneously manage colonial populations while reforming individual people's sexual and marital practices.

12. Slaveowners or their representatives were required to provide written permission for their slaves to marry or, if they objected, to give "sufficient proof that such proposed marriage would be injurious to the well-being of the said slave." 1826 slave code, clause 19.

13. 1826 slave code, clauses 19 and 20. The English Marriage Act of 1753 (Lord Hardwicke's Marriage Act) required marriages "to be performed by formal church ceremony and to be officially publicized, witnessed, and recorded. These rules effectively nullified common-law marriage. The act also required parental consent if both parties to the marriage were under twenty-one years of age. Children of marriages that did not meet these requirements could not inherit property and were considered 'base.' Church of England–sanctioned marriage was the requirement until 1836, when the British Marriage Act finally gave official approval to marriages performed by civil authorities and registered ministers of other denominations" (Green, "Vexed Question of Slave Marriage," 24).

14. The law required any slave who claimed "to have a husband or wife, or reputed husband or wife . . . to prove the truth of his or her assertion, either by the evidence of the owner, manager, or overseer . . . or by the evidence of the other slaves belonging to the same estate or plantation." It also stipulated that "in case the assertion is supported by the evidence of slaves only, but contradicted by that of the owner, manager or overseer," separation by sale could proceed provisionally pending an investigation by the protector of slaves. 1826 slave code, clause 26.

15. 1826 slave code, clause 21. For infant mortality in Berbice and other British Caribbean

colonies, where "rates in excess of 400 [deaths] per 1,000 [births] were typical," see Higman, *Slave Populations*, 25–33, 317–18 (quotation, 318).

16. Green, "Vexed Question of Slave Marriage," 39–40; Paugh, "Politics of Childbearing."

17. See Appendix 1.

18. P. Nicholson to Henry Beard, Oct. 26, 1826, in "Reports of the Civil Magistrates in the several districts in the Colony of Berbice on the promulgation of the New Code of the 25th September 1826 for improving the condition of the slave population therein," CO 111/102, 302–3. Edmund Burke's proposed "Negro Code" (1780) would have similarly punished "all acts of adultery, unlawful concubinage, and fornication, amongst negroes." See Burke, "A Letter to the Right Hon. Hendry Dundas . . . with the Sketch of a Negro Code," in *The Writings and Speeches of Edmund Burke*, ed. P. J. Marshall (Oxford: Oxford University Press, 1991), 6:285.

19. "No. 1., Abstract of Offences committed by Male and Female Plantation Slaves in the Colony *Berbice* . . . from 1st July to 31st December 1828 . . . ," in *Return to an address to His Majesty, dated 15 December 1830; for, copy of any reports which may have been received from the protectors of slaves in the colonies of Demerara, Berbice, Trinidad, St. Lucia, the Cape of Good Hope and Mauritius* . . . , Parliamentary Papers, House of Commons (hereafter PP) (1831), 19–20.

20. "No. 2., Abstract of Offences committed by Male and Female Plantation Slaves in the Colony *Berbice* . . . from 1st January to 30th June 1829 . . . ," in ibid., 62–63.

21. "Offences committed by Male and Female Plantation Slaves on the Island of Trinidad . . . from 24th June 1821 to 24th June 1824 . . . ," and "List of Offences committed by Male and Female Plantation Slaves in the Island of Trinidad . . . from the 24th June 1824 to the 24th June 1826 . . . ," Feb. 24, 1827, in *Papers in explanation of the measures adopted by His Majesty's government for the melioration of the condition of the slave population in His Majesty's possessions* . . . , PP (1827), 261–64; "Demerara and Essequebo, List of Offences committed by Male and Female Plantation Slaves . . . from the 1st of January 1828 to the 30th of June 1828 . . . ," Nov. 1, 1828, in *Protectors of slaves reports. Return to an address of the Honourable House of Commons, dated 11 March 1829, for, copy of any reports which may have been received from the protectors of slaves in the colonies of Demerara, Berbice, Trinidad, St. Lucia, and the Cape of Good Hope* . . . , PP (1829), 4–6; "Abstract of Offences committed by Male and Female Plantation Slaves in the Island of St. Lucia . . . between the 1st July and 31st December 1828, showing the Nature Number of Offences," PP (1831), 4–6.

22. Only 33 of the 142 plantations (23 percent) that submitted punishment record books in 1827 recorded any marital-related offenses. On 20 of the plantations that did report marital-related offenses, moreover, less than 5 percent of reported offenses were marital-related. J. H. Lean, "The Secret Lives of Slaves: Berbice, 1819 to 1827" (Ph.D. diss., University of Canterbury, New Zealand, 2002), 165. In the antebellum U.S. South, where slaveowners liked to believe they were paternalists and smaller slaveholdings often meant that slaveowners interacted directly with their slaves in ways that were uncommon on the large plantations of the Caribbean, owners may have intervened more regularly in enslaved people's domestic conflicts. See Morris, "Violence in Mississippi Slave Families."

23. For "gender frontier," see note 5.

24. Anthony Hamilton, Codrington estate chaplain, "Progress of Religious Instruction in the West Indies," *Barbadian*, June 9, 1829, quoted in Melanie J. Newton, *The Children of Africa in the Colonies: Free People of Color in Barbados in the Age of Emancipation* (Baton Rouge: Louisiana State University Press, 2008), 92n17. See also Newton, "'New Ideas of Correctness': Gender, Amelioration and Emancipation in Barbados, 1810s–50s," *Slavery & Abolition* 21, no. 3 (2002): 113.

25. 1826 slave code, clauses 19 and 20.

26. For slaveowner resistance to slave marriages, see Green, "Vexed Question of Slave Marriage." As Green notes, resistance stemmed in part from slaveowners' "desire to avoid having to endow black male heads—perceived through patriarchal lenses as the chief potential rivals of ruling class men—with an *independent* and *communal* base of authority and property, that might, moreover, mediate, limit, and generally interfere with exploitative planter-class access to their women and children" (ibid., 38).

27. David Power to Henry Beard, Jan. 21, 1827, CO 116/143, 149–52 (quotations, 150).

28. "Protector of Slaves Report, to 31 August 1828, Extract of a Dispatch from Governor Beard,...," PP (1829), 29. An estimated 20,700 slaves lived in Berbice in 1830. See Higman, *Slave Populations*, Table S1.2, "Estimated Annual Slave Populations by Colony, 1807–34," 418.

29. Alvin O. Thompson, *A Documentary History of Slavery in Berbice, 1796–1834* (Georgetown, Guyana, 2002), 216n8.

30. Goderich to George Murray, April 21, 1832, CO 116/148, 12.

31. Birth rates in West Indian colonies (excluding non-plantation societies like the Bahamas) in the late 1820s ranged from a high of 58.2 births per 1,000 in Barbados (1829–32)—the only sugar colony with a consistently self-reproducing slave population in the nineteenth century—to a low of 27.4 per 1,000 in Jamaica (1826–29). These figures do not include the many infants who died soon after birth and were not registered. See Higman, *Slave Populations*, Table 9.1, "Slave Birth Rates, Death Rates, Rates of Natural Increase, and Sex Ratios by Colony, 1815–1834," 308–10.

32. For wealth in people in pre-colonial Africa, see John Thornton, *Africa and Africans in the Making of the Atlantic World, 1400–1800* (Cambridge: Cambridge University Press, 1998), 72–97.

33. Sex ratios varied and became more balanced as the slave population became more creolized closer to emancipation, but men outnumbered women throughout the period examined here. In 1817, there were 128.4 males per 100 females; by 1831, 114.5 males per 100 females. See Higman, *Slave Populations*, Table 5.7, "Slave Sex Ratios and Percentages African and Colored by Colony, c. 1817 and c. 1832," 116.

34. In 1827, for example, 139 of the 570 white colonists in Berbice were women. Meanwhile, there were nearly 10,000 enslaved women and 980 free women of color. Higman, *Slave Populations*, Table S1.1, "Registered and Mean Slave Populations by Colony and Sex, 1813–34," 415, and Table S2.1, "White and Freedman Populations by Sex and Colony, c. 1830," 433.

35. B. W. Higman, "The Slave Family and Household in the British West Indies, 1800–1834," *Journal of Interdisciplinary History* 6, no. 2 (1975), 270.

36. A sample of nearly 1,900 enslaved people from nine plantations—documented in the 1817 slave registration returns—revealed that over half of all adult men (over age twenty) lived in family groups with wives and/or children. See Randy M. Browne and Trevor Burnard, "Husbands and Fathers: The Family Experience of Enslaved Men in Berbice, 1819–1834," *New West India Guide* (forthcoming 2017).

37. Evidence suggests that enslaved men provided material support in exchange for women's labor. At the very least, men expected their wives to perform most domestic chores. An enslaved man named Quaby, for example, cited his wife Arsenia's failure "to perform her duties as a wife" as his reason for submitting a divorce petition. "She will not cook, wash, or even speak to [me]," he testified. When Arsenia answered the protector's summons, he "made [her] sensitive of the obligations she owed to her husband." Nov. 9, 1830, CO 116/147, 104–6 ("to perform," "she

will not," 104; "made [her] sensitive," 106); and David Power, "General Observations," Sept. 15, 1831, CO 116/148, 328–30. Another enslaved man, Brutus, complained to the protector when his owner ordered the women who had been cooking for the men on the estate to pick coffee instead. Brutus explained that "the loss of this we all felt, as we have no wives on the Estate." "Complaint of the negro Brutus belonging to J. F. Linde," Nov. 25, 1827, CO 116/141. Jeannette, an enslaved woman on plantation Providence, reported that she woke up each morning at 4:00 to "boil plantains for my man, myself and little child," and that "the men on the estate get better allowance than the women." "Complaint No. 13," Feb. 9, 1827, CO 116/143, 184. See also Higman, "Slave Family," 284–85; Bush, Slave Women, 98; and Altink, Representations of Slave Women, 95.

38. Higman, "Slave Family," 275, 284–85; Higman, Slave Populations, 370–71; Marietta Morrissey, Slave Women in the New World: Gender Stratification in the Caribbean (Lawrence: University Press of Kansas, 1989), 89; Lean, "Secret Lives of Slaves," 173. Despite skewed sex ratios and opposition from European colonists, polygyny was not uncommon in Berbice, though the exact prevalence is impossible to establish. A sample of 1,247 slaves on five well-documented plantations owned by James Blair in 1817 revealed that 7.7 of all slaves lived in polygynous families. See Browne and Burnard, "Husbands and Fathers." Richard Price calculated that in neighboring Suriname in the eighteenth century about 20 percent of adult male maroons had two or more wives at any given time, though "most men—for demographic, not ideological reasons—were limited to one or two." Price, Alabi's World (Baltimore: Johns Hopkins University Press, 1990), 382.

39. "Complaint of the female slave Minkey belonging to L. F. Gallez," Jan. 14, 1828, CO 116/142, 1–3.

40. "Complaint of the woman Cecilia belonging to the Winkel Department," Feb. 1, 1830, CO 116/142, 20–21.

41. "Examination Report of the Death of the negro Richmond . . . ," March 18, 1822, CO 116/138, 97–98.

42. "INVESTIGATION Complaint of Nine Negro Men, belonging to Mrs. Ibon Sanders, residing in Upper Berbice . . . ," Feb. 1, 1819, CO 116/138, 26 ("never get any allowance," "if they steal," "ha[d] to give"), 27 ("that his wife").

43. "Examination of a Complaint preferred by the negress Sankey . . . ," July 21, 1822, CO 116/138, 127. The fiscal determined that Sankey's husband had not been sold, only sent to work for a few days in New Amsterdam, where his owners "had a large mercantile establishment." He sent Sankey back to the estate with her husband and "remanded [her] for making such a frivolous complaint."

44. Dec. 14, 1826, entry, "Punishment Record Book of Plantation La Prudence," CO 116/143, quoted in Lean, "Secret Lives of Slaves," 167.

45. March 27, 1827, entry, "Punishment record book of Pl^n De Resolutie . . . ," CO 116/143.

46. "Complaint of the Negro Claas belonging to plantation Op Hoop van Beter in Berbice River," June 22, 1824, CO 116/140; "Return of Slaves attached to Plantation Op Hoop van Beter . . . ," Dec. 22, 1817, T 71/437, 78–80. The manager and driver claimed they did not know Claas's wife, Santje, was pregnant, and the doctor who treated Santje claimed that she "miscarried at an early period of pregnancy from the usual causes—there was not the slightest violence" ("Complaint of the Negro Claas").

47. "Complaint of the Negro Willem Belonging to Plantation Ma Retraite on the River Berbice, Property of Fullerton," April 12, 1824, CO 116/140.

48. "Return of Slaves attached to Plantation Herstelling . . . ," Feb. 26, 1819, T 71/438, 627–33 (quotation, 630).

49. "Examination Report of the Death of the negro *Richmond*," March 18, 1822, CO 116/138, 97–98 (quotations, 97).

50. Ibid., 97. Plantation managers occasionally punished enslaved people who jeopardized slaves' marriages, probably because they were aware of the dangers such conflicts posed. The manager of Op Hoop van Beter, for example, ordered a man named Adriaan flogged for "attempting to seduce the woman Lucia in absence of her husband Daniel." Dec. 2, 1826 entry, "Punishment Record Book of Plantn Op Hoop van Beter . . . ," CO 116/143, 108–9.

51. "Examination Report of the Death of the negro *Richmond*," 97–98 (quotations, 97). "Self-divorce" was also common in England—where divorce was illegal until 1857—and in Britain's North American colonies. For England, see Samuel Pyeatt Menefee, *Wives for Sale: An Ethnographic Study of British Popular Divorce* (New York: St. Martin's Press, 1981); and Lawrence Stone, *Road to Divorce: England, 1530–1987* (New York: Oxford University Press, 1990). For British America, see Dorothy A. Mays, *Women in Early America: Struggle, Survival, and Freedom in a New World* (Santa Barbara, Calif.: ABC-CLIO, 2004), 111–14; Clare A. Lyons, *Sex Among the Rabble: An Intimate History of Gender and Power in the Age of Revolution, Philadelphia, 1730–1830* (Chapel Hill: University of North Carolina Press, 2006), 14–58.

52. "Examination Report of the Death of the negro *Richmond*," 98. For obeah and sexual rivalry, see Diana Paton, *The Cultural Politics of Obeah: Religion, Colonialism and Modernity in the Caribbean World* (Cambridge: Cambridge University Press, 2015), 110–15.

53. No. 46, April 1, 1831, PP (1830–31), 175–76 (quotations, 175). Punishment records offer other hints of similar conflicts. An August 18, 1827, entry from plantation Gebroeders recorded two men (Holland and Corridon) and one woman (Africa) punished in the bedstocks overnight for "fighting about Africa, who is the reputed wife of Corridon, but a great whore, and frequently detected with other men. Corridon has also another wife." "Punishment record Book of Pln Gebroeders . . . ," Jan. 14, 1828, CO 116/144.

54. Dec. 11, 1826, entry, "Punishment Record Book of Pl. Belair . . . ," CO 116/143, 170–71.

55. "Return of Slaves, attached to Plantation Providence . . . ," Feb. 22, 1819, T 71/438, 329 ("well made").

56. May 24, 1831, CO 116/148, 191–93 ("in the habit," "secure [Mark]," 192; "in consequence," "orders to bring," "negro yard," 193). The use of terms such as "seduction" and "disturbance" suggest that Mark may have attempted to sexually coerce Hebe. As scholars like Garthine Walker have noted, in early modern Europe even forms of sexual coercion that involved physical force were not always considered rape, and "distinctions between 'persuasion,' 'seduction' and 'rape' were particularly muddy." Walker, "Sexual Violence and Rape in Europe, 1500–1750," in *The Routledge History of Sex and the Body: 1500 to the Present*, ed. Sarah Toulalan and Kate Fisher (New York: Routledge, 2013), 433.

57. Jan. 1, 1829, entry, "Punishment Record Book of Pln Goldstone Hall . . . ," CO 116/145.

58. "Examination of a Complaint preferred by the negro *Felix*," Aug. 23, 1822, CO 116/138, 131.

59. As Garthine Walker has argued, "early modern patriarchalism endorsed violence as a means of maintaining gender and social hierarchy. Righteous violence therefore included 'reasonable correction' of wives by husbands" (Walker, *Crime, Gender and Social Order*, 49). See also Susan Dwyer Amussen, " 'Being Stirred to Much Unquietness': Violence and Domestic Violence in Early Modern England," *Journal of Women's History* 6, no. 2 (1994): 70–89. Even in the early nineteenth century, as a new model of "companionate" marriage challenged certain patriarchal ideals, physical abuse of women remained common in working-class marriages and was

legally and popularly accepted. See Anna Clark, *The Struggle for the Breeches: Gender and the Making of the British Working Class* (Berkeley: University of California Press, 1995), 73–74.

60. Dec. 24, 1828, entry, "Punishment Record Book of Plantation Philadelphia . . . ," CO 116/145, 64–65.

61. May 14, 1832, CO 116/150, 172–75 (quotations, 174). For the association between torn garments and gendered struggles in early modern England, see Walker, *Crime, Gender, and Social Order*, 42–43, 59.

62. Clark, *Struggle for the Breeches*, 83–84.

63. May 14, 1832, CO 116/150, 174 ("requested"), 175 ("reprimanded").

64. Green, "Vexed Question of Slave Marriage," 38.

65. "Complaint No. 5," Sept. 16, 1829, CO 116/145, 232 (quotations); "Return of Slaves, the Property of Andrew Ross," Feb. 21, 1831, T 71/444, 495–98; "Return of Slaves attached to Plantation Cruysburg . . . ," T 71/438, Feb. 18, 1819, 555–62.

66. "Complaint No. 5," Sept. 16, 1829.

67. For the long-term stability of patriarchy in Western civilization, see Gerda Lerner, *The Creation of Patriarchy* (New York: Oxford University Press, 1986); and Judith M. Bennett, *History Matters: Patriarchy and the Challenge of Feminism* (Philadelphia: University of Pennsylvania Press, 2006).

68. Bush, *Slave Women*, 97. James H. Sweet argued that in early colonial Brazil, where there were few African women, "the jealousies and disorders among male slaves that were caused by female infidelity suggest that polyandry may have been as common as polygyny." Sweet, *Recreating Africa: Culture, Kinship, and Religion in the African-Portuguese World, 1441–1770* (Chapel Hill: University of North Carolina Press, 2003), 43. For the increase in polygyny in African societies during the era of the slave trade due to unnaturally high female-to-male ratios and the impact of the transatlantic slave trade on African family structures, see Herbert S. Klein, "African Women in the Atlantic Slave Trade," in *Women and Slavery in Africa*, ed. Claire C. Robertson and Martin A. Klein (Madison: University of Wisconsin Press, 1983), 29–38; and John Thornton, "Sexual Demography: The Impact of the Slave Trade on Family Structure," in *Women and Slavery in Africa*, 39–48.

69. "Complaint of the Woman Named Mary Belonging to L. F. Gallez," May 19, 1826, CO 116/141. Rosie, enslaved on a coffee plantation, similarly took advantage of the surplus of men in the colony. Described by her manager as "young but of the most abandoned character, generally having 4 husbands at time," Rosie refused, despite the manager's repeated efforts, to "attach herself to one man." She was punished and transferred to another estate for "whoring with America," the driver, and "creating a disturbance on the Estate." Jan. 10, 1827, entry, "Punishment record Book of Plantation Gebroeders . . . ," CO 116/143.

70. Dec. 22 and Dec. 26, 1826, entries, "Punishment Record Book of Pl^n De Standvastigheid . . . ," CO 116/143, 100.

71. "Complaint of the Negress Carolina belonging to Pl. Rotterdam," Sept. 27, 1825, CO 116/140.

72. Ibid.

73. Some managers took more interest than others in punishing men who abused their wives, if the wide variation in recorded punishments is any indication. See Lean, "Secret Lives of Slaves," 162–63.

74. Jan. 7, 1827, entry, "Punishment Record Book of Pl. Best Coffee Land . . . ," CO 116/143.

75. Dec. 3, 1827, entry, "Punishment Record Book of Plantations Sandvoort & Goed Bananaland . . . ," Jan. 14, 1828, CO 116/144.

76. Aug. 1, 1828, entry, "Punishment Record Book of Pl^n Noord Holland . . . ," CO 116/145, 200–201.

77. July 9, 1827, entry, "Punishment record Book of Plantation Eliza and Mary . . . ," Jan. 6, 1828, CO 116/144.

78. July 20, 1828, entry, "Extract from the punishment Record Book of Plant^n Skeldon . . . ," Jan. 15, 1829, CO 116/145, 119–20.

79. Sept. 9, 1828, entry, "Punishment record Book of Pl^n No^s 19 & 20 . . . ," Jan. 9, 1829, CO 116/145, 33–34.

80. "Enquiry instituted by authority of His Honor N. Musgrave President of the courts of Justice, into the circumstance of thirty five negroes (14 men & 25 women) belonging to the Sugar Plantation Herstelling, Situated up the river Berbice, having absconded from said property, and taken refuge, in the woods aback of said estate . . . ," April 14, 1825, CO 116/140. The number of slaves involved in this case is difficult to determine. The fiscal recorded either "thirty five" or thirty-nine (fourteen plus twenty-five), though the report named thirty-seven slaves. The driver, meanwhile, counted thirty-four, and the manager's letter to the attorney listed "twenty women and eleven men."

81. Aug. 25, 1828, entries, "Punishment Record Book of Plant^n Overyseel . . . ," CO 116/145, 104–5.

82. Sept. 24, 1828, entry, "Punishment Record Book of Pl^n Nieuw [sp?] Hoop . . . ," CO 116/145, 109–10.

83. Oct. 10, 1828, entry, "Punishment Record Book of Pl^n Bellevue . . . ," CO 116/145, 142–43.

84. Sept. 15, 1828, entry, "Punishment Record Book of Plant^n Ma Retraite . . . ," CO 116/145, 195–96.

85. In early modern England, women were expected to either cry out for help or run away when attacked. Those who physically defended themselves, however, were perceived as threats to the gendered social order. See Walker, *Crime, Gender and Social Order*, esp. 49–51. For similar representations of physically assertive women in nineteenth-century Britain, see Clark, *Struggle for the Breeches*, 72–74.

86. "Complaint No. 39," Jan. 4, 1830, CO 116/145, 242. This plantation's name is rendered "New Vigilantie" in some documents.

87. I borrow "informal public" from Nancy F. Cott, *Public Vows: A History of Marriage and the Nation* (Cambridge, Mass.: Harvard University Press, 2000), 29–30, 37, 40, 48, 54.

88. Annatje had successfully turned to the colonial government four years earlier—when an enslaved woman stole several articles of her clothing—and it is possible that this previous experience encouraged her to complain against Frantz. See "Complaint of the negress Annatje belonging to the Winkel Department attached to the Governor's House," May 12, 1826, CO 116/141.

89. Nov. 15, 1830, CO 116/147, 114.

90. Nov. 15, 1830, CO 116/147, 116–17 ("admitted the charge," "shewed much contrition," 116; "at the recommendation," "reprimanded Frantz," 117).

91. "Complaint of the woman Cecilia," 20–21 (quotations, 20).

92. Ibid., 21. For "the conflation of household and bodily boundaries" in men's attacks against women, see Walker, *Crime, Gender, and Social Order*, 52–55 (quotation, 52).

93. "Complaint of the woman Cecilia," 21.

94. For female support networks in the U.S. South, see Deborah Gray White, *Ar'n't I a Woman?: Female Slaves in the Plantation South* (New York: W. W. Norton, 1999 [1985]. Steve Stern stressed the importance of similar female alliances in *The Secret History of Gender*, 103–7.

95. "Examination of the negro woman *Susanna*, belonging to and in the employ of his Excellency the Governor," May 16, 1821, CO 116/138, 82.

96. Oct. 6, 1830, CO 116/147, 90–93 (quotations, 90).

97. The 1826 slave code, clause 24, required "every proprietor of slaves, or his or her attorney, [to] employ a legally qualified medical practitioner, duly authorised to practise, by a certificate from the Lieutenant Governor or acting Lieutenant Governor, to attend their sick slaves, and [to] provide such medicines, food, and other necessaries as such medical practitioner shall from time to time reasonably order and direct." Legal and medical experts in late eighteenth- and early nineteenth-century England "wished to establish definitions of rape based on 'scientific' criteria such as ejaculation," which supposedly allowed them to determine whether or not a rape had occurred without relying on women's testimony (Anna Clark, *Women's Silence, Men's Violence: Sexual Assault in England, 1770–1845* [New York: Pandora, 1987], 61).

98. Oct. 6, 1830, CO 116/147, 90 ("the person"); Nov. 8, 1830, CO 116/147, 278–79 ("no evidence," 279). In a similar case from 1819, an enslaved man named Telemachus, aided by his wife and his daughter's "adopted mother," went to colonial authorities after his eleven- or twelve-year-old daughter, Elizabeth, died after having been allegedly raped by the manager of plantation Waaxhaamheid (or Warksaamheid), J. D. Luykens. The fiscal prosecuted Luykens in criminal court, where he presented compelling evidence that Luykens had raped Elizabeth and that he had conspired with the estate doctor and militia officers to cover up the crime. But Luykens succeeded in convincing authorities that Elizabeth had been "deflowered" by a young enslaved man, Jenkye, and that she died of "a great nervous debility." Luykens was acquitted of rape. CO 116/139, 195–219.

99. For the history of rape in Europe, see Clark, *Women's Silence, Men's Violence*; Walker, "Sexual Violence and Rape"; and Shani D'Cruze, "Sexual Violence Since 1750," in *Routledge History of Sex and the Body*, 444–59. In England, a legal precedent established in the late eighteenth century required proof of ejaculation to convict a man of rape. An 1828 law abolished this requirement. See Clark, *Women's Silence, Men's Violence*, 60–63.

100. "No. 18," Oct. 21, 1829, CO 116/142, 86–105 ("Sambo girl," 90). In this context, "sambo" or "samboe" was a racial classification for someone who was, as John Gabriel Stedman explained, "between a Mulatto and a black, being of a deep Copper-Colour'd Complexion, with dark hair that curls in large ringlets." Stedman, quoted in *John Gabriel Stedman: Narrative of a Five Years Expedition Against the Revolted Negroes of Surinam*, ed. Richard Price and Sally Price (Baltimore: Johns Hopkins University Press, 1988), 266. I cite the Prices' version of Stedman's narrative rather than the first published edition (1796) because it is a transcription of Stedman's original manuscript; his editor made several changes and additions to the published version. Berbice slave registration returns used several dozen skin color descriptions, including "sambo," "samba," and "dark sambo." For a complete list, see Higman, *Slave Populations*, Table S5.3, "Color of Slaves by Sex and Birthplace: Berbice, 1819," 529.

101. "Return of Slaves, the Property of Joseph Thubou Matthews," Feb. 25, 1819, T 71/438, 509–10.

102. "No. 18," Oct. 21, 1829 ("became very abusive," "I am quiet," "told me," 87; "a damned sow," "a drunken," 91).

103. Ibid. ("second," "half stripped," 86; "mother hearing," "began to fight," "a considerable time," 88; "the most dreadful agony," "a bit of rag," "mother seeing," 89; "guilty of breach," 104–5). This was the typical way colonial authorities handled fights between women over men. In July 1831, for example, a New Amsterdam domestic named Petite "quarreled with . . . and beat" a woman named Nanny because, Nanny claimed, "Petite is jealous of her, as [Petite] thinks Nanny intrigues with her husband." The protector "reprimanded the parties, and dismissed the case" without questioning Petite's husband. July 8, 1831, CO 116/149, 64–66 ("quarreled," 64; "Petite is jealous," 65; "reprimanded," 66). See also April 22, 1831, CO 116/148, 177–79.

104. "Complaint No. 6," July 10, 1827, CO 116/143, 250–52 ("shamefully beaten," 250; "Mr. Gallez (my husband)," "Mr. Gallez held," "barracks," 251); "A Return of Slaves made by Mrs. Frances Beresford, proprietor," Feb. 27, 1819, T 71/438, 101–2.

105. "Complaint No. 6," July 10, 1827 ("that Mrs. Gallez," 250; "should not attempt," "raised [her] hand," "master's negroes," 251).

106. Ibid., 251.

107. Ibid., 251–52 ("Mrs. Gallez acted intemperately," "had she," "in language," 251; "Let me hope," 252).

108. Ibid., 251.

109. For "grooming" and the sexual abuse of children, see Samantha Craven, Sarah Brown, and Elizabeth Gilchrist, "Sexual Grooming of Children: Review of Literature and Theoretical Considerations," *Journal of Sexual Aggression* 12, no. 3 (2006): 287–99.

110. "Complaint No. 22," July 22, 1829, CO 116/145, 223.

111. Ibid.

Chapter 5. Spiritual Power and the "Bad Business" of Obeah

1. *Trial of a Slave in Berbice, for the Crime of Obeah and Murder: Return to an Address to His Majesty, by The Honorable House of Commons, dated 29th of July 1822; for, Copy of any Information which may have been received concerning the Trial of a Slave, for the Crime of Obeah, in the Colony of Berbice,* Parliamentary Papers, House of Commons (hereafter PP) (1823), 13–14 (quotation, 13), 23. Vigilant lived on a plantation bordering Op Hoop van Beter. An 1819 slave registration return listed 172 enslaved people on Op Hoop van Beter. See "Return of Slaves, attached to Plantation Op Hoop van Beter . . . ," Feb. 1, 1819, Treasury series (hereafter T) 71/438, 119–24, National Archives, Kew, London, United Kingdom. "Minje" was the word for "water" in Ijo, an African language and one of the major roots of Berbice Dutch. See Gordon Eton Gill, "Labor, Material Welfare, and Culture in Hydrologic Plantation Enterprises: A Study of Slavery in the British Colony of Berbice (Guyana)" (Ph.D. diss., Howard University, 2004), 318–20, 330.

2. "Obeah" was a "catchall term used to describe a complex of shamanistic practices derived from various parts of Africa and conducted by ritual specialists working largely outside of formal institutions." Vincent Brown, *The Reaper's Garden: Death and Power in the World of Atlantic Slavery* (Cambridge, Mass.: Harvard University Press, 2008), 145. On the etymology of obeah, see Jerome S. Handler and Kenneth M. Bilby, "On the Early Use and Origin of the Term 'Obeah' in Barbados and the Anglophone Caribbean," *Slavery and Abolition* 22, no. 2 (2001): 87–100; Jerome S. Handler and Kenneth M. Bilby, *Enacting Power: The Criminalization of Obeah in the Anglophone Caribbean, 1760–2011* (Kingston: University of the West Indies Press, 2012), 4–5; Diana Paton, *The Cultural Politics of Obeah: Religion, Colonialism and Modernity in the Caribbean World* (Cambridge: Cambridge University Press, 2015), 27–31. On the evolution of obeah as a legal category and the challenges of defining it, see Diana Paton, "Obeah Acts: Producing and

Policing the Boundaries of Religion in the Caribbean," *Small Axe*, no. 28 (2009): 1–18; Diana Paton and Maarit Forde, eds., *Obeah and Other Powers: The Politics of Caribbean Religion and Healing* (Durham, N.C.: Duke University Press, 2012), 6–11; Handler and Bilby, *Enacting Power*, esp. 1–15, 106–8; Paton, "Witchcraft, Poison, Law, and Atlantic Slavery," *William and Mary Quarterly* 69, no. 2 (2012): 235–64; Paton, *Cultural Politics of Obeah*.

3. For the prohibition of obeah, see "Proclamation," April 2, 1810, T 1/3482 Part 3, 34–35 (repr. in part in Alvin O. Thompson, *A Documentary History of Slavery in Berbice, 1796–1834* [Georgetown, Guyana: Free Press, 2002], 149). The proclamation, issued by the Governor and Court of Policy and Criminal Justice, stated that any enslaved person found guilty of practicing obeah, "or pretending to exercise any secret arts, to possess any supernatural powers whereby the life, health, or happiness of any other slave or individual may be endangered . . . shall suffer Death or such other punishment as the exigency of the case shall appear to require." It also required every slaveowner or manager to explain the prohibition to their slaves and ordered that copies of the proclamation (in English and Dutch) be given to every estate. Such proclamations in Berbice carried the force of law, as a British Commission of Enquiry observed during their 1824 visit. "There are certain Ordinances . . . having the effect of law, which have time to time been framed in the mother country (Holland) or in the Colony, for the government and protection of the slaves." *Second Report (Second Series) of the Commissioners of Enquiry into the Administration of Criminal And Civil Justice in the West Indies and South American Colonies . . .*, PP (1825–29), quoted in Handler and Bilby, *Enacting Power*, 123–24n21. See also Thompson, *Colonialism and Underdevelopment in Guyana, 1580–1803* (Bridgetown, Barbados: Carib Research Publications, 1987), 132, 136; Handler and Bilby, *Enacting Power*, 61.

4. For Wray's observations on Willem's trial, see Wray to William A. Hankey, Treasurer of the London Missionary Society, Feb. 6, 1822, in Council for World Mission/London Missionary Society Archives, West Indies, B. Guiana-Berbice, Incoming Letters, box 1A, 1813–1822, folder 6, School for Oriental and African Studies, London.

5. "*W. Ross*, attorney, plantation Demtichem, complainant, against the negro *Hans*, belonging to Beerenstein, on charge of Obiah," June 17, 1819, Colonial Office series (hereafter CO) 116/138, 60–63, National Archives, Kew, London, United Kingdom.

6. For other interpretations of the Hans and Willem cases, see B. W. Higman, "Terms for Kin in the British West Indian Slave Community: Differing Perceptions of Masters and Slaves," in *Kinship Ideology and Practice in Latin America*, ed. Raymond T. Smith (Chapel Hill: University of North Carolina Press, 1984), 66–70; Michael Mullin, *Africa in America: Slave Acculturation and Resistance in the American South and the British Caribbean, 1736–1831* (Urbana: University of Illinois Press, 1992), 180–81; Emília Viotti da Costa, *Crowns of Glory, Tears of Blood: The Demerara Slave Rebellion of 1823* (New York: Oxford University Press, 1994), 107–13; J. H. Lean, "The Secret Lives of Slaves: Berbice, 1819 to 1827" (Ph.D. diss., University of Canterbury, 2002), 238–43; Alvin O. Thompson, *Unprofitable Servants: Crown Slaves in Berbice, Guyana, 1803–1831* (Kingston: University of the West Indies Press, 2002), 181–82, 197–200; Juanita De Barros, "'Setting Things Right': Medicine and Magic in British Guiana, 1803–38," *Slavery and Abolition* 25, no. 1 (2004): 28–50; Gordon E. A. Gill, "Doing the Minje Mama: A Study in the Evolution of an African/Afro-Creole Ritual in the British Slave Colony of Berbice," *Wadabagei* 12, no. 3 (2010): 7–29; and Paton, *Cultural Politics of Obeah*, 83–88.

7. The very investigation of these two cases, along with the severe punishments enacted on those involved, underscores their exceptional nature. Enslaved people's use of obeah and other forms of spiritual healing were rarely documented, and thus evidence taken from criminal

investigations such as these should not be used to construct meanings of "obeah" as a whole. As the opposition Hans and Willem faced from other slaves shows, moreover, these cases were not normative in their use of spiritual power.

8. "Proclamation," April 2, 1810, 34–35 (quotation, 34). According to missionary John Wray, there was also an 1801 anti-obeah law, though I have been unable to locate it. Wray explained that the death penalty for practicing obeah was "founded on the Jewish Law Exo[dus] 22.18." See Wray to William Wilberforce, Oct. 29, 1819, in Council for World Mission/London Missionary Society Archives, West Indies, B. Guiana-Berbice, Incoming Letters, box 1A, 1813–1822, folder 5, School for Oriental and African Studies, London (Exodus 22:18 reads, "Thou shalt not suffer a witch to live"). As Diana Paton has shown, the era of amelioration was when the idea of obeah was consolidated and when it "became a firmly entrenched part of Caribbean law" (*Cultural Politics of Obeah*, 77).

9. Jamaica's 1760 "Act to Remedy the Evils Arising from Irregular Assemblies of Slaves" was the only anti-obeah legislation until 1788, but between 1788 and 1838 at least ten other colonies passed laws against obeah. See Paton, "Obeah Acts," 4–5 (quotations, 4); Handler and Bilby, *Enacting Power*, 16, 46. By emancipation, nearly all British Caribbean colonies had enacted anti-obeah legislation, and many anti-obeah laws remain on the books into the twenty-first century, though they are rarely enforced. See Dianne M. Stewart, *Three Eyes for the Journey: African Dimensions of the Jamaican Religious Experience* (New York: Oxford University Press, 2005), 36–40, 44–46, 76–79; Paton, "Obeah Acts," 4–5; Handler and Bilby, *Enacting Power*, xi–xiii, 16–17, 21–24. In the late eighteenth and early nineteenth centuries, obeah was usually prosecuted when authorities believed it was "undertaken in the context of broader anti-slavery activity or it led, or was thought to lead, to harm to the health of other enslaved individuals" (Paton, *Cultural Politics of Obeah*, 101).

10. "Ordinance to Repress the Commission of Obeah Practices," Jan. 8, 1855, CO 111/304. The missionary presence was particularly weak in Berbice and Demerara-Essequibo, where planter opposition was significant—especially after an 1823 rebellion in Demerara that was blamed on missionary John Smith. As late as 1829, colonial officials in Berbice lamented the lack of progress made in converting enslaved people. As Henry Beard wrote to George Murray, "it certainly is deeply to be lamented that no measures should yet have been adopted to afford Religious Instruction to the generality of the Slave Population, more particularly to the junior part of it. There are but two Clergymen, one of the Established Church, and the other from the London Missionary Society, in the Colony; and as it is impossible for them to extend their labours beyond the town, the great mass of the slave population is unavoidably left in its original state of profound ignorance." Beard to Murray, Sept. 25, 1829, CO 116/145, 23. See also Raymond T. Smith, "Religion in the Formation of West Indian Society," in *The African Diaspora: Interpretive Essays*, ed. Martin Kilson and Robert Rotberg (Cambridge, Mass.: Harvard University Press, 1976), 312–42; Thompson, *Colonialism and Underdevelopment*, 133–34; Viotti da Costa, *Crowns of Glory*, 3–37; Gill, "Labor, Material Welfare, and Culture," 331.

11. See, for example, "Complaint of the negro man Willem belonging to J. A. Dehnertt," Feb. 1, 1824, CO 116/140; "Complaint of the negro La Rose, belonging to pl. Broer's lust property of J. P. Broer," July 10, 1826, CO 116/141; "*Complaint No. 12*," Dec. 28, 1826, CO 116/143, 157.

12. The literature on obeah in the pre-emancipation Caribbean is vast, but some of the most influential work has been done by Kenneth M. Bilby, Jerome S. Handler, and Diana Paton. See especially Bilby and Handler, "Obeah: Healing and Protection in West Indian Slave Life," *Journal of Caribbean History* 38, no. 2 (2004): 153–83; Handler and Bilby, *Enacting Power*; and Paton,

Cultural Politics of Obeah. Bilby and Handler's argument that obeah was "primarily concerned with divination . . . healing and bringing good fortune, and protection from harm," and that "the supernatural/spiritual force (or forces) that the obeah practitioner attempted to control or guide was essentially neutral, but was largely directed toward what the slave community defined as socially beneficial goals," is echoed by many other scholars ("Healing and Protection," 154 ["primarily concerned"], 155 ["supernatural/spiritual force"]).

13. Peter Geschiere made a similar argument for the ambiguity of witchcraft—which could be a constructive or a destructive force—in late twentieth-century West Africa (Cameroon) in Geschiere, *The Modernity of Witchcraft,* trans. Geschiere and Janet Roitman (Charlottesville: University of Virginia Press, 1997), 196–99, 219. "Healers," Geschiere explains, "are always highly ambivalent figures: they can only heal because they have killed. One is, in the end, never sure that healers will use their redoubtable forces only to cure." Ibid., 196. Obeah practitioners also provoked a range of reactions among enslaved people, as colonials recognized. A 1791 report to the House of Commons on Jamaican obeah, for instance, explained that "Negroes in general, whether Africans or Creoles, revere, consult, and abhor [obeah practitioners]." In Vincent Brown, "Spiritual Terror and Sacred Authority: The Power of the Supernatural in Jamaican Slave Society," in *New Studies in the History of American Slavery,* ed. Edward E. Baptist and Stephanie M. H. Camp (Athens: University of Georgia Press, 2006), 179–210 (quotation, 191). See also Jerome S. Handler, "Slave Medicine and Obeah in Barbados, circa 1650 to 1834," *New West Indian Guide* 74, nos. 1–2 (2000): 78; Bilby and Handler, "Healing and Protection," 160.

14. *Trial of a Slave in Berbice,* 22. Primo was head driver and Mey was second driver. Ibid., 9 (quotations), 25. Anglo-American doctors—trained in the humoral or miasmatic theories of medicine—often employed treatments such as bloodletting, purging, and blistering, which harmed their patients more than they helped them. Enslaved people were understandably more likely to rely on their own healers. See Richard B. Sheridan, *Doctors and Slaves: A Medical and Demographic History of Slavery in the British West Indies, 1680–1834* (Cambridge: Cambridge University Press, 1985), 70, 73, 320, 330; Handler, "Slave Medicine and Obeah," 58–60. Enslaved people thought Anglo-American medicine was particularly ineffective when it came to people who had fallen victim to malevolent supernatural forces, as the lyrics of a so-called negro song—attributed to a wife whose husband had been " 'Obeahed' by another woman, in consequence of his rejecting her advances" and described by Jamaican planter Matthew Gregory "Monk" Lewis—suggest: "Doctor no do you good. When neger fall into neger hands, buckra [white] doctor no do him good more." See Lewis, *Journal of a West India Proprietor Kept During a Residence in the Island of Jamaica* (London: J. Murray, 1834), 253. For the use of diviners to detect "unnatural" deaths in neighboring Suriname, see Natalie Zemon Davis, "Judges, Masters, Diviners: Slaves' Experience of Criminal Justice in Colonial Suriname," *Law and History Review* 29, no. 4 (2011): 925–84.

15. Drivers also used obeah to enhance their authority. Vincent Brown, for example, observed that drivers buttressed their status by "presid[ing] over unsanctioned judiciaries" in which obeah often played a central role in determining guilt or innocence. Brown, "Spiritual Terror and Sacred Authority," 197.

16. Bryan Edwards, *The History, Civil and Commercial, of the British Colonies in the West Indies in Two Volumes* (1794; repr. London, 1807), 2:96.

17. John Wray to Charles Bird, Aug. 25, 1829, CO 116/145, 218–19.

18. "Examination of a Complaint preferred by the negro *Tobias,* belonging to plantation Friends," Sept. 4, 1822, CO 116/138, 132–33.

19. Lewis, *Journal of a West India Proprietor,* 237 ("reputed Obeah-man"), 147 ("most

dangerous fellow"), 350 ("was accused," "strongly suspected"), 352 ("threatened the lives"), 353 ("principal negroes," "as their lives"). When Lewis found "a considerable quantity of materials for the practice of Obeah" in Adam's house, he had Adam "immediately committed to the gaol" and then brought him to a slave court where Adam was tried "for Obeah & having materials used in Obeah." He was convicted of "possessing Obeah materials" (though found not guilty of practicing obeah) and was sentenced to be transported, probably to Cuba. Ibid., 354 ("considerable quantity"), 237; "Slave Trials in the Parish of Westmoreland from 1st July 1814 to 30th June 1818," Jamaica, Return of Trials of Slaves, 1814–1818, CO 137/147, 25–29 ("for Obeah," 27). See also Mullin, *Africa in America*, 179–80; Paton, "Witchcraft, Poison, Law," 262–63. Obeah practitioners were frequently accused of using poison but, as Handler and Bilby have shown, "Poison was and is not an intrinsic feature of obeah—some obeah practitioners were accused of employing poison while others were not—and it appears that people who did not consider themselves obeah practitioners also used poison." Legislation in several colonies, including Jamaica, linked poison to obeah. *Enacting Power*, 20 (quotation), 21. See also John Savage, "Slave Poison/Slave Medicine: The Persistence of Obeah in Early Nineteenth-Century Martinique," in Paton and Forde, *Obeah and Other Powers*, 149–71; Sasha Turner Bryson, "The Art of Power: Poison and Obeah Accusations and the Struggle for Dominance and Survival in Jamaica's Slave Society," *Caribbean Studies* 41, no. 2 (2013): 61–90.

20. Willem was between twenty-one and twenty-three years old in 1819. See "Return of Slaves attached to Plantation Buses Lust . . . ," T 71/438, 654–58.

21. *Trial of a Slave in Berbice*, 22–23 ("Attetta"), 23 ("Monkesi"), 25–27 ("God Almighty's," 26; "Abdie Toboko," 27; "Obiah man," 25).

22. For the meaning and etymology of these terms, see Frederic G. Cassidy and Robert B. Lepage, eds., *Dictionary of Jamaican English* (1967; repr. Cambridge: Cambridge University Press, 1980), 433; Higman, "Terms for Kin," 69–70; Brian L. Moore, *Cultural Power, Resistance, and Pluralism: Colonial Guyana, 1838–1900* (Montreal: McGill Queen's University Press, 1995), 138; Richard Allsopp, ed., *Dictionary of Caribbean English Usage* (New York: Oxford University Press, 1996), 165; Monica Schuler, "Liberated Africans in Nineteenth-Century Guyana," in *Central Africans and Cultural Transformations in the American Diaspora*, ed. Linda M. Heywood (Cambridge: Cambridge University Press, 2002), 346n57; De Barros, " 'Setting Things Right,' " 41–42; Gill, "Labor, Welfare, and Material Culture," 351–52; Handler and Bilby, *Enacting Power*, 26, 126n35. Gill, "Doing the Minje Mama," 22. An "Act for Punishing, with Death, All Negroes and Coloured Persons Whatsoever, Who Shall Practise What Is Called Confu, or Obeah Doctor, or Who Shall Take Away, or Attempt to Take Away, the Life, or Injure the Health, of Any Person or Persons Whatsoever," passed in Nevis sometime between 1818 and 1823, suggests that "Obeah" and "Confou" may have been interchangeable in some parts of the British Caribbean. See Handler and Bilby, *Enacting Power*, 126n35.

23. Paton, *Cultural Politics of Obeah*, 84–87.

24. *Trial of a Slave in Berbice*, 24 ("Willem . . . came," "she found herself"), 22 ("made her eyes turn"), 26 ("had been two"), 28 ("came to the hospital"), 25.

25. Higman, "Terms for Kin," 66; Gert Oostindie and Alex van Stipriaan, "Slavery and Slave Culture in a Hydraulic Society: Suriname," in *Slave Cultures and the Cultures of Slavery*, ed. Stephan Palmié (Knoxville: University of Tennessee Press, 1995), 92; De Barros, " 'Setting Things Right,' " 40; Handler and Bilby, *Enacting Power*, 32–33, 116–17n3. For Mami Wata, see Henry John Drewal, ed., *Sacred Waters: Arts for Mami Wata and Other Divinities in Africa and the Diaspora* (Bloomington: Indiana University Press, 2008).

26. Gordon Gill has argued that the pervasiveness of water in the ecology of the Guianas had important implications for slave culture in Berbice, including the Minje Mama dance. See Gill, "Doing the Minje Mama," 8–9. According to John Wray, enslaved people in Berbice consulted the "Minggie or Water Mama (the Mermaid) whom they suppose resides in the River and Creeks of Berbice and who makes known to these Men who it is, that inflicts sickness on their children." Wray to Hankey, Feb. 6, 1822. Written references to the Minje Mama dance, however, are rare, probably because it was illegal and enslaved people tried to keep it secret. In 1834 two people were charged with dancing the "Makizie water or minji mama dance" on plantation Waterloo. They stood accused of "pretending and feigning to have had an inspiration or revelation or intercourse with ghosts relative to poisoners or certain persons suspected of the crime of poisoning." Prosecutions Book of the Court of Criminal Justice, Berbice, British Guiana, 1832–37, in Higman, "Terms for Kin," 66–67 ("Makizie," 66, "pretending," 67). In the late nineteenth century, missionary Charles Daniel Dance reported that people of African descent in British Guiana still performed the "Water Mamma" ritual and worshipped the "Minje Mamma, Water Spirit, or Mermaid." Dance also described "devotion to the Water Mama" as the "kindred faith" of obeah. See Dance, *Chapters from a Guianese Log-Book* . . . (Georgetown, Guyana: The Royal Gazette Establishment, 1881), 77–79. According to British traveler George Pinckard, some whites in Berbice also believed in "mermaids," which they claimed had been seen regularly "by negroes, by Indians, and by whites." "It was maintained," Pinckard wrote, "that these lady-like animals, of fabulous note, do really exist in the Berbische river, and I confess that I experienced some surprise, when I heard the governor, who is a sensible and intelligent man, give his sanction to the opinion." Pinckard, *Notes on the West Indies* . . . (London: Longman, Hurst, Rees, and Orme, 1806), 3:7 (quotations), 8.

27. Stedman, quoted in Richard Price and Sally Price, eds., *John Gabriel Stedman: Narrative of a Five Years Expedition against the Revolted Negroes of Surinam* (Baltimore: Johns Hopkins University Press, 1988), 457. I cite the Prices' version of Stedman's narrative rather than the first published edition (1796) because it is a transcription of Stedman's original manuscript; his editor made several changes and additions to the published version.

28. Alex van Stipriaan, "The Ever-Changing Face of Watramama in Suriname: A Water Goddess in Creolization Since the Seventeenth Century," in Drewal, *Sacred Waters*, 525–47, esp. 529.

29. Price and Price, *Narrative of a Five Years Expedition*, 521. For other references to the Minje Mama that compare the spirit to a mermaid, see Oostindie and Van Stipriaan, "Slavery and Slave Culture," 92–93. For Winti, an Afro-Surinamese religion in which spirit possession plays an important role, see C. J. Wooding, "Traditional Healing and Medicine in Winti: A Sociological Interpretation," *Issue: A Journal of Opinion* 9, no. 3 (1979): 35–40; Price and Price, *Narrative*, 660.

30. Price and Price, *Narrative*, 521. Stedman's description of the Minje Mama dance is similar to John K. Thornton's description of spirit possession in Afro-Atlantic cultures: "In the case of human possession, a being from the other world would enter the medium's body and speak with his or her voice. . . . Typically possession would occur after the medium had fallen into a trance, for . . . the other world seems to have found it easiest to communicate with people in an unconscious state or an altered state of consciousness. Such a trance might be induced by drugs or hypnotic dancing, singing, or drumming." See Thornton, *Africa and Africans in the Making of the Atlantic World, 1400–1680* (Cambridge: Cambridge University Press, 1992), 243. The Minje Mama dance also resembles the ritual dance at the heart of myal or myalism, a term usually associated with spirit possession in Jamaica. Although earlier historians perpetuated a simplistic

dichotomy—established in the nineteenth century by colonial missionaries and other writers—of myal as "good" or "anti-obeah" and obeah as "bad," in recent years scholars have made convincing arguments that "obeah and myal were never inherently opposed; rather, they have long formed complementary parts—one concerned primarily with spiritual power of various kinds, the other with spirit possession—of a single Afro-Creole cultural system" (Handler and Bilby, *Enacting Power*, 10–11 (quotation, 11). See also Monica Schuler, "Myalism and the African Religious Tradition in Jamaica," in *Africa and the Caribbean: The Legacies of a Link*, ed. Margaret E. Crahan and Franklin W. Knight (Baltimore: Johns Hopkins University Press, 1979), 65–79; De Barros, "'Setting Things Right,'" 40–41; Stewart, *Three Eyes for the Journey*; Brown, *Reaper's Garden*, 146–47.

31. Van Stipriaan, "Ever-Changing Face of Watramama," 527 ("watermama"); *Trial of a Slave in Berbice*, 42 ("read and explained"); Alex van Stipriaan, "Watramama/Mami Wata: Three Centuries of Creolization of a Water Spirit in West Africa, Suriname and Europe," in *A Pepper-Pot of Cultures: Aspects of Creolization in the Caribbean*, ed. Gordon Collier and Ulrich Fleischmann (Amsterdam: Rodopi, 2003), 323–37, esp. 327. I have not located a law that specifically criminalized the Minje Mama dance in Berbice, but in the prosecution of Hans and his collaborators on Demtichem, the fiscal referenced laws against "Obeah & the dancing of the Makizie Water Mother," which suggests that the Minje Mama dance was illegal because colonial officials considered it an obeah ritual. See "Declaration and demand in a Criminal Case presented to the Honourable Court of Criminal Justice of the Colony Berbice at the Instance of M. S. Bennett Fiscal of the Colony R.O. Plaintiff Versus the Negroe January head driver . . . ," Aug. 4, 1819, Court of Policy and Court of Civil and Criminal Justice Proceedings, Berbice, AB 6 1C, 12, Walter Rodney Archives, Georgetown, Guyana.

32. "*W. Ross* . . . complainant, against the negro *Hans*," 60–63 (quotations, 61). Among enslaved people, "bad" was often shorthand for malicious obeah or witchcraft, and to "do bad" meant to cause someone "to become incurably sick or mentally ill through the use of evil powers." Allsopp, *Dictionary of Caribbean English*, 64. The name of the plantation where Hans organized the Minje Mama dance is spelled differently in different sources—for example, Deutichem, Deutichen, or Duidichim—but I have elected to spell it Demtichem because that is how it is spelled in the fiscal's record, the major source for the Hans case.

33. Wray to Wilberforce, Oct. 29, 1819.

34. "*W. Ross* . . . complainant, against the negro *Hans*," 61 ("to put every thing"); Wray to Wilberforce, Oct. 29, 1819 ("point out," "they suspected").

35. "*W. Ross* . . . complainant, against the negro *Hans*," 61 (quotations).

36. Ibid., 62 (quotations).

37. Wray to Wilberforce, Oct. 29, 1819.

38. "*W. Ross* . . . complainant, against the negro *Hans*," 62 ("My head"), 60 ("minds of the negroes").

39. Ibid., 62 (quotations).

40. Wray to Wilberforce, Oct. 29, 1819 (quotations).

41. "*W. Ross* . . . complainant, against the negro *Hans*," 62 (quotations).

42. Wray to Wilberforce, Oct. 29, 1819.

43. "Declaration and demand in a Criminal Case presented to the Court of Criminal Justice of the Colony Berbice at the Instance of M. S. Bennett Fiscal of the Colony R.O. Plaintiff Versus the negro woman Venus . . . ," Aug. 4, 1819, AB 6 1C, 9 ("rid themselves"); "Complaint, No. 9," Dec. 12–13, 1826, CO 116/143, 155 ("joe"); "Complaint, No. 7," Sept. 29, 1829, CO 116/145, 232; "Complaint, No. 19," Oct. 26, 1829, CO 116/145, 237; Gill, "Doing the Minje Mama," 18.

44. Africans, especially in West Central Africa, suspected people who accumulated unusual wealth or illegitimate power, especially at their community's expense, of practicing witchcraft. For African notions of witches as selfish consumers (both literally and figuratively), see Ralph A. Austen, "The Moral Economy of Witchcraft: An Essay in Comparative History," in *Modernity and Its Malcontents: Ritual and Power in Postcolonial Africa,* ed. Jean Comaroff and John L. Comaroff (Chicago: University of Chicago Press, 1993), 90–91; John K. Thornton, *The Kongolese Saint Anthony: Dona Beatriz Kimpa Vita and the Antonian Movement, 1684–1706* (Cambridge: Cambridge University Press, 1998), 42–44; Thornton, "Cannibals, Witches, and Slave Traders in the Atlantic World," *William and Mary Quarterly* 60, no. 2 (2003): 275–77.

45. "*W. Ross* . . . complainant, against the negro *Hans*," 62 (quotations).

46. Ibid., 60 (quotations).

47. Wray to Wilberforce, Oct. 29, 1819 ("from the smell," "bad thing"); "*W. Ross* . . . complainant, against the negro *Hans*," 60–63 ("the girl," "pot of obiah," 62).

48. Wray to Wilberforce, Oct. 29, 1819.

49. "*W. Ross* . . . complainant, against the negro *Hans*," 63.

50. Wray to Wilberforce, Oct. 29, 1819. The items allegedly found in Frederick's house correspond to the "instruments of obeah" described in colonial laws. Such items included: blood, bones, skulls, amulets, charms, feathers, grave dirt, shells, eggs, broken glass, potions, and poison. See Handler and Bilby, *Enacting Power,* 19–21, 113n2. For *minkisi,* see Wyatt MacGaffey, *Religion and Society in Central Africa: The BaKongo of Lower Zaire* (Chicago: University of Chicago Press, 1986), 137–48; and Jason R. Young, *Rituals of Resistance: African Atlantic Religion in Kongo and the Lowcountry South in the Era of Slavery* (Baton Rouge: Louisiana State University Press, 2007), 105–45.

51. "*W. Ross* . . . complainant, against the negro *Hans*," 61 ("numerous," "a handkerchief"). In addition to Hans, the fiscal prosecuted La Fleur, Benjamin, Lindsay Harry, Venus, and January. See "Declaration and demand in a Criminal Case made and delivered to the Honourable Court of Criminal Justice of the Colony Berbice at the Instance of M. S. Bennett Fiscal of the Colony R.O. Plaintiff Versus the Negroes La Fleur, Benjamin (Driver) and Lindsay Harry field Negro . . . ," Aug. 4, 1819, AB 6 1C, 3–6; "Declaration and demand . . . Versus the negro woman Venus . . . ," Aug. 4, 1819, 7–10; and "Declaration and demand in a Criminal Case . . . Versus the Negroe January."

52. Wray to Wilberforce, Oct. 29, 1819 (quotations); "*W. Ross* . . . complainant, against the negro *Hans*," 60–63; Thompson, *Unprofitable Servants,* 199–200.

53. As late as 1829, January remained angry with the manager, whom he blamed for losing his position as driver. See Chapter 3.

54. *Trial of a Slave in Berbice,* 14 ("small *coriaal* "), 21 ("he inquired"), 29 ("made the people"), 23 ("man Cuffey").

55. Ibid., 32 ("bad woman"), 25 ("drive the bad story"). Described by witnesses as "a Congo woman" and "rather advanced in years, but otherwise a healthy woman," Madalon was about forty years old at the time of her death, according to an 1819 slave registration return that listed her age as thirty-seven. See *Trial of a Slave in Berbice,* 14 ("Congo woman"), 21 ("rather advanced"); "Return of Slaves, attached to Plantation Op Hoop van Beter." No one described Madalon as an obeah practitioner, but enslaved women across the Caribbean did practice obeah. Enslaved men, however, accounted for the majority of obeah prosecutions. See Barbara Bush, *Slave Women in Caribbean Society, 1650–1838* (Bloomington: Indiana University Press, 1990), 73–77; Handler, "Slave Medicine and Obeah," 62n14; Diana Paton, "Punishment, Crime, and the

Bodies of Slaves in Eighteenth-Century Jamaica," *Journal of Social History* 34, no. 4 (2001): 932; Brown, "Spiritual Terror and Sacred Authority," 194–95; and Paton, *Cultural Politics of Obeah*, 100–101.

56. *Trial of a Slave in Berbice*, 15 (quotations). This cleansing ritual resembles the treatment of suspected witches in late nineteenth-century British Guiana, as described by missionary Charles Dance. "It is inconvenient to the old women of a village when a child becomes suddenly ill; for the mother, in such case, unhesitatingly attributes its illness to the influence of witchcraft, and the oldest neighbour is *prima facie* adjudged to be the offender. She must then be flogged with calabash switches (for none other can she feel) until she restores the child's health, or is rescued from her merciless tormentors." Dance, *Chapters from a Guianese Log-Book*, 81.

57. *Trial of a Slave in Berbice*, 34 ("negro-yard"), 25 ("first person," "was nothing").

58. Ibid., 15.

59. It is unclear what relationship existed between Quashee and Madalon. Frederick stated that Quashee "also had her"—Berbician slang for sex. Ibid., 15.

60. Ibid., 17 ("driver asked"); Wray to Hankey, Feb. 6, 1822 ("some blood").

61. *Trial of a Slave in Berbice*, 17.

62. Ibid., 15 ("administered"), 29 ("he was too much afraid," "the scars"). For Caribbean loyalty oath ceremonies, see Kenneth Bilby, "Swearing by the Past, Swearing to the Future: Sacred Oaths, Alliances, and Treaties Among the Guianese and Jamaican Maroons," *Ethnohistory* 44, no. 4 (1997): 655–89.

63. *Trial of a Slave in Berbice*, 14 ("was present," "performed"), 21–22 ("flogged by the orders," after [David]," "three ells," "struck him," 22), 9 ("punishment").

64. "W. Ross . . . complainant, against the negro *Hans*," 60–63 ("guinea pepper," "recover," 62).

65. *Trial of a Slave in Berbice*, 29 ("beat me"), 43–44 ("influence of dread," 44).

66. John Wray, in Thomas Rain, *The Life and Labours of John Wray, Pioneer Missionary in British Guiana* . . . (London: John Snow & Co., 1892), 114.

67. *Trial of a Slave in Berbice*, 20. The Water Mama healing ceremony in Suriname also featured clients being struck with tree branches. See Handler and Bilby, *Enacting Power*, 33.

68. For witchcraft in early modern Europe, see Brian P. Levack, *The Witch-Hunt in Early Modern Europe* (Harlow: Longman, 1987); Lyndal Roper, *Oedipus and the Devil: Witchcraft, Religion and Sexuality in Early Modern Europe* (London: Routledge, 1994); Diane Purkiss, *The Witch in History: Early Modern and Twentieth-Century Representations* (London: Routledge, 1996); and Ian Bostridge, *Witchcraft and Its Transformations, c. 1650–c. 1750* (Oxford: Oxford University Press, 1997).

69. *Trial of a Slave in Berbice*, 20 ("she fainted," "said it was," "tied [her] up,"), 15 ("in one of the negro-houses," "the persons who"), 37.

70. Ibid., 37 ("negroes would not"), 27 ("Willem called him," "He saw").

71. A total of 308 slaves were registered for plantation Demtichem in 1819. See "Return of Slaves attached to Plantation Deutichem . . . ," Jan. 1, 1819, T 71/438, 669–76.

72. Though many African societies killed suspected witches—sometimes by forcing them to consume poison as part of a trial by ordeal—I have found no evidence that they whipped or beat them. For anti-witchcraft or witch-cleansing practices in Africa, see Jan Vansina, "The Bushong Poison Ordeal," in *Man in Africa*, ed. Mary Douglas and Phyllis M. Kaberry (London: Tavistock, 1969), 245–60; Alison Redmayne, "Chikanga: An African Diviner with an International Reputation," in *Witchcraft Confessions and Accusations*, ed. Mary Douglas (London: Tavistock, 1970), 103–28; R. G. Willis, "Instant Millennium: The Sociology of African

Witch-Cleansing Cults," in Douglas, *Witchcraft Confessions*, 129–39; Paton, "Witchcraft, Poison, Law," 247–48.

73. Natalie Zemon Davis made a similar observation about the Saramacca Maroons' introduction of torture to solicit confessions from people suspected of using sorcery or poison. Under the supervision of a priest-diviner, the accused person "was strung by the thumbs from the branch of a tree, with the feet weighted down by a stone, and beaten by the victim's kinfolk until a detailed confession was forthcoming"—a strategy that was unknown in West and Central Africa. Davis, "Judges, Masters, Diviners," 965.

74. *Trial of a Slave in Berbice*, 26 ("which made her"), 25 ("You are killing me"). Willem's claim echoed Edward Long's description of a Jamaican myal dance in which participants fell into a trance (with the aid of a potion) so deep that they appeared lifeless before being brought "back" to life. See Long, *The History of Jamaica . . .* (London: T. Lowndes, 1774), 2: 416–17.

75. *Trial of a Slave in Berbice*, 26 ("it was going too far," "said nothing").

76. Multiple witnesses told the fiscal that Willem had flogged Primo and suggested that "if Primo would take off his jacket, the marks would be seen where Willem had struck him with a whip, for interfering when the punishment became too severe." The fiscal ordered Primo to take off his jacket, and "his shoulder exhibited the mark of a stroke of a whip." Ibid., 35 (quotations), 21, 26.

77. *Trial of a Slave in Berbice*, 40 ("utter astonishment"), 22 ("bring things").

78. Ibid., 21 ("marks"), 29 ("grew angry"), 25 ("Willem said").

79. Ibid., 23 (quotations).

80. "Investigation into the probable circumstances of the death of the negro Mamadoe . . . ," Nov. 8, 1824, CO 116/140.

81. *Trial of a Slave in Berbice*, 19 ("told the driver," "driver said"), 20 ("they had buried," "had sunk").

82. Ibid., 35.

83. Ibid., 5 ("promoter"), 13 ("Something I have heard"), 19 ("manager himself knew," "said he must"). Adolff, an enslaved man on Op Hoop van Beter, also claimed that "we were informed by the drivers that the manager knew of it." Ibid., 22.

84. Ibid., 6, 17–18 ("preconcerted," 18), 20 ("cause").

85. Ibid., 14.

86. Wray to Wilberforce, Oct. 29, 1819. Hans was probably an *nganga*, a diviner or spirit medium who helped others locate lost items or identify the cause of death or sickness. See Thornton, *Africa and Africans*, 243; Thornton, "Religious and Ceremonial Life in the Kongo and Mbundu Areas, 1500–1700," in Heywood, *Central Africans and Cultural Transformations*, 71–90, esp. 81; Gill, "Doing the Minje Mama," 16. The extent to which Kongolese people embraced Christianity has been the source of vigorous debate. For contrasting views, see Thornton, *Africa and Africans*, 259–61; Young, *Rituals of Resistance*, 58–59.

87. Wray to Wilberforce, Oct. 29, 1819. Coolness in this context might have been associated with the restoration of social stability or tranquility. See Robert Farris Thompson, "An Aesthetic of the Cool," *African Arts* 7, no. 1 (1973): 41–43, 64–67, 89–91; Gill, "Labor, Material Welfare, and Culture," 343–44.

88. *Trial of a Slave in Berbice*, 34.

89. Ibid., 10. The fiscal also prosecuted Corydon and Allegro, two enslaved men who had helped beat Madalon, because they had "los[t] sight of the duty and obedience due to their proprietors, and submitt[ed] themselves to the authority of the negro Willem." Allegro was "ill, and

unable to attend and take his trial at the present session," but the court sentenced Corydon "to receive *One Hundred Lashes.*" Ibid., 44 ("los[t] sight"), 10 ("ill"), 11 ("to receive").

90. Ibid., 44 ("stand with a rope"), 32 ("but a boy," "had not the authority,"), 33 ("go to the field," "if not ordered").

91. Ibid., 11. Kees had been "Overseer on the Logie" since at least 1819, when he was twenty-six years old, according to "Return of Slaves, attached to Plantation Op Hoop van Beter," 119–24.

92. *Trial of a Slave in Berbice*, 41 ("subjecting themselves"), 42 ("authority confided"), 10 ("brand-marked"); "Declaration and demand . . . Versus the Negroe January," 13 ("that any evil," "offence"), 14 ("consequently far").

93. Ibid., 39–41 ("treasonable practices," "proceeded to inflict," "used every means," 39; "taken it upon himself," "the power of taking," 41).

94. *Trial of a Slave in Berbice*, 8 ("dancing"). Diana Paton has argued that the trial record makes it "clear that Willem was not tried for obeah" but rather tried for having killed Madalon and organized the Minje Mama dance. Paton hypothesized that the case has been interpreted as an obeah case because John Wray's letter—which may have been read by William Wilberforce—described Willem as an obeah practitioner, drawing on British understandings of Caribbean spiritual power and thus "set[ting] in motion an interpretation of the events as an 'obeah case' that has dominated the historiography." Paton, *Cultural Politics of Obeah*, 84–88 ("clear that Willem," 84, "set[ting] in motion," 88). However, colonial authorities in Berbice used "Minje Mama" and "obeah" interchangeably, and at least some enslaved people appear to have considered the Minje Mama dance an obeah ritual. See Gill, "Doing the Minje Mama," 20, 24.

95. *Trial of a Slave in Berbice*, 9 ("delivered into the hands").

96. In Britain, the last execution for high treason punished by hanging and decapitation occurred in 1820—a year before Willem's execution. See V. A. C. Gatrell, *The Hanging Tree: Execution and the English People, 1770–1868* (New York: Oxford University Press, 1994), 281, 298–99.

97. Diana Paton found that many people prosecuted for obeah in the late eighteenth and early nineteenth centuries "were individuals who acted not just as individual rebels but as combined spiritual and political leaders," like Willem and Hans (*Cultural Politics of Obeah*, 101).

98. Brown, "Spiritual Terror and Sacred Authority," 186–88; Paton, "Punishment, Crime, and the Bodies of Slaves," 940 ("symbolics of mutilation").

99. Brown, *Reaper's Garden*, 130–42.

100. Wray to Hankey, Feb. 6, 1822 (quotations); *Trial of a Slave in Berbice*, 12.

Chapter 6. The Moral Economy of Survival

1. "Investigation of a Complaint preferred by *A. J. Glasius . . . ,*" June 2–3, 1819, Colonial Office series (hereafter CO) 116/138, 50, National Archives, Kew, London, United Kingdom. The clothing was measured in ells, with the men given three ells, the women five, the house people six, and the children one and a half ells. An ell is about 1.25 yards.

2. Ibid., 50; "Return of Slaves, attached to Plantation Recumzigt . . . ," March 12, 1819, Treasury series (hereafter T) 71/438, 293–86, National Archives, Kew, London, United Kingdom.

3. "Complaint preferred by *A. J. Glasius . . . ,*" 50 ("ringleaders"), 51 ("they have had," "he took his osnaburgs"), 52 ("refused to take," "create[d] much uneasiness").

4. E. P. Thompson used the concept of "moral economy" to understand the notions of economic justice that underlay popular protest in eighteenth-century England, specifically regarding food. The concept spawned rich scholarship in many fields beyond early modern European

history, most notably in scholarship on peasants. See Thompson, "The Moral Economy of the English Crowd in the Eighteenth Century," *Past and Present* 50 (1971): 76–136; James C. Scott, *The Moral Economy of the Peasant: Rebellion and Subsistence in Southeast Asia* (New Haven: Yale University Press, 1976); and Thompson, "The Moral Economy Reviewed," in *Customs in Common* (London: Merlin, 1991), 259–351. Historians of slavery have also made use of the concept to illuminate enslaved people's notions of fairness and the strategies they used to protect and expand their customary rights. See, among others, Marvin L. Michael Kay and Lorin Lee Cary, "'They Are Indeed the Constant Plague of Their Tyrants': Slave Defence of a Moral Economy in Colonial North Carolina, 1748–1772," *Slavery & Abolition* 6, no. 3 (1985): 37–56; Alex Lichtenstein, "'That Disposition to Theft, With Which They Have Been Branded': Moral Economy, Slave Management, and the Law," *Journal of Social History* 21, no. 3 (1988): 413–40; John Edwin Mason, "Hendrik Albertus and His Ex-Slave Mey: A Drama in Three Acts," *Journal of African History* 31, no. 3 (1990): 423–45 (esp. 428–32); Silvia Hunold Lara, "'Blowin' in the Wind': E. P. Thompson e a Experiência Negra no Brasil," *Projeto História*, no. 12 (1995): 43–56; and Alex Lichtenstein, "Theft, Moral Economy, and the Transition from Slavery to Freedom in the American South," in *Slave Cultures and the Cultures of Slavery*, ed. Stephan Palmié (Knoxville: University of Tennessee Press, 1995), 176–86.

5. As Ira Berlin and Philip D. Morgan observed, customary agreements between enslaved people and their enslavers were regarded by both sides "as temporary truces in a continuing battle, not as the basis of a permanent peace." Berlin and Morgan, "Labor and the Shaping of Slave Life in the Americas," in Berlin and Morgan, eds., *Cultivation and Culture: Labor and the Shaping of Slave Life in the Americas* (Charlottesville: University of Virginia Press, 1993), 7.

6. Berbice slave code, clause 28, in *The Berbice Royal Gazette*, Sept. 30, 1826 (reprinted in Alvin O. Thompson, *A Documentary History of Slavery in Berbice, 1796–1834* [Georgetown, Guyana: Free Press, 2002]; hereafter 1826 slave code).

7. 1826 slave code, clause 22. An 1806 law specified that slaves were to receive at least two bunches of plantains each week, or two coffee baskets of "roots" (tubers such as yams or cassava). See Alvin O. Thompson, *Colonialism and Underdevelopment in Guyana, 1580–1803* (Bridgetown, Barbados: Carib Research & Publications, 1987), 120. An 1833 law included more specific regulations and increased the quantity of allowances for people over twelve years old. See Alvin O. Thompson, *Unprofitable Servants: Crown Slaves in Berbice, Guyana, 1803–1831* (Kingston: University of the West Indies Press, 2002), 157–58.

8. For enslaved people's labor bargaining, see Mary Turner, ed., *From Chattel Slaves to Wage Slaves: The Dynamics of Labour Bargaining in the Americas* (Bloomington: Indiana University Press, 1995).

9. In her analysis of enslaved people's complaints to the fiscal in Demerara, Da Costa argued that "slaves perceived slavery as a system of reciprocal obligations. They assumed that between masters and slaves there was an unspoken contract, an invisible text that defined rules and obligations, a text they used to assess any violations of their 'rights.'" Emília Viotti da Costa, *Crowns of Glory, Tears of Blood: The Demerara Slave Rebellion of 1823* (New York: Oxford University Press, 1994), 73. See also Kelly A. Ryan, *Regulating Passion: Sexuality and Patriarchal Rule in Massachusetts, 1700–1830* (New York: Oxford University Press, 2014), 59, 68–74.

10. Thompson, *Unprofitable Servants*, 157.

11. B. W. Higman, *Slave Populations of the British Caribbean, 1807–1834* (Baltimore: Johns Hopkins University Press, 1984), 209, 217–18.

12. According to British soldier George Pinckard, at Christmas enslaved people "usually

receive[d] some indulgence of food, and some present of clothing to augment the happiness of the festival." Pinckard, *Notes on the West Indies* . . . (London: 1816), 3:140.

13. The men also told the fiscal that they were "always ridiculed and laughed at by the gangs on other properties," presumably because they had to work when others did not. The attorney-manager maintained that he only ordered his slaves to be "lightly employed" and that he did so to make sure everyone was on the estate and "to prevent any of them being guilty of further excess in drinking." "Complaint of the Negroes Bernard, Primo, Jacob, Adolf, Damon, Quashy, Basta, La Rose, Amsterdam, & Johannes belonging to Plan Nieuw Vigilantie," Jan. 3, 1825, CO 116/140.

14. Ibid.

15. Italics mine. "*Complaint No. 10*," April 24, 1827, CO 116/143, 218.

16. "Complaint of the Negroes . . . belonging to Plan Nieuw Vigilantie."

17. Sept. 22, 1832, CO 116/151, 130 ("their grog," "in the darkroom," "went to cut," "did not come"), 132 ("abused," "very insolent"); "Return of Slaves attached to Plantation La Fraternite . . . ," Feb. 25, 1819, T 71/438, 595–600 ("country marks").

18. Sept. 22, 1832, CO 116/151, 133.

19. "Complaint of *Grace, Eliza, Flora, Eve, Daphna, Silvia,* and *Hannah,* belonging to plantation Prospect . . . ," Sept. 4, 1823, CO 116/138, 107 ("too much punished," "badly treated"), 108 ("the men"); "Return of Slaves attached to Plantation Prospect . . . ," Feb. 25, 1819, T 71/438, 357–60.

20. In August 1822, for instance, three men told the fiscal that they went to him because they "do not wish to go into the bush like bad negroes." "Examination of a Complaint preferred by the negroes *Frederick, Jem,* and *Davy,* belonging to the plantation Profit . . . ," Aug. 6, 1823, CO 116/138, 128, 129 (quote).

21. "Complaint of *Grace, Eliza, Flora, Eve, Daphna, Silvia,* and *Hannah* . . ."

22. "Examination of a Complaint preferred by the negro *Klaas,* the property of J. V. Mittle-holzer, against him," Jan. 3, 1823, CO 116/138, 134 ("in the bush," "two bunches"), 135 ("that they had not," "remained in the bush").

23. "Examination of a Complaint preferred by the negro *Klaas,*" 135.

24. "Examination of the negro *Bristol,* the property of Plantation New Forest . . . ," June 3, 1822, CO 116/138, 119.

25. Ibid.

26. "EXAMINATION of a Complaint preferred by the negroes *Quashy, Sharp, Dick, Thomas,* and *Spencer,* against Dr. *Munro,* their owner," May 30, 1822, CO 116/138, 118 (quotations), 119.

27. Ibid., 118 ("some irregularities"), 119 ("they were," "a copy," "two of").

28. 1826 slave code, clause 22.

29. Thompson, *Unprofitable Servants,* 85.

30. Charles Bird to Henry Beard, Sept. 1830, CO 111/110 (quotation); Thompson, *Unprofitable Servants,* 85, 163–71.

31. "Investigation of a Complaint preferred by the Negroes *Nelson, Milton, Simon, Ned, Cupid, Trim,* and *Jack,* belonging to Plantation Rosehall . . . ," May 27, 1819, CO 116/138, appx. 15.

32. July 15, 1830, CO 116/146, 145 ("told them"), 146, 147 ("If they . . . experienced"). Two men from Golden Grove made a similar complaint in February 1834. They were about to be hired out and "they would prefer remaining on their own plantation, but if they received their proper allowance of clothing they would go." They claimed they had only received one hat, one jacket, and one pair of trousers, and the protector ruled that they "must forthwith have the other

articles of clothing" they were entitled to. Feb. 6, 1834, CO 116/153, 211 ("they would prefer"), 213 ("must forthwith").

33. July 8, 1833, CO 116/152, 171 ("that they had not," "what they were"), 169 ("neither she," "had received"), 170 ("been fed").

34. Jan. 29, 1834, CO 116/153, 200 ("that his owner," "last year"), 201–2 ("1 lined jacket"), 203 ("the ten canisters," "directed to give").

35. My interpretation is informed by Alex Lichtenstein's argument that enslaved people's "thefts" were part of "the struggle between slaves and masters to define conflicting notions of authority, property and customary rights," and that "theft served as a potential means with which slaves could redefine and extend the bounds of paternalism." See Lichtenstein, "Moral Economy, Slave Management, and the Law" (quote, 415); and, "Theft, Moral Economy, and the Transition from Slavery to Freedom."

36. Pinckard, *Notes on the West Indies*, 2:118.

37. March 12, 1833, CO 116/152, 106 ("only gets one," "and others," "went to cut"), 107 ("American Corn," "were stolen"), 108.

38. "No. 4," July 8, 1829, CO 116/142, 9 ("been flogged"), 10 ("I did not think," "a very worthless character"), 11 ("the crime"); "Return of Slaves attached to Plantation Mary's Hope . . . ," Feb. 9, 1819, T 71/438, 407–8.

39. "Complaint of the negress Prudence . . . ," Feb. 18, 1825, CO 116/140.

40. For the ways that the ration-allotment system, as opposed to the provision ground system, influenced enslaved people's labor bargaining, see Mary Turner, "Slave Workers, Subsistence and Labour Bargaining: Amity Hall, Jamaica, 1805–1832," *Slavery & Abolition* 12, no. 1 (1991): 92–106.

41. July 20, 1832, CO 116/151, 85. The acting protector noted that Jacob's registered age was forty-one, but "in appearance he is above 60." A packall was a small basket used to transport and store various items. Crab oil was "a whitish, slightly smelly oil" made from the crushed nuts of the crabwood tree and used in Berbice as an insect repellent. See Richard Allsopp, ed., *Dictionary of Caribbean English Usage* (Kingston: University of the West Indies Press, 2003 [1996], 423, 175 (quote). Enslaved people in Berbice objected to intrusions into their homes, which they saw as private spaces. The enslaved man Quamino, for example, complained to the fiscal about an owner who was "often in the habit of breaking open the doors and windows of their houses when they are absent." "Examination of the negro, *Quamino,* complaining against his master, F. Brittlebank," Jan. 2, 1821, CO 116/138, 74.

42. July 20, 1832, CO 116/151, 86. Buckra (or backra) was a generic term for white colonists, especially those with high status. Allsopp and Allsopp, *Caribbean English Usage*, 61.

43. July 20, 1832, CO 116/151, 87.

44. Dylan C. Penningroth, *The Claims of Kinfolk: African American Property and Community in the Nineteenth-Century South* (Chapel Hill: University of North Carolina Press, 2003). See also Philip D. Morgan, "The Ownership of Property by Slaves in the Mid-Nineteenth-Century Low Country," *Journal of Southern History* 49, no. 3 (1983): 399–420.

45. 1826 slave code, clause 27. An 1810 governor's proclamation, reprinted in the *Berbice Gazette* in 1822 because people paid "little or no attention" to it, stipulated that "no Slave, under any pretence whatever, shall be permitted to own a Corjaal, or other small Boat, however named." *Berbice Gazette*, July 3, 1822.

46. Higman, *Slave Populations*, 208. In many Caribbean colonies, unlike Berbice, the provision ground system was the primary source of food for enslaved people. See Michael Mullin,

"Slave Economic Strategies: Food, Markets, and Property," in Turner, *Chattel Slaves to Wage Slaves*, 68–78.

47. For nutritional deficiencies, see Higman, *Slave Populations*, 217–18, 294–98; Kenneth F. Kiple, *The Caribbean Slave: A Biological History* (Cambridge: Cambridge University Press, 1984), 76–103.

48. The variety of items enslaved people produced is suggested by a clause in the 1826 slave code that mentioned "the sale of . . . meat, poultry, vegetables, provisions, fruits, herbs, wares, merchandize," and other goods at Sunday markets. 1826 slave code, clause 11.

49. Scholars have long debated the extent to which Caribbean enslaved people's independent economic activities—commonly lumped together as "the slaves' economy"—constituted a "peasant breach," as Tadeusz Lepkowski posited, or made them "proto-peasants," a term popularized by Sidney Mintz. Given that enslaved people in Berbice had limited access to land for cultivation and that they did not provide the majority of their own subsistence but instead relied on slaveowner-provided rations in exchange for their labor, it may be more useful to think of them as "proto-proletarians," as Mary Turner and others have argued. See Tadeusz Lepkowski, *Haiti*, vol. 1 (Havana: Casa de las Americas, 1968), 59–60 ("peasant breach"); Sidney Mintz, "The Question of Caribbean Peasantries: A Comment," *Caribbean Studies* 1, no. 3 (1961): 31–34; Mintz, *Caribbean Transformations* (Chicago: Aldine, 1974), 131–56; Mintz, "Was the Plantation Slave a Proletarian?" *Review* 2, no. 1 (1978): 81–98; Ira Berlin and Philip D. Morgan, eds., *The Slaves' Economy: Independent Production by Slaves in the Americas* (London: Frank Cass, 1991); and Turner, *Chattel Slaves to Wage Slaves*.

50. Vincent Brown, *The Reaper's Garden: Death and Power in the World of Atlantic Slavery* (Cambridge, Mass.: Harvard University Press, 2008), 120–21.

51. "Complaint of the negro Baron belonging to Plan Augsburg," Jan. 19, 1825, CO 116/140; "Return of Slaves, attached to Plantation Augsburg . . . ," Feb. 18, 1819, T 71/438, 441–42. For a similar case, see June 25, 1832, CO 116/150, 183–85.

52. Every plantation was required to dedicate one acre of land for every five slaves to provision grounds. 1826 slave code, clause 22.

53. Enslaved people needed the consent of their owners or managers to raise livestock. 1826 slave code, clause 27.

54. "Examination of the negroes *Philip* and *Leander*, belonging to plantation Bestendigheid . . . ," July 25, 1821, CO 116/138, 85–86. Philip was a mason and Leander was the head carpenter. "Return of Slaves belonging to Plantation Bestendigheid," Feb. 27, 1819, T 71/438, 711–12.

55. "Complaint of the negro *Bethune*, belonging to plantation Tain," Feb. 10, 1819, CO 116/138, 34; "Return of Slaves, attached to Plantation Tain . . . ," Feb. 26, 1819, T 71/438, 159.

56. "Return of Slaves the property of John Quarles . . . ," April 30, 1822, T 71/440, 575; "Examination of a Complaint preferred by the negroes *Mourant, Joseph, Secondo, Frank, Mackay, Fanny, Susan, Louisa, Daly, Cuba, Coffy, Quajo, Elias, Quamy*, and *Fanny*, a girl, the property of John Quarles, plantation Plegt Ankar," July 5, 1822, CO 116/138, 124 ("belonged to Quarles"), 125 ("while the gang").

57. Ibid., 125.

58. "Note by the Protector," CO 116/145, 13.

59. David Power to Henry Beard, Nov. 18, 1828, CO 116/145, 6.

60. Ibid. For the burden that relocation placed on enslaved people who were moved, see Justin Roberts, "The 'Better Sort' and the 'Poorer Sort': Wealth Inequalities, Family Formation

and the Economy of Energy on British Caribbean Sugar Plantations, 1750–1800," *Slavery & Abolition* 35, no. 3 (2014), 467.

61. David Power to Henry Beard, Nov. 18, 1828.

62. Ibid. Abolitionists also seized on the Catharinasburg case to criticize amelioration. See *Anti-Slavery Monthly Reporter*, no. 46 (March 1829), 439–40.

63. "Fifty four slaves Men and Women belonging to Plantation Ithaca, the property of L. F. Gallez, having attended at the Fiscal's Office to complain . . . ," Feb. 14, 1828, CO 116/142, 13–25; "Return of Slaves, attached to Plantation Ithaca . . . ," Feb. 26, 1819, T 71/438, 25.

64. "Fifty four slaves Men and Women belonging to Plantation Ithaca . . ."

65. Ibid.

66. Ibid.

67. Ibid.

68. Roberts, " 'Better Sort.' "

69. Complaint No. 9," Dec. 12–13, 1826, CO 116/143, 155–56; "Complaint, No. 7," Sept. 29, 1829, CO 116/145, 232.

70. April 9, 1825, CO 116/140.

71. Ira Berlin and Philip Morgan similarly noted the "divisive effect" of slaves' economic activities, which "unleashed a variety of conflicts, great and petty, among slaves, as some tried to gain advantages at the expense of others." See Berlin and Morgan, "Introduction," in Berlin and Morgan, *Slaves' Economy*, 17.

72. Enslaved people made an ethical distinction between people who took from whites and people who took from other slaves. A woman named Kitty, for example, admitted that she was "ashamed" when other slaves discovered that she had stolen clothing from another enslaved woman. "Complaint of the Negress Annatje Belonging to the Winkel Department . . . ," May 12, 1826, CO 116/141. Slaves who stole from one another often had a poor reputation within their communities. One man, for example, was known as "a very bad character amongst the negroes," according to the manager, because they "accused him of taking their fowls to procure rum." "Complaint of negro *Philip*, the property of plantation Canefield Carye," June 14, 1819, CO 116/138, 54. See also Lichtenstein, "Moral Economy, Slave Management, and the Law"; Kay and Cary, "Slave Defence of a Moral Economy," 38; and Natalie Zemon Davis, "Judges, Masters, Diviners: Slaves' Experience of Criminal Justice in Colonial Suriname," *Law and History Review* 29, no. 4 (2011), 954.

73. Sept. 4, 1827, entry, "Punishment Record Book of Plantation Deutichem . . . ," CO 116/144.

74. Aug. 25, 1827, entry, "Punishment Record Book of Plantation Eliza and Mary . . . ," CO 116/144.

75. Sept. 7, 1828, entry, "Punishment Record Book of Plantn Albion . . . ," CO 116/145, 45–46.

76. Dec. 27, 1828, entry, "Punishment Record Book of Plantn Vryheid . . . ," CO 116/145, 55–56.

77. "No. 11," Aug. 29, 1829, CO 116/142, 39; "Return of Slaves . . . attached to Plantations Nos. 5 & 7 . . . ," Feb. 25, 1819, T 71/438, 69–70.

78. "No. 11," Aug. 29, 1829, 40 ("saw the woman," "brandish[ed] it," "cried out"), 44 "whole of the men"), 45 ("holding the bayonet"), 51 ("to work on the Estate").

79. Ibid., 40 ("about some fowls"), 42 ("began to quarrel," "asked him how," "said [she] would not").

80. See, for example, Steve J. Stern's discussion of Andean Indians' use of the Spanish colonial legal system. Stern, *Peru's Indian Peoples and the Challenge of Spanish Conquest: Huamanga to 1640* (Madison: University of Wisconsin Press, 1982), esp. 132–37, 187–88.

81. "Examination of a Complaint preferred by the negro *James*, belonging to Dr. Smith," Aug. 20, 1822, CO 116/138, 130; "Return of Slaves the Property of John Smith . . . ," April 25, 1822, T 71/440, 639–40.

82. "Examination of a complaint made by the negro *Harry* against the negro *Quaco* . . . ," Oct. 28, 1820, CO 116/138, 69; "Return of Slaves attached to the Winkel Department . . . ," Feb. 22, 1819, T 71/438, 723, 727.

83. Jan. 6, 1831, CO 116/148, 107 ("he would see," "she had purchased"), 109 ("avail himself"). Even the secretary of state recognized that Leander had gotten a raw deal. "I am unable to discover upon what grounds this complaint was summarily dismissed," he wrote. "No principle of law can be more fully established than that the purchaser of stolen goods can acquire no title in opposition to that of the rightful owner." See Viscount Goderich to George Murray, April 21, 1832, CO 116/148, 6.

84. "Complaint of the negro Baron belonging to Pln. Herstelling," Jan. 16, 1826, CO 116/140; "Return of Slaves, attached to Plantation Herstelling . . . ," Feb. 27, 1819, T 71/438, 627–29.

85. "Complaint of the negro Baron."

86. "Complaint of the Negro Trim belonging to W. Scott . . . ," Jan. 7, 1826, CO 116/140; "Return of Slaves the Property of Wm. Scott," Feb. 9, 1825, T 71/442, 673.

87. Ibid.

88. "Return of Slaves attached to the Winkel Department . . . ," Feb. 16, 1819, T 71/438, 723 ("elderly," "very stout").

89. "Henry Stocking Manager over the slaves attached to the Winkel establishment . . . informed the Fiscal that a young man named Paul . . . was accused of stealing two turkies from an elderly woman named Toetoe," Jan. 19, 1830, CO 116/142, 9–15 (10, "in possession of," "bought them," "Paul came"; 15, "work").

90. Michael maintained that he was innocent and had proof someone else had broken into Jenny's trunk. After he was flogged, he claimed, Jenny "found a string of corals on the neck of a girl named Peggy," the manager's housekeeper. But "nothing was said to her," and when Michael "went to the manager to be indemnified for a punishment he had received for nothing," the manager ordered him to be quiet or be put in the stocks. Whether the fiscal believed Michael's innocence or not, he chastised the manager for having handled the suspected robbery himself. "The manager was informed," according to the fiscal's notes, "that if he really considered [Michael] guilty of the robbery, he ought to have sent him to the Fiscal for trial." "Examination of a Complaint preferred by the negro *Michael*, belonging to plantation Providence, . . . ," April 24, 1823, CO 116/138, 137 ("some money"), 138 ("inspected the chest," "was evidently," "he had committed"); "Return of Slaves the Property of William Henerey . . . ," Feb. 22, 1819, T 71/438, 339; "Return of Slaves attached to Plantation Providence . . . ," April 4, 1822, T 71/440, 239.

91. "Complaint No. 18," Jan. 3, 1829, CO 116/145, 15. Bella also emphasized the damage done to her property. As she told the protector, Maria "broke [exhibiting part of a string of coral beads] my rings and beads." Ibid., 16.

92. Ibid., 16.

93. "Investigation of a Complaint preferred by the Negroes *Nelson, Milton, Simon, Ned, Cupid, Trim*, and *Jack* . . "; "Return of Slaves, attached to Plantation Rose Hall . . . ," Feb. 27, 1819, T 71/438, 151–54.

94. As Mary Turner has argued, certain economic rights enslaved people gained during amelioration challenged the fundamental assumptions behind slavery as an economic system. "To require the exchange of cash for work," Turner writes, "struck at the heart of the slave labour system which in essence denied labour exchange value" ("The 11 O'Clock Flog: Women, Work and Labour Law in the British Caribbean," *Slavery & Abolition* 20, no. 1 [1999], 53).

95. 1826 slave code, clause 9. In 1830, the deputy protector of slaves and lieutenant governor established the following wages for Sunday labor by official proclamation: "One bitt per hour for potting sugar. One bitt per hour for turning and drying coffee or cotton. For picking coffee—three bitts for a basket weighing 70 lbs. gross. For picking cotton—three bitts for a basket weighing 30 lbs. gross." April 27, 1830, *Berbice Gazette*, June 9, 1830. Although wages and cash rewards provided some enslaved people an opportunity to accumulate small amounts of cash, owners and managers also used them to stimulate overwork. See O. Nigel Bolland, "Proto-Proletarians? Slave Wages in the Americas: Between Slave Labour and Free Labour," in Turner, ed., *From Chattel Slaves to Wage Slaves*, 123–47.

96. 1826 slave code, clause 27.

97. J. H. Lean, "The Secret Lives of Slaves: Berbice, 1819 to 1827" (Ph.D. diss., University of Canterbury, 2002), 114.

98. "*Complaint No. 6*," April 20, 1827, CO 116/143, 216.

99. "Complaint of the Negro *London*, the property of W. Kewley, against *Napier*, a pioneer . . . ," Feb. 8, 1819, CO 116/138, 32.

100. "Mary Jane Campbell complains by letter . . . ," June 14, 1826, CO 116/141.

101. Ibid. For a similar case, see "Complaint No. 28," Nov. 21, 1827, CO 116/144, 63–65.

102. "Complaint No. 4," July 10, 1827, CO 116/143, 250.

103. "Complaint, No. 12," Nov. 18, 1828, CO 116/145, 13; "Return of Slaves belonging to Elizabeth Fraser . . . ," Feb. 25, 1819, T 71/438, 283. In 1820 de Vry was also accused of assaulting an enslaved woman, her infant, and her free black owner. See "Examination of the negro woman *Marencia*, belonging to the free black woman Sarah Bourgeois," Dec. 6, 1820, CO 116/138, 71; and "Examination of the free woman *Sarah Bourgeois*, preferring a complaint against the free man *Johannes de Vry* for assault, &c. &c.," Dec. 6, 1820, CO 116/138, 71–72.

104. "Complaint, No. 31," Dec. 18, 1829, CO 116/145, 241.

105. "Complaint, No. 6," Oct. 13, 1828, CO 116/145, 12.

106. Charles Bird to Henry Beard, March 1, 1830, CO 116/145, 230.

107. Ibid.

108. David Power to Henry Beard, Sept. 1, 1828, CO 116/144, 29–30. Power also argued "that manumission can possibly confer no benefit on the Negro unless his industry accompanied his change of condition; and I know of no more active stimulus to that industry, than the certainty of his being paid for his labour." Ibid., 30.

109. For the governor's proclamation, see *Berbice Gazette*, Oct. 7, 1829. For the imperial government's support of Power's suggested "Court of Summary Jurisdiction for the recovery of small debts due to slaves" and its criticism of the Berbice government's delay in establishing such a court, see George Murray to Henry Beard, Sept. 1, 1829, CO 116/145, 22–23. See also Thompson, *Unprofitable Servants*, 43–44.

110. Jan. 1, 1832, CO 116/148, 103 ("Cumba White"), 104 ("were quarreling"), 105 ("Susette was not pleased," "laid hold," "changed the money"); "Return of Slaves attached to the Winkel Department . . . ," Feb. 22, 1819, T 71/438, 727.

111. Nov. 29, 1830, CO 116/147, 141 ("C. Kraan tore"), 142 ("gave him several"), 143.

112. "Complaint No. 43," Jan. 25, 1830, CO 116/145, 242.

113. May 12, 1830, CO 116/146, 99 ("offer[ed] his acceptance"), 101 ("It was at Hannibal's"), 102 ("acknowledgment").

114. As Mary Turner observed, amelioration reforms entailed "beginning the transition to wage work, preparing slave workers and slave-owners to become servants and masters, employees and employers. This process required first and foremost that owner–slave relationships be defined by law and systematically applied to both parties by enhancing the powers of the colonial state. The imperial government's 1824 blueprint consequently made implementation of the law its priority. Within the proposed new structural framework the labour laws modified customary methods of slave labour exaction and introduced elements of wage work." See Turner, "The 11 O'Clock Flog,'" 49. For slave codes as "a recognition of the concessions that slaves had wrung from their owners through constant struggle," see Berlin and Morgan, "Labor and the Shaping of Slave Life," 7.

115. Mary Turner similarly concluded that enslaved people's labor bargaining was "usually directed to securing immediate practical modification of the terms of labour extraction, not to overturning the slave system" (*Chattel Slave to Wage Slaves*, 12).

Epilogue

1. "No. 2, Complaint of the Slave Fortuin belonging to Andrew Ross," Jan. 13, 1831, Colonial Office series 116/142, 5–11 ("seeing my," "beg," 6; "taken ill," 7; "had brought," 8; "although the," 11), National Archives, Kew, London, United Kingdom.

2. Quoted in Laurent Dubois, *Avengers of the New World: The Story of the Haitian Revolution* (Cambridge, Mass.: Harvard University Press, 2004), 40.

3. For Saint Domingue, see Dubois, *Avengers*, 39–40. For Jamaica, see Vincent Brown, *The Reaper's Garden: Death and Power in the World of Atlantic Slavery* (Cambridge, Mass.: Harvard University Press, 2008), 50–51, 55–56. For Brazil, see Stuart B. Schwartz, *Sugar Plantations in the Formation of Brazilian Society: Bahia, 1550–1835* (Cambridge: Cambridge University Press, 1985), esp. 338–78; João José Reis, *Death Is a Festival: Funeral Rites and Rebellion in Nineteenth-Century Brazil*, trans. H. Sabrina Gledhill (Chapel Hill: University of North Carolina Press, 2003); and James H. Sweet, *Recreating Africa: Culture, Kinship, and Religion in the African-Portuguese World, 1441–1770* (Chapel Hill: University of North Carolina Press), 60–66.

4. For the demographic differences between slave populations in the sugar-producing regions of Latin America, the Caribbean, and the United States, (where sugar was not cultivated on a large scale outside of Louisiana), see Michael Tadman, "The Demographic Cost of Sugar: Debates on Slave Societies and Natural Increase in the Americas," *American Historical Review* 105, no. 5 (2000): 1534–75. An important consequence of the North American slave population's self-reproduction was that there was a creole majority by 1740 and less than 1 percent of all slaves in the United States were African by the 1860s. Ibid., 1536.

5. The slave population of the Chesapeake began to reproduce itself in the 1720s and that of the Lowcountry in the 1740s–50s. From a population of 1.1 million slaves in 1810, two years after the importation of African captives to the United States legally ended, the slave population nearly quadrupled to almost four million by 1860—about ten times the number of African captives imported to North America in the transatlantic slave trade. Peter Kolchin, *American Slavery: 1619–1877* (New York: Hill and Wang, 2003 [1993]), 22, 38–39.

6. For the internal slave trade in the United States, see Michael Tadman, *Speculators and Slaves: Masters, Traders, and Slaves in the Old South* (Madison: University of Wisconsin Press,

1989); Walter Johnson, *Soul by Soul: Life Inside the Antebellum Slave Market* (Cambridge, Mass.: Harvard University Press, 2009); and Damian Pargas, *Slavery and Forced Migration in the Antebellum South* (Cambridge: Cambridge University Press, 2014).

7. I borrow "Second Middle Passage" from Ira Berlin, *Generations of Captivity: A History of African-American Slaves* (Cambridge, Mass.: Harvard University Press, 2003). For the relationship between slavery, cotton, and capitalism, see Walter Johnson, *River of Dark Dreams: Slavery and Empire in the Cotton Kingdom* (Cambridge, Mass.: Harvard University Press, 2013), and Sven Beckert, *Empire of Cotton: A Global History* (New York: Knopf, 2014).

8. Kolchin, *American Slavery*, 125–26; Berlin, *Generations*, 214–15, 226–27.

9. For Jamaica, see B. W. Higman, *Plantation Jamaica, 1750–1850: Capital and Control in a Colonial Economy* (Kingston: University of the West Indies Press, 2005), and Brown, *Reaper's Garden*, 21–22. For the West Indies in general, where absenteeism was widespread but varied by colony, see Douglas Hall, "Absentee-Proprietorship in the British West Indies to About 1850," *Jamaican Historical Review* 4 (1964): 15–34; Gad Heuman, "The Social Structure of Slave Societies in the Caribbean," in Franklin W. Knight, ed., *General History of the Caribbean* (London: UNESCO, 1997): 153–54; and Justin Roberts, *Slavery and the Enlightenment in the British Atlantic, 1750–1807* (New York: Cambridge University Press, 2013).

10. An earlier generation of scholarship on comparative slavery, inspired by Frank Tannenbaum, drew sharp distinctions between the law of slavery in British colonies and the United States versus Latin America, often exaggerating the protections available to enslaved people in societies where legal protections existed and failing to account for the large gap between the law and its enforcement. For a recent overview of the debate Tannenbaum sparked, see Alejandro de la Fuente, "Slave Law and Claims-Making in Cuba: The Tannenbaum Debate Revisited," *Law and History Review* 22, no. 2 (2004): 339–69, and María Elena Díaz, "Beyond Tannenbaum," *Law and History Review* 22, no. 2 (2004): 371–76. See also Frank Tannenbaum, *Slave and Citizen: the Negro in the Americas* (New York: A. A. Knopf, 1946).

11. See, for example, Sherwin K. Bryant, "Enslaved Rebels, Fugitives, and Litigants: the Resistance Continuum in Colonial Quito," *Colonial Latin American Review* 13, no. 1 (2004): 7–46; Brian P. Owensby, "How Juan and Leonor Won Their Freedom: Litigation and Liberty in Seventeenth-Century Mexico," *Hispanic American Historical Review* 85, no. 1 (2005): 39–80; Alejandro de la Fuente, "Slaves and the Creation of Legal Rights in Cuba: Coartación and Papel," *Hispanic American Historical Review* 87, no. 4 (2007): 659–94; Manuel Barcia, *Seeds of Insurrection: Domination and Resistance on Western Cuban Plantations, 1808–1848* (Baton Rouge: Louisiana State University Press, 2008), 84–104; Marcela Echeverri, "'Enraged to the Limit of Despair': Infanticide and Slave Judicial Strategies in Barbacoas, 1788–98," *Slavery & Abolition* 30, no. 3 (2009): 403–26; Malick W. Ghachem, *The Old Regime and the Haitian Revolution* (New York: Cambridge University Press, 2012); and Rachel Sarah O'Toole, *Bound Lives: Africans, Indians, and the Making of Race in Colonial Peru* (Pittsburgh: University of Pittsburgh Press, 2012), esp. 122–56.

12. For a good overview of laws regulating slavery in the antebellum South, see Kolchin, *American Slavery*, 127–32. As Kolchin observed, "antebellum legislation gave considerably more attention than had colonial-era laws to regulating the masters as well as the slaves," but whites were rarely held accountable for crimes against enslaved people, in part because no southern state allowed enslaved people to testify against whites. Ibid., 129–30 (quote), 131. David Brion Davis similarly concluded that state laws regulating the treatment of enslaved people "were difficult to enforce, especially in sparsely populated rural areas where slaveowners monopolized

political power." Davis, *Inhuman Bondage: The Rise and Fall of Slavery in the New World* (New York: Oxford University Press, 2006), 193. For earlier laws, see Sally Hadden, "The Fragmented Laws of Slavery in the Colonial and Revolutionary Era," in Michael Grossberg and Christopher Tomlins, eds., *The Cambridge History of Law in America*, vol. 1: *Early America (1580–1815)* (New York: Cambridge University Press, 2007), 253–87.

13. As Dylan C. Penningroth has written, "Both the resistance framework and its counterre-visionist critics focus on conflict between the races, especially the master-slave relationship. That emphasis tends to obscure the experiences of black people, whose understanding of economic and social life involved far more than their relations with white people." Penningroth, "My People, My People: The Dynamics of Community in Southern Slavery," in *New Studies in the History of American Slavery*, ed. Edward E. Baptist and Stephanie M. H. Camp (Athens: University of Georgia Press, 2006), 167.

INDEX

People with identical names are distinguished by additional identifying information in parentheses, such as the name of the plantation where they lived or their owner.

ACKNOWLEDGMENTS

_____

Like the Berbice River, the path that led to this book had many twists and turns. And some of its tributaries only became clear in hindsight. The project began at Eckerd College, long before I knew it, where my professors sparked a fascination with the history of slavery and introduced me to the craft of history. Carolyn Johnston and Barnet Hartson were model teachers and advisers—I am eternally grateful for their patience, guidance, and encouragement.

This book first took shape at the University of North Carolina at Chapel Hill, where I had the good fortune to study with an extraordinary group of people. Although I had every intention of working on slavery in the American South, the pull of the Atlantic was strong—and so was the support of my professors who encouraged me to think about the history of slavery broadly and comparatively. I am particularly indebted to Kathryn Burns, Kathleen DuVal, Jerma Jackson, Lisa Lindsay, and Heather Williams for stimulating seminars and individual conversations in my early years. Vincent Brown, Laurent Dubois, Lisa Lindsay, John Sweet, and Heather Williams had high expectations and plenty of enthusiasm for this project. Vince Brown challenged me to think deeply about what I wanted to say and why it mattered, and his own scholarship has had a large impact on the way I think about Atlantic slavery. Laurent Dubois showed me just how important the Caribbean was to the field of Atlantic history (and reminded me, whenever he sensed that I sounded defensive about dedicating so much time to a little-known colony on the fringes of the Caribbean, that colonial Berbice was much more important than colonial North Carolina—not that he recommended me sharing that with Tar Heels). Lisa Lindsay taught me more than anyone else about African history and the transatlantic slave trade, and her encouragement helped me overcome not a few obstacles in the years since. Heather Williams believed in me and my work from the beginning, but was always a tough critic who forced me to explain—repeatedly—why it was important.

My largest debt—for his help with the book and so much else—is to John Sweet, who has done more than anyone to shape my vision of the field and development as a scholar. From the beginning, John has been there, reading multiple drafts, asking famously tough questions, encouraging me to take risks and experiment, and—especially when I did not necessarily welcome it—holding me to high standards. I treasure the many conversations we had, plenty of them on the patio of Caffé Driade, as well as John's continued friendship.

In Chapel Hill, I also relied on many friends in and out of the academy for advice and support. Among those who kept me going were Matt Daley, Jeff Erbig, Rob Ferguson, Katherine French Fuller, Hilary Green, Anna Krome-Lukens, Alicia and Jeremy Lange, Christy Mobley, Brad Proctor, Alex Protzman, Ben Reed, Jeff Richey, Tony Sabbagh, Katy Smith, and Erika Wilson. Chris Cameron and Laura Premack, my writing partners and confidants, deserve special mention for their steadfast support. Frank Gullo's friendship meant more to me then and now than he knows.

I presented much of the material that appears here at conferences, seminars, and other universities on both sides of the Atlantic, where I was forced to engage questions and comments that helped improve the book. I am grateful for the opportunity to have presented at King's College London in 2012; the 2013 annual conference of the Society for Caribbean Studies, held at the University of Warwick; the Omohundro Institute of Early American History and Culture's Conference on Africans in the Americas, held in 2013 at the University of the West Indies–Cave Hill in Barbados; the Kentucky Early American Seminar in 2014; Bowdoin College in 2014; the Triangle Early American History Seminar in 2014; the Library Company of Philadelphia in 2014; Eckerd College in 2014; the 2015 annual conference of the Omohundro Institute of Early American History and Culture, held in Chicago; and the 2016 annual conference of the Association of Caribbean Historians, in Havana, Cuba. Among those who offered helpful critiques, questions, and comments at those events were Krystal Appiah, Trevor Burnard, Peter Coclanis, Richard Drayton, Kathleen DuVal, Bronwen Everill, Gad Heuman, David Lambert, Jane Landers, Melanie Newton, Diana Paton, Susan Pennybacker, Kelly Ryan, Jenny Shaw, Katy Smith, Brad Wood, Peter Wood, and Jason Young.

At Xavier University, I have benefited from the encouragement and advice of my colleagues in the History Department. I am particularly grateful to Rachel Chrastil, Kathleen Smythe, and Amy Whipple. John Fairfield has been a staunch advocate and generous friend, providing rich conversations (and plenty of good food and drink, too). Karim Tiro, as both colleague and department chair, made sure I got the resources I needed to complete this book, especially as the tenure clock ticked away. In the dean's office, Janice Walker and David Mengel offered financial and logistical support for conferences and research travel, including a much-appreciated semester of leave to take a residential fellowship at the Library Company of Philadelphia.

Historians know better than anyone just how valuable the support of archivists, library curators, and local guides is. I owe a special thanks to the staff of the School for Oriental and African Studies, the Walter Rodney Archives in Georgetown, Guyana, the Walter Royal Davis Library at the University of North Carolina, the McDonald Library at Xavier University, and above all the National Archives of the United Kingdom. The librarians at the Library Company of Philadelphia, where I spent a semester completing the research for this book and rewriting several chapters, were especially helpful. My thanks there to Krystal Appiah, Jim Green, and Connie King. In Guyana, Margaret Chan-a-Sue was an exceedingly helpful guide who helped with everything from introductions to local academics and where to find the best roti to arrangements to travel some ninety miles up the Berbice River. Also in Guyana, Alex Mendes graciously invited me to spend several days at his family's remote Berbice River cattle ranch, Dubulay, which we reached via Alex's expertly piloted 4×4 pickup truck. From Dubulay, I was able to explore the upper Berbice River—where the colony's first plantations were established— and come face to face with everything from eighteenth-century graves to a jaguar. Alex and Margaret showed me things and shared stories I never could have discovered in any archive or book. I am also grateful for the conversations I had in Jamaica with the Maroons of Moore Town and Accompang, who told me about their history and challenged me to reconsider much of what I thought I knew about the legacies of slavery in the Caribbean.

Generous financial support came from several corners. While at UNC, a Jacob K. Javits Fellowship from the U.S. Department of Education allowed me the rare gift of unrestricted time to research and write. Also at UNC, funding from the History Department, the Program in Medieval and Early Modern Studies, and the Institute for the Study of the Americas funded trips to Guyana and the United Kingdom. I am also grateful for fellowships from the American Historical Association and the International Seminar on the History of the Atlantic World at Harvard University. A National Endowment for the Humanities fellowship enabled me to spend a very productive semester at the Library Company of Philadelphia. There I not only benefited from the Library Company's extraordinary collections but also enjoyed the comradery of colleagues in and around Philadelphia, not least of all those clustered around the McNeil Center for Early American Studies under the energetic leadership of Dan Richter.

A wide network of friends and colleagues—in addition to those already mentioned above—helped make the completion of this book possible, in various and important ways. Marjoleine Kars, my fellow traveler in the very small circle of historians of Berbice, generously shared resources, citations, and travel advice about Guyana. Alvin Thompson similarly discussed his rich knowledge of slavery in Guyana with me and read early stages of my work. Phil Morgan, Vince Brown, and Diana Paton read an earlier version of what is now Chapter 5, which originally appeared as "The 'Bad Business' of Obeah: Power, Authority, and the Politics of Slave Culture in the British Caribbean," *William and Mary Quarterly* 68, no. 3 (2011): 451–80. They offered incisive comments that not only improved the article but helped me conceptualize the broader project. Chris Grasso, then Editor at the *WMQ*, also offered very helpful suggestions. Thanks to the Omohundro Institute of Early American History and Culture for permission to reproduce parts of that article. Justin Roberts made key suggestions that helped me transform my manuscript into a much better book. He has also championed the project ever since (and even agreed to read the manuscript again for the Press). Thomas Callan was my extraordinary London host year after year and even located sources for me at one point when I could not travel across the Atlantic. Corey Gibson copyedited an early draft of the manuscript with astonishing speed. Rachel Walker verified the citations with a precision that was enviable. Jeff Erbig and Meghan Cohorst helped with the maps. I am also grateful to Armando Azmitia, Jack Baird, Raja Torres Browne, Ben Cabrera, Gary Collins, Matt D'Antonio, Matt and Heidi Hudson-Flege, Barry Gaspar, Aston Gonzalez, Jerry Handler, Kelly Kennington, Zach Kincaid, Scott Licardi, Chris Luessen, Brian MacHarg, Jim McGinnis, Matt Price, Heidi Scott-Giusto, and Nic Wood.

At Penn Press, Bob Lockhart has been an ideal editor. Bob was excited about this project from our first conversation about it and helped me shape it at every stage since then, in some cases reading several drafts and always making smart suggestions for improving the text. I am grateful for his editorial guidance and vision, and for allowing me the freedom to make my own decisions. Kathy Brown, the Press's Early American Studies series editor, commented on the book manuscript multiple times with an enthusiasm and precision that gave me much-needed motivation to undertake major revisions. Her ambition for the book and willingness to devote so much of her own precious time to it was crucial. Diana Paton and Justin Roberts served as external reviewers for the Press and wrote extensive, thoughtful reports that helped me clarify my arguments and reframe key portions of the manuscript. They also graciously waived their anonymity, which allowed me to reach out to them with follow-up questions about issues large and small. Taken together, I could not have asked for a better group of readers and critics. At Penn Press, I also thank Amanda Ruffner and Noreen O'Connor-Abel for their assistance in ensuring a smooth publication process and Joyce Ippolito for copyediting the final text.

In the beginning and at the end, I could not have written this book without the encouragement of my family. Thanks to my Mom and Dad, and to my other parents, Martha and Juan. I am also grateful for the love, support, and humor of the extended Browne, Ness, Pfeifer, Torres, and Velasquez families. Finally, there are no words to properly thank Mafe for everything she has done for me—and everything that I have learned from her.